OXFORD STUDIES IN DIACHRONIC AND
HISTORICAL LINGUISTICS

GENERAL EDITORS
Adam Ledgeway and Ian Roberts, *University of Cambridge*

ADVISORY EDITORS
Cynthia Allen, *Australian National University*; Ricardo Bermúdez-Otero, *University of Manchester*; Theresa Biberauer, *University of Cambridge*; Charlotte Galves, *University of Campinas*; Geoff Horrocks, *University of Cambridge*; Paul Kiparsky, *Stanford University*; Anthony Kroch, *University of Pennsylvania*; David Lightfoot, *Georgetown University*; Giuseppe Longobardi, *University of York*; David Willis, *University of Cambridge*

PUBLISHED

[For a complete list of books published and in preparation for the series see pp. 321-22.]

The Boundaries of Pure Morphology

The Boundaries of Pure Morphology

Diachronic and Synchronic Perspectives

Edited by
SILVIO CRUSCHINA
MARTIN MAIDEN
JOHN CHARLES SMITH

OXFORD
UNIVERSITY PRESS

OXFORD
UNIVERSITY PRESS

Great Clarendon Street, Oxford, OX2 6DP,
United Kingdom

Oxford University Press is a department of the University of Oxford.
It furthers the University's objective of excellence in research, scholarship,
and education by publishing worldwide. Oxford is a registered trade mark of
Oxford University Press in the UK and in certain other countries

British Library Cataloguing in Publication Data

Data available

ISBN 978-0-19-967886-0

As printed and bound by
CPI Group (UK) Ltd, Croydon, CR0 4YY

Contents

Series preface

Modern diachronic linguistics has important contacts with other subdisciplines, notably first-language acquisition, learnability theory, computational linguistics, sociolinguistics, and the traditional philological study of texts. It is now recognized in the wider field that diachronic linguistics can make a novel contribution to linguistic theory, to historical linguistics, and arguably to cognitive science more widely.

This series provides a forum for work in both diachronic and historical linguistics, including work on change in grammar, sound, and meaning within and across languages; synchronic studies of languages in the past; and descriptive histories of one or more languages. It is intended to reflect and encourage the links between these subjects and fields such as those mentioned above.

The goal of the series is to publish high-quality monographs and collections of papers in diachronic linguistics generally, i.e. studies focusing on change in linguistic structure, and/or change in grammars, which are also intended to make a contribution to linguistic theory, by developing and adopting a current theoretical model, by raising wider questions concerning the nature of language change, or by developing theoretical connections with other areas of linguistics and cognitive science as listed above. There is no bias towards a particular language or language family, or towards a particular theoretical framework; work in all theoretical frameworks, and work based on the descriptive tradition of language typology, as well as quantitatively based work using theoretical ideas, also feature in the series.

Adam Ledgeway and Ian Roberts
University of Cambridge

List of abbreviations

1PL	first person plural
1SG	first person singular
2PL	second person plural
2SG	second person singular
3PL	third person plural
3SG	third person singular
A	adjective
ACC	accusative
Adv.	adverb
Amp.	Ampezzano
Bad.	Badiotto
Br.	Brach
BS	basic stem
Caz.	Cazet
CL	clitic
coll.	colloquial
Coll.	Collese
COND	conditional
conj.	conjugation
COP	copula
DAT	dative
DIC	doubly inflected construction
DM	Distributed Morphology
ExclF	exclusion feature
F	feminine
Fass.	Fassano
FIP	future in the past
Fod.	Fodom
Fr.	French
FUÈC	future and conditional
FUT	future

Gard.	Gardenese
GEN	genitive
GER	gerund
Germ.	Germanic
IE	Indo-European
IMP	imperative
IMPF	imperfect
IND	indicative
INF	infinitive
intr.	intransitive
It.	Italian
L1	First Language
Lat.	Latin
LOC	locative
Log.	Logudorese
M	masculine
Mar.	Marebbano
MIr.	Middle Iranian
Moen.	Moenat
MPers.	Middle Persian
N	noun
NEUT	neuter
NOM	nominative
NT	Northern Talyshi
OBL	oblique
OCSl	Old Church Slavonic
OFr.	old French
OIr.	Old Iranian
OLog.	old Logudorese
OSp.	old Spanish
PL	plural
PLPF	pluperfect
PN	person and number markers
PRET	preterite
PRF	perfect

PRom	Proto-Romance
PRON	pronoun
PRS	present
PST	past
Pt.	Portuguese
PTCP	participle
PYTA	'perfecto y tiempos afines'
Rom.	Romanian
SBJ	subject
SBJV	subjunctive
SC	synthetic conditional
SCL	subject clitic
SF	synthetic future
SG	singular
Sp.	Spanish
ST	Southern Talyshi
Surm.	Surmiran
SVC	serial verb construction
TAM	tense–aspect–mood
ThV	thematic vowel
TMA	tense–mood–aspect
tr.	transitive
V	verb
VP	verb phrase
VR	verb root

Notes on contributors

STEPHEN R. ANDERSON is Professor of Linguistics and Cognitive Science at Yale University. He has been President of the Linguistic Society of America and is Vice-President of the Comité International Permanent des Linguistes. His main research interests lie in general linguistic theory, historical linguistics, the history of linguistics, and the biological bases of human language. He has developed a view of word structure known as A-Morphous Morphology. His research includes fieldwork on the Surmiran form of Rumantsch, as well as a number of other languages.

MARK ARONOFF is Distinguished Professor of Linguistics at Stony Brook University, where he has taught since receiving his Ph.D. many years ago from MIT. The central focus of his research has always been on morphology. For the last decade, he has also worked on sign language, with special interest in the emergence of structure in new sign languages and its relation to the evolution and nature of languages. Besides his research and teaching, he has served as Editor of the journal *Language*, President of the Linguistic Society of America, and Chair of the section on Linguistics and the Language Sciences of the AAAS. He is a Fellow of both the AAAS and the Linguistic Society of America.

CHIARA CAPPELLARO is a British Academy Post-doctoral Fellow in the Faculty of Linguistics, University of Oxford and a Research Fellow at St John's College. Her research interests focus on morphological theory, historical linguistics, language typology, and Romance linguistics and dialectology.

SILVIO CRUSCHINA studied Linguistics at the University of Siena and at the University of Cambridge. His Ph.D. thesis (Cambridge, 2008/2009) focused on the interaction between syntax and discourse-related features in Romance. He worked at the University of Oxford as a Research Assistant on the research project 'Autonomous Morphology in Diachrony: Comparative Evidence from the Romance Languages', and he is currently working at the University of Manchester as a Research Associate on the research project 'Existential Constructions: An Investigation into the Italo-Romance Dialects'. His research interests include generative syntax, morphology, phonology, evidentiality, historical linguistics, and morphosyntactic change.

MARTINA DA TOS recently completed her Ph.D. in Romance linguistics at the University of Padua. Her research interests include Italo-Romance dialectology, historical linguistics, and morphological theory. Her dissertation focuses on the role of thematic vowels in the paradigm of Italian verbs.

LOUISE ESHER is a Junior Research Fellow in Modern Languages at St John's College, Oxford. Her main research interests are in Romance historical morphology and morphosyntax. Her current project, 'A Cartography of Morphomic Space', investigates the internal structure of the morphomic level, and the interaction of autonomous morphology with extramorphological components of the grammar.

STEVEN KAYE is a D.Phil. student at Magdalen College, University of Oxford, and an associate member of UMR 7192 ('Proche-Orient – Caucase : langues, archéologie, cultures'), CNRS. His interests include morphological change, Indo-European linguistics, and language documentation. His doctoral research is on the rise and fall of mixed ('heteroclite') inflection in the Italic and Romance verb.

MICHELE LOPORCARO is Professor of Romance Linguistics at the University of Zurich and a Fellow of Academia Europaea. His research interests include the phonology, morphology, and syntax of Italo-Romance varieties, historical Romance linguistics, and linguistic historiography. He is the author of the following monographs: *Grammatica storica del dialetto di Altamura*, Pisa 1988; *L'origine del raddoppiamento fonosintattico*, Basel–Tübingen 1997; *Sintassi comparata dell'accordo participiale romanzo*, Turin 1998; *Cattive notizie. La retorica senza lumi dei mass media italiani*, Milan 2005 (3rd edn, 2010); *Profilo linguistico dei dialetti italiani*, Rome-Bari 2009 (2nd edn, 2013).

MARTIN MAIDEN is Professor of the Romance Languages at the University of Oxford, the Director of the Research Centre for Romance Linguistics, University of Oxford, and Fellow of Trinity College, Oxford. He is also a Fellow of the British Academy. His main research interests are historical and comparative linguistics of the Romance Languages, especially Romanian and Italo-Romance linguistics, and morphological theory.

CLAIRE MEUL is a researcher at the University of Leuven and holds a postdoctoral fellowship of the Research Foundation—Flanders (FWO-Vlaanderen). Her research interests include verbal morphology, sociolinguistics, and Italo- and Gallo-Romance dialectology. Within the context of her Ph.D. project, she investigated the verb system in Dolomitic Ladin. Her current post doctoral project focuses on the expression of futurity in Gallo-Romance.

PAUL O'NEILL is a University Lecturer in Hispanic Linguistics at the University of Sheffield. His research interests include the history of Romance, Ibero-Romance dialectology, and the interface between phonetics and phonology and morphological theory.

JOHN CHARLES SMITH has been Fellow and Tutor in French Linguistics at St Catherine's College, Oxford since 1997. Before returning to Oxford, where he was an undergraduate and graduate student, he held appointments at the Universities of

Surrey, Bath, and Manchester. He has also held visiting appointments in Paris, Limoges, Berlin, Melbourne, and Philadelphia. His main field of interest is historical morphosyntax, and he has published widely on agreement, refunctionalization, deixis, and the evolution of case and pronoun systems, with particular reference to Romance, although he has also worked on other language families, including Germanic and Austronesian. He is Secretary of the International Society for Historical Linguistics, Deputy Director of the University of Oxford Research Centre for Romance Linguistics, and co-editor of *The Cambridge History of the Romance Languages*. In 2007, he was created *chevalier dans l'ordre des Palmes académiques* by the French government, for services to the French language and French culture.

NIGEL VINCENT is Professor Emeritus of General and Romance Linguistics at the University of Manchester, following his retirement from the Mont Follick Chair in Comparative Philology in October 2011. His theoretical interests lie in exploring feature-based systems, in particular Lexical–Functional Grammar, as models of language change, with a special focus on the interface between morphology and syntax. His specialist languages are Latin, Italian, and the dialects of Italy, and he has published on a variety of topics in the historical morphosyntax of Italo-Romance. He was elected a Fellow of the British Academy in 2006, where he is currently the Vice-President for Research and Higher Education Policy.

1

Introduction

'Arbitrariness' is an uncontested fundamental of linguistic science. The form of what we may call 'roots' and 'affixes' usually stands in an arbitrary, conventional, language-specific relation to the meanings (lexical or grammatical) that those roots and affixes express. In the general case this arbitrariness of the sign is circumscribed, however, by a measure of *iconicity*: one meaning has as its exponent one (arbitrary) form. Yet very often (and especially in languages of the so called 'fusional' type, as are all of those discussed in this book) the arbitrariness of the form–meaning relationship may be, so to speak, 'exacerbated' by the fact that the relation is not one of 'one meaning to one arbitrary form', but of 'one meaning to more than one arbitrary form' or, sometimes, 'more than one arbitrary form to one meaning'. Linguists have an instinct when faced with such facts, and that is to attempt to 'rein in' such profligacy by analysing *allomorphy* as a function either of phonological or of semantic context, thereby factoring out variation in such a way that form–meaning relationships in morphology remain maximally iconic. Often such a procedure is both justified and successful, but some manifestations of allomorphy may prove wholly recalcitrant to such a reductive approach (the highly erratic morphology of the verb 'to be' in many European languages might be taken as a case in point), and here there may be nothing more to do than simply to list the variant forms and their paradigmatic distribution for the relevant lexeme. Such facts are rather an analytical 'dead end'. Most of the studies in this book arise, in contrast, from the awareness that certain instances of allomorphy (or syncretism) are neither reducible wholly to extramorphological causes nor a matter of 'one-off' lexical idiosyncrasy. We are sometimes in the presence of a different dimension of arbitrariness, such that differences of form are systematically correlated with *arbitrary*, 'incoherent' contexts, irreducible to any common, distinctive feature or set of features. The past two decades have seen the emergence of powerful (if sometimes controversial) claims, both synchronic and diachronic, for the existence of such phenomena, which may be considered 'autonomously morphological', or 'morpho-mic', in the sense that their existence (and diachronic persistence) cannot be plausibly ascribed to any coherent 'extramorphological' (phonological or morpho-syntactic) determinants.

The idea that there exist phenomena which are (synchronically) unique to morph-ology, and not determined by extramorphological factors such as phonology or syntax, finds its seminal articulation in Mark Aronoff's book *Morphology by Itself* (1994). Central to this claim is the 'morphome', conceived as a function, lacking any inherent connection with a specific form or a specific meaning, which nonetheless serves systematically to relate form and meaning. Stating that there are autonomously morphological phenomena does not necessarily exclude the possibility that these phenomena could be conditioned in part by, for example, phonological form or morphosyntactic function. 'Autonomy' is not an inherently absolute notion, and it is perfectly conceivable that some morphological phenomenon can be in some measure 'autonomous', yet also sensitive to extramorphological conditioning which, neverthe-less, falls short of fully determining its characteristics. Demonstration of the existence of morphomes initially requires really clear-cut cases for which no extramorphological conditioning can reasonably be postulated. This is what Aronoff (1994) mainly deals with, while making it explicit that the autonomy of morphology may be far more pervasive in language than his principal examples suggest. There is a danger of falling into the error of identifying the morphomic solely with the absolutely morphomic (a tendency which, for example, Vincent in this volume discerns in the early work of Maiden on the diachrony of morphomes). Such a perspective could in turn lead to the isolationist and perhaps sterile position that morphomic structure is simply 'orthogonal' to other components of the grammar, existing, so to speak, 'in a world of its own',[1] in which the only point of contact with (say) phonology or morphosyntax might lie in the past.

The contributors to this volume all believe, so far as we know, that it has been established beyond reasonable doubt that some autonomously morphological phe-nomena exist. The next question must be, therefore, 'How pervasive are they in languages?'. For *any* given morphological phenomenon we should be prepared, at the outset, to contemplate three general possibilities: that it is wholly determined by phonology or morphosyntax, that it is purely morphological, or that it is somewhere in between. With our minds open in this way, we need to identify criteria which will enable us to detect different types of conditioning, and we need careful empirical sifting of data from across a range of languages, with these criteria in mind.

---

[1] Maiden (forthcoming) suggests, in effect, that the way in which all synchronically autonomous morphomic phenomena remain 'anchored' in the grammar is via the lexicon and by virtue of their recurrence. A pattern of allomorphy, however idiosyncratic and however variable its phonological manifestation, offers a predictable and therefore *transparent* relation between form and lexical meaning if it is systematic and recurrent. In other words, given that there is allomorphy, there is a semiotic advantage in being able to predict the pattern of deviation between form and meaning.

Vincent, in his study, articulates a salutary warning for those who may be tempted too readily to discern morphomic structure for phenomena (e.g. the morphology of the Romance synthetic conditional) which, on more careful scrutiny, still reveal functional motivation (in this case compositional). The morphology of the Romance synthetic future and conditional, particularly as manifest in Occitan, is in fact the object of the study by Esher. Here we indeed have close empirical scrutiny of a phenomenon which displays a two-way mismatch, both from form to function and from function to form, and for which neither an exclusively functional motivation nor an exclusively morphomic account seems satisfactorily to fit the data. Perhaps at the other extreme, O'Neill, in a bold and provocative essay, makes a point which all morphologists need to bear in mind. This is (in effect) that we should not allow our analysis to be conditioned by the labels conventionally given to morphological forms. O'Neill argues that the morphological entity in Spanish labelled 'imperfect indicative' is in fact a morphome, irreducible, despite the conventional label, to any coherent set of features. O'Neill seeks to demolish any notion that the uses of the 'imperfect' (in Spanish—but the arguments apply broadly across Romance) have a common semantic denominator, thereby opening up the possibility that many of the labels for tense-forms and similar categories conventionally used by linguists are actually cover terms for morphomes. At the same time, Aronoff takes aim at what might seem yet another redoubt of 'semantic motivation' in morphology, namely the 'lexical root', traditionally viewed as the seat of lexical meaning, demonstrating, for Semitic languages in particular,[2] that it can have a morphological status independent of such meaning.

Kaye's synchronic and diachronic analysis of possibly morphomic stems in the north-western Iranian language Talyshi is an object lesson in how an awareness of morphomic structure can inform the study of morphological change; at the same time, it is tempered by a sober and judicious appreciation of the problems inherent in extricating morphomic phenomena from possible extramorphological determinants of the observed historical developments. Cappellaro's chapter, dealing with the emergence of the phenomenon of 'overabundance' (cf. Thornton 2011) in the Italo-Romance third-person pronominal system, is a reminder that morphological phenomena which are not synchronically determined by any extramorphological factor may arise in ways other than the typical sources of such phenomena. These are loss of phonological or functional motivation, but Cappellaro shows that speakers' 'uncertainty' over the realization of a particular paradigm cell, combined with low frequency or salience, is a determinant of overabundance (cf. also Maiden and O'Neill, 2010, for the role of 'speaker uncertainty' in the incidence of morphomic defectiveness).

The issue of the relation between the autonomously morphological and synchronic phonological conditioning is to the fore in the essays by Anderson and Maiden. The former defends and refines his view (cf. the debate between Anderson

---

[2] Compare also Maiden (2008*a*).

and Maiden in Maiden *et al.* 2011), that certain patterns of allomorphy in the Swiss Rumantsch (or Romansh) of Savognin are examples of 'phonologically conditioned allomorphy', adducing new comparative data from other Swiss Romansh dialects and contesting Maiden's 'morphomic' analysis of data from Savognin and elsewhere. Regardless of which point of view readers judge the more persuasive in this debate, Anderson provides a beautiful example of close engagement with complex morphological data and of the application of sophisticated theoretical tools in their analysis. Maiden's chapter, while not this time addressing Anderson's arguments, in fact represents a concession to the 'phonologizing' perspective with regard to a set of phenomena which he had previously maintained to be autonomously morphological. This concession is empirically driven and bears crucially on the analytical tools for the identification of phonological conditioning. Putative morphomic phenomena often arise historically through phonological conditioning, and not infrequently the original conditioning environment persists intact long after the phonological process has ceased to be productive. This is the case with certain kinds of alternation in the Italian verb which, given evidence for the unproductivity of the original phonological process and the existence of phenomena suggesting that as early as the Middle Ages the alternation was positively insensitive to the phonological environment, Maiden had earlier proclaimed to have been 'morphomic' for centuries. On the other hand, new historical data have come to light which are very difficult to explain unless speakers did indeed (at least in the Middle Ages) attribute the distributional pattern of the alternants in some degree to their phonological environment. Again, phonological conditioning *underdetermines* the observed morphological behaviour, and an autonomously morphological component seems undeniable, but at the same time it seems that if clear phonological cues are available, speakers will exploit them in addition to assigning abstract morphological conditioning to some alternation.

A study at the boundary between the purely morphomic, on the one hand, and morphosyntactic conditioning, on the other, is Loporcaro's, which brings to light, especially in the Bonorvese variety of Logudorese Sardinian, some cases of 'breakdown' in entities which elsewhere have been identified, for example by Maiden, as prime examples of morphomes. This involves the so-called 'L-pattern' (a distributional pattern comprising the first person singular present indicative and the whole of the present subjunctive), which in the relevant variety shows signs of aligning itself functionally just with the 'present subjunctive'. This observation suggests a continual tension between the morphomic 'L-pattern' (strikingly robust across most Romance varieties) and an extramorphological functional motivation with which the L-pattern is very nearly aligned. In Bonorvese, the functional element seems to have prevailed. The sense that extramorphological pressures continue to exercise an influence even on phenomena which are, prima facie, morphomic also emanates from Da Tos's examination of the structure of Italo-Romance 'augments' which are demonstrably sensitive to morphomic patterns of distribution yet are also subject to form–meaning matching in respect of the 'theme vowel' of the verbs in which they occur. Returning to Loporcaro's study, it also calls intriguingly into question an assumption made by Maiden with regard to what we may call the 'temporal' boundaries of a morpheme: what can precede a morpheme—that is, where can a morpheme come from? Most Romance languages are characterized by a morphomic pattern of allomorphy (the 'N-pattern') comprising a subset of present tense forms and due, historically, to the regular effects of certain stress-related sound changes acting on vowels. Maiden claims that the N-pattern can only arise as a historical successor to such sound changes, and adduces as evidence the fact that the one Romance variety in which such a sound change is historically absent—Logudorese— correspondingly lacks any examples of the N-pattern. But Loporcaro illustrates precisely an apparent case of analogical creation of an N-pattern alternation in Logudorese.

So far we have discussed studies which might be said to explore the 'conventional' boundaries of the purely morphological—namely the boundaries with phonological conditioning and those with morphosyntactic or other syntactic conditioning. While 'classic' (or, in Smith's term, 'overt') morphomic phenomena are by definition independent of functional conditioning, there is a further possibility that needs, however, to be considered. Smith, in his essay, points out that while an overt morpheme is irreducible to any 'coherent' set of functions, the functional 'incoherence' of a morpheme may be a matter of degree, measurable in terms of the markedness relations between the set of cells over which some morpheme is defined and its complement. Moreover, he suggests, intriguingly, that there may exist a correlation between the *type* of phenomenon which exhibits a morphomic distribution (specifically, in his study, suppletion and defectiveness) and the degree of motivation of the morpheme. The notion that morphomes, despite their continued irreducibility to any extramorphological causation, may accrue some correlation with factors wholly external to the morphology appears also, in a quite different form, in Meul's chapter, where the 'augments' (generally empty formatives in Romance verbs distributed in many varieties according to purely morphomic patterns) are shown, for Ladin, not only to have a general correlation with polysyllabicity in the root (even though not all polysyllabic root-forms of the relevant verbs take an augment), but also in some dialects with the sociolinguistic function of marking 'distance' from other languages such as Italian, or with certain kinds of aspectual meaning. These observations suggest an intriguing synchronic complementarity between a morphomic pattern of distribution of the augment, insensitive to phonological characteristics of the root or aspectual meaning, and a tendency for speakers to associate the augment, *wherever it does occur in the paradigm*, with extramorphological determinants (and even with particular sociolinguistic[3] factors).

---

[3] For the notion that morphomes may have sociolinguistic significance, see also Smith (2011*b*).

Most examples of morphomes in the literature involve synthetic word-forms (and usually, if not exclusively, within what is conventionally considered as the 'inflectional paradigm'). Any notion that morphomic phenomena may be in some way 'bounded' by synthetic word-forms dissolves in Cruschina's study of certain grammaticalized periphrastic constructions in Sicilian which occur only in a morphomic 'N-pattern' distribution, being otherwise defective. Cruschina—in addition to raising the question of the boundary between phenomena which are purely morphological and those dependent on syntax—stresses the extent to which the relevant constructions are 'grammaticalized'. Another way of looking at this is, of course, to say that morphomes exist where there is only one lexical meaning present in these constructions—a fact which may have some bearing on Maiden's suggestion (forthcoming) that *unity of lexical meaning* provides a bounding domain for morphomic phenomena and that morphomes offer speakers a systematic and predictable way of regulating and restraining the relation between the unitary meaning of a lexeme and its otherwise multiple and idiosyncratic manifestation in paradigms.

The present volume brings together thirteen scholars (seven of whom also contributed to Maiden *et al.* 2011) with interests in autonomously morphological phenomena, from both diachronic and synchronic perspectives.[4] The orientation is strongly towards the data, rather than necessarily to theory or formalism, for the first stage of any sophisticated theoretical analysis must be a mapping out of those domains in which the 'boundaries' between pure morphology and other components of language lie. The central message which emerges from the following chapters is the need for a cautious, judicious, open-minded approach in the analysis of those phenomena which show signs of being purely morphological. Morphologists must always be prepared to take seriously the possibility not only that 'clearcut' morphomic phenomena could be independent of any extramorphological conditioning but that the same could in principle be true of familiar and apparently fully extramorphologically conditioned phenomena. Indeed, a willingness to take such a stance is necessary as a corrective to the reductionist instincts of those who would seek at all costs to force all morphological phenomena into the Procrustean bed of synchronic phonological or functional conditioning. However, those who are convinced that the close analysis of linguistic data (particularly from a diachronic perspective—whose fecundity is demonstrated by many of the studies in this book) establishes beyond doubt the psychological reality of morphomic phenomena are certainly not thereby licensed to dismiss alternative views of putative morphomes which seek to relate them to other types of determinant. It needs to be recognized (see,

---

[4] Much work on the diachrony of morphomes has been done with respect to Romance languages, and this fact is reflected in the large number of chapters in this book concerned with those languages. However, the studies by Aronoff (as in his earlier work) and Kaye clearly show the applicability of the issues to languages well beyond Romance.

for example, the comments by Smith or Vincent in this volume) that Aronoff (1994) allows for morphomic phenomena to permeate language far beyond the 'clear-cut', unambiguous, cases of morphomehood. This does not mean, of course, that 'everything is morphomic', but it is construable as an invitation to stay constantly alert to the role and place of systematic but idiosyncratic structure in morphology, and as a warning against the urge to seek at all costs to subjugate all morphology to extramorphological causes (cf. Aronoff, this volume). Indeed it is our duty to stay rooted in the data and to be ready to accept the implications of new data which may contradict our earlier positions. What emerges quite often is a compromise, in which certain morphological facts have a morphomic component yet also manifest, to varying degrees, correlations with phonological, morphosyntactic, semiotic, or even sociolinguistic factors. Probably most morphomic phenomena possess an element of extramorphological conditioning; and probably many phonologically and functionally conditioned phenomena possess an element of the purely morphological.

2

Stem alternations in Swiss Rumantsch

STEPHEN R. ANDERSON

The present chapter continues an extended conversation with Martin Maiden (Anderson 2008, Maiden 2008*b*, Anderson 2010, 2011, Maiden 2011*d*) about the analysis of stem alternations in one form of Swiss Rumantsch, Surmiran as spoken in the area of Savognin and the surrounding communities.[1] Over time, our analyses have shown some convergence, but important differences remain. Some of these, such as the status of the verb *dueir* (viewed as defective by me, and as suppletive by Maiden) will not be addressed here, because there are no new facts available, and Maiden and I simply disagree on some points in the interpretation of what is known.

My intention here is to provide some further context and interpretation in support of the analysis I have offered in previous work, suggesting: (a) that the corresponding facts in other Swiss Rumantsch languages call for an analysis similar to that which is motivated for the Surmiran of Savognin; and (b) that some additional facts from forms of Rumantsch provide additional support for that analysis and do not undermine it as Maiden suggests.

2.1 The story so far: Surmiran stems (Anderson 2011)

The stems of many verbs (nearly all, on the analysis being defended here) in the Surmiran of Savognin and related areas in the valley of Julia in Graubünden display an alternation between two distinct phonological shapes. The facts concerning this pattern have been presented in previous papers (Anderson 2008, 2010, 2011); the data

[1] This work was supported in part by NSF awards #BCS-0418410 and #BCS 98–76456 to Yale University, and by awards from the Social Sciences Research Fund at Yale. Discussion with Martin Maiden (and others at the OxMorph meetings) has been extremely important in the development of the analyses presented here, as will be evident, even if I find myself in the end unable to agree with him on some important points.

are not in dispute, and will not be rehearsed again in detail here. Representative alternating verbs include *ludar* [luˈdar] 'to praise', 3SG *loda* [ˈlodə]; *entrar* [ənˈtrar] 'to enter', 3SG *aintra* [ˈai̯ntrə]; *vurdar* [vʊrˈdar] 'to watch', 3SG *varda* [ˈvardə], etc.

2.1.1 *Stem alternation: the basics*

Let us refer to the two stem shapes associated with a verb 'Stem 1' and 'Stem 2' for the moment. For the verb *ludar,* for example, Stem 1 is /lud-/ and Stem 2 /lod-/; for *entrar,* /əntr-/ and /ai̯ntr-/; for *vurdar,* /vʊrd-/ and /vard-/, etc. One of these stems (Stem 1) appears in one set of morphological categories of the verb: in the 1,2PL of the present indicative, throughout the imperfect, the future, and the conditional, as well as in the 2PL imperative and the present and past participles. The other (Stem 2) appears in a complementary set of categories: in the 1–3SG and the 3PL of the present indicative, plus the entire present subjunctive and the 2SG of the imperative. The infinitive is generally based on Stem 1 as illustrated by the verbs cited above, but verbs of the type descended from the Latin third conjugation have Stem 2 in the infinitive instead: e.g. *discorrer* [dɪʃˈkorər] 'speak'; 1SG.PRS *disˈcor*; 1PL.PRS *discurˈrign*.

Although grammatical descriptions of Surmiran such as Signorell *et al.* (1987*a*) and Thöni (1969) imply that 'alternating' verbs are a limited class, once we consider differences of vowel quality, it is reasonable to say that 'regular' verbs also have two stems, although the two are not distinguished orthographically. The stem of *cantar* 'to sing', for example, appears as /kənt-/ in just those environments where Stem 1 is called for, and as /kant-/ in those calling for Stem 2.

Although the differences between the two stem shapes can often be reconstructed as based on predictable and purely phonological regularities in earlier stages of the language, the alternations between Stem 1 and Stem 2 are not simply a matter of phonology today, because it is not possible to predict either stem from the other. For any given vowel quality appearing in Stem 1 the vowel of the corresponding Stem 2 can have any of a number of different qualities, and vice versa, such that it is impossible to predict either stem from the other in the general case.

In the majority of instances, the difference between the two stems rests on different qualities of a single vowel, but other patterns characterize many verbs, including some consonantal differences (e.g. *s'anclinar* 'to bend', 3SG.PRS.IND *s'an-clegna*), variation in more than a single vowel (e.g. *misirar* 'to measure', 3SG.PRS.IND *maseira*), and vowel/Ø alternations (e.g. *luvrar* 'to work', 3SG.PRS.IND *lavoura*). These patterns reflect the complex interplay of a variety of phonological changes in the histories of individual words, changes that are now quite opaque from the point of view of the language's synchronic phonology.

The set of circumstances in which Stem 2 is found as opposed to Stem 1 is of course reminiscent of what Maiden, in a series of studies of a variety of Romance languages, has called the 'N-pattern' (modified to include the infinitives of original

Latin third conjugation verbs, and expanded to include the entire present subjunctive rather than just the singular and third person plural). With this pattern in mind, Maiden (2011*d*) argues that we should continue to consider the distribution of these stem alternants as defined in morphological terms. The N-Pattern (or the particular variant we see here) is a *morphome*, a purely morphological construct whose unity is not based on a coherent phonological, morphosyntactic, or semantic definition but rather functions solely in the morphology.

Such an analysis has been shown to be plausible and motivated for similar stem alternations in several Romance languages, but in the present case there is a straightforward alternative. Although the alternations cannot be (synchronically) reduced to the operation of phonological rules in the language, there is nonetheless a clear phonological factor which differentiates the environments in which the two variants of each stem occur: Stem 2 occurs when main stress falls on the stem, while Stem 1 occurs when main stress falls on a desinence.

As argued in previous papers (Anderson 2008, 2010, 2011), stress in Surmiran is phonologically predictable (apart from some vocabulary borrowed from German and treated as synchronically foreign) on the basis of the rule in (1).

(1) **Stress:** Main stress falls on the penult if the rhyme of the final syllable consists of [ə], possibly followed by [r], [l], [n], or [s]. If the final rhyme contains a non-ə vowel, or [ə] followed by some other consonant, the main stress falls on this syllable instead.

The verbal forms calling for Stem 1 are precisely those whose endings contain a syllable attracting stress by this rule, while those calling for Stem 2 are just those with no such syllable in the ending, allowing stress to retract onto the stem. Accordingly, it seems reasonable to refer to the stem alternants as the 'unstressed stem' as opposed to the 'stressed stem' rather than as the less informative Stem 1 vs. Stem 2.

The distinction between the presence and the absence of stress in Surmiran has consequences for the range of vowels found in a syllable. Stressed syllables can contain a variety of full vowels (long and short) and diphthongs. Unstressed syllables, in contrast, generally contain only short [ə] (written *a* or *e*), [ɪ] (*i*), or [ʊ] (*u*), though unstressed [ɛ, ɔ] are not rare. We can formulate the relation between stress and vowel quality as a system of constraints, as in (2).

(2) Constraints:
    a. Avoid stressed [ə,ɪ,ʊ].
    b. Avoid unstressed [a,i,u] (as well as unstressed long vowels and diphthongs).
    c. Avoid unstressed short mid vowels (ranked lower than those above).
        Ranking: **Stress** ≫ **a, b** ≫ **c**

Verbal stem alternations reflect these facts about the distribution of vowels, in that the vocalism of the stressed stem will contain an appropriate vowel in the position where stress can fall, while the corresponding unstressed stem will generally have a different vowel (drawn from the set of those possible in unstressed syllables) in the corresponding position. Unstressed stem [ɛ] and [ɔ] commonly either (a) alternate with long stressed (open or closed) similar mid vowels, or else (b) do not alternate, belonging to the class of verbs in *esch* (see the discussion of this pattern below). Roughly two dozen verbs (out of several hundred) with stressed ['ɛ] or ['ɔ] show an unstressed vowel with the same quality, while in a few verbs unstressed [ĕ] alternates with ['ai̯] or ['ei̯].

On this basis, the description of the stem alternation system is straightforward. The lexical representation of a given verbal stem has two phonological shapes, one of which is suitable for having stress placed on it, and the other of which is suitable for remaining unstressed. In the latter of these, the last vowel in the representation is drawn from the set [ə, ɪ, ʊ] (ignoring the case of mid vowels, which is more complicated but not fundamentally different), and in the former the last vowel is a full vowel or diphthong. Verbal desinences, similarly, have a phonological shape which either attracts stress or fails to do so. The morphology then combines the (complex, bipartite) representation of a stem with the representation of an ending, and the constraint system eliminates one or the other potential stem shape on the basis of the degree of well-formedness of the two alternatives. An example of how this works is provided by the tableaux for the infinitive and 3SG present indicative forms in (3).

(3) *vurdar* 'watch', 3SG. *varda* = {/vʊrd/ , /vard/} + /-ar/ or /-ə/

a.

/{vʊrd,vard}-ar/	Stress	*'ʊ,'ɪ,'ə	*ă,ĭ,ŭ
'vʊrdăr	!*	*	*
'vardăr	!*		*
☞ vŭr'dăr			
văr'dar			!*

b.

/{vʊrd,vard}-ə/	Stress	*'ʊ,'ɪ,'ə	*ă,ĭ,ŭ
'vʊrdə		!*	
☞ 'vardə			
vŭr'də	!*	*	
văr'də	!*	*	*

2.1.2 *The augment* -esch

Related to these matters is the presence or absence in certain inflected verbal forms of the stem extension -*esch*, comparable to elements found under similar conditions in other Romance languages (e.g. the -*isc* in Italian *fiˈnisco* from *finire*, cf. *finiˈamo* 'I/ we finish'), illustrated in (4).

(4)   *gratular* ([ˌgratʊˈlar]) 'beat, shake'

1SG	ˌgratʊˈlesch
2SG	ˌgratʊˈleschas
3SG	ˌgratʊˈlescha
1PL	ˌgratʊˈlagn
2PL	ˌgratʊˈlez
3PL	ˌgratʊˈleschan
1SG.PRS.SBJV	ˌgratʊˈlescha

A substantial number of Surmiran verbs show this *-esch,* precisely in those forms of the finite paradigm where the stressed stem would be called for. My account of this posits the semantically vacuous rule of finite inflection in (5).

(5) $/X/ \rightarrow /X\varepsilon\int/\ [\overline{+\text{VERB}}]$
       (limited to tensed first and fourth conjugation verbs)

Since the marker introduced by this rule does not serve to express any of the semantic or morphosyntactic content of the form, it should normally be seen as producing a violation of the natural condition in (6).

(6)   **Dep$_\mathcal{M}$**: (Introduced) phonological material in the output should be the realization of morphological content in the Input.

However, the application of rule (5) is not pointless. Since it has the effect of introducing stress-attracting phonological material precisely where stress would otherwise fall on the stem, a consequence of its operation is that verbs with which it appears never show any alternation in the stem shape: the unstressed stem (augmented with *-esch* exactly where necessary) will always be phonologically appropriate.

Verbs that take the *-esch* augment can thus be lexically listed with only a single stem, one whose shape is such that the vowel on which stress would otherwise fall in stem-stressed forms is one that should not be stressed according to the constraints in (2). Under exactly these circumstances, the violation of (6) which the introduction of *-esch* by rule (5) produces is less serious than the violation of the constraints in (2). This implies the constraint ranking in (7).

(7)   (2a, b, c) $\gg$ **Dep$_\mathcal{M}$**

As a result, the application of rule (5) is sanctioned exactly where its operation will avoid the occurrence of stress on a vowel that resists stress in a verb whose lexical representation does not provide an alternative stressable shape for this purpose.

Rule (5) is restricted to finite forms of verbs from two of the six conjugation classes of Surmiran, and so can be said to involve morphological conditions. Maiden (2011d: 45) argues that the appearance of *-esch* is thereby morphologically determined, but I would emphasize that the conditions on this rule have nothing to do with the N-pattern or any other morpheme. The apparent 'N-pattern effects' follow entirely from the phonology of stress and its relation to vowel quality.

2.1.3   *Stem alternations beyond the verb*

Important evidence that the patterns of stem alternation just discussed cannot be tied to a morpheme defined by a set of morphological categories of the verb is provided by that fact that the same alternations are found robustly in virtually all word classes in the language as a consequence of derivation. Across the lexicon, stems with shapes characteristic of the stressed stems of verbs appear when stress falls on them, but when derivation has the effect of shifting stress away from the stem, a different shape appears, one whose form is that characteristic of the unstressed verbal stems. The examples in (8) illustrate the fact that, in general, when the stem of a verb is used as the basis for such derivation, the alternations that appear are the same as those arising within the paradigm of the verb involved.

(8)   a. *burscha'nar* 'brush' 3SG.PRS *bar'schunga*
         bar'schung 'brush (N)'; *(la) burscha'neda* '(process of) brushing'
      b. *cuglia'nar* 'swindle' 3SG.PRS *cu'gliunga*
         cu'gliung 'swindler'; *(la) cuglia'nada* '(act of) swindling'
      c. *gut'tar* 'to drip' 3SG.PRS *'gotta*
         'got 'drop (N)'; *gu'tella* 'drip (N), (eye)drop'; *gutta'rada* 'sudden snow-melt'
      d. *li'ier* 'to bind, tie, combine' 3SG.PRS *'leia*
         'leia 'union, alliance'; *ˌleiabar'schung* 'brush-binder'; *lia'deira* '(ski) bind-ing'; *li'om* 'string, garter'
      e. *'neiver* 'to snow' 3SG.PRS *'neiva*, PST.PTCP *na'via*
         'neiv 'snow'; *na'vaglia* 'big snowfall'; *na'vada* '(lots of) snow'
      f. *tschur'rar* 'to curl, frizz' 3SG.PRS *'tschorra*
         (erva) 'tschorra 'curly mint, *Mentha spicata* var. *crispa*'; *tshcur'richel* 'curl (N)'; *tshcur'riglia* 'crumpled, as slept-in clothes'
      g. *tuf'far* 'to stink' 3SG.PRS *'toffa*
         'tof 'fart'; *tuf'fous* 'stinky'
      h. *'veiver* 'to live' 3SG.PRS *'veiva*, 2PL.PRS *vi'vagn*
         'veiv 'alive'; *vi'vent* 'one who lives'

In some instances, an alternation appears in non-verbal forms which is distinct from that appearing in a related verb, as illustrated in (9). The choice of stems is still conditioned by the location of stress, however, suggesting that related verbs and non-verbs can have distinct stem sets.

(9)   *sua'rar* 'to smell' 3SG.PRS *sa'voira*
      sa'vour 'smell (N)'; *savu'rous* 'fragrant'

Non-verbs derived from the same stems as some of those that show the augment *-esch* as described in Section 2.1.2 above show a stem alternation. This suggests that while the verb has only a single stem in its lexical entry, the non-verbs are built on a set containing two stems. Once again, the stem appearing in non-verbs with non-stem stress is the same as that appearing in the (non-stem stressed) verbal forms, while the other stem appears in stem-stressed forms of the derived non-verbs.

(10) a. *favo'réir* 'to favour' 3SG.PRS *favo'rescha*
         fa'vour 'favour'; *favo'revel* 'favourable'
      b. *flu'drar* 'line (clothing)' 3SG.PRS *flu'drescha*
         'flodra 'lining (of an article of clothing)'; *flu'drader* 'one who lines (clothes)'
      c. *murti'rar* 'to torment' 3SG.PRS *murti'rescha*
         mar'toir 'torment (N), trouble'; *murti'rem, murti'rada* 'torments (coll.)'
      d. *sbli'tgier* 'to bleach' 3SG.PRS *sbli'tgescha*
         'sblatg 'bleach(ed) (N, A)'; *sbli'tgider* 'one who bleaches'
      e. *saraman'tar* 'put someone under oath' 3SG.PRS *saraman'tescha* (*sar-a'mainta* in Sonder and Grisch 1970)
         sara'maint 'oath'; *saraman'to* 'sworn'
      f. *tschurriclar* 'to curl (hair)' 3SG.PRS *tschurriclescha*
         [from *tschurrichel* 'curl (N)'; cf. *tschurrar/tschorra* 'curl (V)']

The same alternations also appear, again in a way correlating with the location of stress, in some non-verbs for which no corresponding verb exists that could serve as their base (although some of these words serve in their turn as the bases for derived verbs).

(11) a. *'meir* 'wall'; *mi'raglia* 'walling, stonework'; *mi'rader* 'wall-maker'
      b. *'deir* 'hard'; *di'raglia* 'hardness; *di'rezza* 'very hard'
      c. *'freid* 'cold (N, A)'; *far'daglia* 'great cold'; *far'dour* 'coolness'
         sfar'dar 'to get cold' 3SG.PRS *'sfreida*; *sfar'dour* 'frost-shower'; *sfardan'tar* 'to cool (tr.)' 3SG.PRS *sfar'dainta*

A class of apparent problems for the analysis maintained here is presented by derived words in which the 'stressed' stem (identifiable by comparison with a related verb) is found inappropriately in a derived word where it does not in fact have stress. Some examples are given in (12), where the 'inappropriate' vowels are underlined.

(12) a. *sa'tger* '(to) dry [intr.]' 3SG.PRS *'setga*
         'setg(a) 'dry (A)'; *setgan'tar* '(to) dry [tr.]'
      b. *preschen'tar* '(to) present' 3SG.PRS *pre'schainta*
         preschentazi'un 'presentation'; *pre'schaint* 'present (A)'; *preschainta'maintg* 'presently'
      c. *accumpa'gner* 'accompany' 3SG.PRS *accum'pogna*
         accumpa'gneder 'accompanist'; *accumpogna'maint* 'accompaniment'

d. *acccuma'dar* 'adjust' 3SG.PRS *accu'moda*
   accumo'dabel 'adjustable' *accumoda'maint* 'adjustment'
e. *'sfend[ər]* '(to) split' 1PL.PRS *sfan'dagn*
   sfan'dia 'cracked (A)'; *sfen'dibel* 'splittable'
f. *dur'meir* '(to) sleep' 3SG.PRS *'dorma*
   durmi'gliun 'late riser'; *dormu'lent* 'sleepy'
g. *anga'nar* 'defraud' 3SG.PRS *an'giona*
   anga'nous 'fraudulent'; *an'gion* 'fraud (N)'; *angiona'reia* 'deceit (coll.)'

Maiden (2011d) argues that the existence of such words suggests that stem shape is not, in fact, correlated with the location of stress, but is rather determined by a complex of morphological conditions. A closer examination of the facts concerning these forms, however, shows that this conclusion is unwarranted.

Words displaying such inappropriate stem shapes constitute a decided, and limited, minority. Note first of all an asymmetry in the set of such forms: all involve the appearance of a 'stressed' stem that does not bear stress. No examples are found of words in which an 'unstressed' stem shape appears with stress. Furthermore, all of the words with the 'wrong' stem are derived from other full words, and not from basic stems. The bases from which they are derived are words in which the stressed stem is appropriate, since stress falls on that stem in the base, but is displaced onto a derivational ending in the more complex form. This suggests that the appearance of the stressed stem without stress in words such as those illustrated in (12) results from the fact that this stem was selected (appropriately) in the construction of the base word, and remains unchanged in other words derived from that.

This suggests a hypothesis based on the conception of morphological structure as constructed in a cyclic fashion. On that account, basic, underived lexemes are characterized phonologically by a pair of 'stressed' and 'unstressed' stems.[2] The choice of one or the other stem allomorph takes place on the first cycle to which a stem is subject; once the stem shape is determined, that decision is not revisited on subsequent cycles. As a result, if the 'stressed' base is chosen on the first stem cycle, and this form is subsequently extended by further endings so that the vowel stressed on the first cycle no longer bears stress, the original stem will appear to be inappropriate.[3]

The distinction suggested here between morphological formations built on the basis of the (two stem) lexical base and those built on existing words is similar to the effect of the 'Level I' vs. 'Level II' distinction within Lexical Phonology (Kaisse and Shaw 1985, Kiparsky 1982, 1985) and its descendant, Stratal Optimality Theory (Bermúdez-Otero, forthcoming, Kiparsky 2000), between two classes of morphological formation in English.

---

[2] Verbs of the class that take the *-esch* augment where the stressed stem is called for have only a single stem shape, as discussed above in Section 2.1.2.

[3] See Kamprath (1987) for discussion of motivations for cyclic interaction in a closely related form of Rumantsch.

One set of these, the Level I formations, take roots or basic stems as their input. In such words, phonological material comprising an affix is taken into account in assigning stress, conditioning vowel alternations, etc. Examples include both derivational and (non-productive) inflectional material such as the affixes in (13).

(13)   a. -*ity* (*profound, profundity; final, finality*), -*al*, -*ous*, -*th*, -*ation*, -*atory*, -*ize*, etc. [Derivational]

      b. -*t* (*keep, kept; lose, lost; leave, left;* etc.) [Inflectional]

In contrast, Level II affixes are *neutral*, in that they leave their base unchanged. Stress, vowel quality, and other phonological properties of the base are computed entirely in terms of the content of the base itself, and are not altered by the addition of affixal material. Again, both derivational and inflectional formations can behave in this way, as in the examples in (14).

(14)   a. -*ness* (*profound, profoundness; final, finalness;* etc.), -*hood*, -*er*, -*ism*, -*ist* [Derivational]

      b. -*d* (*heap, heaped; doze, dozed; believe, believed*) [Inflectional]

Some instances of -*able* appear as level I affixation and others as level II. Thus, *cómparable* 'roughly equal' is a level I form, while *compárable* 'suitable for comparison' is a level II form. This dual possibility is similar to variation cited by Maiden in some cognate affixes in Surmiran.

In English, stress computed at Level I remains unchanged at later levels of the lexical phonology, while in Surmiran, stress is a predictable property of the surface phonological word, and so is recomputed at later levels. Its presence in an initial formation, however, determines the distribution of vowels and stem shapes, phonological properties that are retained as further affixes are added. This effect accounts for nearly all exceptional stem shapes of the sort illustrated in (12). Since further affixation can only shift stress away from a stem, and not result in the assignment of stress to a syllable that was unstressed on an earlier cycle, this accounts for the asymmetric pattern of anomaly in stem shapes.

The basic point of contention between my account and Maiden's is whether we should prefer a phonological account of the stem alternations in Surmiran, as offered here, to one based on autonomously morphologized dimensions. However valid the case for such an analysis may be in other Romance languages, I think it is not motivated here.

Maiden's (2011*d*) preference is to see the two possible stems of a lexeme as distributed on the basis of a morphome (Aronoff 1994): a morphophonological function that does not have a single (or coherent) morphosyntactic value, such as the English 'perfect participle' which is used to form (a) passives and (b) perfect tenses. He has justified the positing of the morphomic N-pattern ([1SG.PRS + 2SG. PRS + 3SG.PRS + 3PL.PRS] vs. the rest of the paradigm) in a series of studies (Maiden 1992, 2004*a*, 2005*a*), and I do not question the utility of that notion in the examples for which it has been argued there.

In Surmiran, though, the choice of a stem is clearly correlated with a phonological factor (location of main stress), entirely transparently in most cases and easily recoverable in the small set of cyclically derived words derived from other words illustrated in (12). A morphomic analysis, in contrast, needs to invoke a set of categories (present indicative singular and third plural except for verbs that take -*esch*, singular imperatives, third conjugation infinitives, and a heterogeneous collection of non-verbal categories) as the environment for Stem 1 or its equally complex complement as the environment for Stem 2. The analysis as 'phonologically conditioned allomorphy' (Carstairs 1987, 1988) seems clearly indicated here.

2.2 Some other Swiss Rumantsch languages

The analysis of stem alternations presented in Section 2.1 is based entirely on the facts of Surmiran as spoken in Savognin and the surrounding area, and it is this language that I have explored in some detail. From a consideration of the available descriptive literature on other Rumantsch languages of Switzerland, however, it appears that parallel accounts may well be more broadly applicable.

2.2.1 *Surselvan*

Spescha (1989: 473–8) lists some twenty-eight patterns of alternation in Surselvan verbs, making it clear that (as in Surmiran) it is not possible to predict either alternant from the other. Some of these are illustrated in (15).

(15)

INF	3SG
clamar	cloma
tschintschar	tschontscha
purtar	porta
alzar	aulza
filtschar	faultscha
ludar	lauda

As in Surmiran, the stem variants are distributed such that a stem shape whose last vowel is suitable to bear stress appears in rhizotonic forms, while forms with desinential stress have a final vowel limited to unstressed variants of [a, i, u, e, o]. The 'stressed' stem appears in the singular and the third plural of the present (indicative and subjunctive), in the singular imperative, and in the infinitive of class 3 verbs; the 'unstressed' stem appears elsewhere. The only difference between this system and that of Surmiran is that the first and second person plural present subjunctive forms in Surselvan have desinential stress (and thus require the 'unstressed' stem). The two stems can be lexically differentiated by the quality of the final vowel, and stem choice can be accomplished by regularities of the phonology comparable to those presented in (2) above for Surmiran. The augment *-esch* appears with the only stem shape in otherwise-rhizotonic forms of some verbs.

Again as in Surmiran, forms derived from alternating stems generally show the stem alternant appropriate to the position of stress in the derived form. Among these are derived factive verbs such as *buentar* 'cause to drink' from *beiber* 'drink' (2PL *buein*) and *stunclentar* 'make tired' from *staunchel* 'tired', and deverbal nouns such as *la lavur* 'the work' from *luvrar* 'to work' (3SG *lavura*), *la dumonda* 'the question' from *dumandar* 'to ask' (3SG *dumonda*), etc.

Notice that if we thought of stem alternation as conditioned by purely morphological categories, we might expect some verbs like *buentar* to show it: that is, to have 3SG.PRS forms like **beibenta*, etc. This never occurs, however: the presence of the causative formative *-ent* will always prevent stress from falling on the preceding stem, so there is never any way to get the 'stressed' stem in the N-pattern forms. Stem choice in Surselvan thus appears to be phonologically conditioned allomorphy, as in Surmiran.

2.2.2 *Engadine languages*

The two closely related languages spoken in the Engadine display similar systems. Both of these languages have somewhat different vowel systems from that of Surmiran, including front rounded vowels. The relations between the vowel systems of stressed and unstressed syllables are otherwise similar to what we find in Surmiran, and alternations along the same lines as what we find in that language are characteristic. To some extent (especially in Puter) these alternations are being levelled in contemporary speech, and it is probably the case that two-stem (alternating) verbs are increasingly a minority in the lexicon. This implies that the class of verbs taking the augment *-esch* (also *-isch* in Vallader) cannot be identified as simply as in Surmiran, as verbs with a single stem inappropriate for taking stress. Nonetheless, within the remaining (and still substantial) class of items showing stem alternations, the distinction between one stem and the other tracks the distribution of rhizotonic vs. non-rhizotonic forms rather than an otherwise arbitrary collection of morphological categories. In addition, within this class the phonological correspondences between stressed and unstressed stems are still idiosyncratic enough to support an analysis of the sort proposed above.

2.2.2.1 *Puter*   This form of Rumantsch, spoken in the upper Engadine (cf. Ganzoni 1977, Scheitlin 1962, Urech-Clavuot 2009), displays at least eighteen distinct patterns of stem alternation involving a single vowel in the stem, and others that are more complex.

Some unusual alternation patterns in Puter do not have direct parallels in Surmiran or Surselvan. One of these is a group of verbs including *couscher* 'cook', 1SG *cousch*, 1PL *cuschains*; *volver* 'turn', 1SG *volv*, 1PL *vulvains*; *vaindscher* 'defeat', 1SG *vaindsch*, 1PL *vandschains*, among others, displaying a third stem variant in the past participle: *cot(ta), vout(a), vint(a)*. In some cases, these verbs have both the unusual participle and the expected form: thus, Urech-Clavuot (2009) gives both *vint(a)* and the expected *vandschieu/vandschida* as past participle forms for *vaindscher*. In some cases these three-stem forms have been regularized: Ganzoni (1977) gives the forms above for *couscher* 'cook', but Urech-Clavuot (2009) gives the 1PL form as *coschains*, perhaps regularized on the model of the participle. Ganzoni (1977: 132f. [my transla-tion]) notes that 'a good portion of the irregular verbs earlier had two past participles, an irregular and a regular: *tais, tendieu* ["tightened"]; *promoss, promovieu* ["pro-moted"]. Many of these irregular past participles are still used today only as adjectives: *commoss* "moved, touched, deeply affected"; *stret* "tight".' This development would appear to be a straightforward instance of Kuryłowicz's (1949) 'fourth law of analogy'.

Another interesting development in Puter is an alternation pattern involving verbs whose 'unstressed' stem has no vowel corresponding to the final vowel of the 'stressed' stem: *mner* 'lead', 1SG *main*; *tmair* 'fear', 1SG *tem*; *trer* 'pull', 1SG, *tir*; *cusglier* 'advise', 1SG *cussagl*; *artschaiver* 'receive', 1PL *arvschins*. Although the stressed vowel corresponding to such a Ø is not predictable, the two stems can still be distinguished by the quality (or absence) of the final vowel, as in other dialects. In the case of verbs whose unstressed stem contains no vowel at all (e.g. /mn-/ 'lead', /tm-/ 'fear', /tr-/ 'pull'), while the stressed stem contains a final vowel that can bear stress (/main-/, /tem-/, /tir-/), the choice between stems can be made straightfor-wardly by the constraint system along the same lines as in Surmiran, on the basis of stress. The same is true for stem pairs such as {/kŭsʎ-/, /kŭsaʎ-/} 'cook', {/ərvʃ-/, /ərtʃai̯v-/} 'receive', etc., on the assumption that vowel qualities associated with unstressed syllables characterize the unstressed stems of such words.

Apart from such phenomena, the 'stressed' stem is used as in Surmiran in the singular and third person plural of the present indicative, the singular imperative, and the entire paradigm of the present subjunctive (also used as a polite imperative). The 'unstressed' stem is used elsewhere; and again the difference corresponds directly to the difference between forms with root vs. desinential stress. The augment *-esch* appears in otherwise rhizotonic (finite) forms of many verbs of the first and fourth conjugations.

Derived forms display the stem appropriate to their surface stress, as in *stanglanter* 'to tire', from *staungel* 'tired'. More research is necessary to establish the generality of the phenomenon, but it appears that stress-conditioned stem choice is robustly attested throughout the Puter lexicon, and not only in the verbal paradigm.

2.2.2.2 *Vallader*   The facts characterizing the language of the lower Engadin (cf. Ganzoni 1983, Tscharner 2003) differ from those in Puter primarily in that the augment has two forms: *-esch* for first conjugation verbs (e.g. *evitar* 'avoid', 1SG *evitesch*) but *-isch* for verbs of the fourth conjugation (e.g. *impedir* 'hinder', 1SG *impedisch*).

Here too we find that when a verb has two stems, the stem that shows up in related derivational forms is generally predicted by the location of the stress. Some examples are given in (16).

(16) a. *mas'dar* 'to mix', 1SG *'maisda*
           'maisda 'mixture, blend'; *mas'düra* 'mixture'
      b. *dur'mir* 'to sleep', 1SG *'dorma*
           dur'mind 'sleeping (Adv.)', *durmi'gliunz* 'sleepyhead', *dur'mida* 'long nap';
           'dorma 'narcotic, soporific'
      c. *ran'tar* 'to tie up (especially livestock)', 1SG *'raint*
           ran'tam 'halter'
      d. *re'cuorrer* 'to appeal, seek redress', 1SG *re'cuor*, 1PL *recur'rin*
           re'cuors 'recourse, redress'; *recur'rent* 'complainant'

As in Surmiran, we find some examples in which the stressed stem appears 'inappropriately' when a derived form is built not on the alternating verbal base but on an existing word for which that stem is appropriate, as in the set of words in (17).

(17) *sco'lar* 'to educate', 1SG *'scoula*
      scola'ziun 'education', *sco'lar* 'scholar; *'scoulas* 'educational system'
      'scoula 'school', *scou'lina* 'kindergarten', *scou'letta* 'crafts school'

While more restricted in its lexical extension than is the case in Surmiran, then, the stem alternation system in Puter and Vallader displays essentially the same character for those lexemes to which it applies.

2.2.2.3 *Val Müstair*   The language of this side valley of the Engadine, as documented by Schorta (1938), differs in many details from other forms of Swiss Rumantsch. One of these is cited by Maiden (2011d: 45) as presenting a difficulty for the present analysis, arguing that 'Anderson's analysis implies that if, in a verb taking –*esch*, stress underwent an obligatory shift from the ending onto the root, then that stress shift would duly be accompanied by –*esch*'.

In Val Müstair, stress in first conjugation (-*ár*) infinitives systematically shifts onto the root: *láydər* 'to spread manure' (Surm. *ladár/léida*); *fílər* 'to spin' (Surm. *filár/féila*). The stem alternant that appears is the one normally used for rhizotonic forms, as expected. Where the verb normally takes the augment (here -*áj* rather than -*ésch*), however, this element does not appear in the infinitive, and instead stress remains on the ending: *batjár* 'to baptize' (3SG *batjája*). In augmenting verbs, then, the shift of stress expected on the basis of verb class does not result in the introduction of the augment, but rather is blocked.

As Maiden notes, this is accommodated on the present analysis by saying that verbs taking the augment only have a single stem, which is not able to take stress, while other verbs have two stems. The expected 'stressed' stem occurs when stress falls on the root of the infinitive, as in the third conjugation. The fact that the augment does not appear under these circumstances falls out from the fact that the rule introducing it (the local analogue of rule (5) above) is limited to finite inflection. In fact, the augment (Surm. -*esch*, Val Müstair -*aj*) never appears except in tensed forms: never in related non-verbal forms, never in participles or infinitives. Therefore this rule is not available to 'save' verb stems like Val Müstair *bătj-* in the infinitive from bearing stress, and the only alternative to impermissible stem stress appears to be to stress the infinitival ending instead.

These facts are thus entirely consistent with (the extension to Val Müstair of) the present analysis. They do show that there are morphological conditions on the rule introducing the augment, but they do not compromise the principle that, like stem choice, the appearance of this element *where possible on morphological grounds* is governed by the location of stress.

2.2.3 *Other languages of Surmeir*

Although the speech of the Julia valley around Savognin has served as the basis of the 'standard' form of Surmiran as taught in schools, printed in the local newspaper *La Pagina da Surmeir*, etc., the region of Surmeir is home to a number of other, rather different forms of Rumantsch. One of these presents another instance in which stress normally found on a desinence is shifted onto the stem: in particular, the replacement of 1PL present indicative ending -*áɲ/ájn* by -*ăn* in some areas. This is mentioned by (Haiman and Benincà 1992: 95):

> The only Rhaeto-Romance dialect [in which stress in the 1st plural present indicative is rhizotonic] seems to be that dialect of Surmeiran [*sic*] which is spoken in Bravuogn/Bergün. [...] The most plausible development, given other developments in both the 2nd singular and the 1st plural is the following. First, the 1st plural was expressed by HOMO/UNUS + 3sg. (compare, on the one hand, the use of *on* in colloquial French and other impersonal forms with 1st plural meaning in Tuscan and Friulian; on the other, the use of *we* as the unspecified agent in English). Second, this PRO form appeared post-verbally in inverted word order as a clitic. Finally, -VN was reinterpreted as a bound suffix on the verb stem, obligatory in both direct and inverted word order.

While the fact of the replacement of the 1PL ending is clear enough, Haiman and Beninca's explanation for it is problematic. For one thing, the reflex of impersonal UNUS in Surmiran is *in(s)*, not *ăn* (Grisch 1939). The innovated unstressed form of the 1PL ending would thus not appear to continue this element. Furthermore, the form that does, Surmiran *ins*, does not invert with the verb even under conditions where verb-second would be expected (Anderson 2006). In terms both of its shape and of its syntactic positioning, then, the reflex of earlier UNUS is not likely as the source of the 1PL ending -*ăn*.

There is, however, another possible source for the observed change in this ending, which lies in the fact that in all tenses other than the present indicative, 1PL=3PL=-(ă)n. The replacement of -áɲ/ájn by -ăn might simply be the generalization of this regularity (and thus, the ending -ăn) to the present indicative.

In Bravuogn/Bergün, verbs that take -esch in the rhizotonic forms of their paradigm extend this to the 1PL of the present indicative (Kamprath 1987: 182): *pateir* 'to suffer', 1SG [pətéš], 1PL [pətéšən], 2PL [pətéks], 3PL [pətéšən]. So the prediction Maiden derives from the present analysis is in fact confirmed for this language, unlike the situation in Val Müstair, where other factors intervene to prevent the expected extension of the augment to newly rhizotonic forms.

This does not, of course, exclude the 'morphomic' account: one could simply claim that the morphome including the singular and 3PL of the present indicative is extended here to include the 1PL as well, and continues to condition both the occurrence of one stem rather than the other and also the presence of the augment in verbs that take this. This analysis continues to disregard the obvious generalization that the categories that behave in this way are exactly those where (predictable) stress would fall on the stem (as opposed to those where it would fall on the ending), but in that respect it is no different from the morphomic account of 'standard' Surmiran.

Contrary to Haiman and Benincà's (1992) description, however, Bravuogn/Bergün is not the only area in which these newly rhizotonic forms of the 1PL present indicative are found. The Rumantsch of Vaz (Obervaz, Lenzerheide, Valbella; cf. Ebneter 1981) also displays the replacement of 1PL present indicative -áɲ/ájn by -ăn. Here, however, there is an additional complication. For many verbs, the 1PL ending can be either -ain or -ăn. Ebneter's dictionary indicates for roughly one-third of verbs the 1PL form in -ain, perhaps intending that this form is preferred for these verbs but -ăn for others. Regardless, both here and in Ebneter (1994) he indicates that both forms of the 1PL are possible and to some extent in variation with one another.

When the normal stressed form is specified, this is associated with the stem normally used with stressed endings: *amblidar* 'forget', 1SG *ambloid*, 1PL *amblidain*. This is also true of forms that take -esch: *adorar* 'adore', 1SG *adoresch*, 1PL *adorain*; *sa vastgir* 'get dressed', 1SG *sa vastgesch*, 1PL *sa vastgain*.

When the unstressed, innovative 1PL ending is used, the stem that appears with it is that associated with rhizotonic forms:

(18)	INF	1SG	1PL		gloss
	amprastar	amprest	amprestan		'lend, loan'
	amvarnar	amvearn	amvearnan		'overwinter livestock'
	numnar	nomn	nomnan		'call, name something'
	s-chéuder	s-cheud	s-cheudan	scudáiz (2PL)	'thresh'

Importantly, this also extends to verbs taking *-esch*:

(19)

INF	1SG	1PL	gloss
habitar	habitesch	habiteschan	'live somewhere'
s'anclinar	s'anclinesch	s'anclineschan	'kneel, genuflect'

In all cases, the location of stress correctly predicts both the stem used and also the presence of *-esch*.

Finally, when both endings are possible, each is associated with the stress-appropriate stem; the two forms are in variation, but no forms appear with the 'wrong' stem.

(20)

INF	1SG	1PL		gloss
ampruar	amprov	ampruvain/amprovan		'try'
gudair	giod	giodan/gudain		'enjoy'
scaldar	stgoald	scaldain/stgoaldan		'heat, warm'
baiver	baiv	bavain/baivan	bavaiz (2PL)	'drink'

While these data cannot of course be claimed to render the morphomic account of stem alternation impossible, they do pose a problem for that analysis: it is fairly clear that stem alternation and the appearance of *-esch* (in finite verbal forms) are tied directly to the location of stress, even where this is potentially variable, and not to a fixed set of morphological categories.

2.3 Conclusion

I conclude, therefore, that stem shape (including the possible appearance of *-esch* in finite forms) in Rumantsch is, as previously claimed, a clear instance of phonologically conditioned allomorphy. In the case of Surmiran, the constraint system that governs the location of stress and the relations between vowel quality and stress suffices to describe the stem allomorphy, on the assumption that verbs generally have two stem shapes (and *-esch* verbs only one) differing in their ability to accommodate stress. In some other Swiss Rumantsch systems, the alternation pattern is more restricted, and a diacritic of some sort may be necessary to distinguish the behaviour of verbs that take an augment such as *-esch*; but given this, the variation remains phonologically conditioned. This is not to deny that morphological categories play a role (e.g. in constraining the appearance of *-esch* to tensed forms of first and fourth conjugation verbs), but there is no warrant for invoking the further step of complete and arbitrary morphological categorization that would be implied by associating the variation with a morpheme.

3

'Semi-autonomous' morphology? A problem in the history of the Italian (and Romanian) verb*

MARTIN MAIDEN

3.1 Are the velar–palatal alternations of Italian phonologically, or morphologically, conditioned?

This study is concerned with a *locus classicus* of Italian (and Romance) historical morphology, the alternation between velar and palatal consonants in the lexical roots of verbs. This is a classic example of the emergence of allomorphy in inflectional paradigms as a result of historically regular sound change. It focuses our attention on the delicate question of the relation between sound change and morphologization. At what point does the phonological process cease and purely morphological conditioning take over? If the original phonological conditioning environment has been effaced, the answer is usually (though questionably; cf. Maiden 2009*b*) that morphology must have taken over when that environment was lost. But what is the relationship between morphological and phonological conditioning when, for the most part, the original conditioning environment is still in place? This is the problem posed by the velar–palatal alternation in modern Italian, where the original conditioning front vowels still survive. I have argued in various places that, in effect, the persistence of the phonological environment is synchronically accidental, and that the distribution of the alternation is, and has been for centuries, a purely morphological matter; indeed that the alternation is 'autonomously' morphological in the sense that the distribution is independent equally of the phonological environment and of the functional or semantic conditions under which it occurs, being a function directly of the heterogeneous set of

* Part of the research for this chapter was undertaken within the AHRC-funded project *Autonomous Morphology in Diachrony: comparative evidence from the Romance Languages*, in the Faculty of Linguistics, Philology and Phonetics, Oxford University. The support of the AHRC is gratefully acknowledged.

paradigm cells with which it is associated. The main reason for dismissing the hypothesis of phonological conditioning has been empirical, rather than a matter of theoretical principle; namely the demonstrable demise of the phonological process of palatalization, and the failure of palatalization to occur in the verb even when new environments have arisen with the potential to trigger it, not to mention the persistence of the morphological distribution even where the phonological environment disappears. There has simply been no substantive evidence for the 'phonologizing' view. In what follows I slightly revise this position, not in the sense of abandoning the claim that the alternation is fundamentally and irreducibly morphological, but rather in the sense that there are grounds to postulate an additional phonological element in the conditioning of the alternation (at least, as I shall explain, during the acquisition process). The reasons for taking this revised position are again empirical, and emerge from some highly significant fragments of historical and comparative data. In conclusion, I shall reflect on the kind of relationship between autonomously morphological phenomena and their phonological pendants towards which such data may point.

In Italian morphology the root-final velar consonants /g/ and /k/ alternate, respectively, with the palatal-alveolar affricates /tʃ/ and /dʒ/ (and /sk/ alternates with /ʃʃ/). This kind of alternation is common in the inflectional morphology of the verb. Usually, the velar alternant occurs when followed by a non-front vowel in the inflectional ending, while the 'palatal alternant' (as I shall call it henceforth) occurs when followed by a front vowel in the inflectional ending. Thus the verbs vin/tʃ/ere 'win', pian/dʒ/ere 'weep', cono/ʃʃ/ere 'know'.[1]

(1)	PRS.IND	PRS.SBJV	PRS.IND	PRS.SBJV	PRS.IND	PRS.SBJV
1SG	vin/k/o	vin/k/a	pian/g/o	pian/g/a	cono/sk/o	cono/sk/a
2SG	vin/tʃ/i	vin/k/a	pian/dʒ/i	pian/g/a	cono/ʃʃ/i	cono/sk/a
3SG	vin/tʃ/e	vin/k/a	pian/dʒ/e	pian/g/a	cono/ʃʃ/e	cono/sk/a
1PL	vin/tʃ/iamo	vin/tʃ/iamo	pian/dʒ/iamo	pian/dʒ/iamo	cono/ʃʃ/iamo	cono/ʃʃ/iamo
2PL	vin/tʃ/ete	vin/tʃ/iate	pian/dʒ/ete	pian/dʒ/iate	cono/ʃʃ/ete	cono/ʃʃ/iate
3PL	vin/k/ono	vin/k/ano	pian/g/ono	pian/g/ano	cono/sk/ono	cono/sk/ano

I have argued in various places[2] that this type of alternation—in Italian and across the Romance languages generally—is now (and has been for centuries) purely

---

[1] For clarity of exposition, I have replaced the orthographic representation of these alternants with a phonological one both in the Italian and (later) in the Romanian examples. Both languages systematically distinguish velars and palatals orthographically (and have done so for centuries), but the sounds /k/ and /g/ are spelled c and g before back-vowel letters, and ch and gh before front-vowel letters; the sounds /tʃ/ and /dʒ/ are spelled c and g before front-vowel letters, and ci and gi before back-vowel letters. The sound /ʃʃ/ is spelled sc before front-vowel letters and sci before back-vowel letters in Italian.

[2] See, e.g., Maiden (1992, 2005a, 2011b).

morphological, indeed 'morphomic' in the sense of Aronoff (1994). The distribution of the velar (but also of other root allomorphs) is and has long been a function of a heterogeneous set of paradigm cells, comprising the first person singular and third person plural present subjunctive and most or all cells of the present subjunctive. Now this is not the obvious conclusion to reach: readers seeing the data for the first time are likely to have assumed that the alternation is triggered by a phonological process of palatalization, the velar being the 'input', and palatalization being triggered by the adjacent front vowel. This conclusion seems all the more plausible for apparently involving a 'common or garden' type of 'natural' phonological process, repeatedly attested in the history of the world's languages. Historically this assumption is quite right; synchronically it is at best in need of adjustment, since Italian has accrued, throughout its attested history and much earlier, and from various sources, very large numbers of counterexamples to the putative process. There are countless cases of /tʃ/, /dʒ/, and /ʃʃ/ before back vowels, and a multitude of words containing the strings /ke/ and /ki/, /ge/ and /gi/, /ske/ and /ski/ all quite immune from palatalization: e.g. *stan*/k/*i* 'tired.M.PL', *stan*/k/*e* 'tired.F.PL', *fun*/g/*i* 'mushrooms', *al*/g/*e* 'seaweed'. Palatal consonants may equally and freely be followed by 'non-palatalizing' vowels: e.g. *ca*/ttʃ/*a* 'hunting', *ra*/ɲɲ/*o* 'spider', *fa*/ʃʃ/*a* 'strip'. It is fair to say that the original palatalization process has been 'dead' for many centuries.

In fact palatalization is thoroughly compromised in potentially alternating, as well as non-alternating, environments. The feminine plural ending *-e* in nouns and adjectives never triggers palatalization of a preceding velar, while the plural ending *-i* in nouns and adjectives seldom does so (for analyses of the historical reasons for this situation, see Maiden 1996*a*, 2000). As for the verb, the palatalization of velars is wholly excluded from the first conjugation (the largest, and now the only productive, inflection class in the verb, characterized by thematic /a/ in various parts of the paradigm), even though the 2SG present, the whole of the present subjunctive, and the future and conditional all show a front vowel immediately following the root-final consonant. Nor is there any sign (Maiden 2011*a*: 209–11), at any point in the history of Italian, or in any Italo-Romance dialect (or indeed Ibero-Romance, 'Raeto-Romance', or southern Gallo-Romance varieties, to bring in Italian's outlying neighbours) that historically expected palatalizations before front vowels ever took place in the first conjugation.

A more promising approach to modern Italian, and one still maintaining the insight that the alternation is phonologically conditioned, might be to say that the presence of a velar–palatal alternation has to be specified lexically, but that once it is so specified the distribution of the alternants is automatically effected as a function of the phonological identity of the endings, those containing front vowels selecting the palatal alternants, and the velar appearing elsewhere by default (or vice versa). In this way, we can continue to claim that the *conditioning* of the alternation is phonological. In verbs, nouns, and adjectives, if we specify that the root has the velar–palatal alternation, then the observed distribution of the alternants falls out naturally as a function of the frontness of the following vowel. This type of approach, involving 'phonologically conditioned allomorphy', has been applied both to consonantal and vocalic alternations in the Romance verb (see Carstairs 1988, 1990, Anderson 2008, 2011), but it is not in fact supported in the case of the velar–palatal alternation in modern Italian by *historical evidence or by comparison with closely cognate dialects*.

Now many readers may at this point be asking: 'So what? Modern Italian is not old Italian, nor is it some other Italian dialect—so the evidence of history and of comparative dialectology can be safely disregarded.' I believe (and the point is essential to the following arguments; see also Maiden 2011d: 37f.) that this kind of dismissal of comparative and historical evidence would be a methodological error. It is certainly true that evidence from one (albeit genetically related) variety cannot be probative for the analysis of another one, but it should not follow from that fact that such evidence can be disregarded. In our Italian case it is impossible to tell from the synchronic evidence taken in isolation whether the velar–palatal alternation is purely phonologically conditioned or purely morphologically conditioned; but the existence of very closely similar varieties (indeed of well-nigh identical varieties in the immediately relevant phonological and morphological respects), separated from modern Italian only by time or space, and in which the hypothesis of phonological conditioning is contradicted, will turn out to show—at the very least—that a purely phonological analysis of the modern Italian data has a serious chance of being wrong.

The fact is that for most of the history of Italian there has been an enduring counterexample which contradicts even the hypothesis that lexically specified allomorphs might be selected by the phonological environment, and supports instead the 'morphological' hypothesis. This is that the inflectional ending of the second person singular present subjunctive consists of a front vowel, but the alternant that occurs there is consistently, and without exception,[3] the velar and not the palatal (Rohlfs 1968: 296f., Vanelli 2010a: 1447). For example:

(2)   PRS.SBJV   PRS.SBJV
    1SG   *vin/k/a*   *pian/g/a*
    2SG   *vin/k/i*   *pian/g/i*
    3SG   *vin/k/a*   *pian/g/a*

The historical explanation for this fact may be briefly summarized as follows (see Maiden, 1996a, for a fuller exposition of the historical phonological background). The ending of the second person singular present subjunctive (in non-first conju-

---

[3] This claim is made not merely for Italian and old Tuscan, but for the history of *all* Italo-Romance dialects in which this ending occurs. See also *AIS* maps 1653, 1654, 1695.

gation) verbs was originally *-as (< Lat. -AS). At the time when phonetic palatal-ization was operative, this ending still contained /a/, and therefore no palatalization was produced. Subsequently (or perhaps contemporaneously), *-as became *-aị, later monophthongizing as -e. These second person singular present subjunctives in -e, and without palatalization, are well attested in early Tuscan and elsewhere. Later still, the 2SG ending -i—already the dominant desinence for the second person singular present—comes to replace -e. Notwithstanding the fact that in the present indicative -i is firmly correlated with selection of the palatal, the analogical introduction of -i into the 2SG present subjunctive shows no sign of selecting a palatal in the present subjunctive. Surely the conclusion must be that the allomorphy is *not* a function of the phonological environment, but is rather *morphologically* conditioned, being specified as occurring (among other places) in the present subjunctive.

The fact that in the more recent history of Italian the 2SG present subjunctive ending has been replaced by -a (thereby creating a state of syncretism with 1SG and 3SG present subjunctive; see example (1)), might yet be adduced as evidence of an adjustment showing sensitivity to the phonological environment, such that the incompatibility of the velar with the front vowel is eliminated by replacing that front vowel with /a/. This kind of argument is not especially convincing, because one would have to give reasons to exclude first a perfectly plausible alternative explanation for the emergence of -a, along purely morphological lines: the distinc-tion for person happens to be wholly neutralized in the first conjugation (all singular present subjunctive forms end in -i), and this model of neutralization seems to have been transferred into other conjugation classes, so that the -a already characteristic of the 1SG and 3SG is also introduced into 2SG. There is certainly nothing to make us think that phonology must have played any role in this development.

There is an even more serious counterexample to the 'phonological conditioning' hypothesis, and one which is present not only in many modern central Italian dialects but in substandard varieties of modern Italian as well. This is the fact that the present subjunctive-marker -i, historically characteristic of the first conjugation, has been analogically extended to the present subjunctive of *all* verbs, yielding the type:

(3)		PRS.SBJV	PRS.SBJV
	1SG	*vin/k/i*	*pian/g/i*
	2SG	*vin/k/i*	*pian/g/i*
	3SG	*vin/k/i*	*pian/g/i*
	3PL	*vin/k/ino*	*pian/g/ino*

This phenomenon never triggers the palatal alternant. Burzio (2004: 36) makes the curious claim that what is involved is merely characteristic of what he believes to be a 'working class dialect' of Italian, in which the velar is inherited from an immediate ancestor in which the environment was a non-front vowel. He states (Burzio 2004: 38) that the phenomenon 'constitutes a type of language change from the standard, which must therefore have provided the input data'. The assumption seems to be that, somehow, the inflectional -a is still present and known to those speakers who use -i, and that this knowledge is manifested in a re-ranking of morphological over phonological conditioning. The trouble is that the phenomenon is both old and geographically widespread in Italy, and that the idea of a 'working class dialect' of Italian scarcely makes sense. To the extent that there are 'substandard' forms (hardly 'dialects') of Italian (such as so-called 'italiano popolare': see, e.g., Lepschy and Lepschy 1981: 33f.), they are overwhelmingly a product of twentieth-century history. It is characteristic of the Italian language from the sixteenth century until the twentieth that it was, precisely, the language of a literate elite, marked by a particularly high degree of morphological conservatism and remoteness from everyday speech. Yet the phenomenon of extension of -i has actually been attested since the Middle Ages, across the dialects of southern Tuscany, and of Umbria and Lazio west of the Tiber and in some dialects of Corsica: cf. Rohlfs (1968: 297–9); Hirsch (1886: 416f.); Bianchi (1888: 50); Bianconi (1962: 110); *AIS* map 1695. The facts stand, quite simply, in flat contradiction of the 'phonological' hypothesis. The environment of the front vowel is clearly irrelevant to the distribution of the alternants.

    In addition, there is an aspect of modern standard Italian itself which seriously undermines the phonological hypothesis, and simply cannot be dismissed as marginal or merely historical. This is the fact the past participle in -*uto* of verbs with the root alternations /sk/–/ʃʃ/, such as *cono/ʃʃ/ere* 'know', *cre/ʃʃ/ere* 'grow', *pa/ʃʃ/ere* 'graze' displays not the alternant /sk/ phonologically predicted before a back vowel, but the palatal /ʃʃ/:

(4)   3SG.PRS.IND   3SG.PRS.SBJV   past participle
      cono/ʃʃ/e   *cono/sk/a*   *cono/ʃʃ/uto*
      cre/ʃʃ/e   *cre/sk/a*   *cre/ʃʃ/uto*

Burzio (2004: 34–6) attempts to deal with the *cono/ʃʃ/uto* type by invoking an 'Output-to-Output Faithfulness' constraint relating past participles to their infinitives, which outranks palatalization, adducing 'independent evidence that past participles are in strong correspondence with their infinitives'. I find this argument unpersuasive for two reasons. First, the root /konoʃʃ/ etc. is found in *most* cells of the paradigm, and no reason is given for privileging the relation of the past participle with the infinitive rather than with any other part of the verb in which the allomorph appears. Second, Burzio's evidence comes down to the observation that third conjugation past participles tend to share root-stress with infinitives (e.g. infinitive *vincere* 'win', past participle *vinto*). But they do not significantly share *segmental* content with the infinitive; actually, most Italian rhizotonic past participles display segmentally *different* roots from their infinitive (e.g. *prendere* 'take' – *preso*; *trarre* 'draw' – *tratto*; *correre* 'run' – *corso*; *rompere* 'break' – *rotto*; *fondere* 'melt' – *fuso*; *stringere* 'squeeze' – *stretto*). There would be far better reason to claim that in the great majority of Italian verbs there exists an 'Output-to-Output Faithfulness constraint' among present-tense stems, since for the most part they do not have alternating stems (cf. Burzio 2004: 20), yet 'palatalization' is certainly not 'overridden' in this part of the paradigm. In reality, the emergence and persistence of *cono/ʃʃ/uto* etc. strongly indicates again that speakers *do not analyse the alternation as syntagmatically conditioned by phonological environment*. The historically underlying form was *kono'skuto (actually attested in old Tuscan *conoscuto, cognoscuta*),[4] and the most likely explanation for the disappearance of the velar root is purely morphological; the fact that, in the overwhelming majority of verbs, the velar alternant is characteristic just of certain cells of the present indicative and subjunctive, and not encountered elsewhere.

A final reason for rejecting 'phonologizing' approaches to the velar–palatal alternation in the verb is that this alternation is far from being the only one paradigmatically distributed in this way in Italian. Historically (see Maiden, 2011*b*, for more detail), two, separate and unconnected, types of sound change had the *fortuitous* effect of producing the *same* alternation pattern in the verb. Of these, the palatalization of velars appears to have been the more recent, while an earlier change (both seem dateable to the first half of the first millennium AD) involved various kinds of palatalization, affrication, and lengthening of consonants when immediately followed by yod. Some regular effects of this change can be seen in the following examples, from *pia/tʃ/ere* 'please' and *volere* 'want':

(5)		PRS.IND	PRS.SBJV	PRS.IND	PRS.SBJV
	1SG	*pia/ttʃ/o*	*pia/ttʃ/a*	*vo/ʎʎ/o*[5]	*vo/ʎʎ/a*
	2SG	*pia/tʃ/i*	*pia/ttʃ/a*	*vuoi*	*vo/ʎʎ/a*
	3SG	*pia/tʃ/e*	*pia/ttʃ/a*	*vuole*	*vo/ʎʎ/a*
	1PL	*pia/ttʃ/amo*	*pia/ttʃ/amo*	*vo/ʎʎ/amo*	*vo/ʎʎ/amo*
	2PL	*pia/tʃ/ete*	*pia/ttʃ/ate*	*volete*	*vo/ʎʎ/ate*
	3PL	*pia/ttʃ/ono*	*pia/ttʃ/ano*	*vo/ʎʎ/ono*	*vo/ʎʎ/ano*

---

[4] See also Laurent (1999: 148).   [5] The orthographic representation of /ʎʎ/ is *gli*.

As these examples show, the conditioning environment for this change is extinct. The typical development involves, in effect, a historical 'absorption' of the yod into the preceding consonant (yielding, indeed, a whole new class of palatal consonants which had been absent from Latin). Scarcely any trace of the original yod exists (or has existed for centuries) in Italian, and to the extent that any trace does persist, it happens not to have the same distribution.[6] There can be no justification for assuming (as Burzio, 2004: 23f., does) that what is in effect the original conditioning element, described by him as a 'pre-affixal insert *i*' is somehow underlyingly present but neutralized in modern Italian and continues to trigger the alternation phonologically.[7] The last evidence for the presence of a *sound* of this kind with the relevant distribution in the relevant phonological environments dates from, perhaps, a millennium and a half ago. The fact is that the velar–palatal alternation actually belongs to a much larger class of (phonologically very heterogeneous) alternation types all sharing the same paradigmatic distribution, and this certainly seems to dilute any argument from 'phonological naturalness'. A velar–palatal alternation may be very 'natural' in correlation with a back- vs. front-vowel alternation, but the same could hardly be said for the alternant *poss-* found in *potere* 'be able' and following the same distribution (e.g. 1SG.PRS.IND *posso*, 3PL.PRS.IND *possono*, PRS. SBJV *possa*, etc.) or for *pia*/tʃ/- – *pia*/ttʃ/- described above.

The answer to the question posed at the beginning of this section seems to be that the velar–palatal alternation is plainly morphologically, not phonologically, conditioned.

3.2 Why the velar–palatal alternations might be phonologically conditioned after all

3.2.1 *The 1/2PL present subjunctive*

Everything I have said so far supports the view that the velar–palatal alternation in the Italian verb is purely morphological, indeed *morphomic*. The distribution of the alternants bespeaks blithe unawareness on the part of speakers of the phonological environment with which they are often (but, precisely, not always) correlated. In the view of Maiden (1992, 2001*a*, 2005*a*, 2009*a*; cf. also Pirrelli

---

[6] The verbs *sapere* 'know' and *avere* 'have' have present subjunctive *sappia* /ˈsappja/, etc. and *abbia* /ˈabbja/, etc. But these alternants with yod are not found anywhere else in the paradigm. It is true, by the way, that yod is apparently deleted after palatal consonants in Italian (cf. *valiamo* /vaˈljamo/ 'we are worth' but *vogliamo* /voʎˈʎamo/ 'we want') but it does not follow from this that palatal consonants such as /ʎ/ can generally be ascribed an underlying following yod.

[7] One should not be distracted by orthography. In the verbs given above, the spelling is *piaccio, piaccia*, etc., *voglio, voglia*, etc., but the *i* is merely a diacritic indicating the palatal pronunciation of the preceding consonant(s). Even if we were to postulate an underlying /i/, we would still have to account for its synchronic distribution.

2000: 79f., 178–84, and Pirrelli and Battista 2000), the velar alternant is defined as occupying a heterogeneous set of paradigm cells comprising present subjunctive + 1SG present indicative + 3PL present indicative. There appears to be nothing more to be said, and any lingering correlation with the frontness of the following vowel has apparently been synchronically accidental for centuries. It may therefore come as a surprise that I shall now argue the opposite, that the alternation actually may be—in some sense to which I shall return—'phonologically conditioned' after all.

Burzio's general line (2004: 38) in the face of counterexamples to the hypothesis of conditioning by the phonological environment is that 'the fact that syntagmatic relations do not obtain in this case [...] does not mean [...] that they do not exist, but rather only that they are outranked'. The trouble is that a statement of this kind is simply a declaration of faith: how can anybody know whether 'syntagmatic relations' (i.e. phonological conditioning) are at work or not?[8] One very reasonable answer might be that it hardly seems plausible that in the face of what is, after all, a fairly consistent, if far from perfect, correlation between alternant and phonological environment, speakers could fail to internalize a systematic connection between them. There would seem to be something almost perverse in the idea of their *not* doing so. Yet to show that they do do this we still need 'substantive evidence' (cf. Skousen 1975), and that kind of evidence can only come in the form of psycholinguistic experimentation (which we do not as yet have for Italian), for example by using nonce-forms in palatalizing environments, or from the testimony of historical change, all of which so far turns out to be negative.

However, I have hitherto left out of consideration an additional piece of evidence adduced by Burzio which, especially when viewed historically, perhaps does suggest some role for phonological conditioning. This involves the first and second persons plural of the present subjunctive. In Italian the endings have the form -'jamo, -'jate, with an initial yod in principle refractory to a root-final velar. These endings originate in second and fourth conjugation verbs (and a handful of verbs of the third conjugation), but in many verbs with velar–palatal alternations they are a matter of—probably very early—analogical extension, the original endings having been -'amo, -'ate.[9] In this environment, indeed, the velar consonant *never* occurs in modern Italian (see example (1)):

<hr/>

[8] See also, from a different perspective, Fanciullo (1998), and the responses in Pirrelli (2000) and Maiden (2001a). Recently, Krämer (2009: 56–84) develops an essentially phonological analysis of the Italian facts, yet concedes at the very outset of his discussion that the facts could equally support a purely 'grammatical' account.

[9] See also, for example, Rohlfs (1968: 297), and Maiden (1995a: 128f.).

(6)

INF	3 SG.PRS.SBJV	1 PL.PRS.SBJV	2 PL.PRS.SBJV
fare 'do'	*fa/*ttʃ*/a*	*fa/*ttʃ*/iamo*	*fa/*ttʃ*/iate*
sapere 'know'	*sappia*	*sappiamo*	*sappiate*
potere 'be able'	*possa*	*possiamo*	*possiate*
piacere 'please'	*pia/*ttʃ*/a*	*pia/*ttʃ*/iamo*	*pia/*ttʃ*/iate*
avere 'have'	*abbia*	*abbiamo*	*abbiate*
volere 'want'	*vo/*ʎʎ*/a*	*vo/*ʎʎ*/iamo*	*vo/*ʎʎ*/iate*
salire 'go up'	*salga*	*saliamo*	*saliate*
dire 'say'	*di/*k*/a*	*di/*tʃ*/iamo*	*di/*tʃ*/iate*
*vin/*tʃ*/ere* 'win'	*vin/*k*/a*	*vin/*tʃ*/iamo*	*vin/*tʃ*/iate*
*cono /*ʃʃ*/ere* 'know'	*cono /*sk*/a*	*cono /*ʃʃ*/iamo*	*cono /*ʃʃ*/iate*
*pian/*dʒ*/ere* 'weep'	*pian/*g*/a*	*pian/*dʒ*/iamo*	*pian/*dʒ*/iate*
*giun/*dʒ*/ere* 'join'	*giun/*g*/a*	*giun/*dʒ*/iamo*	*giun/*dʒ*/iate*
*fu/*ddʒ*/ire* 'flee'	*fu/*gg*/a*	*fu/*ddʒ*/iamo*	*fu/*ddʒ*/iate*
venire 'come'	*venga*	*veniamo*	*veniate*
vedere 'see'	*vegga / veda*	*vediamo*	*vediate*
tenere 'hold'	*tenga*	*teniamo*	*teniate*
rimanere 'stay'	*rimanga*	*rimaniamo*	*rimaniate*

In Maiden (2009a: 64f., 70) I suggest that even this case had a purely morphological explanation. In a wider, comparative-historical perspective (see Maiden 2010a), there is a clear tendency for elimination of the expected present subjunctive root allomorph in the first and second persons plural, not only in central and northern Italo-Romance but in fact well beyond (in Gallo-Romance and some varieties of Ibero-Romance). This tendency affects all present subjunctive root allomorphs and is quite independent of phonological environment. In some dialects (e.g. in Liguria or Istria) this pattern is absolutely systematic. It is, in short, a *purely morphological* adaptation. In Italian it is apparent also in some verbs with kinds of root allomorphy other than velar–palatal. For example *morire* 'die' and *parere* 'seem', where the alternant in root-final -*i* (/j/) is attested well into the historical period in 1/2PL present subjunctive as well, but is now generally absent from those cells:

(7)

	PRS.SBJV	PRS.SBJV
1SG	*muoia*	*paia*
2SG	*muoia*	*paia*
3SG	*muoia*	*paia*
1PL	*moriamo*	*pariamo*
2PL	*moriate*	*pariate*
3PL	*muoiano*	*paiano*

Consider also the verb *dolere* 'hurt', which has the form *do/ʎʎ/a* in the subjunctive, but either *do/ʎʎ/iamo, do/ʎʎ/iate*, or *doliamo, doliate* in 1/2PL. Other verbs, which in modern Italian show velar alternants in the present subjunctive, do not merely lack that alternant in the 1/2PL present subjunctive; rather, they attest to historical *eviction* of the present subjunctive alternant. Many verbs which historically possessed a root allomorph in -/ʎʎ/ or -/ɲɲ/ have in the past few centuries replaced that allomorph with /lg/ and /ng/ (see Maiden 1992, 2005a): e.g. the singular present subjunctive forms *ve/ɲɲ/a* 'come' becomes *venga*, *rima/ɲɲ/a* 'stay' becomes *rimanga*, *sa/ʎʎ/a* 'go up' becomes *salga*, *va/ʎʎ/a* 'be worth' becomes *valga*. Given the observed aversion of speakers for combining the *-iamo -iate* with allomorphs containing root-final velars, it is of course unsurprising that 1/2PL present subjunctive does not show the velar. But this fact fails to predict the absence of the older subjunctive allomorph. In principle, there is no reason why modern Italian could not have present subjunctives of the following type:

(8)
1SG	*tenga*	*salga*	
2SG	*tenga*	*salga*	
3SG	*tenga*	*salga*	
1PL	****te/ɲɲ/iamo**[10]	****sa/ʎʎ/iamo**	
2PL	****te/ɲɲ/iate**	****sa/ʎʎ/iate**	
3PL	*tengano*	*salgano*	

The fact that we do not get such a pattern indicates a prior *eviction* of the subjunctive alternants in the first and second persons plural present subjunctive. In this light, the absence of the velars themselves in these morphological contexts seems less obviously a matter of phonology, and much more like a manifestation of an extensively attested morphological tendency.

Still, the facts present an awkward problem for the 'morphologizing' view: while there is indeed a general, and, I submit, morphologically motivated, trend in central Italo-Romance, including Italian, for the present subjunctive root allomorph to be evicted from the first and second person plural, only in the case of the velar–palatal alternant is this development *systematic*. There is absolutely no case in modern Italian, and virtually no trace in the medieval language (or at any intermediate stage),[11] of a velar alternant before *-iamo, -iate*. Consider the verb morphology of the Tuscan Giovanni Villani (mid fourteenth century), which is quite typical of its period:

---

[10] The orthographic representation of /ɲɲ/ is *gn*.

[11] The only examples from the *OVI* database of the velar before *-iamo -iate* from Tuscany are three of *di/k/iamo* (vs. one of *di/tʃ/iamo*) and four of *di/k/iate* (vs. three of *di/tʃ/iate*) in the anonymous *Tristano riccardiano* of c.1300.

(9)   Old Tuscan (G. Villani)

INF	3SG.PRS.SBJV	1PL.PRS.SBJV	2PL.PRS.SBJV[12]
fare 'do'	*fa*/ttʃ/*a*	*fa*/ttʃ/*iamo* 17	*fa*/ttʃ/*ate* 2
sapere 'know'	*sappia*	*sappiamo* 3	
potere 'be able'	*possa*	*possiamo* 6	
pia /tʃ/*ere* 'please'	*piaccia*	*piacciamo* 2	
avere 'have'	*abbia*	*abbiamo* 25	
volere 'want'	*vo*/ʎʎ/*a*	*vo*/ʎʎ/*iamo* 11	

INF	3SG.PRS.SBJV	1PL.PRS.SBJV
dire 'say'	*di*/k/*a*	*di*/tʃ/*iamo* 14
cono/ʃʃ/*ere* 'know'	*cono*/sk/*a*	*cono*/ʃʃ/*iamo* 3
le/dd ʒ/*ere* 'read'	*le*/gg/*a*	*le*/ddʒ/*iamo* 7

The non-co-occurrence of velars and the *-iamo, -iate* endings in modern Italian is not only systematic today, but can be shown to have been so continuously over time. Moreover, the suspicion that this is a matter of phonological sensitivity turns out to be reinforced by a second type of development, in a quite different morphological environment, attesting to exactly this postulated sensitivity. This involves the old Italian *gerund*.

3.2.2 *The gerund in old Italian*

In Italian the gerund of non-first conjugation verbs ends in *-endo* (< Lat. -ENDO). This ending has an initial front vowel, and verbs having the velar–palatal alternation duly show the palatal, not the velar, before it. In this respect, the gerund shares a root allomorph with the majority of other cells of the paradigm, for example the verbs *vin*/tʃ/*ere* 'win' and *pian*/dʒ/*ere* 'weep':

(10)

	PRS.IND	PRS.SBJV	GER	PRS.IND	PRS.SBJV	GER
1SG	*vin*/k/*o*	*vin*/k/*a*		*pian*/g/*o*	*pian*/g/*a*	
2SG	*vin*/tʃ/*i*	*vin*/k/*a*		*pian*/dʒ/*i*	*pian*/g/*a*	
3SG	*vin*/tʃ/*e*	*vin*/k/*a*		*pian*/dʒ/*e*	*pian*/g/*a*	
1PL	*vin*/tʃ/*iamo*	*vin*/tʃ/*iamo*	*vin*/tʃ/*endo*	*pian*/dʒ/*iamo*	*pian*/dʒ/*iamo*	*pian*/dʒ/*endo*
2PL	*vin*/tʃ/*ete*	*vin*/tʃ/*iate*		*pian*/dʒ/*ete*	*pian*/dʒ/*iate*	
3PL	*vin*/k/*ono*	*vin*/k/*ano*		*pian*/g/*ono*	*pian*/g/*ano*	

This state of affairs in respect of the gerund has consistently held throughout the history of Italian and of other Italo-Romance varieties. Moreover, it is a pattern repeatedly found in other verbs showing root allomorphy in the present: if there is a distinctive root allomorph in the first person singular and third person plural present indicative and in (at least) the singular and third–person forms of the present

---

[12] It is in the nature of the texts that second-person examples are very rare.

subjunctive then that is *not* the root found in the gerund (cf. *tenere* 'hold', PRS.
SBJV.3SG *tenga* but gerund *tenendo*; *volere* 'want', PRS.SBJV.3SG *voglia* but gerund
volendo). Forms such as *vin/tʃ/endo, pian/dʒ/endo* therefore seem wholly unremark-
able, but the consistency with which this pattern holds for such verbs is not to be taken
for granted, in the light of another, albeit ephemeral, development attested in the
Middle Ages.

Italo-Romance displayed a small number of (very frequently used) verbs in which,
as a result of historical inheritance from Latin, the alternant found in the present
subjunctive was also encountered in the gerund. Like the alternant found in the
present subjunctive, that found in the gerund is the result of the (exceptional)[13]
historical presence of a yod. The following old Tuscan forms of the verbs *venire*
'come', *fare* 'do', *sapere* 'know' reflect (among other things) the effects of yod in the
Latin subjunctives UENIAM, etc., FACIAM, etc., SAPIAM, etc., and the gerunds[14]
UENIENDO, FACIENDO, SAPIENDO:

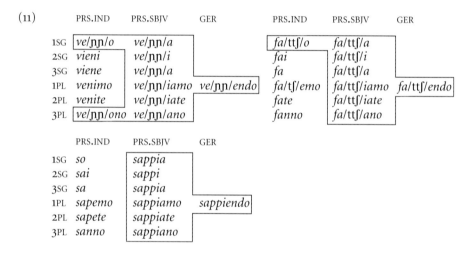

This small nucleus of forms furnished, in the thirteenth and fourteenth centuries,
the basis of a sporadic analogical extension, such that the root allomorph associated
with present subjunctive (and forms of the present indicative) began to be introduced into the gerund. While extensively attested (see the *OVI* data for medieval
Tuscan), at no stage did this innovatory pattern become definitively established, and

---

[13] The Latin *fourth* conjugation gerund regularly ended in -IENDO (as opposed to second and third
conjugation -ENDO), which should regularly have produced gerunds in yod (*-jɛndo). In general, and with
the apparent exception of the (very frequent) UENIENDO 'coming', however, -IENDO (e.g. FINIENDO
'finishing') seems to have been replaced at an early date by -ENDO. FACIENDO and SAPIENDO are third
conjugation verbs which, unusually, had -I- (> -j- before a vowel) as part of their root.

[14] There is reason to believe that the Italo-Romance forms derive from the ablative of the Latin gerund,
and that is the form given here.

eventually it did not prosper in Tuscan. It operated regardless of the phonological identity of the present subjunctive allomorph, but with one striking qualification: *there are absolutely no examples of it in the case of the velar alternants* (see also Vanelli 2010*b*: 1467f.). The following illustrates the position in the writings of Giovanni Villani. The corresponding present subjunctive form is given (where Villani gives no present subjunctive for the relevant words, we have taken forms from other texts of the period from Tuscany, given in square brackets; the numbers indicate the number of tokens):

(12)	INF	3SG/PL.PRS.SBJV	GER	
	venire 'come'	*ve/ɲɲ/a(no)* 2 *ven/g/a(no)* 3	*ve/ɲɲ/endo* 161	*venendo* 16
	fare 'do'	*fa/ttʃ/a(no)* 45	*fa/ttʃ/endo* 439	*fa/tʃ/endo* 1
	sapere 'know'	*sappia(no)* 3	*sappiendo* 70	*sapendo* 4
	potere 'be able'	*possa(no)* 38	*possendo* 53	*potendo* 136
	vedere 'see'	[1PL *ve/ddʒ/iamo* 3]	*ve/ddʒ/endo* 564	*vedendo* 27
	tenere 'hold'	*tenga(no)* 2	*te/ɲɲ/endo* 49	*tenendo* 63
	rimanere 'stay'	*rimanga(no)* 2	*rima/ɲɲ/endo* 12	*rimanendo* 80
	pia/tʃ/ere 'please'	*pia/ttʃ/a(no)* 10	*pia/ttʃ/endo* 6	*pia/tʃ/endo* 17
	avere 'have'	*abbia(no)* 30	*abbiendo* 2	*avendo* 486
	volere 'want'	*vo/ʎʎ/a(no)* 31	*vo/ʎʎ/endo* 5	*volendo* 151
	dolere 'pain'	*do/ʎʎ/a(no)* 2	*do/ʎʎ/endo* 20	*dolendo* 11
	porre 'put'	[1PL *po/ɲɲ/amo* 3]	*po/ɲɲ/endo* 4	*ponendo* 7
	chiedere 'ask'	[*ch(i)e/ddʒ/a* elsewhere]	*ch(i)e/ddʒ/endo* 8	*chiedendo* 2
	cadere 'fall'	[*ca/ddʒ/a* elsewhere]	*ca/ddʒ/endo* 2	*cadendo* 0
	salire 'go up'	[*sa/ʎʎ/a* elsewhere]	*sa/ʎʎ/endo* 1	*salendo* 6
	dire 'say'	*di/k/a* 10	*di/tʃ/endo* 221	
	vin/tʃ/ere 'win'	[*vin/k/a* elsewhere]	*vin/tʃ/endo* 6	
	cono/ʃʃ/ere 'know'	*cono/sk/a(no)* 3	*cono/ʃʃ/endo* 48	
	pian/dʒ/ere 'weep'	[*pian/g/a* elsewhere]	*pian/dʒ/endo* 1	
	le/ddʒ/ere 'read'	*le/gg/a(no)* 17	*le/ddʒ/endo* 81	
	giun/dʒ/ere 'join'	[*giun/g/a* elsewhere]	*giun/dʒ/endo* 2	
	fu/ddʒ/ire 'flee'	*fu/ddʒ/a* 6 *fu/gg/a* 21	*fu/ddʒ/endo* 54	

The expected variants ***di/k/endo* and ***pian/g/endo* (and the like) simply do not occur, either in Villani's writing or in any other text of the period. Needless to say, there is absolutely nothing 'impossible' about such putative forms, since /ke/ and /ge/ are abundantly attested, then as in modern Italian (e.g. /k/*eto* 'quiet', *an/k/e* 'also', /g/*ermire* 'grasp', *lar/g/e* 'broad'.F.PL). It seems rather that this innovation really is sensitive to the phonological environment, the velar being rejected in the environment of a front vowel in favour of the palatal.

This evidence from an earlier stage in the history of Italian—but one at which the morphological and phonological system was already very close indeed to that found today—brings further support to the position that the velar–palatal alternant actually is, after all and in some sense, 'sensitive to the phonological environment'.

But what kind of 'sensitivity' is involved? Clearly, since the vocalic environment is the same for all verbs with any kind of consonantal root allomorphy in the present tense, it must be the specific phonological identity of the alternants that is relevant: it is just velar alternants that are rejected before front vowels in the gerund, in favour of palatals, and presumably this happens because (and indeed cross-linguistically) palatal alternants have a high degree of phonological 'naturalness' over velars in such an environment.

3.2.3 *The gerund in Romanian*

I argued earlier that a comparative-historical perspective can legitimately inform our analysis of the morphological organization of any single variety. In this spirit, I now widen our purview to include Romanian, where once again the behaviour of the gerund turns out to throw crucial light on our analysis.

Romanian is, of course, a Romance language, and one whose historically underlying system of inflectional verb morphology is in many relevant respects closely similar to that historically underlying Italian. Like Italian (and like nearly all other Romance languages except Sardinian), Romanian underwent a palatalization/affrication of velar consonants when they were immediately followed by front vowels. As in Italian, the original palatalization process is long defunct and massively contraexemplified by surface sequences of velar + front vowel and palatal + back vowel; however, in inflectional morphology, given a velar–palatal alternation, the distribution of the alternants can be *unfailingly* predicted from the character of the following vowel. This applies not only in the verb (see example (12)), but equally in nouns and adjectives, where the plural inflections spelled -*i* and -*e* always select a palatal alternant (e.g. F.SG *poar*/k/*ă* 'sow', F.PL *poar*/tʃ/*e*—cf. Italian *por*/k/*a* – *por*/k/*e*). The Romanian velar–palatal alternation looks, then, like a first-class candidate (and a far better one than its Italian counterpart) for analysis in terms of phonologically conditioned allomorphy, with the phonological environment distributing the alternants.[15]

I do not propose to describe in detail here the morphological effects of palatalization of velars in Romanian (see, e.g., Maiden 2011c). Suffice it to say that the normal outcome is such that the velar appears in the first person singular and third person plural present indicative, and in the third-person forms of the subjunctive (the remaining person–number forms of the subjunctive were historically replaced by those of the present indicative). However, in addition and quite unlike Italo-Romance, *the velar regularly appears also in the gerund*. Consider the verbs *a plânge* 'weep' and *a zice* 'say':

---

[15] Maiden (2011c) is sceptical about this conclusion for various reasons, the most telling of which will be addressed shortly. For the time being, however, we shall assume its correctness.

(13)

	PRS.IND	SBJV	GERUND	PRS.IND	SBJV	GERUND
1SG	plân/g/	plân/g/		zi/k/	zi/k/	
2SG	plân/dʒ/i	plân/dʒ/i		zi/tʃ/i	zi/tʃ/i	
3SG	plân/dʒ/e	plân/g/ă	plân/g/ând	zi/tʃ/e	zi/k/ă	zi/k/ând
1PL	plân/dʒ/em	plân/dʒ/em		zi/tʃ/em	zi/tʃ/em	
2PL	plân/dʒ/eţi	plân/dʒ/eţi		zi/tʃ/eţi	zi/tʃ/eţi	
3PL	plân/g/	plân/g/ă		zi/k/	zi/k/ă	

The reason for the appearance of the velar in the gerund should be apparent from these examples: the ending of the gerund contains a non-front vowel â (/ɨ/), and not a front vowel as in Italian. I shall assume for present purposes (although the chronology is not certain) that the ending -ând represents a very early analogical generalization of a gerund ending originally associated with first conjugation verbs, and that this generalization chronologically 'bled' (i.e. removed potential input to) the palatalization process.

There is, however, one verb in Romanian with a velar–palatal alternation which does not show the velar in the gerund. This fact has a simple and obvious historical explanation. The verb in question, a fugi 'run, flee', belongs to the fourth conjugation, and it happens to be the sole[16] member of that conjugation to show a velar–palatal alternation. Now the gerund of fourth conjugation verbs ends not in -ând (as in all other conjugations), but in -ind (cf. a dormi 'sleep' – dormind; a veni 'come' – venind; a auzi 'hear' – auzind; a simţi 'feel' – simţind). Since -ind contains a front vowel, the principle that the alternants are phonologically selected predicts that the palatal, not the velar, alternant should appear in the gerund—and that is just what we find:

(14)

	PRS.IND	SBJV	GERUND
1SG	fu/g/	fu/g/	
2SG	fu/dʒ/i	fu/dʒ/i	
3SG	fu/dʒ/e	fu/g/ă	fu/dʒ/ind
1PL	fu/dʒ/im	fu/dʒ/im	
2PL	fu/dʒ/iţi	fu/dʒ/iţi	
3PL	fu/g/	fu/g/ă	

Now while the pattern of alternation in a fugi is regular from a phonological point of view, it is quite anomalous from a morphological perspective. In all other verbs having the velar–palatal alternation, the gerund shows the same (velar) root allo-

---

[16] In principle there is also a mugi 'low (of a cow)', but it tends to follow a different inflectional pattern in which /dʒ/ is present throughout the paradigm, and in any case it has much lower frequency of use and attestation than a fugi.

morph as the relevant forms of the present and subjunctive. Yet it appears to be in order to 'correct' this anomaly that, repeatedly across the Romanian dialects, speakers have introduced the velar into the gerund of this verb as well (see, for example, Lombard 1954–1955: 651f.; *ALRII* map 2153 *fugind* and the responses to question 543 *fugind* in the regional Romanian linguistic atlases such as Neiescu *et al.* 1969, Teaha *et al.* 1984; see also Maiden 2011c). In respect of this phenomenon, the Romanian dialects are a patchwork, but a patchwork such that there are attested scores of examples of the older type of gerund [fuˈdʒind] and scores of examples of the newer type /fuˈɡɨnd/, not infrequently existing side by side in the same dialect.

The innovatory type /fuˈɡɨnd/ reveals a detail which actually looks like splendid and irrefutable confirmation of the view that the alternants are a function of phonological environment. If the velar is introduced into the gerund of *a fugi*, then the gerund ending is no longer *-ind*, with a front vowel, but *-ând* (/ɨnd/), with a non-front vowel: there is not one single example, in all the copious attestations of this phenomenon, in which the outcome is (the entirely pronounceable) **/fuˈɡind/. Any celebration of these facts as vindication of the 'phonologizing' view of the alternation would, however, be short-lived. What they actually, and inescapably, show is that speakers have analysed the distribution of the velar alternant *morphologically*, indeed *morphomically*, in that a pattern comprising the first person singular and third person plural present, the first person singular subjunctive, and the third person subjunctive together with the gerund (hardly a 'natural class') has provided the basis for an adjustment in the verb *a fugi*. Were the alternation assigned by speakers to purely phonological conditioning, such a change would be inexplicable.

What needs to be emphasized is that the change in the ending of the gerund must *follow*, and cannot precede, the analogical adjustment of the root allomorph. It is practically inconceivable that *-ind* in this verb for some reason first became *-ând* and that phonological principles thereafter automatically selected the velar root alternant. This would involve a change of conjugation class marker just in the gerund and just in one verb, a development of a kind otherwise wholly unattested in Romanian. The only reason to postulate such a change would be in order to preserve intact the hypothesis of a phonologically conditioned change. Rather, if *-ind* has been replaced by *-ând*, this is a consequence of the morphological change in the root. Of course, the sequence of events I have in mind is in 'psychological' rather than 'chronological' time. Given that the velar is selected, the speaker's sense that the velar is incompatible with the front vowel probably triggers automatic selection of the gerund ending compatible with the velar. This development is indeed powerful confirmation of speakers' awareness of a tight correlation between velar alternants and non-front vowel endings, but it is also inescapable confirmation of speakers' sense that the distribution of the velar is *morphological*.

3.3 Conclusion

What do the Romanian and Italian data tell us? As I have presented the Romanian facts here[17] they are almost shocking, for speakers seem recklessly to have snatched morphology from the jaws of phonology. The velar–palatal alternation is correlated with unfailing consistency with the frontness or otherwise of the immediately following vowel, this recurrent syntagmatic fact is clearly quite obvious to speakers, *and yet* the alternation is revealed by the analogical change also to be directly associated by them with a heterogeneous set of morphologically specified paradigm cells. What the Romanian data do is to subvert the apparently quite reasonable assumption that the exceptionless occurrence, or even the predominance, of a phonological environment for some alternation precludes a morphological (or indeed morphomic) analysis.[18]

The data from central Italo-Romance involve a more subtle balance between phonology and morphology: phonological causation looks prima facie plausible, while the facts generally speak for a morphological analysis. *And yet* there are unmistakeable historical signs that speakers are also aware of systematic phono-logical cues to the distribution of the allomorphs. The Italian developments rather give the impression, in fact, of speakers' resorting to phonological cues 'in case of doubt'—where some morphological innovation (notably, the short-lived extension of present-tense allomorphs into the gerund) is tentative and 'experimental'. The Romanian data from the gerund perhaps have a similar quality, the tentative and still by no means firmly established innovation in the gerund needing, so to

---

[17] In Maiden (2011c) the data appear in a broader context, in which the velar–palatal alternation has much the same distribution as other types of root allomorphy, for which a phonological account seems less immediately plausible.

[18] Romanian dialects, indeed, provide some remarkable evidence for speakers' analysing in terms of a *morphological* distribution a pattern of alternation whose distribution is a classic example of a highly 'natural' *phonetic* process, and a matter of allophony. As in many languages, Romanian nasals are homorganically assimilated for position of articulation before an immediately following velar. This means, in the verb, that velar nasals will appear before root-final velar alternants, but not elsewhere (e.g. ['liŋɡə] 'lick'3SG.SBJV vs. ['lindʒe] 'lick'3SG.PRS.IND). In some dialects of the southern Romanian region of Oltenia (see Maiden, 2009b, for a more detailed account), the velar alternant /g/ has been analogically eliminated in a number of verbs, and replaced by a non-velar root-final consonant; yet the putatively allophonic nasal retains its velar articulation in the relevant *morphological* environment (and despite the fact that homorganic assimilation of nasals continues to be a productive, automatic, phonetic process): e.g. ['tuŋɡə] 'shear'3SG.SBJV > ['tuŋdə], not **['tundə]. This is clear evidence that speakers pick up *redundant* contextual distributional cues to the distribution of alternants, and may even reanalyse them as basic to the alternation.

speak, to be 'retrospectively licensed' by the phonological environment, if it is to go through.

This chapter began with a question about Italian morphology which is probably unanswerable simply from synchronic observation of the utterances of modern Italian speakers. What is suggested by the comparative-historical perspective I have proposed is that in our approach to Italian, or to any other language, our analysis should avoid being *reductionist*. Maiden (1992, 2001a, 2009a), Pirrelli (2000), and Pirrelli and Battista (2000) argue for a purely morphological analysis of the Italian facts, and they do so because the phonological one is clearly contra-exemplified, whereas the morphological one is not. This stance is expressed by Pirrelli and Battista (2000: 323) in the assumption that: 'All alternating stem roots which are not accountable in terms of exceptionless phonological rules of Italian are to be considered as independent B[asic] S[tems] in Aronoff's sense.' In contrast to this position, Burzio (2004) takes an approach grounded in Optimality Theory, invoking the notion of violability of constraints to accommodate the view that the Italian alternations are indeed phonologically conditioned with occasional morpho-logically specified examples. Interestingly, Burzio (2004: 38) does concede that 'paradigmatic relations enter into the mental computation', but on his account a phonological analysis seems to be sufficient, save in those cases where it is 'out-ranked' by morphological conditions. The metaphor of 'outranking' seems itself to be ultimately reductionist and exclusivist: on this view alternations are phonologic-ally conditioned by default, except in cases where the facts force us to accept a morphological analysis. But what we see in Italo-Romance and Romanian looks more like a scenario in which morphological and phonological conditioning factors seem to coexist and *collaborate*, not to compete.

Speakers seem much untidier than us linguists. Phonology and morphology do not appear to be mutually exclusive in the diachronic behaviour of the velar–palatal alternations, but rather redundantly co-present. Everything I have surveyed here really is *autonomously morphological*—that is 'morphomic': the alternants occupy a heterogeneous set of paradigm cells and if we removed specification of that set of cells from our account of the distribution of the alternants, and relied purely on phonological cues, we simply could not explain the diachronic behaviour we ob-serve. But the morphological autonomy of the alternations is not absolute and detached from phonological information. We can no more allow ourselves a *reduc-tionist* attitude in respect of the *morphomic* analysis than we can with any other account. In addition to an array of morphological specifications (in terms of number, person, tense, mood, and even finiteness) my diachronic analyses of the Italo-Romance and Romanian facts suggest that we should recognize that the phonological identity of the desinences can play an *ancillary* role in the distribution of the morphological alternation, no more. The phonological element certainly does not 'trigger' the alternations in the sense that one could postulate a unique underlying input subject to modification in a particular phonological environment, nor (assuming direct specification of the alternants in the lexical entry for each verb) does it 'select' the appropriate alternant: such accounts would be massively contra-exemplified by the Italo-Romance facts and strikingly undermined by the example of Romanian *fugând*, where the distribution of the thematic vowel can be shown to *presuppose* the distribution of the alternants, not vice versa.

The facts I have reviewed are not 'autonomously morphological' to the extent that to account for them in fine detail we need to make some additional reference to the phonological environment of the alternation. In this respect we might want to call them 'semi-autonomous' or 'partially autonomous': that such things should exist is a not unexpected finding, given that Aronoff (1994: 25, 166–7) was at pains to stress that his illustrations of morphomes were the most 'clear cut' cases, with the plain implication that morphomic phenomena were not, so to speak, outlandish exceptions which existed only when all possibility of phonological or phonologial conditioning had been ruled out, but were potentially present, to a greater or lesser degree, even in the presence of phonological or other kinds of 'extramorphological' conditioning.

We need, however, to be very clear about the kind of thing I have been describing here. The foregoing study makes some inferences from *diachrony*. It can certainly throw light, therefore, on the strategies at work in language change and principally, one supposes, in the acquisition process. What we have seen confirms that learners do internalize abstract and autonomously morphological distribution patterns, but also suggests that they may attempt to modify those distributions as they acquire their language and that in the process of doing so they make use also of phonological cues as to the plausibility of any given innovation. An innovation apparently has a better chance of survival when it is phonologically 'natural' (as in the case of the old Italian gerund) and/or when it occurs in a phonological environment which is consistently correlated with the relevant alternant (as in the case of Romanian *fugând*). Such observations do not necessarily tell us anything about the adult grammar,[19] and more particularly they do not necessarily show that *established* (i.e. non-innovatory) morphomic distributions involve any kind of extramorphological conditioning at all, although the evidence from diachrony/acquisition surely increases the plausibility of the inference that the phonological environment has a role in the adult grammar as well. If we are to get a clearer understanding of the exact nature of the relation between the exclusively morphomic and phonological conditioning in synchrony, then neither static observa-

---

[19] In so far as innovations are integrated into the system and become the norm, the adults' sense of what is 'natural' in their language presumably plays a role. Note, however, that neither of the two main phenomena discussed here have become fully established, and the innovation in the old Italian gerund ultimately failed to take root.

tion of synchronic outputs, nor a purely diachronic approach, are enough. We shall need proper psycholinguistic testing of speakers under laboratory conditions.[20] The diachronic and comparative evidence from Italian and Romanian underscore that it will be well worth investigating in this direction.

---

[20] Very little experimental work on putative morphomes has been conducted, an interesting exception being some recent and still unpublished work by Andrew Nevins and Cilène Rodrigues on the modern Portuguese manifestations of the Romance morphome labelled by Maiden (e.g. 2011a) as 'L-pattern'. It has to be said that their results suggest that modern Portuguese speakers do not recognize the putative morphomic distribution (even if the *diachronic* evidence in its support is very robust). Whether (as I suspect) such findings confirm my suspicion that the acquisition process and what ends up in the adult grammar may be different, or whether they mean that this morpheme is simply 'extinct' in Portuguese, remains to be seen.

4

The Italian FINIRE-type verbs: a case of morphomic attraction

MARTINA DA TOS

4.1 Introduction

The label 'N-pattern' (cf. Maiden 2004*b*, 2011*b*) designates a recurrent pattern of alternation in the inflectional paradigm of most Romance verbs such that 'the present tense first, second and third persons singular, the second person singular imperative, and the third person plural share a [common element, mostly a] root distinct from that of the remainder of the paradigm'.[1] The Italian third conjugation verbs (the label I give to those with 'thematic vowel' /i/), show several instances of N-pattern. Consider, for example, the verbs MORIRE 'die' and USCIRE 'go out'. As Table 4.1 shows, these two verbs are inflectionally equivalent and both exhibit allomorphy in their lexical roots.[2] Notice that, although the phonetic substance of their alternations is different, the alternation pattern is one and the same.

TABLE 4.1 N-pattern

	MORIRE 'die'		USCIRE 'go out'	
	Present indicative	Present subjunctive	Present indicative	Present subjunctive
1SG	*muoi-o*	*muoi-a*	*esc-o*	*esc-a*
2SG	*muor-i*	*muoi-a*	*esc-i*	*esc-a*
3SG	*muor-e*	*muoi-a*	*esc-e*	*esc-a*
1PL	*mor-iamo*	*mor-iamo*	*usc-iamo*	*usc-iamo*
2PL	*mor-ite*	*mor-iate*	*usc-ite*	*usc-iate*
3PL	*muoi-ono*	*muoi-ano*	*esc-ono*	*esc-ano*

[1] Maiden (2011*b*: 241).
[2] Notice that the present analysis only deals with alternation in root-vowels. Consonantal alternations (in MORIRE mwo/mo[r] vs. mwo[j] and in USCIRE u/e[ʃʃ] vs. e[sk]) are not taken into account here.

The N-pattern is generally regarded as a manifestation of a morpheme (see Aronoff 1994: 25f.). A definition of the morpheme is certainly outside the scope of the present work;[3] for the present purposes, this can be conceived as a morphologically abstract function, grouping together some of the cells of a paradigm and marking the word-forms in those cells as sharing a formal element (cf. O'Neill 2011*b*: 70). Aronoff (1994), who first acknowledged morphomic structures in the inflectional paradigm, claims that morphomes are endowed with psychological reality, that is, are part of a native speaker's competence. In this sense, morphomes can prove the existence of an autonomously morphological level of linguistic analysis: going back to the N-pattern above, it is easy to see that the paradigm cells of the singular and third plural of the present indicative and subjunctive do not constitute a natural class in morphosyntactic or semantic terms.

It is traditionally recognized that the principal source of the N-pattern is the historical differentiation in quality between stressed and unstressed vowels (cf. Maiden 2011*b*: 242). Actually, as Table 4.1 shows, the word-forms of the present tense singular and third plural are stressed on the root ('rhizotonic'), while the word-forms of the rest of the paradigm are stressed elsewhere ('arrhizotonic'). Indeed, a phonetic differentiation between stressed and unstressed vowels can easily account for the alternation observed in the verb MORIRE 'die' above: in the earlier stages of Italian, the vowel /o/ diphthongized to [wɔ] in stressed position, yielding the alternation *muòio/morìte* (see, for instance, Loporcaro 2011: 119f.). Although the diphthongization rule is no longer active in modern Italian, it could be claimed that it left a residual mark which speakers simply memorized as a lexical idiosyncrasy of the verb at issue, without any distributional generalization at the paradigmatic level.

However, this is not the case with the verb USCIRE 'go out', since no phonological rule—either synchronic or diachronic—could account for the alternation between *esc-* and *usc-*. Rather, Maiden (1995*b*) accounts for that alternation in terms of a suppletive conflation of two distinct etyma, i.e. the verb *exire* (old Italian *escire* 'go out'), and the noun *uscio* 'doorway'. Clearly, the idea that the N-pattern can serve as a distributional template guiding a suppletive replacement supports the claim that this morpheme is endowed with psychological reality.[4] It is true that suppletive verbs such as USCIRE are few and far between in Italian.[5] Accordingly, even though it seems plausible that the N-pattern might have played some kind of role in the paradigmatic arrangement of the root alternants of USCIRE, it could still be objected

---

[3] On the notion of morpheme, cf. O'Neill (2011*b*, this volume).

[4] As pointed out by Smith (2011*a*: 294), although the N-pattern is not the only morphomic structure identified in the Italian verb system, it is actually the only one which can serve as a template for suppletive alternations.

[5] That is, the abovementioned USCIRE 'go out' and ANDARE 'go'.

TABLE 4.2 N-pattern

	FINIRE 'end, finish'	
	Present indicative	Present subjunctive
1SG	*fin-isc-o*	*fin-isc-a*
2SG	*fin-isc-i*	*fin-isc-a*
3SG	*fin-isc-e*	*fin-isc-a*
1PL	*fin-iamo*	*fin-iamo*
2PL	*fin-ite*	*fin-iate*
3PL	*fin-isc-ono*	*fin-isc-ano*

that this template just lends itself to the accommodation of a few sporadic lexical exceptions.

But consider now the verb FINIRE 'end, finish' in Table 4.2, again from the Italian third conjugation. In this verb, the N-pattern manifests itself through an element *-isc-* occurring between the (invariant) root and the (regular) inflectional endings. Notice that this element, while obviously contributing to the formal structure of at least some word-forms in the paradigm of the verb, does not seem to contribute in a similar way in terms of meaning.

Here again, an account on phonological grounds seems implausible: to my knowledge, there is no natural phonological rule which could add (or delete) an element like *-isc-* whenever a given context is met.[6]

It would also be hard to claim that the element *-isc-* is a lexical idiosyncrasy of the verb under discussion. In fact, a close inspection of the Italian third conjugation reveals that the vast majority of verbs in this class exhibits this characteristic feature: out of about 450 basic third conjugation verbs, only 19 fail to have *-isc-* in their inflection.[7] Notice also that this element turns out to be involved in the inflection of all third conjugation verbs derived from adjectives or nouns (e.g. *chiarire* 'explain, make clear', from *chiaro* 'clear'; *ingiallire* 'yellow, make yellow', from *giallo* 'yellow'). This extremely high type-frequency suggests that *-isc-* should be more than a simple root-extender, helping to characterize a given alternant in a given pattern of allomorphy: rather, *-isc-* seems to be part of an actual, though peculiar, pattern of inflection. Henceforth, I will use the label 'FINIRE-type' to refer to this peculiar inflectional pattern, including not only the regular third conjugation endings, but also the element *-isc-* in the relevant paradigm cells. Clearly, if it were possible to

---

[6] Cf. Vogel (1994: 224) and Burzio and Di Fabio (1993: 24f.). Carstairs (1988) accounts for the phenomenon as an instance of 'phonologically conditioned suppletion'.

[7] The list of these nineteen verbs will be provided below (see §4.5). For the moment, notice that MORIRE 'die' and USCIRE 'go out' (whose paradigms are illustrated in Table 4.1) are two of them.

demonstrate that the N-pattern played a role in the diachronic development of the FINIRE-type, this morpheme could no longer be associated with isolated idiosyncrasies in the verbal system.

In view of this, the present study investigates the origin of the FINIRE-type, taking early Latin as a starting point and focusing on the development of its characteristic element -*isc*-. This topic is certainly not new: in one interesting paper, Ramat (1992) points out the rise of the FINIRE-type as an instance of degrammaticalization.[8] After losing its semantic function the suffix -SC-, which in the Latin verbal system was involved in a derivational pattern creating new verbs from verbs, adjectives, and nouns, is thought to have been incorporated into the inflectional system of Italian as a relic, an 'empty morph' providing no additional meaning to the word-forms in which it appears. This analysis, though convincing, cannot account for the fact that the suffix, in its development from Latin to Italian, also undergoes a significant paradigmatic redistribution. In fact, while in the Latin verbal system -SC- is found to characterize all the forms of the *infectum* tenses, its Italian reflex is restricted ('downgraded', as Ramat puts it) to the singular and third plural of the present tenses (and imperative). Following Maiden (2004*b*, 2011*b*), I will suggest that this paradigmatic redistribution should be viewed as an instance of the attractive force of the 'N-pattern'.

A more innovative aspect of this contribution is the analysis of the vowel preceding -*sc*-. While in Italian this vowel is only -*i*-, in Latin, as we will see, it could vary among -*a*-, -*e*-, and -*i*-. My claim is that in its development from Latin to Italian, the -*i*- of the Italian -*isc*- was reanalysed as a 'thematic vowel', namely the vowel identifying, among other things, the verbal conjugation. We will see that this reanalysis process is the key point in the integration of -*isc*- into the inflectional system.

After an analysis of -*isc*- in a synchronic perspective (§4.2), I will deal with the diachronic development of the element. First, I will consider its evolution from early to late Latin (§4.3) and then its subsequent adaptation (§4.4). As we will see, this involves its paradigmatic redistribution according to the N-pattern as well as the reanalysis of the vowel before -*sc*- as a thematic vowel. This reanalysis, in turn, triggers the shift of -*isc*- to the domain of inflection, making the FINIRE-type a true inflectional pattern. In Section 4.5 I will discuss the advantages of this new inflectional pattern, which can account for its productivity in the system.

4.2 The Italian word-forms with -*isc*-: synchronic analysis

Following a suggestion by Vincent (1987*a*: 289) and Maiden (1995*a*: 122),[9] I will assume that all word-forms of the Italian verb system have to conform to the canonical structure (1):

---

[8] See also Allen (1995).   [9] See also Meinschaefer (2011: 52).

(1)   ROOT (**THEMATIC VOWEL**) (FORMATIVE) ENDING

In this structure, the parentheses mark the units which can be missing without compromising the well-formedness of the resulting word-form. In other words, according to structure (1), each word-form of the Italian verb system has to be provided with a ROOT and an ENDING; in addition, it may (but need not) have a THEMATIC VOWEL and a FORMATIVE. Finally, the part in bold indicates that stress has to fall on the thematic vowel, if there is one.[10] With structure (1) in mind, let us try to analyse two word-forms of the paradigm of FINIRE 'end, finish', i.e. the first singular present indicative *finisco* 'I finish', involving the sequence *-isc-* under discussion, and the first singular imperfect indicative *finivo* 'I finished / was finishing', without *-isc-*. The first step in the analysis, segmentation, is illustrated in (2):

(2)   **ROOT   THV   FORMATIVE   ENDING**
    a.   *fin*   *i*   *sc*   *o*
    b.   *fin*   *i*   *v*   *o*

According to this analysis, the two forms at issue are supposed to have one and the same morphological structure. The analysis of the form *finivo* outlined in (2b) is quite traditional and uncontroversial (cf. Vincent 1987a: 289). The informational content expressed by each of the four morphological units can be illustrated as follows:

(3) | ROOT | THV | FORMATIVE | ENDING | **Structure** |
|---|---|---|---|---|
| *fin* | *i* | *v* | *o* | **Form** |
| Lexeme | Conjugation | Tense & Mood | Person & number | **Categories** |
| 'FINISH, END' | Third | Imperfect indicative | First singular | **Content** |

In contrast, an analysis of the form *finisco* 'I finish' like that in (2a), treating the element *-isc-* as a morphologically significant sequence 'THEMATIC VOWEL + FORMATIVE', is rather unusual and certainly open to several objections. To begin with, in the Italian verb system the first person singular of the present indicative is generally found to have a structure '(stressed) ROOT + ENDING', i.e. a structure without any THEMATIC VOWEL or FORMATIVE (e.g. *àm-o* 'I love', *tèm-o* 'I fear', *dòrm-o* 'I sleep'). In a system where the morphological structure of a word-form seems to be directly associated with the paradigm cell which the form occupies—that is, where word-forms occupying the same paradigm cell are usually found to exhibit one and the same structure—the analysis in (2a), if correct, has the disadvantage of making a form like *finisco* 'irregular' with respect to all others in the system.[11]

---

[10]   On the link between thematic vowels and stress in the Italian verb system, see Meinshaefer (2011: 58).

[11]   Notice that this 'structural irregularity' affects not only the first person singular present indicative but, more generally, all the other word-forms with *-isc-*.

TABLE 4.3 **Formatives**

Root	ThV	Formative	Sub-paradigm
fin	*i*	*v*	Imperfect indicative
fin	*i*	*ss*	Imperfect subjunctive
fin		*(i)r*	Future
fin		*(i)re*	Conditional
fin	*i*	*t*	Perfect participle

Another problem concerns the treatment of *-sc-* as a FORMATIVE. In the analysis of the form *finìvo* above (cf. (3)), the FORMATIVE *-v-* was associated with the expression of the grammatical categories of Tense and Mood, i.e. imperfect indicative. This analysis is supported by the fact that this item appears in all and only the word-forms of the sub-paradigm imperfect indicative: *finìvo, finìvi, finìva, finivàmo, finivàte, finìvano*. Notice that the same is true for the other Formatives of the system. Table 4.3 illustrates them, together with the sub-paradigms in which they occur. This suggests that any Formative in the Italian verbal system, if present, should express a given property-combination for the morphosyntactic categories of Mood and Tense.

Yet this is not the case with the *-sc-* of the element *-isc-*: as a Formative, *-sc-* cannot be associated with a specific sub-paradigm, in that it appears only in some forms of two distinct sub-paradigms, i.e. present indicative and present subjunctive. Although all evidence suggests that a morphological analysis of the element *-isc-* as 'THEMATIC VOWEL + FORMATIVE' is to be rejected, one of the aims of this study is actually to defend it, by showing its advantages.

4.3 The evolution of the suffix -SC- in the Latin verbal system

As discussed earlier, the *-sc-* appearing in the inflection of the Italian FINIRE-type verbs is traditionally acknowledged as the continuant of a Latin suffix *-SC-*. In early Latin, where the present analysis begins, this suffix is found to be involved in a derivational pattern whereby new verbs (henceforth referred to as *sco*-verbs)[12] are formed from verbs, adjectives, or nouns. In a *sco*-verb paradigm, the suffix *-SC-* is found only in the forms of the so-called *infectum* tenses (i.e. the forms built on Aronoff's, 1994, Present Stem),[13] where it occupies the position before the inflectional endings. Table 4.4 shows the relevant paradigm portion of the Latin verb *sentisco* 'become aware of', derived from the verb *sentio* 'feel, perceive'.

---

[12] Cf. Haverling (2000). In this chapter, vowel length on Latin verbs will be generally only marked on the thematic vowels of infinitive forms. It will be marked on other vowels only when this is relevant to the argument.

[13] Cf. Aronoff (1994: 56).

TABLE 4.4 Latin *sentisco*

INFINITIVE
Present
sentiscĕre

IMPERATIVE		INDICATIVE			SUBJUNCTIVE	
		Present	Imperfect	Future	Present	Imperfect
1SG		*sentisco*	*sentiscebam*	*sentiscam*	*sentiscam*	*sentiscerem*
2SG	*sentisce*	*sentiscis*	*sentiscebas*	*sentisces*	*sentiscas*	*sentisceres*
3SG		*sentiscit*	*sentiscebat*	*sentiscet*	*sentiscat*	*sentisceret*
1PL		*sentiscimus*	*sentiscebamus*	*sentiscemus*	*sentiscamus*	*sentisceremus*
2PL	*sentiscite*	*sentiscitis*	*sentiscebatis*	*sentiscetis*	*sentiscatis*	*sentisceretis*
3PL		*sentiscunt*	*sentiscebant*	*sentiscent*	*sentiscant*	*sentiscerent*

A closer look at the *sco*-verbs of early Latin reveals that the vowel before -SC- can vary among -a-, -e-, and -i-. In the *sco*-verbs derived from verbs the vowel before -SC- varies depending on the conjugation of the base verb (we have, for instance, *amasco* 'fall in love', from the first conjugation *amo* 'love'; *augesco* 'increase, grow', from the second conjugation *augeo* 'increase, intensify'; *vivesco* 'come to life, grow stronger', from the third conjugation *vivo* 'be alive, live'; and *sentisco* 'become aware of', from the fourth conjugation *sentio* 'feel, perceive'). This suggests that in a *sco*-verb of a deverbal kind, the vowel before -SC- should be analysed as the 'thematic vowel' of the base verb. In this view, the derivational strategy involving -SC- seems to require that this suffix be added to the STEM (i.e. the sequence ROOT + THEMATIC VOWEL) of the base verb, the morphological structure of, for instance, *sentisco*, being therefore (4):

(4) **Structure** ROOT-THV SUFFIX ENDING
  Example *sent-i* *sc* *o*

However, the label 'thematic vowel' for the *sc*-preceding vowel in a form like *sentisco* might be misleading. Generally, a thematic vowel—as a unit in the morphological structure of a verb form—has to do with inflection: by signalling conjugation, a thematic vowel can be used for inflecting a verb correctly (cf. Aronoff 1994: 45f.). In contrast, the 'thematic vowel' that we are faced with here should rather have a 'derivational content': in the form *sentisco*, going back to the example above, the -i- before -SC- signals the inflection class of *sentio*, i.e. the verb from which *sentisco* derives, and not the inflection class of *sentisco* itself. Inflectionally, all Latin *sco*-forms belong to only one conjugation, i.e. the third.

The *sco*-verbs derived from adjectives or nouns, in contrast, only display the vowel -e- before -SC- (e.g. *crudesco* 'become raw, fierce, or savage', from *crudus* 'uncooked, raw, rough, unripe'; *arboresco* 'grow into a tree', from *arbor* 'tree'). This vowel cannot be analysed as the 'thematic vowel' of the base.[14] Rather, it is plausible to suppose that this might be segmented along with -SC-, being interpreted as the 'onset' of the derivational suffix.[15] Example (5) illustrates the morphological structure of *crudesco*:

(5)   ROOT   SUFFIX   ENDING
        crud   *esc*   *o*

Usually, the *sco*-verbs are intransitive and have dynamic value. When the base is a verb, the *sco*-verb matches its base in the opposition dynamic vs. non-dynamic (e.g. *amo, -āre* 'love, be in love' vs. *amasco, -ĕre* 'fall in love'; *sileo, -ēre* 'be silent' vs. *silesco, -ēre* 'grow more silent'; *vivo, -ĕre* 'be alive, live' vs. *vivesco, -ĕre* 'come to life, grow stronger'; *scio, -īre* 'know, be aware of' vs. *scisco, -ĕre* 'try to get to know, find out about'; *sentio, -īre* 'be aware of, hear, perceive' vs. *sentisco, -ĕre* 'be becoming aware of'; *dormio, -īre* 'be asleep, sleep' vs. *(con)dormisco, -ĕre* 'fall asleep') or, less frequently, in the opposition intransitive vs. transitive (e.g. *augeo, -ēre* 'increase, intensify' vs. *augesco, -ĕre* 'increase, grow'; *frango, -ĕre* 'break, smash' vs. *frangesco, -ĕre* 'become subdued or tractable'). When the base is an adjective or a noun, the *sco*-verb usually expresses the acquisition of the quality denoted by the base (e.g. *macresco* 'become thinner, waste away', from *macer* 'thin, meagre'; *herbesco* 'become covered with grass, spring up', from *herba* 'grass').

In some cases, *sco*-verbs related to adjectives or nouns are found to have verbal counterparts. Tables 4.5a and 4.5b show a sample of the two largest families of this kind, i.e. intransitive *sco*-verbs matching transitive verbs mostly of the first conjugation (in Table 4.5a), and dynamic *sco*-verbs matching stative verbs of the second conjugation (in Table 4.5b).

As pointed out by Haverling (2000: 178), in such cases it can be difficult to decide whether a *sco*-verb is derived 'directly' from the adjective (or noun), or else from a verb which is in its turn derived from the adjective. The vowel before -SC- can be a cue in this sense: a verb like *integrasco*, for instance, displaying -a- before -SC-, will reasonably derive from the first conjugation verb *integro*.[16] The analysis of *rubesco* is more difficult. Is it derived from *rubeo*, or directly from the adjective *ruber*? Given the 'default' character of the vowel -e-, it is actually impossible to decide. Clearly, both the verbs *rubeo* and *rubesco* are related to the adjective *ruber*, and *rubesco* can

---

[14] Here I assume that nouns and adjectives, contrary to verbs, do not have any thematic vowel. For a different position, cf. Scalise (1994).

[15] In this view, *-e-* should be taken as a 'default' vowel in the position before -SC-. On the grammaticalization of *-esc-*, see Allen (1995: 3–4).

[16] Here the derivational path should involve two steps: step one, whereby a simple verb is derived from an adjective or noun (so, *integro, -āre* 'restore to a former condition' from *integer* 'untouched, whole'), and step two, whereby a *sco*-verb is derived from the erstwhile verb (so, *integrasco, -ĕre* from *integro, -āre*).

TABLE 4.5a

Base adjective or noun	Verb (Transitive)	Sco-Verb (Intransitive)
ferus 'wild'	*effero, -āre* 'make wild'	*efferasco, -ĕre* 'become wild'
gravis 'heavy'	*aggravo, -āre* 'weigh down'	*aggravasco, -ĕre* 'become heavier'
integer 'untouched, whole'	*integro, -āre* 'restore to a former condition'	*integrasco, -ĕre* 'begin anew, break out afresh'
maturus 'ripe, mature'	*maturo, -āre* 'make mature'	*maturasco, -ĕre* 'become ripe, ripen, mature'
genus 'birth, origin, kind'	*genero, -āre* 'beget, create'	*generasco, -ĕre* 'come to birth'
purpura 'purple dye'	*purpuro, -āre* 'make purple, make rosy or bright'	*purpurasco, -āre* 'become stronger'
robur 'an oak-tree, firmness, strength'	*roboro, -āre* 'make stronger, give strength'	*roborasco, -ĕre* 'become stronger'
unus 'one'	*unio, -īre* 'join together, unite'	*unisco, -ĕre* 'grow into one'

TABLE 4.5b

Base adjective or noun	Verb (Non-dynamic)	Sco-Verb (Dynamic)
aeger 'sick, ill'	*aegreo* 'be ill or sick'	*aegresco* 'become physically ill, sicken, grow worse'
albus 'white'	*albeo* 'be white, light, pale'	*albesco* 'become white, pale, be growing white'
canus 'white'	*caneo* 'be white'	*canesco* 'grow white'
calvus 'bald, bare'	*calveo* 'be bald'	*calvesco* 'lose one's hair, grow bald'
clarus 'clear'	*clareo* 'be clear'	*claresco* 'become bright, shine, clear'
flaccus 'drooping, floppy'	*flacceo* 'have no strength, languish'	*flaccesco* 'lose strength'
flavus 'yellow'	*flaveo* 'be yellow'	*flavesco* 'grow golden, yellow'
hebes 'blunt, obtuse, weak'	*hebeo* 'be dull, feeble'	*hebesco* 'grow blunt or faint'
lentus 'flexible, clinging'	*lenteo* 'be slow'	*lentesco* 'become slow, sticky'
mucus 'mucus, snot'	*muceo* 'be mouldy'	*mucesco* 'become mouldy'
niger 'black'	*nigreo* 'be dark'	*nigresco* 'grow dark, blacken'
piger 'lazy, slow'	*pigreo* 'be reluctant'	*pigresco* 'grow sluggish'
putris 'decomposed, rotten'	*putreo* 'be in a state of decay'	*putresco* 'grow rotten'
ruber 'red'	*rubeo* 'be red'	*rubesco* 'grow red'
senex 'old'	*seneo* 'be old'	*senesco* 'grow older, age'
anus 'old woman'	*aneo* 'be an old woman'	*anesco* 'grow older'
ignis 'fire'	*igneo* 'be on fire'	*ignesco* 'catch fire'
lac, lactis 'milk'	*lacteo* 'be full of milk or juice'	*lactesco* 'become milk, gradually develop into milk'
pubes 'the age or condition of puberty'	*pubeo* 'be physically mature'	*pubesco* 'grow towards physical maturity'
tabes 'wasting away, decay, corruption'	*tabeo* 'be in a state of decay, rot away'	*tabesco* 'waste or dwindle away'

be seen as the 'dynamic counterpart' of the (stative) *rubeo*. Nonetheless, *rubesco* is admittedly open to a twofold interpretation.

In one of the most detailed studies on the diachronic development of the Latin *sco*-verbs, Haverling (2000) shows that the system of early Latin described above— where it was possible to derive *sco*-verbs from other verbs—decays over time. In the diachronic development from early to late Latin, the semantic relationship between the *sco*-verbs and their base verbs becomes blurred: in the latest periods of Latin, we find several *sco*-verbs used in a non-dynamic sense (e.g. *paresco* 'be clear, visible', *placesco* 'please', *pollesco* 'be powerful', *caresco* 'lack, be without', *lippesco* 'be red-eyed'), as well as new *sco*-verbs formed from dynamic verbs from which they do not differ semantically (e.g. *cadesco* = *cado* 'fall', *labiscor* = *labor* 'fall', *fluesco* = *fluo* 'flow, melt', *frendesco* = *frendo* 'grind one's teeth'). This suggests that the suffix -SC-gradually ceases to be seen as a mark of a derivation from one verb to another, losing its original derivational function. Notice that this has a significant consequence for the analysis of the vowel before -SC-. In late Latin, several *sco*-verbs are found in which the vowel before -SC- does not correspond to the thematic vowel of the original base verb, for instance *obsopesco* 'put or lull to sleep' (originally derived from *obsopio, -īre*), *gemisco* 'sigh' (originally from *gemo, -ĕre*), *lippesco* 'be red-eyed' (from *lippio, -īre*). As will be recalled from the above, in the system of early Latin this vowel had been analysed as the thematic vowel of the verb from which a given *sco*-verb derives (cf. structure (4) above). Clearly, such an analysis makes sense only in a system where a *sco*-verb is understood as a secondary formation from another verb. But when the semantic relationship between a *sco*-verb and its original base verb becomes blurred, the formal relationship between the two gets compromised too: to take one of the examples above, whereas *obsopesco* is no longer understood as a secondary formation from *obsopio*, the analysis of the vowel before -SC- as the thematic vowel of *obsopio* simply becomes pointless. For this reason, it is plausible to suppose that, when the original derivational system breaks down, the vowel before -SC- might be included in the -SC- formation, losing its original morphological autonomy and becoming the 'onset' of the suffix (cf. Rudes 1980, Aronoff and Fudeman 2011: 88). Notice that in a verb like *obsopesco*, the whole element -*esc*-seems to be reanalysed as a simple root-extender, performing no particular derivational function; it should also be noted that in the course of time the vast majority of *sco*-verbs of this kind gradually disappear from the system.

In the light of this change in the use of -SC-, let us consider the development of the *sco*-verbs listed in Tables 4.5a and 4.5b, namely those related to verbs which are themselves derived from an adjective or a noun. I have said that a verb like *albesco* 'become white' naturally lends itself to a twofold interpretation: it can be seen as a formation from the second conjugation verb *albeo, -ēre* 'be white', but it can also be related directly to the adjective *albus* 'white'. Clearly, this implies a different analysis of the vowel before -SC-: whereas *albesco* is seen as a deverbal formation from *albeo*, the vowel before -SC- will be analysed as the thematic vowel of the base verb, as shown by (6):

(6)   ROOT-ThV   SUFFIX   ENDING
       albe   *sc*   *o*

In contrast, if the *sco*-verb is interpreted as a deadjectival formation from *albus*, the vowel before -SC- cannot be treated as a thematic vowel.

It is probable that, when the original derivational system creating *sco*-verbs from verbs breaks down, a verb like *albesco* ceases to be regarded as a deverbal formation from *albeo*. However, it can be retained in the system as a deadjectival formation from *albus*, as the other interpretation is available. In this reanalysis, the vowel before -SC- ceases to be regarded as the thematic vowel of the base verb, and is taken as the onset of a derivational suffix -esc-, whereby *sco*-verbs are derived from adjectives or nouns. This suggests a possible explanation for several 'parallel forms' attested in Haverling's corpus, i.e. pairs of *sco*-verbs meaning the same but displaying different vowels before -SC-, e.g. *corporasco/corporesco* 'become physical', *gelasco/gelesco* 'freeze, coagulate', *maturasco/maturesco* 'become ripe, ripen, mature', *callesco/callisco* 'acquire a thick skin', *pauperasco/pauperesco* 'become poor, lose wealth'.

In the verb-pair *gelasco/gelesco*, to take one of the examples above, *gelasco* can be analysed as a formation from the first conjugation verb *gelo, -āre,*[17] while *gelesco*, displaying -e- before -SC-, should derive 'directly' from the noun *gelu* 'cold'. Examples (7a) and (7b) illustrate the morphological structures of the forms under discussion:

(7)   a.   ROOT-ThV   SUFFIX   ENDING
             gela   *sc*   *o*
       b.   ROOT   SUFFIX   ENDING
             gel   *esc*   *o*

Summing up so far, while in the system of early Latin the suffix -SC- had been involved in the derivation of verbs from verbs, adjectives, or nouns, in late Latin the possibility of creating *sco*-verbs from existing verbs gets gradually lost. As a consequence, the vowel before -SC-, which in the deverbal formations had been analysed as the 'thematic vowel' of the base verb, completely loses its morphological autonomy, and is systematically segmented along with -SC-. The whole suffix -esc-, where -e- is to be interpreted as a 'suffix-onset', survives in late Latin as a mark of a derivational strategy forming verbs from adjectives or nouns.

---

[17] Cf. Haverling (2000: 407).

TABLE 4.6 'Mixed' paradigm

	Present indicative	Present subjunctive	Imperative
1SG	*grandēsco*	*grandēscam*	
2SG	*grandēscis*	*grandēscas*	*grandēsce*
3SG	*grandēscit*	*grandēscat*	
1PL	*grandīmus*	*grandiāmus*	
2PL	*grandītis*	*grandiātis*	*grandīte*
3PL	*grandēscunt*	*grandēscant*	

4.4 On the subsequent adaptation of -*esc*-

4.4.1 *A blending process*

The derivational strategy involving the suffix -*esc*-, whereby new verbs are formed from adjectives or nouns, is not the only one available for this purpose in Latin. Indeed, verbs derived from adjectives or nouns via conversion are found in the first, the second, and the fourth conjugation of Latin.[18] Among these formations, Maurer (1951: 138) draws particular attention to a group of fourth conjugation verbs (with thematic vowel -i-) extremely close to the *sco*-verbs under discussion, in both form and function: in addition to being themselves derived from adjectives or nouns, those verbs likewise denote a change of state. So in late Latin we would have two closely related derivational types: *sco*-verbs expressing a change of state with middle action (e.g. *grandesco* 'I become large'), and fourth-conjugation verbs expressing a change of state often with causative value (e.g. *grandio* 'I increase'). According to Maurer, the closeness of these derivational processes is proved by the fact that several adjectives and nouns are found to give rise to derivatives in both classes (e.g. *mollesco* 'become soft or yielding' and *mollio, -īre* 'make softer', both from *mollis* 'soft'; *inanesco* 'become empty, be emptied, decrease' and *inanio, -īre* 'make empty', both from *inanis* 'empty, hollow'; *grandesco* 'increase in size, grow, swell' and *grandio* 'increase').

It is Maurer's claim that this formal and semantic compatibility between the denominative verbs in -*ĕsco -escere* and those in -*io -īre* resulted in a blending between the two types, yielding a paradigm like that illustrated in Table 4.6.

In this 'mixed' paradigm—to be understood as the antecedent of the Italian FINIRE-type—the present tense singular and third plural should come from the *grandesco* type, the remainder of the paradigm being replaced by the forms of the *grandio* type. In my opinion, a weak point in Maurer's analysis is the way he

---

[18] Cf. Dressler (2002: 98–9).

accounts for the paradigmatic distribution of the forms of the *grandesco* type in the 'mixed' paradigm of Table 4.6. According to Maurer, the presence of these forms in only a few cells of the present tense depends on a gradual restriction of their use. Over the course of time, as Maurer claims, the forms of the *sco*-type become 'limited in their use almost entirely to the present tense'. The problem with this explanation is that it is unsupported by any independent evidence: after all, as Maurer himself admits, the *sco*-formations show great vitality in the later periods of Latin, so that such a restriction in use seems quite improbable. The paradigm of the *grandesco*-type was subject to a paradigmatic restriction, in fact, the element *-esc-* appearing only in the forms of the *infectum* tenses (as seen in §4.3). However, this leads us to suppose the presence of a mixed paradigm with the forms of the *grandesco*-type throughout the *infectum* tenses and the forms of the *grandio*-type elsewhere.

In sum, although Maurer's idea of a blending process between the *grandesco*- and *grandio*-type sounds interesting, his account of the paradigmatic arrangement of the forms involved looks quite unsatisfactory.

It is plausible to suppose that the blending process claimed by Maurer might be an instance of attraction by the N-pattern: in the resulting paradigm, the forms of the *grandesco*-type display the well-known N-shaped distribution, while the remainder of the paradigm has forms of the *grandio*-type. Indeed, the idea that the N-pattern might have guided the blending process illustrated above is not implausible: after all, we know that this very template in the history of Italian could shape suppletive alternations as well, as in the case of the conflation of the etyma *escire* 'go out' and *uscio* 'doorway' yielding the paradigm of the modern Italian USCIRE 'go out' (cf. §4.1). In this framework, a blending between the paradigms of the verbs *grand-esco* and *grandio* should be conceived of as something close to the suppletive conflation of *uscio* and *escire*, except that here the items involved are not two distinct etyma, but rather two secondary verbs derived from the same adjective.

Admittedly, however, such a solution leaves some questions open. These concern: (i) the phonological content of the vowel before *-sc-*: in the 'mixed' paradigm of Table 4.6, the forms of the *grandesco*-type exhibit *-e-* in the position before *-sc-*, while in Italian we always find *-i-* (i.e. *finisco*, *finisci*, etc., and not **finésco*, **finésci*, etc.);[19] (ii) the great productivity of the resulting type. As shown earlier (cf. §4.1), in Italian the FINIRE-type characterizes the vast majority of third-conjugation verbs, including not only derivational formations from adjectives or nouns, but also a large number of 'basic' (i.e. non-derived) verbs. It is true that the verb-pair *grandesco* and *grandio* considered above is not the only one lending itself to a blending process like that illustrated in Table 4.6, since we know that there are several verb-pairs like

---

[19] Note that Romanian preserves the alternation *e – i* in the present indicative, as exemplified by *a citi* 'read': *citesc, citești, citește, citim, citiți, citesc.*

grandesco/grandio in late Latin; nonetheless, the great productivity of the FINIRE-type in 'basic' verbs still needs to be further justified.

In the rest of this section, I will try to account for this further step in the development of the FINIRE-type, showing how a proper inflectional-type could arise from a paradigm like that of Table 4.6. We will see that a key point in this process is the reanalysis—due to paradigmatic pressure—of the word-forms of the *grandesco*-type, whereby the vowel before *-sc-* was reinterpreted as a thematic vowel.

4.4.2 *The reanalysis of the vowel before* -sc-

As will probably have been noticed, the 'mixed' paradigm illustrated in Table 4.6 has a striking peculiarity: it exhibits 'columnar' or 'vertical' stress on the root-following syllable throughout the present tenses. In Latin, such a stress pattern is unprecedented, as Latin verbs are generally characterized by stress alternation in the present. In fact, it falls on the root in the singular and third plural (rhizotonic forms) and after the root in the first and second plural (arrhizotonic forms). A different stress pattern is exhibited by the Latin third conjugation, in which the root is stressed throughout the present indicative tenses; here again, however, the stress falls on the root, and not after it.

An important effect of this exceptional 'columnar' stress is that it can trigger a reanalysis of the word-forms of the *grandesco*-type. To see this process, let us focus on the present indicative of the 'mixed' paradigm shown in Table 4.7.

As the table shows, the aligned stress increases the contrast between the vowel -e-occurring after the root in the forms of the singular and third plural, and the -i- occurring in the first and second plural. Notice that despite their 'structural compatibility' these vowels have a different morphological status: the -i- of the first and second plural is the thematic vowel for Latin fourth-conjugation verbs, while the -e- before -sc- has no morphological autonomy (cf. §4.3). That is, while in the morphological structure of a form like *grandítis* 'you (PL) become bigger', the tonic -i- should occupy a dedicated slot (as shown in (8a) below), the tonic -e- of, for

TABLE 4.7 **Reanalysis**

		Present indicative	
1SG	*grand*	ḗ	*sco*
2SG	*grand*	ḗ	*scis*
3SG	*grand*	ḗ	*scit*
1PL	*grand*	ī	*mus*
2PL	*grand*	ī	*tis*
3PL	*grand*	ḗ	*scunt*

instance, *grandēsco* 'I become bigger' would have no dedicated position, as shown in (8b):

(8) a. ROOT   THV   ENDING
         grand   ī   te
     b. ROOT   ENDING
         grandēsc o

I claim that the contrast between the thematic vowel -*i*- and the -*e*- of -*esc*-, which in the present indicative of the 'mixed' paradigm is increased by their stressed position, caused the reanalysis of the vowel before -*sc*- as a thematic vowel, and its subsequent replacement by -*i*-. This shift can be regarded as a sort of 'analogical levelling': once the vowel before -*sc*- is identified as a thematic vowel, its phonological content tends to conform to that of the thematic vowel found elsewhere in the paradigm.[20] Whether this analysis is correct or not, it is undeniable that in Italian the element characterizing the FINIRE-type verbs is -*isc*-, not -*esc*-, and that the FINIRE-type is a subclass (indeed, the largest one) of the conjugation with thematic vowel *i*.

In this view, the element -*esc*- would be reanalysed as a morphologically significant structure 'THEMATIC VOWEL + sc'. In a system where all word-forms have to conform to the canonical structure 'ROOT + (THEMATIC VOWEL) + (FORMATIVE) + ENDING' (cf. §4.2), a form like *grandisco*, having the tonic -*i*- analysed as a THEMATIC VOWEL and the final -*o* analysed as an ENDING, can be easily accepted providing that the element -*sc*- is analysed as a FORMATIVE. Schematically, the reanalysis of the erstwhile suffix would be (9):

(9)   *esc*
          ↓
     THV   FORMATIVE
     -*i*-   -*sc*-

At this point, I claim that the reanalysis of the vowel before -*sc*- as a thematic vowel is the key factor for the integration of the sequence -*isc*- into the inflectional system.[21]

To understand this claim, let us look back once more to the canonical structure 'ROOT + (THEMATIC VOWEL) + (FORMATIVE) + ENDING' introduced in Section 4.2, focusing on the thematic vowel. This structure requires that the thematic vowel, if there is one, should occur between the ROOT and the FORMATIVE; if there is no FORMATIVE, the thematic vowel should stand between the ROOT and the ENDING.

---

[20] In the words of Maurer (1951: 143): 'in a paradigm where the overwhelming majority of the endings were characterized by the vowel ī, the vowel ē of -ēsco must have sounded strange.'

[21] Cf. Ramat (1992) and Allen (1995), as well as Blaylock (1975: 444) who, commenting on the origin of the FINIRE-type in Romance, claims that 'Though we have grown accustomed to speaking of stem augments, we should perhaps think more in terms of desinence-augments.'

Thinking of roots as 'lexical' items and endings as 'inflectional' (i.e. 'grammatical') items is certainly nothing new. As far as formatives are concerned, I showed in Section 4.2 that the formatives of the Italian verbal system generally express a given property-combination for the categories of Tense and Mood. Since these categories are morphosyntactic, I claim that formatives should also be regarded as part of a verb's inflection. In a word-form displaying a formative, the distinction between 'lexicon' and 'grammar' would therefore be (10):

(10)   ROOT   (THV)   (FORMATIVE)   ENDING   **Structure**
       Lexical   Grammatical   Grammatical   **Level of interpretation**

This schema suggests that the thematic vowel, if present, should mark the boundary between the 'lexical' and the 'inflectional' (or, 'grammatical') portion of a word-form. Once these premises have been set, the idea that the identification of the vowel before -*sc*- as a thematic vowel might have triggered the incorporation of the sequences -*isco*, -*isci*, etc. into the inflectional system becomes more understandable.

That the sequences -*isco*, -*isci*, etc. are really seen as an inflectional pattern is also proved by the fact that this pattern was used to integrate a large number of new verbs in the system. Theorists of Natural Morphology (cf. Dressler 2002: 96f.) have drawn up a list of criteria which can prove the productivity of an inflectional type. Actually, the FINIRE-type turns out to meet all of these criteria, in that it includes:[22]

(a)   loans that originally lack the marker of inflection class characterizing Italian verbs (i.e. a thematic vowel): e.g. *arrostire* 'roast' < Germanic **raustjan*; *smaltire* 'digest, work off' < Gothic *smaltjan*

(b)   loans that already have a suitable marker of inflection class (i.e. the thematic vowel *i*): e.g. *accudire* 'look after' < Spanish *acudir*; *trasalire* 'flinch' < old French *tressaillir*

(c)   conversions (including verbs created by parasynthesis): e.g. *chiarire* 'make clear' < *chiaro* 'clear'; *colpire* 'strike' < *colpo* 'stroke'; *addolcire* 'sweeten' < *dolce* 'sweet'; *arrugginire* 'rust$_V$' < *ruggine* 'rust'

(d)   verbs which have undergone a class shift from Latin second or third conjugation: e.g. *abolire* 'abolish' < *abolēre*;[23] *capire* 'understand' < *capere*.

It will have been noticed that the FINIRE-type, as an inflectional pattern of the Italian verb system, turns out to be doubly irregular with respect to all others: in fact, it preserves the peculiar 'columnar' stress after the root throughout the present tenses and, in addition, exhibits a thematic vowel in the present tense singular and third plural, while Italian verbs are generally found to have forms with the structure '(stressed) ROOT + ENDING' in these paradigm cells (cf. §4.2). Therefore, in terms

---

[22] A list of the Italian verbs following the FINIRE-type is given in the Appendices.
[23] Cf. Davis and Napoli (1994: 58).

of language-specific system-congruity (cf. Wurzel 1989), the FINIRE-type seems to be doubly disadvantageous. Should we conclude that this peculiar inflectional pattern, being productive, simply spreads irregularity in the system? Despite its irregular character, the FINIRE-type admittedly has a great advantage, as it avoids allomorphy in the lexical part of the word-form. In a system where root allomorphy in the present can arise just because of the differentiation in quality between stressed and unstressed vowels (as discussed in §4.1), an inflectional pattern avoiding the typical alternation between rhizotonic and arrhizotonic forms can in principle guarantee root-invariance.

4.5 On the advantages of the FINIRE-type

A paradigm having multiple root alternants (i.e. the phenomenon known as root allomorphy) is definitely more complex than one exhibiting one root, both in terms of word-production (in that all root alternants have to be stored in the verb's lexical entry) and in terms of word-analysis (root allomorphy notoriously contravenes the ideal 'one-meaning–one-form' principle).[24] As will be recalled from the above, the characteristic alternating stress-positions in the present are the major source of root allomorphy in the Italian verb paradigm, in that rhizotonic and arrhizotonic forms can be subject to a different phonetic treatment (cf. the paradigm of the verb MORIRE 'die', in Table 4.1).

As noted by Maiden (2011a: 211f.),[25] in the Italian verb system the phenomenon of root allomorphy, whatever its source, appears to be conjugation-dependent. In particular, first-conjugation verbs, while retaining the characteristic alternating stress pattern of their Latin antecedents, have been showing a tendency from the beginning of their history to eliminate root allomorphy. Accordingly, even those first-conjugation verbs which happen to have any form of root alternation due to stress are found to restore invariant roots in the course of their diachronic development. This is the case, for instance, of the verb NEGARE 'deny', in which the original alternation *niégo* 'I deny' / *neghiàmo* 'we deny' was levelled as *négo/neghiámo* (cf. Maiden 2011a: 211).[26] Yet such a strong tendency towards root-invariance seems to be a characteristic feature of first conjugation verbs, i.e. those with thematic vowel /a/: as far as the conjugation with thematic vowel /i/ is concerned, its verbs not only tend to preserve root allomorphy patterns which have arisen because of stress alternation (as in the case of the verb MORIRE illustrated above), but may also be found to introduce root-variation into originally invariant paradigms. The verb

---

[24] Cf. Crocco-Galèas (1998). Notice that Corbett (2007a) explicitly states root-invariance as one of the characteristic features of a 'canonical paradigm'.

[25] See also Maiden (1995a).

[26] Other cases are provided by Aski (1995: 411).

FUGGIRE 'flee', for instance, acquires an unprecedented alternation in the root-final consonant, as shown by the comparison between old Italian *fuggio/fuggi* 'I/you flee' and modern Italian *fuggo/fuggi*.[27]

In a conjugation showing no inherent tendency towards root-invariance, any device helping to counteract stress alternation (i.e. the major source of root allomorphy) should therefore be welcome. It is easy to see that the peculiar 'columnar' stress of the FINIRE-type appears to be particularly apt for this purpose: by fixing stress immediately after the verbal root, this novel inflectional pattern can prevent the latter from undergoing any differentiation in shape due to the characteristic stressed/ unstressed alternation. Notice that there is a clear correlation in Italian between the avoidance of root allomorphy, on the one hand, and the productivity of an inflectional type, on the other: the first conjugation, with its peculiar tendency toward root-invariance, is notoriously the most productive inflection class in the system. However, we have seen that the FINIRE-type too, with its peculiar 'anti-allomorphic' stress (cf. Maiden 2011b: 251f.), shows great productivity in the history of Italian.

Interestingly enough, the FINIRE-type as an innovation of the Italian verb system seems not to attract Latin 'base verbs' with thematic vowel -i-.[28] In other words, it seems as if basic verbs which enter the Italian verb system endowed with a thematic vowel /i/ avoid taking -*isc*- as part of their inflection. The list of Italian third-conjugation verbs at issue, i.e. inflecting without -*isc*-, is the following: *aprire* 'open', *coprire* 'cover', *cucire* 'sew', *dire* 'say', *dormire* 'sleep', *empire* 'fill', *fuggire* 'flee', *inghiottire* 'swallow', *offrire* 'offer', *morire* 'die', *partire* 'leave', *salire* 'rise', *seguire* 'follow', *sentire* 'feel, hear, perceive', *servire* 'serve', *soffrire* 'suffer', *udire* 'hear', *uscire* 'exit', and *venire* 'come'. The overwhelming majority of these verbs either had thematic vowel /i/ in Classical Latin (among them are *aprire*, *coprire*, *dormire*, *partire*, *salire*, *sentire*, *servire*, *udire*, and *venire*), or acquired it quite early in the course of their diachronic development—that is, already in Latin, in such a way that they could enter the Italian verb system provided with thematic vowel /i/, in accordance with the hypothesis above. Among them are *cucire*, *empire*, *fuggire*, *inghiottire*, *morire*, *offrire*, *seguire*, and *soffrire*.[29] The last two verbs in the list, *dire*

---

[27] The real point here is not that non-first-conjugation verbs do not restore root-invariance if affected by phonological changes modifying their roots, as some verbs doing so are actually found outside the first conjugation (e.g. *mietere* 'reap', *chiedere* 'ask', *cuocere* 'cook', in the conjugation with thematic -e-; *coprire* 'cover' and *seguire* 'follow', in the conjugation with thematic -i-; see Maiden 1992: 293f.). The point is that while in first-conjugation verbs root-invariance seems to be pursued categorically, verbs in the other conjugations are not so categorical in this regard: they may restore one root-form throughout, but may also be found to retain (or even increase) root allomorphy.

[28] By 'base verb' I mean verbs which are neither derived from adjectives or nouns, nor of onomatopoeic origin.

[29] Cf. Cortelazzo and Zolli (1979–1988); see also Väänänen (1982: 235).

and *uscire*, come from Latin *dīcĕre* and *exīre* (a prefixed form of *īre*), in which /i/ is actually not a thematic vowel, being rather part of the root.

At first glance, the FINIRE-type cannot be claimed to represent the best of all possible solutions: while the ideal situation is for a paradigm to have no allomorphy at all, the presence of *-isc-* only in some word-forms is, actually, a kind of allomorphy. However, if the analysis above is correct, the kind of allomorphy that we are faced with here has the advantage of leaving the lexical portion of the word-form, i.e. the root, untouched.

After all, the apparent disadvantage of the allomorphy involving the element *-isc-* might even be argued to be another advantage, in the following terms. We know that the FINIRE-type, as a peculiar allomorphy pattern, becomes a characteristic feature of a group of third conjugation verbs in Italian. It is easy to see that this is consistent with the already mentioned tendency of Italian non-first-conjugation verbs to tolerate (and even increase, when possible) allomorphy in their inflection.[30] Moreover, the fact that the allomorphy pattern at issue manifests itself not by a formal modification of the root, but rather by an autonomous formal marker (i.e. the element *-isc-*) recurring in all verbs of the relevant kind, seems to confer yet another advantage on it, in terms of predictability. This also supports the claim that it should be ascribed to the grammatical system of Italian verbs.

As will be recalled from above, one of the problems with the morphological analysis of the element *-isc-* concerns the treatment of *-sc-* as a Formative. The problem is that *-sc-* appears in a morphosyntactically nonsensical set of paradigm cells, i.e. the 'N-pattern', while the other Formatives of the Italian verbal system are associated with specific sub-paradigms. I suggest that the element *-sc-* might be analysed as a mark of the N-pattern,[31] as illustrated in (11) by the analysis of the word-form *finisco* 'I finish':

(11)	ROOT	THV	FORMATIVE	ENDING	**Structure**
	fin	*i*	*sc*	*o*	**Form**
	Lexeme	Conjugation	Morpheme	Person & Number	**Categories**
	'FINISH, END'	Third	N-pattern	First Singular	**Content**

According to this analysis, the peculiar formative *-sc-* is a kind of 'dedicated exponent' of the morpheme N-pattern. In other words, it is a *signans* whose *signatum* is not morphosyntactic (as in the case of the other Formatives), but rather 'purely morphological'. Also, the fact that *-sc-* appears after the thematic vowel

---

[30] That, by contrast, would also contribute to reinforcing the idea that lack of allomorphy is a characteristic feature of first conjugation verbs.

[31] Cf. Giacalone Ramat (1998: 110f.).

suggests that its *signatum* N-pattern should be understood as part of the grammatical system of Italian verbs.

4.6 Conclusion

In investigating the origin of the Italian FINIRE-type, this study has tried to emphasize the crucial role of the 'N-pattern' morphome. It is this abstract paradigmatic template that guides the blending between the derivational types *grandio* and *grandesco*, yielding a mixed paradigm *grandēsco/grandītis*. In this sense, it can be claimed that the rise of the FINIRE-type is morphologically motivated from the very beginning. The resulting 'mixed' paradigm has a peculiar 'columnar' stress, which was acknowledged as doubly advantageous: first, it can trigger the reanalysis of the vowel before -*sc*- as a thematic vowel, causing the shift of the element -*isc*- into the inflectional system of Italian verbs, and therefore making the sequences -*isco*, -*isci*, etc. a true inflectional pattern. Second, it can prevent the verbal root from undergoing any variation in shape due to stress. Actually, the correlation between the peculiar stress pattern of the FINIRE-type and the avoidance of root allomorphy has not gone unnoticed. Various linguists have even tried to account for the origin of the FINIRE-type in these terms, according to the so-called 'anti-allomorphic approaches'.[32] Those scholars see the introduction of the element -*isc*- in the paradigm of the FINIRE-type verbs as a device to have stress aligned in the present tenses. In its turn, stress alignment should guarantee an identical phonological treatment of the root throughout the paradigm.

Although the peculiar stress pattern of the FINIRE-type is undoubtedly advantageous in terms of 'root allomorphy avoidance', the 'anti-allomorphic approaches' seem to confuse cause and effect. In the present analysis, the stress alignment of the FINIRE-type arises as a consequence of a blending between two formally and semantically compatible derivational types, i.e. those exemplified above by the verbs *grandesco* and *grandio*. This blending is guided by the N-pattern and there is nothing teleological in it. True, the peculiar stress pattern of the resulting paradigm turns out to be particularly advantageous, since it can prevent the root from undergoing any variation in shape due to stress. Nonetheless, the origin of this paradigm is nothing but a fortuitous effect of the (independent) attractive force of the N-pattern.

---

[32] Cf. Maiden (2004b: 34), who also provides a detailed bibliography on the topic.

Appendix 1

FINIRE-type verbs: **loans** that originally lack the marker of inflection class characterizing Italian verbs, i.e. a thematic vowel (data from Cortelazzo and Zolli 1979–1988).

LEMMA	ORIGIN
arrostire 'roast'	Germanic **raustjan*
attecchire 'take root'	Gothic **thikjan*
bandire 'publish, banish'	Gothic *bandwjan*
candire 'candy'	Arabic *qandī*
forbire 'furbish'	Franconian *forbian*
ghermire 'claw, grab'	Lombard **krimmjan*
gremire 'fill (up), cram'	Lombard **krammjan*
gualcire 'crease, crumple'	Lombard *walkan*
guarire 'recover'	Germanic **warjan*
guarnire 'decorate, garnish'	Germanic **warnjan*
schermire 'protect, shield'	Lombard *skirmjan*
schernire 'mock'	Lombard *skirnjan*
smaltire 'digest, work off'	Gothic *smaltjan*
stormire 'rustle'	Franconian *sturmjan*

Appendix 2

FINIRE-type verbs: **loans** that already have a suitable marker of inflection class, namely thematic vowel -i-.

LEMMA	ORIGIN
accudire 'attend (to), look after'	Sp. *acudir*
agire 'act, behave'	Fr. *agir* < Lat. *agĕre*
ardire 'dare'	OFr. *hardir* < Frankish **hardjan*
bramire 'bell, growl, bellow'	OFr. *bramir* < Germ. **brammon*
brunire 'burnish, tarnish'	OFr. *brunir*
deperire 'lose strength, wither'	Fr. *dépérir* < Lat. *de* + *perīre*
evoluire 'manoeuvre'	Fr. *évoluer*
farcire 'stuff, fill'	Fr. *farcir* < Lat. *farcīre*
fornire 'furnish, provide'	Fr. *fournir* < Franconian **frumjan*
garantire 'pledge, vouch for'	Fr. *garantir*
gioire 'be glad'	OFr. *joir*
imbottire 'stuff, fill'	Sp. *embutir*

imbutire 'draw'	Fr. *emboutir*
interferire 'interfere'	Fr. *s'interferir*
sortire 'achieve, be drawn'	Fr. *sortir* < Lat. *sortīre*
trasalire 'start, be startled'	OFr. *tressaillir*

Appendix 3

FINIRE-type verbs: **conversions** (sample)

subclass A – conversion from **adjectives** with **parasynthesis**	
LEMMA	BASE
addolcire 'sweeten'	*dolce* 'sweet'
arrossire 'turn red'	*rosso* 'red'
incuriosire 'make curious'	*curioso* 'curious'
indebolire 'weaken'	*debole* 'weak'
ingiallire 'yellow, make yellow'	*giallo* 'yellow'
irrancidire 'go rancid'	*rancido* 'rancid'
schiarire 'make clear'	*chiaro* 'clear'

subclass B – conversion from **nouns** with **parasynthesis**	
appuntire 'sharpen, point'	*punta* 'point'
arrugginire 'rust'	*ruggine* 'rust'
impaurire 'frighten'	*paura* 'fear'
impietrire 'petrify, be turned to stone'	*pietra* 'stone'
insaporire 'flavour, make tasty'	*sapore* 'taste, flavour'

subclass C – conversion from **adjectives** without parasynthesis	
chiarire 'explain, make clear'	*chiaro* 'clear'
sveltire 'quicken'	*svelto* 'quick'

subclass D – conversion from **nouns** without parasynthesis	
colpire 'strike'	*colpo* 'stroke'
finire 'finish, end'	*fine* 'end'

Appendix 4

FINIRE-type verbs: verbs which have undergone a **class shift** from Latin second or third conjugation.

LEMMA	LATIN ANTECEDENT
abolire 'abolish'	ABOLĒRE
aderire 'adhere, stick'	ADHAERĒRE
affluire 'flow, crowd'	AFFLUĔRE
aggredire 'assail'	AGGREDI
annuire 'nod (in assent)'	ANNUĔRE
attribuire 'attribute'	ATTRIBUĔRE
capire 'understand'	CAPĔRE
comparire 'appear'	COMPARĒRE
compatire 'pity'	COMPATI
conferire 'confer, award'	CONFERRE
costituire 'constitute'	COSTITUĔRE
costruire 'build'	CONSTRUĔRE
digerire 'digest'	DIGERĔRE
diluire 'dilute'	DILUĔRE
diminuire 'reduce, diminish'	DIMINUĔRE
esibire 'exhibit'	EXHIBĒRE
fluire 'flow'	FLUĔRE
influire 'influence'	INFLUĔRE
inserire 'insert'	INSURĔRE
istruire 'teach, instruct'	INSTRUĔRE
ostruire 'obstruct'	OBSTRUĔRE
percepire 'perceive'	PERCIPĔRE
preferire 'prefer'	PRAEFERRE
proibire 'forbid, prohibit'	PROHIBĒRE
rapire 'kidnap'	RAPĔRE
regredire 'go backwards, regress'	REGREDI
scandire 'scan'	SCANDĔRE
scolpire 'sculpt, carve'	SCULPĔRE
sostituire 'replace, substitute'	SUBSTITUĔRE
stupire 'astonish'	STUPĒRE
suggerire 'suggest'	SUGGERĒRE
tradire 'betray, be unfaithful to (someone, something)'	TRADĔRE

5

The fate of the -*ID(I)*- morpheme in the Central Dolomitic Ladin varieties of northern Italy: variable conditioning of a morphological mechanism

CLAIRE MEUL

5.1 Introduction

In a few Romance and Raeto-Romance varieties, the *first* conjugation (< Latin -ĀRE) contains a subclass of verbs that are susceptible to the insertion of a stressed morpheme—henceforth also referred to as 'infix'[1]—between the verb root and endings of the originally *rhizotonic* (root-stressed) forms of the verbal paradigm. Etymologically, this intercalated segment derives from the Latin (derivational) morpheme -*ID(I)*-. The fact that first-conjugation infixation in Romance is essentially a *dialect*-related matter makes it the locus 'par excellence' of linguistic variation. In this study, it will be shown that a morphological mechanism such as first-conjugation infixation can be exploited for multiple purposes, some of which reach far beyond morphology. Our analysis rests on an in-depth dialectological examination of the fate of -*ID(I)*- in Dolomitic Ladin.

---

[1] Usually the 'infix' is defined as a (consonantal) element inserted into roots (cf. Brugmann 1887, vol. I: 188). The example par excellence is the intrusion of the Latin nasal /n/ or /m/ into present stem formations (e.g. PRS.IND. *RU-M-PO* 'I break' vs. PRF.IND. *RUPI* 'I broke'). However, the segment on which we will concentrate in this study, i.e. -*ID(I)*-, crucially differs from the nasal infix in Latin, for the reason that it *follows* the lexical verb root, rather than interrupting it. Although we are aware of the descriptive inappropriateness of the label 'infix' in the present application, we nevertheless think that it has the advantage of highlighting the singularity (and indefiniteness) of the morphological status of -*ID(I)*-.

5.2 Short historical presentation of -*ID(I)*-

The Latin segment -*ID(I)*- goes back to an Ancient Greek coinage, -*ίζ*-, used for the derivation of denominatives (e.g. *κερματίζω* 'to make small, divide, split up' ← *κέρμα* '(small) change, coins') and deverbatives (e.g. *βαπτίζω* 'to immerse, wash, baptize' ← *βάπτω* 'to wet, moisten, paint'). Greek verbs in -*ίζ*- were borrowed into the Latin first conjugation (with theme vowel /a/), where -*ίζ*- was initially repre-sented as -*ISS*- (e.g. MALAC-ISS-ĀRE 'to soften, make weak' < *μαλακ-ίζ-ω*), later reintroduced as -*IZ*- (e.g. BAPT-IZ-ĀRE 'to baptize' < *βαπτ-ίζ-ω*) or -*IDI*- (e.g. CATOM-IDI-ĀRE 'to beat, thrash' < *κατωμ-ίζ-ω*, LACT-IDI-ĀRE 'to stamp one's foot' < *λακτίζω*, GARGAR-IDI-ĀRE 'to gargle' < *γαργαρ-ίζ-ω*), probably with interchangeable or even identical pronunciations (cf. Job 1893: 357–8, Leumann 1948: 371–7, Sturtevant 1940: 176, Stotz 1996, vol. III: 283, Wilkinson 2000: 163). The spelling -*IDI*- is characteristic of vulgar Latin inscriptions (from the second century onwards) and reflects the overall orthographic and phonetic (con)fusion between -*Z*- and (palatalized) -*DI̯*-: e.g. ORIDIA instead of ORYZA, BAPTIDIĀRE instead of BAPTI-ZĀRE, and, conversely, e.g. ZABOLUS, ZETA, OZE instead of DIABOLUS, DIETA, ODIE. These coexistent spellings suggest that -*Z*- and -*DI*- converged into a single sound, probably a voiced alveolar affricate ([dz]) or a post-alveolar affricate ([dʒ]). In late Latin (cf. Job 1893: 361), the suffix in question did not only appear in calques from Greek verbs in -*ίζω*, but could also be used productively, in order to derive verbs from nouns or adjectives borrowed from Greek (e.g. Greek adjective *Γραικός* > Lat. GRAECUS 'Greek' → GRAEC-ISS-ĀRE 'to be Greek, behave like a Greek') or even from 'authentic' Latin bases (AMĀRUS, -A, -UM 'bitter' → AMAR-IZ-ĀRE 'to make bitter'; TĪBĬA 'flute' → TIB-IZ-ĀRE 'play flute' (cf. Funck 1886, Job 1893: 362, Mignot 1969: 335–7, Stotz 1996, vol. III: 386–8).

In the evolution to Romance, the vestiges of Latin -*ID(I)/IZ*- came to fulfil two different functions, each of which corresponds to a different intra-paradigmatic configuration:

(1) On the one hand, as illustrated in Table 5.1, it continues its (Latin) status as a lexically integrated / derivational morpheme, i.e. as part of the verb stem and consequently occurring throughout the verbal paradigm. The 'popular'[2] form -*IDI-(ĀRE)* gave rise to Italian -*eggi-(are)*,[3] Spanish -*e-(ar)*, French -*oy-(er)*,

---

[2] The learned form -*IZ-(ĀRE)* supplies, in Romance and beyond, an 'outburst' of neologisms and cultisms, often with a transitive–causative meaning. It gave rise to Italian -*izz-(are)*, French -*is-(er)*, Romanian -*is-(a)*, and Spanish and Portuguese -*iz-(ar)*: e.g. It. *latin-izz-are* 'to Latinize', *moral-izz-are* 'to moralize', *polver-izz-are* 'to pulverize', *organ-izz-are* 'to organize'; Fr. *latin-is-er*, *moral-is-er*, *pulvér-is-er*, *organ-is-er*; Rom. *latin-iz-a*, *moral-iz-a*, *pulver-iz-a*, *organ-iz-a*; Sp./Pt. *latin-iz-ar*, *moral-iz-ar*, *pulver-iz-ar*, *organ-iz-ar* (cf. Meyer-Lübke 1974, vol. II: 660–1, 663, Tekavčić 1972, vol. III: 118–19, Wilkinson 2000: 163, Alkire and Rosen 2010: 290).

[3] The Italian outcome of -*ID(I)*- has been modelled on the basis of the third singular -*éggia* (< -*ÍDIA(T)*): -*IDIÁRE* would have given -*iáre* (cf. Meyer-Lübke 1974, vol. I: 460, Parodi 1901: 462). In older stages of

TABLE 5.1 The fate of -*ID(I)*- in Romance as a lexically integrated morpheme

Latin		Italian	French	Spanish	Portuguese
UNDA 'wave'	→	*UND-IDI-ĀRE 'to undulate'	ond-eggi-are	ond-oy-er	ond-e-ar	ond-e-ar
VIRIDE 'green'	→	*VIRID-IDI-ĀRE 'to be, grow green'	verd-eggi-are	verd-oy-er	verd-e-ar	verd-e(j)-ar
FLAMMA 'flame'	→	*FLAMM-IDI-ĀRE 'to flame'	fiamm-eggi-are	flamb-oy-er	llam-e-ar	cham-e(j)-ar
LACRIMA 'tear'	→	*LACRIM-IDI-ĀRE 'to weep'	lacrim-eggi-are	larm-oy-er	lagrim-e-ar	lacrim-ej-ar
FESTA 'feast'	→	*FEST-IDI-ĀRE 'to party'	fest-eggi-are	fest-oy-er	fest-e-ar (OSp.)	fest-ej-ar

Portuguese -*e(j)-(ar)*, and Romanian -*ez-(a)* (Mussafia 1883: 9, Lombard 1954–1955, vol. I: 492).[4]

(2) On the other hand, in some Romance varieties, the segment -*ID(I)*- developed, still within the scope of the first conjugation, as an inflectionally bound morpheme. In most of the varieties where the remnants of -*ID(I)*- appear in such a non-lexicalized guise, its occurrence is restricted to the originally rhizotonic forms of the paradigm, which usually coincide with the singular and third plural of the present indicative and of the present subjunctive. In order to account for such a positional 'innovation' of -*ID(I)*-, Rohlfs (1968: 244–5) postulated the following 'proto-Romance' conjugation type: PRS.IND. 1. *VINDIC-ÍDI-O 'I revenge', 2. *VINDIC-ÍDI-AS, 3. *VINDIC-ÍDI-AT, 4. VINDICĀ-MUS, 5. VINDICĀTIS, 6. *VINDIC-ÍDI-ANT. In the following sections we will focus on this type of 'grammaticalized' outcome of -*ID(I)*- in Romance.

Tuscan, several verbs in -*eggi-are* indeed had an alternant in -*i-are* (e.g. *al-eggi-are* vs. *al-i-are*, *guerr-eggi-are* vs. *guerr-i-are*). Even variants in -*e-are* occurred as a result of the influence exerted by the Provençal outcome of the suffix (e.g. *guerr-e-are*, *man-e-are* vs. *man-eggi-are*, *cort-e-are* vs. *cort-eggi-are*, etc.) (cf. Parodi 1901: 465, 467, Tekavčić 1972, vol. III: 119).

[4] In the Lazio dialect of San Leucio del Sannio, the infix developed as a productive derivational morpheme, involved in the creation of deverbatives with an iterative–intensive and/or diminutive lexical–aspectual value. Iannace (1983: 86–7) offers the following examples: *abbruscalà* 'to roast' → *abbruscul-ij-à* 'to bake, roast softly', *ammazicà* 'to chew' → *ammazech-ij-à* 'to chew up slowly', *arresicà* 'to risk' → *arresich-ij-à* 'to risk tentatively', *fumà* 'to smoke' → *fum-ij-à* 'to smoke slowly and little by little', *tuzzulà* 'to knock' → *tuzzul-ij-à* 'to knock repeatedly, drum fingers' (cf. also Maiden 2003: 15).

5.3 Some general observations on inflectionally bound first-conjugation 'infixation' in Romance

Whereas in virtually all Romance languages, reflexes of *-ID(I)-* are applied as lexicalized formants of first-conjugation verbs (cf. §5.2, group (1)), the grammaticalization of *-ID(I)-* as an inflectionally bound morpheme (cf. §5.2, group (2)) is much less common in the Romance-speaking territory: Daco-Romanian is actually the only Romance *standard* language in which a remnant of *-ID(I)-*, viz. *-ez-*, occurs in a non-lexicalized configuration. In Romanian, the segment in question, *-ez-*, is inserted between the verb root and the endings of the singular and third plural of the present indicative and subjunctive, as shown in Table 5.2.

TABLE 5.2 'Infixed' PRS.IND. and PRS.SBJV. of *a lucra* 'to work'

Romanian *a lucra* 'to work'

PRS.IND.	PRS.SBJV.
1. lucr-**ez**[a]	1. lucr-**ez**
2. lucr-**ez**-i	2. lucr-**ez**-i
3. lucr-**eaz**-ă	3. lucr-**ez**-e
4. lucrăm	4. lucrăm
5. lucrați	5. lucrați
6. lucr-**eaz**-ă	6. lucr-**ez**-e

[a] Henceforth, in each conjugation scheme, the stress-bearing vowel will be underlined and the infix will appear in bold and hyphenated between the lexical root and inflectional ending.

Except for Romanian, this particular development of *-ID(I)-* is essentially a *dialect-related* phenomenon. We find it in a handful of Italian and Raeto-Romance dialects, with possible (at least 'functional') ramifications in Gallo-Romance varieties. More particularly, traces of first-conjugation infixation can be documented in the Istro-Romance varieties of south-west Istria (Croatia and Slovenia) (e.g. PRS.IND. 3. *messed-é-a* '(3SG) mixes' in Capodistria) and in Vegliot, i.e. the (extinct) Dalmatian variety spoken on the island of Krk (Croatia) (e.g. PRS.IND. 3. *ton-áj-a* 'it thunders'); in the northern Venetan varieties spoken around Treviso, Feltre, and Belluno (e.g. PRS.IND. 3. *mañuz-é-a* '(3SG) nibbles' in Trevigiano); in the western Friulian varieties of the province of Pordenone (e.g. PRS.IND. 3. *tarlup-é-a* there's lightening'); in almost the entire Central and Peri-Dolomitic Ladin zone, which covers a substantial part of the provinces of Bolzano, Trento, and Belluno (e.g. PRS.IND. 3. *zapol-é-a* '(3SG) crushes, stamps fine' in Agordino (Peri-Ladin); *batul-é-a* '(3SG) chatters' in Gardenese (Central Ladin)) (cf. Mussafia 1883, Bartoli 1906, Zamboni 1980–1981: 173–4, 181, Bernardi 2002). South of the La Spezia–Rimini line, evidence of 'augmented' first conjugation verb forms can be found in the insular varieties of Corsica (e.g. PRS. IND. 3. *biastim-éghj-a* '(3SG) curses') and Sardinia (e.g. PRS.IND. 3. *furr-íghj-a* '(3SG) returns'), and in the southern Italian dialects of Abruzzo (e.g. PRS.IND. 3. *lacrem-ejj-e* '(3SG) weeps'), Puglia (e.g. PRS.IND. 3. *nat-éiiš* '(3SG) swims'), and Basilicata (e.g. PRS. IND. 3. *mattsǝk-i̯y-ǝtǝ* '(3SG) chews') (cf. Yvia-Croce 1979: 81, Corda 1983: 30, Giammarco 1979: 159, Loporcaro 1988a: 251, Lausberg 1939: 156). The hatched areas on the map in Figure 5.1 correspond to the Italo-, Raeto-, and Istro-Romance areas where inflectional first-conjugation 'infixation' is attested.

FIGURE 5.1 View of the dialect-geographical extension of the inflectionally-bound use of *-ID(I)-* in Italo-, Istro-, and Raeto-Romance

Similar first-conjugation patterns occur in some Gallo-Romance dialects, notably in Walloon (e.g. PRS.IND. 3. *calcul-èy-e* '(3SG) calculates' in the variety of Liège (Eastern Walloon)) and in Francoprovençal (e.g. PRS.SBJV. 3. *plyor-ęy-e* 'that (3SG) weep' in Fribourg) (Mussafia 1883: 23, Micheels 1865: 33, Haefelin 1879: 102, Reymond and Bossard 1982: 100, Chenal 1986: 559).[5] Lausberg (1956–1962, vol. III: 189) embedded the geolinguistic spread of the inflectionally bound use of *-ID(I)-* in what he called the 'interadriatische Romanität' ('inter-Adriatic Romanity'), i.e. the Romance varieties clustered around the Adriatic Sea, viz. Romanian, Dalmatian, and the dialects spoken on the east side of the Italian peninsula. This does not, however, account for the occurrence of 'augmented' first-conjugation verb forms in Corsican and Sardinian, as well as in Walloon and Francoprovençal.

Geolinguistically speaking, the transition from a lexically integrated to an inflectionally bound status is neither 'gradual' nor mutually exclusive, by which we mean that it is not the case that in some Romance varieties *-ID(I)-* continues as a lexically integrated morpheme, whereas in others it was eliminated from certain slots of the paradigm. Rather, we are confronted with a true functional 'split', in that the inflectional application of *-ID(I)-* in Romance always coexists with its continuation as a lexically integrated morpheme. More particularly, in those Romance varieties where the reflexes of *-ID(I)-* etched out an inflectional subclass within the first conjugation, it has also been conserved as a lexicalized formative of first-conjugation verbs. This becomes particularly evident in those varieties where the lexicalized/derivational outcome of *-ID(I)-* phonetically coincides with its inflectional outcome. This is the case, for example, in Corsican, where in some verb (forms), the morpheme *-ighj-* (or *-eghj-*) occurs twice: in the rhizotonic forms of the paradigm, derivational *-ighj-* (equivalent to Italian *-eggi-*) is followed by inflectional *-ighj-*; e.g. *festighj-ighj-u* 'I party' (cf. Italian *festeggio*).

As mentioned before, in most varieties in which first-conjugation infixation is known, the infix is confined to the rhizotonic forms of the present indicative, usually[6] the singular and third plural of the present indicative (cf. the infix-distribution laid out in Table 5.2). This conjugational 'template' (or 'morphome' in

---

[5] The phonetic origin of the segment *-èy-* in Walloon and Francoprovençal sparked much speculation among nineteenth-century linguists. Because of the remoteness and isolation of Walloon and Francoprovençal with respect to Romanian and the Italo-, Istro-, and Raeto-Romance varieties in which this type of first-conjugation subclass is attested, several authors (e.g. Meyer-Lübke 1974, vol. II: 210, 274–5, Willenberg 1878: 292–3, Boucherie 1871: 57, Meyer 1878: 229, Apfelstedt 1881, Gilliéron 1880) rejected the link with *-ID(I)-* and instead proposed several other hypotheses with respect to the historical foundations of this segment. In theory, however, one cannot exclude that the Walloon and Francoprovençal segment *-èy-* finds its phonetic origin in *-ID(I)-* (for a critical examination of the various viewpoints on the origins of the Gallo-Romance intercalated segment *-èy-*, cf. Meul 2013: 186–90).

[6] In Corsican and Gallurese, stress is on the verb root *throughout* the present subjunctive, which entails that the infix also appears in the first and second plural (e.g. Corsican *tilifun-éghj-imu* 'that we telephone', *tilifun-éghj-ete* 'that you telephone').

Aronoff, 1994: 25, and Maiden, 2003: 4, 2005a: 137–9), which groups the singular and third plural of the present tense against the rest of the paradigm, is called the 'N-pattern' in Maiden's (2003, 2005a, 2005b) theory.[7] In earlier accounts, this particular intra-paradigmatic configuration of the infix has been coupled with a striving for arrhizotonic stress alignment (cf. Meyer-Lübke 1974, vol. II: 268, Rohlfs 1968: 242, Bourciez 1956: 78, Tekavčić 1972, vol. II: 336) and/or the avoidance of root allomorphy (cf. Gartner 1883: 127, Elwert 1943: 144, Lausberg 1956–1962, vol. III: 249).[8]

5.4 An in-depth exploration of first-conjugation infixation in Dolomitic Ladin

5.4.1 *Area investigated and methodological aspects of the research*

Infixation is not generalized throughout the first conjugation:[9] in each variety in which this morphological mechanism is known, there are first-conjugation verbs that require infixation and others that reject infixation. In order to gain further insight into the intra- and extralinguistic factors that (co-)determine whether a particular first-conjugation verb is susceptible or not of taking the infix, we submitted a questionnaire containing about 140 first-conjugation verbs to 77 informants of **Dolomitic Ladin** varieties.[10] The main task of the informants was to conjugate the verbs of the survey in the third singular of the present indicative, which is a form sensitive to infixation (cf. Table 5.4). The dialect-geographical area of this investigation covered thirteen locations (villages), scattered over five mountain valleys, and took into account nine dialect varieties, viz. **Badiotto**, spoken in the central and lower part of Val Badia; **Marebbano**, spoken in the upper part of Val Badia; **Gardenese**, spoken in Val Gardena; **Fassano** (subdivided into three sub-varieties, i.e. **Brach**, **Cazet**, and **Moenat**) in Val di Fassa; **Fodom**, in the western part of the Val

---

[7] Only in the Gallo-Romance varieties in which first-conjugation infixation is attested does the intra-paradigmatic distribution of the infix deviate considerably from the N-pattern. In the eastern Walloon dialect of Liège, for instance, the first-conjugation infix -*èy*- is not restricted to the rhizotonic forms of the paradigm (PRS.IND./PRS.SBJV. 1–3), but shows up in some of the arrhizotonic forms too, notably the future and the conditional (cf. Lempereur and Morayns 1974: 8). In Francoprovençal, -*éy*- only appears in the subjunctive mood of first-conjugation verbs, whereas it is lacking in the present indicative (cf. Jaquenod 1931).

[8] Cf. Maiden (2003) and Meul (2010) for a critical evaluation of the various interpretations of infix-patterns.

[9] One exception to this is the 'infixation' of the present subjunctive in Francoprovençal (cf. §5.3), which is applied independently of lexical selection: *all* first-conjugation verbs invariably display the segment -*ey*- (or similar) in the present subjunctive.

[10] It was mainly for practical reasons that we chose the Dolomitic Ladin dialect group as the setting for an in-depth case study on first-conjugation infixation: the 'boom' of dialectological interest in this region, evidenced by an extensive number of (recent) dialect dictionaries and grammars and by the presence of several linguistic 'institutes' ('Istitut Ladin'), made this area particularly suitable for our purposes.

Cordevole; **Collese**, in the eastern part of the Val Cordevole; and **Ampezzano**, spoken at (and in the surroundings of) the town of Cortina d'Ampezzo. Except for Collese, all these varieties are part of the **Central Dolomitic Ladin** group. Collese is actually a more 'peripheral' variety, belonging to the Peri-Ladin **Agordino** group, though having affinities with Central Dolomitic Ladin, especially with the contiguous Fodom variety. The survey points were selected, to the maximum extent possible, in conformity with the spatial grid of the *ALD* (*Atlante linguistico del ladino dolomitico e dei dialetti limitrofi* – 'Linguistic Atlas of Dolomitic Ladin and neighbouring dialects') (Goebl *et al*. 1998). The map in Figure 5.2 gives an approximate geographical sketch of the investigated zone.

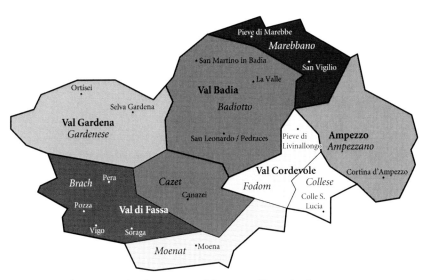

FIGURE 5.2 Dialect-geographical coverage of the area of investigation

Our 77 informants were stratified according to three age categories. In each village, between 4 and 7 informants were interviewed, which corresponded, in 'ideal' circumstances, to 2 informants between twelve and thirty years old, 2 informants between thirty-one and fifty years old, and 2 informants over fifty years old. This principle of stratification was respected as much as possible, but, as appears from Table 5.3, in some villages we were compelled to deviate slightly from homogeneous distribution into equal-sized age groups. Another observation to be made is that for Badiotto, Marebbano, and Gardenese, more than one village was taken into account; as for the other varieties, the investigation was limited to one survey point only. Table 5.3 presents the distribution of the informants according to villages and age groups.

TABLE 5.3 77 informants grouped into 9 dialect varieties, 13 villages, and 3 age groups

Ladin dialects	Villages[a]	Age groups 12-30 y.	31-50 y.	+50 y.	Total/village
Badiot	San Leonardo	1	3	2	6
	San Martino in Badia	3	1	2	6
	La Valle	2	3	1	6
Marebbano	San Vigilio	2	2	2	6
	Pieve di Marebbe	2	3	2	7
Gardenese	Ortisei	1	4	2	7
	Selva Gardena	2	2	3	7
Fassano Brach	Pozza/Pera/Vigo[b]	1	3	2	6
Cazet	Canazei	2	2	1	5
Moenat	Moena	1	2	1	4
Fodom	Pieve di Livinallongo	2	0	4	6
Ampezzano	Cortina d'Ampezzo	2	2	2	6
Collese	Colle Santa Lucia	2	2	1	5
	Total/age group	23	29	25	77

[a] We have used the Italian names of the villages. Most of the villages also have a Ladin name.
[b] We did not differentiate between the neighbouring villages of Pozza, Pera, and Vigo. Pera is (since 1952) a subdivision of the municipality of Pozza di Fassa.

The 141 verbs that we proposed to the informants were selected[11] on the basis of three parameters:

(1) The *etymological origin* of the verbs: in order to obtain a balanced etymological selection of verbs, we subdivided the corpus into (i) 'indigenous' verbs, i.e. verbs that were inherited straightforwardly from Latin; (ii) loan verbs, from Standard Italian, or from neighbouring Italian and German[12] dialect varieties; and (iii) neologisms;[13]

[11] The main sources used for the compilation of the corpus were the various Ladin dictionaries at our disposal: Mischì (2001) for *Badiotto*, Videsott and Plangg (1998) for *Marebbano*, Forni (2003) for *Gardenese*, De Rossi (1999) for *Brach (Fassano)*, Mazzel (1995) for *Cazet (Fassano)*, Dell'Antonio (1972) for *Moenat (Fassano)*, Masarei (2005) for *Fodom*, Colle *et al.* (1997) for *Ampezzano*, and, finally, Pallabazzer (1989) for *Collese*.

[12] Especially for the varieties of Val Gardena and Val Badia the influence of German must be taken into account.

[13] The etymology of the verbs was traced with the *EWD—Etymologisches Wörterbuch des Dolomitenladinischen* (Kramer 1988–1993). The 'neological' character of verbs was established on the basis of the indications of the *DELI* (Cortelazzo and Zolli 1979–1988) and the *LEI* (Pfister 1979–). Ladin verbs borrowed from (Standard) Italian verbs having their first attestation in the literature from the nineteenth century onwards were tagged as 'neologisms'.

(2) The *'pan-dialectal' occurrence* of the verbs: in order to obtain nine *parallel* questionnaires, we primarily selected verbs that were known and used in each of the nine examined dialect varieties;

(3) The *frequency* and *vitality* of the verbs: before going 'into the field', we proposed the lists constituted on the basis of the aforementioned criteria ((1) and (2)) to a small 'control group', composed of several Ladin informants in order to guarantee that the verbs that we selected were known and used in daily language.[14]

In Table 5.4 we present the formation of the 'infixed'[15] paradigm of the verb *ćiacolè* 'to chat', which is attested in all of the examined varieties.

For the complete repertory of 141 Ladin first-conjugation verbs, we obtained a total number of 8,215 responses.[16] By 'response' we mean the verb form of the third singular of the present indicative, which is, as we already noted, a form susceptible of taking the infix. We categorized the answers (i.e. PRS.IND. 3) by assigning them a number expressing the relation to infix-insertion on a scale ranging from 1 to 3:

1 = the speaker accepts, for a given verb, only the form *without* infix;
2 = the speaker accepts both forms, *with* and *without* infix;
3 = the speaker accepts exclusively the form *with* infix.

From the total number of 8,215 responses, 4,691 (= 57.1%) responses fell into category 1 'without infix'; 509 (= 6.2%) into category 2 'double ending'; and, finally, 3,015 (= 36.7%) responses fell into category 3 'with infix'. The distribution of the answers over three response options is shown in Table 5.5.[17]

---

[14] Although the homogeneity of the corpus was our primary concern, there are nevertheless some verbs for which we obtained a very limited number of responses. Mostly, this was due to the fact that the verbs were added (often on the advice of the informants) to the questionnaire at a more advanced stage of the fieldwork.

[15] It should be noted, however, that, in reality, the verb *ćiacolè* also allows for the non-infixed paradigm.

[16] We recall that we did not obtain for each verb of the questionnaire an answer from all our 77 informants ($77 \times 141 = 10,857 > 8,215$) (cf. n. 14).

[17] It should also be stressed that these percentages are based on the '*first*' impression' of the informants with respect to first-conjugation infixation: the total amount of 8,215 responses that we obtained are to be considered as the informants' first idea on what should be the 'correct' form for the third person singular of the present indicative. For 3,587 of the 8,215 observations we asked the 'second opinion' of the speakers, which basically means that we confronted them with the other possibility. For instance, if, for a given verb, an informant uttered the form *without* infix, we asked their opinion on the form *with* infix. Sometimes they rejected this form, but it also happened that they evaluated it as being acceptable, or even better than the one that they had given initially. More particularly, in 824 of the 3,587 cases (= 23%) the informants *modified* their opinion with respect to the first answer they gave. Nevertheless, the quantitative result is based on the *first* impression of the informants, without taking into account the fact that there is a reasonable chance that they would also accept one of the other possibilities with respect to infixation.

TABLE 5.4 'Model' of the infixed paradigm in the examined varieties

	Badiotto *ćiacolè*		Marebbano *ćiacolè*		Gardenese *ciaculé*[a]		Fassano (Cazet) *ciacolè*[b]	
	PRS.IND.	PRS.SBJV.	PRS.IND.	PRS.SBJV.	PRS.IND.	PRS.SBJV.	PRS.IND.	PRS.SBJV.
1	ćiacol-ëi[(aj)][c]-i	ćiacol-ëi-es	ćiacol-ei[ej]-i	ćiacol-ei-i	ciacul-ei[ej]-e	ciacul-ei-e	ciacol-e[e]-e	ciacol-e-e
2	ćiacol-ëi-es	ćiacol-ëi-es	ćiacol-ei-es	ćiacol-ei-i	ciacul-ei-es	ciacul-ei-es	ciacol-e-es	ciacol-e-es
3	ćiacol-ëi-a	ćiacol-ëi-es	ćiacol-ei-a	ćiacol-ei-i	ciacul-e[ej]-a	ciacul-ei-e	ciacol-e-a	ciacol-e-a
4	ćiacolun	ćiacolunse	ćiacolun	ćiacolunse	ciaculon	ciaculonse	ciacolon	ciacolane
5	ćiacolëis	ćiacolëise	ćiacoleis	ćiacoleise	ciaculeis	ciaculeise	ciacolède	ciacolède
6	ćiacol-ëi-a	ćiacol-ëi-es	ćiacol-ei-a	ćiacol-ei-i	ciacul-e-a	ciacul-ei-e	ciacol-e-a	ciacol-e-e

	Fodom *ćiacolè*		Ampezzano *ciacolà*		Collese *ćiakolà*	
	PRS.IND.	PRS.SBJV.	PRS.IND.	PRS.SBJV.	PRS.IND.	PRS.SBJV.
1	ćiacol-ei[ej]-e	ćiacol-ei-e	ćiacol-e[e]-o	ćiacol-e-e	ćiakol-e[ɛ:]-e	ćiakol-e-e
2	ćiacol-ei-e	ćiacol-ei-e	ćiacol-e-es	ćiacol-e-es	ćiakol-e-e	ćiakol-e-e
3	ćiacol-ei-a	ćiacol-ei-e	ćiacol-e-a	ćiacol-e-e	ćiakol-e-a	ćiakol-e-a
4	ćiacolon	ćiacolombe	ćiacolon	ćiacolone	ćiakolon	ćiakolone
5	ćiacolei	ćiacoleibe	ćiacolà	ćiacolade	ćiakolé	ćiakolesà
6	ćiacol-ei-a	ćiacol-ei-e	ćiacol-e-a	ćiacol-e-e	ćiakol-e-a	ćiakol-e-e

[a] In Gardenese, the infix appears as -e- [e] if the verb root ends in a consonant and if the (personal) ending is -a. This is the case in the 3SG and 3PL of the present indicative. If the (personal) ending is not -a but -e, then the infix transforms into -ei- [ej]. This alternation is phonetically determined and also affects nominal inflection: between a stressed -e- followed by an unstressed -e, the palatal approximant [j] is intercalated (e.g. SG. *kurea* 'leather ribbon' → PL. *kureies* 'leather ribbons') (cf. Kramer 1976–1977, vol. I: 71–2; Mourin 1980: 586). When the verb root ends in -i, the infix appears uniformly as -ei-, corresponding to [ɐj] ([ɐj] sounds a little more open than the mid vowel [ə]), e.g. PRS.IND. 3. *cunsi-ei-a* [kun'sjɐja] 'he advises'.

[b] In the two other varieties of Fassano, viz. Brach and Moenat, the infinitives of first-conjugation verbs end in -ar. Other than that, the paradigmatic formation of the present indicative and of the present subjunctive entirely corresponds to what we find in Cazet.

[c] In Badiotto, *ë* corresponds phonetically to a very open *e*, close to [a].

TABLE 5.5 **Distribution of the answers over three response options**

	Answers (PRS.IND.3) given by the informants	Absolute frequency	Relative frequency
1	Without infix	4691	57.10%
2	Double ending	509	6.20%
3	With infix	3015	36.70%
	TOTAL	8215	100%

In order to examine the influence of a few socio- and geolinguistic variables (i.e. the *independent variables*) on the mechanism of first-conjugation infixation in Dolomitic Ladin (i.e. the *dependent variable*), two types of statistical tests were performed: the Mann–Whitney/Kruskal–Wallis test and Pearson's chi-square (χ^2) test. Both tests allow us to verify whether there is a statistically significant relationship between the independent and the dependent variables, though they have a slightly different focus: the **Mann–Whitney/Kruskal–Wallis test** tracks global quantitative differences with respect to the total score levels between the various categories of the independent variable; the **chi-square test** aims to determine whether the distribution of observations over the various categories of the dependent variable differs significantly among the categories of the independent variable. Depending on the variable under study, we will use the output of either the Mann–Whitney/ Kruskal–Wallis test or the chi-square test.[18] Before turning to the sociolinguistic analysis, we will first proceed with the isolation of a few intralinguistic parameters that are fundamental in the lexicological selection of the infix.

5.4.2 *The lexicological distribution of the infix in Dolomitic Ladin: general considerations and intralinguistic parameters*

First of all, it is noteworthy that of the 141 Ladin first-conjugation verbs included in the survey, only 16 verbs (= 11.3% of the entire repertory) were—with no exception (i.e. by *all* our informants, irrespective of their age and dialect)—conjugated *without* the infix, whereas only 2 verbs (= 1.4% of the repertory) were—invariably (i.e. again, by *all* our informants)—conjugated *with* the infix. A schematic overview of these verbs is presented in Table 5.6.[19] This implies that the overwhelming majority of the

---

[18] The data were processed with the statistical software SPSS (*Statistical Package for the Social Sciences*). We used version 17.0 from 2008.

[19] For reasons of space, Table 5.6 only lists the *roots* of the verbs in question. The endings of the infinitives vary according to the dialect (cf. Table 5.4 for the complete paradigms). For the intermediate category ('without/with infix') we randomly picked out two examples out of the 123 verbs that this category actually contains.

TABLE 5.6 Distribution of the proposed verbs, according to the (non-)insertion of the infix: paradigmatic 'stability' for 16+2 verbs vs. paradigmatic 'variability' for 123 verbs

Exclusively *without* infix 16 verbs (=11.35%)		141 Ladin first-conjugation verbs			
		With or *without* the infix 123 verbs (=87.23%)		Exclusively *with* infix 2 verbs (=1.42%)	
Gard.*adurv*-, Bad./Mar.*ador*-, Fod.*dour*-, Coll.*duor*-, Amp./Moen.*dor*-, Br./Caz.*dur*-	'to use'	Bad./Mar./Fod./Coll./Amp./Br./Caz./Moen.*bazil*-	'to rave, talk nonsense'	Gard./Bad./Mar./Fod./Coll./Br./Moen./Caz.*passen*-	'to fit'
Gard./Bad./Mar.*cherd*-, Br./Caz.i/Moen.*crid*-	'to call, scream'	Gard.*blestem*-, Bad./Mar.*blastem*-, Fod./Caz.*bestemi*-, Amp./Coll.*bestem*-, Br.*biastem*-, Moen.*bestiem*-	'to swear'	Bad./Mar./Fod./Coll./Br./Caz./Moen.*plindern*-	'to plunder, to move (house)'
Gard./Bad./Mar./Fod./Amp./Br./Caz./Moen.*ciant*-, Coll.*cent*-	'to sing'				
Br./Caz./Moen.*coman*-	'to command'				
Gard./Bad./Mar.*cunt*-, Fod./Coll./Amp./Br./Caz./Moen.*cont*-	'to tell/to count'				
Gard./Bad./Mar./Fod.*(n)dessen*-	'to get angry'				
Gard./Bad./Fod./Coll./Br./Moen.*devent*-, Mar.*dont*-, Amp.*deent*-, Caz.*dovent*-	'to become'				
Coll./Amp./Br./Caz.*imbroi*-	'to deceive, cheat'				
Br./Caz./Moen.*(e/i)ndrez*-	'to organize'				
lasc-	'to leave, let'				
Bad.*laur*-, Mar./Fod./Coll./Moen.*laor*-, Amp.*lour*-, Br./Caz.*lur*-	'to work'				
Gard./Bad./Fod./Coll./Amp./Br./Caz./Moen.*salud*-, Mar.*salid*-	'to save'				
Gard./Bad./Fod./Coll./Br./Caz./Moen.*scus*-, Mar.*sciis*-	'to please, to taste (good)'				
Fod./Amp./Moen.*sporc(h)*-, Coll.*sporc*-	'to soil, dirty'				
Gard./Fod./Coll./Br./Caz./Moen.*spud*-, Bad.*spod*-, Mar.*spöd*-, Amp.*sbut*-	'to spit'				
Br./Caz./Moen.*zac(h)*-	'to chew, masticate'				

verbs of the corpus, i.e. the 123 remaining verbs (= 87.2% of the repertory), were *susceptible* of taking the infix, which basically means that, for these verbs, both forms, *with* and *without* infix, have been documented. The 'duplicity' of this grey area may be due to one of the following two scenarios: (1) the two possibilities (*with* and *without* infix) for a given verb were produced by one and the same informant ('intrapersonal' or 'individual' variation); (2) the two possibilities (*with* and *without* infix) for a given verb were uttered by different speakers, belonging, for instance (but not necessarily), to different age- or dialect-groups ('interpersonal' or 'idiosyncratic' variability).

It turned out that those verbs that are *eligible* for infixation, i.e. the group of verbs that are *invariably* conjugated *with* the infix, as well as the 'hybrid' category consisting of verbs for which the two options were documented, generally display at least one of the following characteristics: (a) a *non-indigenous* etymology; (b) a *polysyllabic* verb root; and (c) a verb root formed by means of a *derivational suffix*.[20] Table 5.7 is a cross-tabulation (contingency table) of the aforementioned three intralinguistic factors (displayed in the rows of the table) and the (non-)eligibility for infixation.[21] The most salient percentages highlighted in Table 5.7 should be interpreted as follows: if a given verb does not match any of the aforementioned criteria, and thus is characterized by an *indigenous* (Latin) etymology and a *monosyllabic* verb root which *does not contain a derivational suffix*, there is an 88.5% chance that this verb is *not eligible* for infixation and, conversely, there is only an 11.5% chance that this verb would be *eligible* for infixation. Generally speaking, the chance that a given verb of the questionnaire is *eligible* for infixation is highest when this verb

---

[20] Among the verbs of our corpus, the following root-final segments were considered as 'triggering' suffixes for infixation: -*i/e*- (< Lat. -*IC/IG/ID(I)-*), -*is*- (< Lat. -*IZ*-), -*ej*- (< Lat. -*ID(I)-*), -*ul/ol*- (Lat. -*UL*-), -*ud*- (< Lat. -*UT*-), -*ent*- (< Lat. -*ENT*-), -*il*- (< Lat. -*ILL*-), -*ig(h)*- ('savant' outcome of Lat. -*IG*-), -*idl*- (< Lat. -*IC-UL*-), -*(e)n*- (< Germ. infinitive ending -*(e)n*), -*in*- (< Lat. -*IN*-), -*it*- (< Lat. -*IT*-). It should also be noted that only in some *rare* cases does the presence of a derivational suffix not entail that the verb root is polysyllabic. More particularly, in several Ladin varieties, the phonetic evolution of the Latin suffix -*IC/IG-ĀRE* corresponds to an asyllabic [j]: e.g. Lat. *HIRP-IC-(ĀRE)* 'to harrow' > Gard./Bad./Mar./Fod. *arpi*- [arpj-] (but Fass./Amp./Coll. *arp-e*- [arpe-]). Other examples in which the presence of a root-final derivational suffix does not imply the polysyllabicity of the root are the cases in which the derivational suffix has been syncopated: the Gardenese verb *bruntlé* 'to grumble', for instance, is in fact a syncopated version of *brunt-ol-é*, formed with the presence of the root-final suffix -*ol*-. In most of the cases, however, suffixation and the polysyllabicity of the verb root go together.

[21] The three determining factors in question, viz. the etymology of the verb, the number of syllables of the verb root, and the presence/absence of particular root-final suffixes, are susceptible to dialectal variation. A verb that, for instance, has a dissyllabic verb root in one dialect can be monosyllabic in the other dialect: for instance, the Gardenese monosyllabic verb root of *bruntl-* 'to grumble' is dissyllabic in all the other examined varieties (Bad. *bruntor*-, Mar. *brunter*-, Fod. *bruntol*-, Amp./Coll. *bruntol*-). The same is true for the use of suffixes: a verb does not necessarily receive in every dialect the same suffix. For instance, in Badiotto, the root of the verb 'to sneeze' is formed by means of the suffix -*idl*- (< Lat. -*IC-UL-ĀRE*), viz. *strinidlé*, whereas in all the other examined varieties, this verb receives the suffix -*ud*- (< Lat. -*ŪT-ĀRE*).

has a polysyllabic verb root formed by means of a derivational suffix: irrespective of the indigenous or non-indigenous nature of the verb in question, the probability that a verb with a polysyllabic and suffixed verb root is *eligible* for infixation amounts to 71.8%.

The tendency of the infix to graft itself on to this type of polysyllabic and suffixed verb root has also been documented in other varieties in which first-conjugation infixation is known and has been interpreted from two different angles: as the result either of (1) the avoidance of a proparoxytonic stress pattern (compare, in this respect, the Ladin infixed and thus *paroxytonic* PRS.IND. 3 forms *ciacol-e-a* '(3SG) chatters', *peten-e-a* '(3SG) combs', *slisor-e-a* '(3SG) glides' with the corresponding non-infixed and thus *proparoxytonic* forms in Standard Italian: *chiacchiera, pettina, scivola*); or of (2) the 'appeal' of the iterative–intensive value of (many of) these verbs. On the basis of several counterexamples, however, it can be claimed that (1) and (2) are neither sufficient nor necessary conditions to account for the spread of the infix across Ladin first-conjugation verbs. For instance, the corresponding (hypothetical) 'infix-less' form of Ladin *manaj-é-a* '(3SG) handles' would be *man-ája (analogous to the Italian counterpart *maneggia*) rather than the proparoxytonic form **máneja). As to the semantic–aspectual hypothesis, many of the first-conjugation verbs susceptible of taking the infix can hardly (or not) be considered as having an iterative–intensive meaning: e.g. Bad. *passen-ëi-a* '(3SG) fits, adapts', *intossi-ëi-a* '(3SG) poisons', *scioment-ëi-a* '(3SG) cures (meat)', etc. Instead, we presume that the correlation between *polysyllabic* and *suffixed* verb roots, on the one hand, and infix-insertion, on the other, might be considered an instance of 'paronymic attraction', i.e. the exchange of features between two or more words that bear a formal resemblance to each other. As a matter of fact, the lexical spread of the first-conjugation infix seems to be controlled by a formal association established between verbs with a similar morphophonological shape. The 'impetus' for the crystallization of this subgroup of formally related infixed first-conjugation verbs might be given by the original (derivational) domain of the infix itself: from a derivational/lexicalized emergence in Latin verb forms such as *BAPTÍDIAT > *BAPTÉJA, it was grafted as an inflectional segment onto verbs that are formally close to the verbs in -IDI-ĀRE.

As mentioned previously, if a given verb is characterized by a monosyllabic root and an indigenous etymology, there is an 88.5% chance that it is *not eligible* for infixation. The reluctance of 'base verbs' to first-conjugation infixation is common to all other varieties in which this phenomenon is attested. Usually, the infixed first-conjugation subclass does not contain 'base verbs' like 'to work', 'to live', 'to save', 'to use', etc. (cf. also Table 5.6), belonging to the most archaic (Latin) stratum of the lexicon, often with very high token frequencies. On a general scale, it seems that the items of the 'basic vocabulary' are subject to a law of inertia when it comes to first-conjugation infixation.

TABLE 5.7 **Eligibility for infixation on the basis of three intralinguistic parameters**

			Not eligible for infixation	Eligible for infixation	TOTAL
Indigenous verb	Monosyllabic VR	VR without suffix	991	129	1120
			88.5%	11.5%	100.0%
		VR with suffix	162	268	430
			37.7%	62.3%	100.0%
		TOTAL	1153	397	1550
			74.4%	25.6%	100.0%
	Polysyllabic VR	VR without suffix	695	156	851
			81.7%	18.3%	100.0%
		VR with suffix	233	594	827
			28.2%	71.8%	100.0%
		TOTAL	928	750	1678
			55.3%	44.7%	100.0%
		TOTAL	2081	1147	3228
			64.5%	35.5%	100.0%
Loan verb	Monosyllabic VR	VR without suffix	915	232	1147
			79.8%	20.2%	100.0%
		VR with suffix	19	5	24
			79.2%	20.8%	100.0%
		TOTAL	934	237	1171
			79.8%	20.2%	100.0%
	Polysyllabic VR	VR without suffix	1383	1399	2782
			49.7%	50.3%	100.0%
		VR with suffix	291	740	1031
			28.2%	71.8%	100.0%
		TOTAL	1674	2139	3813
			43.9%	56.1%	100.0%
		TOTAL	2608	2376	4984
			52.3%	47.7%	100.0%

On the basis of the foregoing, it can be stated that the mechanism of first-conjugation infixation is fundamentally determined by a series of intralinguistic variables: the etymology of the verb and the morpho-prosodic structure of the verb root determine a priori whether a particular first-conjugation verb is susceptible to infixation or not. However, the extent to which this intralinguistically conditioned principle is observed within the language community varies according to the social and geographical situation. In other words, the interplay with *diatopic, diastratic,* and *diaphasic* variables determines a posteriori whether a verb that meets the intralinguistic requirements in question is effectively conjugated with the infix by the speakers.

5.4.3 *Extramorphological parameters of morphological variation*

5.4.3.1 *Diatopic variability*   The statistical analysis showed that the *productivity* of first-conjugation infixation differs significantly among the investigated dialects. In order to determine where exactly (i.e. between which dialects or dialect groups) quantitative differences with respect to first-conjugation infixation are located, a series of paired Mann–Whitney tests (cf. §5.4.1) was performed. This allowed us to isolate *four* dialect groups among which the productivity of first-conjugation infixation is significantly different. Figure 5.3 is a graphic interpretation of the output of the Mann–Whitney test. The values plotted on the *y*-axis are so-called 'mean ranks', i.e. a numerical abstraction of frequency/productivity, based on the ranking of the data. For our purposes, it suffices to know that the higher the value of the mean rank, the more highly categorized answers (i.e. scores closer to 3, 'with infix'; cf. §5.4.1) the informants gave. In other words, the higher the mean rank, the more productive infixation is. On the *x*-axis are listed the investigated dialect varieties, classified in descending order according to their mean ranks. Dialects among which mean ranks (and thus 'productivity' of infixation) do *not* significantly differ are circled. The first group is composed of Badiotto and Marebbano: they have the highest mean ranks, and thus the highest productivity of first-conjugation infixation. The second homogeneous group comprises Marebbano and Gardenese: the corresponding Mann–Whitney tests revealed that there are *no* significant differences in productivity of infixation between Marebbano and Gardenese, but that productivity does differ between Badiotto and Gardenese. A further position is occupied by Fodom, collocated between the Marebbano–Gardenese group on the one hand, and the Collese–Cazet–Moenat–Ampezzano–Brach group on the other hand. Collese, Cazet, Moenat, Ampezzano, and Brach thus present similar degrees of productivity of infixation.

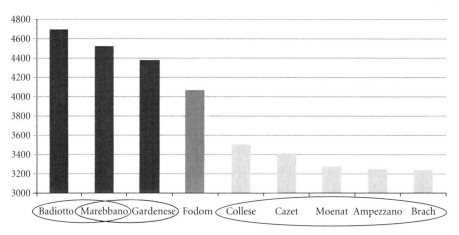

FIGURE 5.3 Bar chart of the descending classification of the dialects with respect to the productivity of infixation (expressed by the mean ranks of the scores)

TABLE 5.8 Frequency distribution of the answers according to the dialect of the informants

			Answers given by the informants			
			Without infix	Without/ with infix	With infix	TOTAL
Dialect of the informants	Badiotto		912 (=43.8%)	116 (=5.6%)	1054 (=50.6%)	2082 (=100%)
	Marebbano		701 (=47.8%)	83 (=5.7%)	684 (=46.6%)	1468 (=100%)
	Gardenese		646 (=51.8%)	45 (=3.6%)	556 (=44.6%)	1247 (=100%)
	Fodom		365 (=58.3%)	32 (=5.1%)	229 (=36.6%)	626 (=100%)
	Fassano	Brach	507 (=76.1%)	54 (=8.1%)	105 (=15.8%)	666 (=100%)
		Cazet	409 (=71.1%)	63 (=11.0%)	103 (=17.9%)	575 (=100%)
		Moenat	343 (=76.7%)	22 (=4.9%)	82 (=18.3%)	447 (=100%)
	Collese		366 (=70.2%)	42 (=8.1%)	113 (=21.7%)	521 (=100%)
	Ampezzano		442 (=75.8%)	52 (=8.9%)	89 (=15.3%)	583 (=100%)
TOTAL			4691 (=57.1%)	509 (=6.2%)	3015 (=36.7%)	8215 (=100%)

Figure 5.3 clearly shows that the biggest 'gap' with respect to the productivity of infixation is situated between Badiotto, Marebbano, and Gardenese on the one hand, and Collese, Cazet, Moenat, Ampezzano, and Brach on the other, with the Fodom variety occupying an intermediate position. More detailed information can be obtained from Table 5.8, which contains absolute and relative frequencies for each response option, listed by the dialect of the informants.

The data in Table 5.8 confirm and further concretize the findings that emerged from Figure 5.3. If we focus on the category 'with infix', we observe that for Badiotto, Marebbano, and Gardenese it contains between 44% and 50% of the answers given by the informants; in Fassano, Collese, and Ampezzano, the percentages for this response option ('with infix') are much lower, fluctuating between 15% and 22%.

Thus, the degree of 'popularity' of first-conjugation infixation is certainly not constant in the entire investigated zone. The question that arises here is, of course, how should these dialect–geographical discrepancies be interpreted? After all, the dialects examined are contiguous and linguistically closely related and, therefore, these rather huge differences in the productivity of a morphological mechanism such as infixation might seem surprising. We presume that the explanation—or, at least, part of the explanation—is to be found in the valleys' divergent **glotto-political** status. More particularly, in Val Badia (which covers the Badiotto and Marebbano varieties), as well as in Val Gardena (Gardenese), both part of the province of Bolzano (cf. Figure 5.4), the Ladin language is much better embedded in the social,

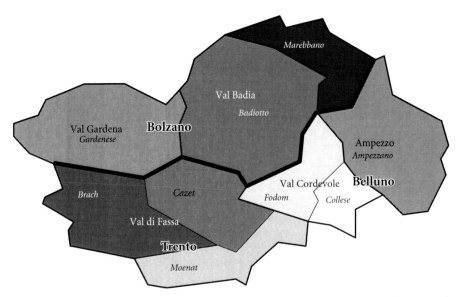

FIGURE 5.4 'Bipartition' of the Dolomitic Ladin zone with respect to the productivity of first-conjugation infixation

administrative, and educational contexts.[22] Several initiatives, ranging from the foundation of several linguistic 'institutes' ('Istitut Ladin') to the introduction of Ladin as an official language at school, have been taken in order to preserve the indigenous Ladin varieties of the valleys and shield them from excessive infiltration of the standard languages (Italian and German). The favourable language policy of these two valleys might also explain the success of a typically 'ladinizing' process such as first-conjugation infixation. In Standard Italian this morphological mechanism is unknown and, as such, its occurrence in Ladin allows to mark distance from the standard language and to emphasize the dialect-specific (Ladin) individuality of verb morphology. The other valleys, viz. Val di Fassa (Fassano), part of the province of Trento, and Val Cordevole (Fodom and Collese) and Cortina (Ampezzano), both part of the province of Belluno, are much more subject to 'Italianization', and Ladin is much less established for administrative and educational purposes. In Figure 5.4, we show the bipartition of the investigated zone with respect to infixation.

The 'bipartition' of the Dolomitic Ladin zone with regard to the productivity of first-conjugation infixation is most obvious in the conjugation of

---

[22] One of the concrete measures taken in this respect is the introduction of the so-called 'insegnamento paritetico' (from 1948 onwards) in the Ladin valleys that belong to the province of Bolzano. This special educational arrangement broadly consists of an equal distribution of hours taught in Ladin, Italian, and German, during nursery and elementary school.

neologisms. Recent loan verbs from Standard Italian (and/or German) were by most speakers of Badiotto, Marebbano, and Gardenese 'automatically' incorporated into the augmented first-conjugation subclass: e.g. Italian *fotografare* 'to photograph', *telefonare* 'to telephone', *programmare* 'to program(me)' > Badiotto PRS.IND. 3. *fotograf-ëi-a, telefon-ëi-a, program-ëi-a*; Marebbano PRS.IND. 3. *fotograf-ei-a, telefon-ei-a, program-ei-a*; Gardenese PRS.IND. 3. *fotograf-é-a, telefun-é-a, prugram-é-a*.[23] Especially in Badiotto, the spread of *-ëi-* to recent acquisitions is so pervasive that it can even affect neologisms with a syllabic structure that is very remote from the prototypical polysyllabic suffixed verb root structure (cf. §5.4.2) that is traditionally the locus for insertion of the infix: neologisms with a monosyllabic verb root, such as *boxé* 'to box', *cloné* 'to clone', *surfé* 'to surf', *filmé* 'to film', call for the insertion of *-ëi-* (PRS.IND. 3. *box-ëi-a, clon-ëi-a, surf-ëi-a, film-ëi-a*). In the other dialects, the first-conjugation morpheme only incorporates neologisms in so far as they have a syllabic structure that conforms more or less to the prototypical one.

As a last remark, we should note that there are practically no differences in the productivity of first-conjugation infixation between villages belonging to the same dialect zone. We recall that for the Badiotto, Marebbano, and Gardenese varieties we took into account *more than one* village (cf. Table 5.3), but the difference in infix 'behaviour' between villages located within one and the same dialect area appeared to be minimal and probably even negligible. Very subtle fluctuations in productivity were found between Ortisei and Selva (Val Gardena), but in this case it is difficult to come up with an explanation.[24]

5.4.3.2 *Diastratic variability*   The diatopically conditioned variation of infixation in Dolomitic Ladin discussed above is intertwined with several diastratic variables, the most important being the *age* of the informants. As noted previously, our 77 informants were subdivided into three age-classes. In particular, we interviewed 23 informants between twelve and thirty years old; 29 informants between thirty-one and fifty years old; and 25 informants over fifty years old. Table 5.9 shows the exact absolute and relative frequency distribution of the answers (i.e. PRS.IND. 3) over three

---

[23] Thirteen out of the 141 first-conjugation verbs that constitute our corpus can be considered 'neologisms'—they correspond to Italian verbs with first attestations in the nineteenth or twentieth century (according to the *DELI*; Cortelazzo and Zolli 1979–1988). In the varieties where first-conjugation infixation appeared to be most flourishing (i.e. in Badiotto, Marebbano, and Gardenese), these verbs were conjugated in 87.7% of the cases *with* the infix. In Fodom, this percentage decreases to 50%, and for the remaining Fassano, Ampezzano, and Collese varieties, the proportions are completely inverted (altogether, in only 19.3% of the cases did the informants conjugate the neologisms *with* an infix).

[24] The geographical distance between the villages certainly has no determining influence: in spite of the fact that in the Badiotto area the distances between the villages were actually bigger than for the other areas, we could not notice any divergences with respect to infixation. For example, between the Badiotto villages San Martino and San Leonardo there is approximately 12 km, whereas Ortisei is only 8 km away from Selva, yet no differences in infixation could be detected between San Martino and San Leonardo, whereas slight differences in infixation were found between Ortisei and Selva.

response options ('without infix', 'without/with infix', 'with infix') according to the age groups. The chi-square test demonstrated that the distributional differences between the age groups are statistically relevant. Table 5.9 also lists the 'standardized residuals', which allow us to track those cells that make a significant contribution to the overall (significant) association measured by the chi-square test. Basically, if the value of the standardized residual lies outside ±1.96 then it is statistically significant. Conversely, standardized residuals with a critical value below ±1.96 are not significant, which entails that the observed frequency does not differ in a significant manner from the frequencies that one would expect if there were *no relation* between the *independent* (in our case, the *age* of the informants) and the *dependent* (i.e. *infixation*) variable, or, to put it differently, if the 'null hypothesis', i.e. the hypothesis that the predicted effect does *not* exist, were true. In Table 5.9, the significant standardized residuals (i.e. those exceeding ±1.96) are highlighted.

Some interesting findings emerge from the data given in Table 5.9. First of all, it appears that the **youngest** generation of informants (12–30 years old) use the infix significantly *less* (cf. the *negative* and *significant* standardized residual of −2.4 in the category '**with infix**') than the informants of the intermediate (31–50 years old) and oldest (50+ years old) age groups. Thus, this leads us to suspect that first-conjugation infixation is declining among the youngest generation of Ladin speakers. The most logical way to interpret this result is to presume that the attitude of the informants towards infixation remains constant in life (irrespective of their age), but that there has been / is an evolution of language in time: the grammar (as internalized by speakers) has gradually lost / is gradually losing the morphophonemic variation (i.e. infixation) affecting verbal stems. In other words, the current youngest generation of Ladin speakers makes the least use of the first-conjugation infix and it is not to be expected that, as these speakers grow older, they will use the infix more than when they were younger. As such, rather than age differences, we are dealing here with *generational* differences.

Another important observation that can be drawn from the analysis of the standardized residuals listed in Table 5.9 concerns the intermediate response option '**without/with infix**'. For the three age groups, the standardized residual is highly significant, but it has a *negative* value for the two extreme age groups (−2.4 for the age group 12–30 years old and −4.4 for the age group 50+ years old) and a *positive* value for the intermediate age group (6.2 for the age group 31–50 years old). Basically, this implies that the informants between twelve and thirty years old, as well as the informants over fifty years old, are significantly *less* inclined to tolerate, for a given first-conjugation verb, the two possibilities 'without/with infix' than the informants between thirty-one and fifty years old. The lowest value of the standardized residual for this response option is found within the oldest age group (−4.4). This might indicate that the principle of first-conjugation infixation is the most 'stable' in the

TABLE 5.9 Distribution of answers (absolute and relative frequencies, standardized residuals) according to the age of the informants

		Informants' answers			
		Without infix	Without/with infix	With infix	TOTAL
12–30 y.	Absolute/relative frequency	1502 (=61.2%)	123 (=5.0%)	829 (=33.8%)	2454 (=100%)
	Standardized residual	2.7	−2.4	−2.4	
	Absolute/relative frequency	1660 (=53.0%)	280 (=8.9%)	1194 (=38.1%)	3134 (=100%)
31–50 y.	Standardized residual	−3.1	6.2	1.3	
	Absolute/relative frequency	1529 (=58.2%)	106 (=4.0%)	992 (=37.8%)	2627 (=100%)
50+ y.	Standardized residual	0.7	−4.4	0.9	
Age of the informants					
TOTAL	Absolute/relative frequency	4691 (=57.1%)	509 (=6.2%)	3015 (=36.7%)	8215 (=100%)

oldest generation of informants: more than the informants of the younger generations, speakers over fifty years old seem to have a clear-cut idea about which verbs
should be conjugated *with* the infix and which verbs ought to be conjugated *without*
the infix. Conversely, the informants that appeared to be the most willing (cf. the
positive standardized residual of 6.2) to admit both possibilities, 'without/with infix',
belonged to the intermediate age group (31–50 years old). This could be interpreted
as the 'linguistic insecurity' of middle-aged speakers with respect to infixation.
These speakers are wedged between the youngest generation, which tends to reject
the infix, and the oldest generation, which is quite neutral, in that it neither particularly rejects nor particularly promotes the use of the infix (cf. the insignificant
standardized residuals in the category 'with infix' and in the category 'without
infix'). As a matter of fact, in sociolinguistics it is commonly attested that the highest
degree of insecurity with respect to linguistic phenomena is reached in middle-aged
speakers, since they experience the influence of both linguistic tradition and renewal
(cf. Labov 2006: 205).

Other 'diastratic' variables that were assessed to evaluate their impact on first-
conjugation infixation in Dolomitic Ladin were the *dialect competence* and *gender* of
the informants. By 'dialect competence', we mean the 'acquaintanceship' of the informants with the Ladin dialect. When selecting informants, we gave preference to
those who had assured us that they used *exclusively* Ladin in private conversation;
nevertheless, 4 of our 77 informants became familiarized with Ladin only at a more
advanced age, within the context of school. Without going into the statistical details, it
might be worth mentioning that these non-native speakers hesitated significantly more
between insertion/deletion of the infix (and thus the 'double' response option 'without/
with infix'). Of course, this should not come as a surprise: it is obvious that non-native
informants, who are less familiar with Ladin, are the most hesitant or insecure with
respect to first-conjugation infixation. Finally, and in line with expectations, it also
appeared that men and women do not perform differently with respect to infixation.

5.4.3.3 *Diaphasic variability*   We have already pointed to the fact that quite often
informants were inclined to accept the two possibilities—*with* or *without* infix—for a
given verb. Interestingly enough, in some dialect varieties, this 'individual'
morphological variation between presence and absence of the infix appeared to be
exploited at a functional level: a considerable number of Fassano, Ampezzano, and
Collese informants used infixation in order to bring in semantic–aspectual shades of
meaning, depending on the semantico-pragmatic context of the communication.
More particularly, confronted with a given verb in the corpus, some informants of
the three dialect varieties in question tended to associate the forms conjugated
without the reflexes of *-ID(I)-* with instantaneous, concrete, punctual events,
whereas they linked the corresponding 'infixed' counterparts with typical, habitual,
generic actions or behaviour, often supported at the syntactic level by adverbs

expressing iteration, continuity, or habituality (e.g. 'often', 'always', 'usually', 'incessantly', 'each day/week/...', etc.).[25] At first sight, it might seem a paradox that we did *not* identify this type of semantic–aspectual exploitation of first-conjugation infixation in those varieties where the infix appeared to be the most productive, notably in Badiotto, Marebbano, and Gardenese (cf. §5.4.3.1). Yet, on the other hand, it is also obvious that in a strongly Ladinized area with a coherent language policy—let us recall the institutionalization of Ladin at school and in administrative contexts—speakers have fewer opportunities to deal 'creatively' with linguistic phenomena such as first-conjugation infixation.

Table 5.10 gives an overview of the examples and context types in which semantic–aspectual differentiation could be documented between infixed and non-infixed doublets.[26] As expected, in many of these examples, the infixed verb forms are used to refer to 'habitual-generic' (Dahl 1985: 95–100) or 'attitudinal' (Bertinetto 1986: 143–52) phenomena, i.e. actions, situations, or behaviours that are 'typical or characteristic properties of a species, kind, or an individual' (Dahl 1985: 99). This becomes particularly evident in examples 1–4, 8–10, and 14–15 on the right-hand side of Table 5.10. In sentences 1, 3, 9, and 15, the habitual–generic content is emphasized by the adverb 'always', which, in this case, should be interpreted as a permanent 'readiness' to participate in the event, without the subject being literally continuously involved in the development of the process (cf. Vendler 1967: 108–9, Bertinetto 1986: 150): e.g. Ampezzano: *El el sošpet-é-a sènpre dùte* 'He is always suspicious about everything'. Cleft constructions of the type 'that's someone who...' (e.g. Collese: *El é un che... se lament-é-a semper* 'That's someone who's always complaining') also appear to be particularly suited for expressing habitual–generic contents with augmented verb forms (cf. examples 2, 8, 10, and 15). Some of the informants explicitly stated that the presence of the adverb 'always' is perceived as 'superfluous', since the infixed verb form in itself has an inherent connotation of habituality or genericity (cf. examples 2, 8, and 10: e.g. Fassano: *L'é un che sospet-é-a* 'He is (always) suspicious'). In examples 4 and 14, the infixed verb forms are used for referring to the habitual action par excellence, viz. the practice of a profession: e.g. Fassano: *El parchej-é-a auto dant l'hotel* 'He parks cars in front of the hotel' (sc.: it's his job).

The above examples point in the direction of a cautious functional–semantic 'revalorization' of the infix in some varieties of Dolomitic Ladin: from a semantically empty morpheme, it has developed into a segment with semi-derivational/aspectual characteristics. This is, however, crucial to observe that it is a 'mixed' status, since, in

[25] In the entire corpus, the habitual–generic differentiation between infixed and non-infixed alternatives was identified for 16.5% of the cases in which the double ending was allowed.

[26] Some of the examples reported in Table 5.10 were spontaneously produced by the informants themselves. In other cases, we asked the informant to translate doublets of sentences that could trigger the semantic–aspectual exploitation of the mechanism.

TABLE 5.10 Semantic–aspectual exploitation of the morphological alternation between infixed and non-infixed first-conjugation verb forms in Fassano, Ampezzano, and Collese

Fassano (Brach, Cazet)

Paradigm without infix

1. Senti co ch'el biastèma 'Listen how he's swearing'
2. El sospeta della vejina 'He suspects the neighbour'
3. El critica el professor 'He criticizes the professor'
4. El parcheja sùa auto dant l'hotel 'He parks his car in front of the hotel'
5. El se abona a la revista 'He subscribes to the journal'
6. El nveléna el giat 'He poisons the cat'
7. L'é do ch'el rónceda 'He's snoring'

Paradigm with infix

1. E semper ch'el biastem-é-a 'He's always swearing'
2. L'é un che sospet-é-a 'He finds everything suspicious'
3. El critich-é-a semper döt 'He always criticizes everything'
4. El parchej-é-a auto dant l'hotel 'He parks cars in front of the hotel' (sc.: it's his job)
5. Ogne an el se abon-é-a a la revista 'Every year he subscribes to the journal'
6. L'é già la terza uta che nvelen-é-a el giat 'It is already the third time that he has poisoned a cat'
7. Mio pare ronced-é-a perché beve massa 'My father snores because he drinks a lot'

Ampezzano

Paradigm without infix

8. Senti cemòdo che beštema 'Listen how he's swearing'
9. El el sóspeta ra vejinànza 'He suspects the neighbour'
10. Il fiol se n'aprofita che sa mare non era 'The boy takes advantage of the absence of his mother'
11. El tosato ciàcola col dotor 'The boy chats with the doctor'
12. El el cálcola ra òga de 'l lustro 'He calculates the velocity of light'
13. El el fotocópia el libro 'He photocopies the book'

Paradigm with infix

8. L'é un che beštem-é-a 'That's someone who's always swearing'
9. El el sošpet-é-a sèmpre dùte 'He suspicious is always/about everything'
10. L'é un che se n'aprofit-é-a 'That person is a profiteer' (free translation)
11. El tosato non laora ma el ciacol-é-a dut el di 'The boy doesn't work but chats the whole day'
12. Sta calcolatrice è ideale par ci che calcol-é-a dut el di 'This calculator is ideal for those who calculate the whole day'
13. De spess el el fotocopi-é-a libre 'He often photocopies books'

Collese

Paradigm without infix

14. Ma fratel organisa na festa 'My brother is organizing a party'
15. L'é daré che se lamenta 'He's complaining'

Paradigm with infix

14. Ma fratel organis-è-a feste 'My brother organizes parties' (sc.: it's his job)
15. El é un che se lament-é-a semper 'That's someone who's always complaining'

spite of its presumed semantic–aspectual coloration, the infix remains confined to the originally rhizotonic forms of the verbal paradigm: in habitual contexts such as '*we* always criticize everything' or '*we* are always cursing', our informants systematically refused to use an infixed verb form. Hypothetically infixed first plural forms with which we confronted them, such as (PRS.IND. 4) **critich-é-on*, **beštem-é-on*, were radically rejected by the speakers. The alleged semantic–aspectual properties are thus curbed by grammatical/morphological constraints: even in habitual context types, the infix does not transgress the boundaries imposed by the grammar.

Moreover, apart from its inflectional limits, the semantic–functional use of first-conjugation infixation in Dolomitic Ladin is also subordinate to the etymological and morphophonological characteristics of the lexeme: on the one hand, indigenous first-conjugation 'base' verbs, in which infixation is traditionally blocked, are excluded from exploitation for semantic–aspectual differentiation; on the other hand, verbs that are destined to receive the infix because of their syllabic structure cannot drop it, even if they figure in contexts that are not specifically habitual or generic. For instance, in Fassano, a 'primitive' base verb like *ciantàr* 'to sing' is never conjugated with the insertion of *-é-* (< *-ID(I)-*), even if used in habitual/generic contexts ('I always sing' → Fassano: *canto semper*, **cant-é-o semper*), whereas a polysyllabic suffixed verb like *passenàr* 'to fit' (with *-en-* originating in the German(ic) infinitival ending *-n*: *passen*) invariably displays the augment *-é-* in the rhizotonic forms of the paradigm (e.g. PRS.IND. 3. *passen-é-a*), whether it is used in a habitual context or not ('it fits' → Fass. *passen-é-a*, **passena*).

5.5 Conclusion

The present study has shown that first-conjugation infixation, understood as the creation of an inflectional subclass within the scope of the first-conjugation by means of the intercalation of a stressed morpheme (< Latin *-ID(I)-*, cf. §5.2) between the root and ending of the verb, is a morphological process with multiple purposes and variable conditioning. Our case study of first-conjugation infixation in Dolomitic Ladin has shown that the infix is first and foremost attracted by verbs with polysyllabic and suffixed roots and/or with a non-indigenous etymology (cf. §5.4.2, Table 5.7). Polysyllabicity/suffixation of the verb root and/or foreign etymology of the verb appeared to be the minimum conditions for infixation. However, the intralinguistic parameters that underlie the lexical selection of the first-conjugation infix are intertwined with a series of *diatopic* (dialect–geographical origin of the speakers), *diastratic* (age and degree of dialect competence of the speakers), and *diaphasic* (the semantic and pragmatic context of communication) parameters (cf. §5.4.3). The fact that first-conjugation infixation is essentially a dialect-related phenomenon makes it particularly suitable for sociolinguistic variation and extramorphological exploitation. We have seen that in Badiotto, Marebbano, and Gardenese the infix has a social 'signalizing' function, in that it is considered by the speakers as a means of empha-sizing the dialect-specific (Ladin) individuality of verb morphology and, as such, of 'marking distance' with the (Italian/German) standard language (cf. §5.4.3.1). In the other varieties, notably in Fassano, Ampezzano, and Collese, the infix serves a semantic–aspectual function, becoming a marker of 'habituality' (cf. §5.4.3.3). These findings testify to the power of the 'freedom' of the (dialect) speaker to deal creatively with morphological phenomena, by assigning them functions that are not merely morphological any more.

6

Future and conditional in Occitan: a non-canonical morphome*

LOUISE ESHER

6.1 Introduction

Varieties of Occitan present several synthetic and periphrastic forms which may be considered 'futures' and/or 'conditionals', covering the semantic fields of future time reference, hypothesis, attenuation, and possibility: these include the Romance synthetic future, the Romance synthetic conditional, the reflex of the Latin pluperfect indicative, and periphrastic constructions such as *anar* 'go' + infinitive, *voler* 'want' + infinitive, and PRS.IND. + *puèi* 'then'. This chapter focuses on the first two of these items, considering the formal and functional relations between them, and the consequences of these relations for the theoretical notion of 'morphome' proposed by Aronoff (1994)—a systematic formal regularity which is not simply due to sound change and which has no unique functional correlate.

I argue that the set of cells formed by the synthetic future and synthetic conditional constitutes a 'weakly morphomic' distribution of the type predicted by Aronoff (1994: 25, 167) and exemplified by Maiden (2011c): partly, but not exhaustively, conditioned by extramorphological, semantic factors. For convenience of reference, I assign to this set of cells the arbitrary and abstract label 'FUÈC',[1] as a means of identifying a particular set of cells without reference to any semantic content postulated for them. For the same reason, I use the abstract labels 'SF' and 'SC' here to designate the morphological forms of the Romance synthetic future and Romance synthetic conditional respectively, independently of the semantic functions associated with either form.

* The research presented here was supported by AHRC doctoral grant 08/140462.
[1] Reflex of Latin FOCUS 'hearth' in eastern varieties of Occitan, now meaning 'fire', and closely approximating to an abbreviation of the Occitan term *futur e condicional* 'future and conditional'.

6.2 Origin of the synthetic future and synthetic conditional

The synthetic future (henceforth SF) found in Occitan derives from a periphrasis involving the infinitive and the present indicative of HABERE 'have' (CANTARE HABEO, etc. > *cantarai*, etc.), while the synthetic conditional (henceforth SC) derives from a parallel construction involving the infinitive and the imperfect indicative of HABERE 'have' (CANTARE HABEBAM, etc. > *cantariái*, etc.). Initially expressing necessity or obligation (Adams 1991), these constructions acquire the meaning of futurity due to the pragmatic inferences that necessary events are highly likely to occur, and that these events, as yet unrealized, will occur at a later point in time, i.e. in the future (see also Hopper and Traugott 2003: 53–5).

It is generally held that the SC originates with the sole, temporal value of 'future in the past' (henceforth FIP), and progressively acquires modal values (see e.g. Fleischman 1982: 64–6). Traditional descriptions of modern French (e.g. Grevisse and Goosse 2011) and modern Occitan (e.g. Alibèrt 1976) now subdivide the paradigm into a screeve 'future' and a screeve 'conditional', suggesting that the two are functionally different items, with little if anything in common. 'Future' is treated as intrinsically temporal, while the SC is assigned to a distinct mood 'conditional', neither indicative nor subjunctive; the position of the future 'tense' with respect to mood or of the 'conditional' with respect to 'tense' is rarely addressed explicitly.

Despite the apparent shift of the SC from a primarily temporal function to a primarily modal function, in the majority of cases the SF and SC are reported as continuing to present a shared stem (see e.g. Maiden 2011*b*: 264–6). In this respect FUÈC appears to present similarities with the canonical morphome PYTA described by Maiden (2001*b*, 2004*b*, 2005*a*), comprising Romance forms whose Latin etyma had perfective stems. Although the reflexes of Latin perfective forms have undergone substantial functional divergence in the transition to modern Romance, such that they no longer present any unique functional correlate, they nevertheless preserve and often reinforce their formal identity. Maiden (2005*a*) discerns two 'symptoms' of morphomehood presented by PYTA, namely 'coherence', the preservation of formal identity between the cells of a morphome, and 'convergence', the tendency for a morphome to acquire a characteristic phonological shape; in Esher (2012*a*) I adduce Occitan data showing that FUÈC presents both coherence and convergence. However, as shown below, more detailed examination of the formal developments undergone by the SF and SC[2] and of the semantic values associated with these

---

[2] This chapter does not explicitly consider the infinitive. Although the infinitive is at the historical source of the SF and SC, there is no a priori reason why in the native speaker's mental representation of the synchronic paradigm these forms should continue to be associated with the infinitive, all the more so since the infinitive presents both semantic and formal characteristics separating it from the SF and SC (Maiden 2011*a*: 208–9, Matthews 1982).

forms reveals that the parallel between PYTA and Fuèc is not absolute: in particular, Fuèc presents greater functional commonality and lesser formal coherence.

6.3 Symmetric and asymmetric stem distributions within Fuèc

The most immediately apparent difference between the behaviour of Fuèc and that which would be expected for a canonical morphome is in the formal relationship of the SF and SC: Fuèc, while usually coherent, is not systematically so.

In the majority of cases, the distribution of stems between the SF and SC in Occitan respects the pattern inherited through regular historical change and familiar from other Romance languages. Identity is preserved between the stem of the SF and that of the SC; this stem is sometimes distinctive and confined to Fuèc. These observations are consistent with the behaviour which would be expected of a morphomic distribution.

Furthermore, innovative developments commonly make reference to Fuèc. Many heteroclite paradigms involve a contrast between Fuèc forms characteristic of the first or second conjugation, and all other forms, which retain their etymological third conjugation shape. Table 6.1 shows just such a distribution for third conjugation *créisser* < CRESCERE 'grow' in the variety of Toulouse (*ALLOc* 31.12):[3] the original Fuèc stem with etymological theme vowel /e/ has been replaced by the theme vowel /a/ characteristic of first conjugation verbs such as *cantar* 'sing', but no other forms are affected.

TABLE 6.1 Heteroclisis affecting Fuèc (*créisser, ALLOc* 31.12)

	PRS.IND	IMPF.IND	PRS.SBJV	PRET	IMPF.SBJV	SF	SC
3SG	*creis*	*creissiá*	*cresque*	*cresquèt*	*cresquèsse*	*creissarà*	*creissariá*

Occasionally, cases of convergence are found. For Fuèc in Occitan, the characteristic shape assumed involves the cluster /dr/. This cluster is initially present for reasons of regular historical change in the Fuèc stems of a number of high-frequency irregular verbs, e.g. *valdrà/valdriá* 'it will/would be worth', *caldrà/caldriá* 'it will/would be necessary', *prendrà/prendriá* 'he will/would take', *voldrà/voldriá* 'he will/would want'. It is subsequently reanalysed as a marker of the set Fuèc, and extended to the Fuèc stems of other lexemes, such as *avudre/agure* 'have' and *veire*

---

[3] I am grateful to Patrick Sauzet and Guylaine Brun-Trigaud for access to unpublished morphological data from the *ALLOc* and *ALLOr*.

'see' in Sète, which the etymological Fuèc forms *aurà, auriá* and *veirà, veiriá* co-occur with innovative forms *audrà, audriá* and *veidrà, veidriá* (Thérond 2002): the consonant /d/ in the innovative forms cannot be traced to regular historical change and must be of analogical origin.

Taken together, these developments appear to indicate that for speakers Fuèc constitutes a meaningful pattern of distribution, which can serve as a template for innovations in the paradigm. Such 'symmetrical' patterns, in which SF and SC continue to share a stem, are the majority pattern across all varieties of Occitan, regardless of the functions attributed to the two screeves.

However, many varieties also present cases of 'asymmetric' stem distribution, in which the stems of the SF and SC differ from each other. The diversity and unsystematic nature of asymmetric distributions indicate that this is a recent phenomenon. Asymmetry may arise as a consequence of morphological analogy, phonological change, conflation of multiple lexemes into a single paradigm, shift of conjugational class, or pragmatic factors. It may involve innovation in the SF or in the SC. Although it is rare for a given asymmetry to be attested over a coherent geographical zone, asymmetric distributions are nevertheless real and widespread, affecting almost all 200 varieties surveyed for the *ALLOc* and *ALLOr*. Occitan may be unique among Romance languages in presenting such distributions, in which the familiar stem identity of SF and SC is disrupted.

6.3.1 *Asymmetric distributions*

Some asymmetries are of phonological origin. Lanly (1971) identifies a number of localities in the Auvergne and Limousin where the etymological -r- typically assumed to be characteristic of the SF and SC stems has been lost from the SC. Although Lanly only describes these for a relatively small area, the true extent of their range is much wider: they are attested not only in the *ALMC* data on which Lanly's study is based, but also across much of Gascony and the Languedoc (*ALLOc, ALLOr*, Kelly 1973, Camps 1985, Laurent 2002a). Most commonly, r-less SC forms are found in the first conjugation, with contrasts such as *cantarà* /kanta'ra/, *canta(r)iá* /kanta'jɔ/. The fall of the -r- is favoured by a specific phonological context—VrjV—which is systematically present in first and second conjugation Fuèc stems, and in certain irregular verbs; the r-less SC forms appear to originate in a regular sound change affecting first conjugation verbs, and are then spread by analogy to other lexemes. These forms are of interest as an example of an asymmetry which is of transparent origin, and which is not subsequently 'repaired': I am not aware of any case in which the -r- of the SF is deleted to realign the SF forms on the SC forms.

Another such asymmetry resulting from phonological processes, and affecting SF and SC stems which were not historically differentiated, concerns verbs which for reasons of historical phonology would be expected to present a diphthong in the stems of the SF and SC, e.g. *veirà/veiriá* 'he will/would see'. In a significant number of cases, the expected -j- in the SC stem falls, leaving a monophthong in the SC stem but a diphthong in the SF stem, e.g. *veirà/veriá* 'he will/would see'. From a phonological point of view, there is no a priori obstacle to restoring symmetry by remodelling the SF on the SC, a solution which has been adopted in some varieties, resulting in monophthongs in both stems. However, in many varieties, no such realignment has taken place: asymmetry between SF and SC is tolerated, and persists. This 'vocalic' asymmetry is attested for approximately half the *ALLOc* sample localities, and as a phenomenon appears to occur across a relatively coherent zone. However, localities in which an individual lexeme presents vocalic asymmetry rarely cluster in a coherent zone, nor is there significant overlap between the localities in which each individual lexeme presents asymmetry, indicating that this change, though of phonological origin, is lexically diffuse.

Other cases involve variant stems which belong to distinct conjugational class types. Occasionally such asymmetry is systematic for a given conjugational class: in the variety of Labretonie (*ALLOc* 47.05), the SF of third conjugation verbs retains a stem due to regular historical change, e.g. *vendrèi* /βen'drɛj/ 'I will sell', while the SC presents the theme vowel /a/ characteristic of the first conjugation, e.g. *venda(r)iái* /βenda'jɔj/ 'I would sell'. More commonly, however, asymmetry of conjugational class is sporadic, and results from morphological analogy operating on either the SF or the SC to produce a heteroclite paradigm, in which the SF or SC alone of all paradigm screeves adopts a form characteristic of a different conjugational class. At Meljac (*ALLOc* 12.24) the SF of *nàisser* 'be born' has assumed the first conjugation theme vowel /a/, while the SC along with all other paradigm cells retains a third conjugation form (Table 6.2); at Saint-Sernin-sur-Rance (*ALLOr* 12.34) for the lexeme *conéisser* 'know', the opposite distribution is found (Table 6.3).

TABLE 6.2 **Asymmetric heteroclisis (*nàisser*, ALLOc 12.24)**

	PRS.IND	IMPF.IND	PRS.SBJV	PRET	IMPF.SBJV	SF	SC
3SG	*nais*	*naissiá*	*nasca*	*nasquèt*	*nasquèssa*	*naissarà*	*naisseriá*

TABLE 6.3 **Asymmetric heteroclisis (*conéisser*, ALLOr 12.34)**

	PRS.IND	IMPF.IND	PRS.SBJV	PRET	IMPF.SBJV	SF	SC
3SG	*coneis*	*coneissiá*	*conesque*	*conesquèt*	*conosquèssa*	*coneisserà*	*coneissariá*

Still other asymmetries result from the incursion of a root or stem already present elsewhere in the paradigm into the SF or SC. In a number of varieties in the Couserans, the stem of the present indicative and imperfect indicative is propagated into the SC of certain irregular verbs, while the SF retains the stem which is the expected result of regular historical change (Table 6.4).

TABLE 6.4 **Asymmetries in varieties of the Couserans (Deledar 2006, Laurent 2001, 2002*a*, 2002*b*)**

lexeme	locality	SF.3SG	SC.3SG
valer 'be worth' < UALERE	Massat, La Ruse	*valdrà*	*valeria*
voler 'want' < *volere	Lescure	*voldrà*	*voleriá*
saber 'know' < SAPERE	Lescure	*saurà*	*saberiá*
poder 'be able' < *potere	Aulus, Bas-Couserans, Castillonais	*poirà*	*poderiá*
víver 'live' < UIUERE	Aulus	*viurà*	*viveriá*
escríver 'write' < SCRIBERE	Lescure	*escriurà*	*escriveriá*
béver/beure 'drink' < BIBERE	Seronais	*beurà, beverà*	*beveria*
béver 'drink' < BIBERE	Volvestre	*beurà, beverà*	*beveria*

The form of the innovative SC stem corresponds to a type of FUÈC stem which is both widespread in Pyrenean varieties of Occitan, and well-represented in the varieties for which asymmetry is listed above. This stem superficially resembles the infinitive, but is more plausibly analysed as resulting from a general process of analogical stem levelling acting across the paradigm. The tendency for such analogical levelling in the relevant area, and the presence of *beverà* alongside *beurà* in some localities, suggest that the asymmetries of the Couserans may be an artefact of change in progress. However, it cannot be assumed with any certainty that these asymmetries represent a transitional state and that they will in the course of time be eliminated by extension of the innovative stem to the SF. They may most usefully be characterized as instances in which a relatively recent, morphological (analogical) change has created an asymmetry which speakers subsequently appear to tolerate, despite it being at variance with the overwhelming norm (i.e. symmetry of SF/SC stems) within the system. The systematic directionality of the Couserans asymmetries suggests that the SC is in general more sensitive to pressure from the remainder of the paradigm than is the SF. This hypothesis is supported by the tendency of the PYTA root to spread into the SC rather than the SF.

In the variety of Fauch (*ALLOc* 81.12), the reflex of CRESCERE 'grow' presents the stem distribution shown in Table 6.5: in the SF, the expected form *creisserà* alongside innovative *creirà*; in the SC, an innovative form *crescriá*, transparently remodelled on the PYTA root /kresk/.

TABLE 6.5 SC remodelled on PYTA root (*créisser, ALLOc* 81.12)

	PRS.IND	IMPF.IND	PRS.SBJV	PRET	IMPF.SBJV	SF	SC
3SG	*creis*	*creissiá*	*cresque*	*cresquèt*	*cresquèssa*	*creirà, creisserà*	*crescriá*

In the variety of Jouels (*ALLOc* 12.22), the SC of this same lexeme has again been remodelled on the PYTA root /kreh/, while the SF retains its expected historical form *creisherá* (Table 6.6).

TABLE 6.6 SC remodelled on PYTA root (*créisher, ALLOc* 12.22)

	PRS.IND	IMPF.IND	PRS.SBJV	PRET	IMPF.SBJV	SF	SC
3SG	*creish*	*creishiá*	*crésca*	*cresquèt*	*cresquèssa*	*creisherá*	*cresqueriá*

In the variety of Foulayronnes (*ALLOc* 47.31), a similar distribution is encountered for the verb *creire* 'believe': the SC is remodelled on the PYTA root /krets/, while the SF retains its expected historical form (Table 6.7).

TABLE 6.7 SC remodelled on PYTA root (*creire, ALLOc* 47.31)

	PRS.IND	IMPF.IND	PRS.SBJV	PRET	IMPF.SBJV	SF	SC
3SG	*crei*	*cregiá*	*cretge*	*cretgeguèt*	*cretgeguèssa*	*creirà*	*cretge(r)iá*

It should, however, be noted that this is no more than a tendency: in the varieties of Donzac (*ALLOc* 82.20) and Massat (Laurent 2001), there are isolated attestations of the PYTA root spreading to the SF but not the SC. In Donzac, the lexeme affected is *anar* 'go': the SC continues, as expected, *andare* x IRE, which would have given first *aniriá* and subsequently the attested form *ani(ri)á* following loss of the -r- from the SC; the SF has been remodelled on the PYTA root (Table 6.8).

TABLE 6.8 SF remodelled on PYTA root (*anar, ALLOc* 82.20)

	PRS.IND	IMPF.IND	PRS.SBJV	PRET	IMPF.SBJV	SF	SC
3SG	*vai*	*anava*	*angue*	*angót*	*angósse*	*anguerà*	*ani(ri)á*

In Massat, this type of asymmetry occurs for *voler* 'want' < *volere: the SC retains its expected Fuèc stem due to regular historical change, while the SF presents a form remodelled on the PYTA root (Table 6.9). The distribution found for *voler* in Massat represents an exception both to the majority pattern of symmetry, and to the relatively systematic type of asymmetry current in this and other neighbouring varieties, since not only are SF and SC asymmetric, but here it is the SC rather than the SF which retains the historical stem in /ldr/; moreover, the innovating stem is modelled on the PYTA root rather than that of the present indicative and imperfect indicative. Although the PYTA root sometimes extends into the infinitive and/or Fuèc in Pyrenean varieties of Occitan, Laurent does not attest any velar infinitive for Massat; in the case of *voler* here it is clear that the PYTA root has propagated directly into the SF without the mediation of the infinitive.

TABLE 6.9 SF remodelled on PYTA root (*voler*, Laurent 2001)

	PRS.IND	IMPF.IND	PRS.SBJV	PRET	IMPF.SBJV	SF	SC
3SG	*vòl*	*volia*	*volga*	*volguèc*	*volguès*	*volguerà*	*voldria*

A more frequent analogical source of innovative SF stems, however, is the root associated with the morphome Maiden labels N-pattern, as in the following examples from Merens-les-Vals (*ALLOc* 09.32) and Rabastens (*ALLOc* 81.06), shown in Tables 6.10 and 6.11 respectively. In both these varieties, for *còser* 'cook', the SF presents a stem vowel /ɔ/ otherwise limited to the present indicative (and, in the case of 09.32, present subjunctive), while the SC presents a vowel /u/ which is the expected result of regular sound change.

TABLE 6.10 SF remodelled on N-pattern stem (*còser*, *ALLOc* 09.32)

	PRS.IND	IMPF.IND	PRS.SBJV	PRET	IMPF.SBJV	SF	SC
3SG	*còtg*	*cosiá*	*còse*	*cosèc*	*cosès*	*còirà*	*cuiria*

TABLE 6.11 SF remodelled on N-pattern stem (*còser*, *ALLOc* 81.06)

	PRS.IND	IMPF.IND	PRS.SBJV	PRET	IMPF.SBJV	SF	SC
3SG	*còi*	*cosiá*	*cosega*	*coseguèt*	*coseguèssa*	*còserà*	*cose(r)ia*

Extension of a stem or stem vowel usually correlated with primary stress and thus with the N-pattern forms into Fuèc is not without precedent in Romance: Maiden (2011e) notes a number of cases in the history of French and Italian, arguing that such extensions are due to analogy with existing patterns, in which the stem found in the N-pattern presents a 'fortuitous' identity with the Fuèc stem. While a similar explanation can be given for the spread of this stem in the lexemes cited above, it fails to account for the non-extension of the stem into the SC. Evidence of variation in the SC (and sometimes SF) may suggest that this is a change in progress, and that symmetry will later be restored. However, this conjecture is by nature uncertain, particularly so in the cases of 'cook', where variation between symmetrical and asymmetrical patterns is apparently unattested.

Overall, in cases of morphological analogy, it may be observed that the SC tends to be remodelled on the stem found in PYTA, while the SF, which is generally more resistant to analogical influence, is most frequently influenced by the present indicative and/or subjunctive. While only a tendency, this finding is interesting since it suggests a more complex internal structure to the set of cells constituting Fuèc: not only are the SF and SC subject to formal pressure holding them together, but each one is subject to a different set of external pressures.

6.4 Functions associated with SF and SC

In French, Dendale (2001: 9) identifies four canonical functions associated with the SC—posteriority (temporal futurity), possibility, attenuation, and evidentiality. As Vet and Kampers-Manhe (2001) show, these functions are likewise associated with the SF, which, in addition to temporal futurity, may express possibility, attenuation, or epistemic modality (this last correlating with the evidential use of the SC, since both express a reserve on the part of the speaker as to the truth value of the proposition at issue). The traditional labels 'future' and 'conditional' thus obscure not only the distinction between a form and its functions, but the fact that the SF and SC each have both modal and temporal uses (Vet and Kampers-Manhe 2001: 90).

For the SF in Occitan, examples of the same four broad categories may be found: temporal posteriority (1), possibility (2), attenuation (3), and conjecture (4).

(1)   Deman me **vendrà** quèrre. Qué que faguèssem o que faguèssem pas. Es antau. (from *Ciutats dins l'Azur* by Jean-Frédéric Brun)
      'Tomorrow he will come to fetch me. Whatever we do, or leave undone. That's how it is.'

(2)   Mas benlèu se demòre aquí, a bèles paucs, aquel lengatge me **vendrà** mai familiar. (from *Ciutats dins l'Azur* by Jean-Frédéric Brun)
      'But perhaps, if I stay here, this language will gradually become more familiar to me.'

(3)   [R]ecomendam de fugir leis autors que serián jamai estats legits s'aguèsson agut l'onestetat d'escriure en francés, en luega d'estremar sa nullitat sota de pelhas dialectalas. Lei Niçards nos **perdonaràn** donc un juste mesprètz per son illustrisme Rancher. (from 'Per un art poëtic occitan' by Michel Miniussi, in *Amiras* 19)

'You should steer clear of those authors who would never have been read had they only had the honesty to write in French, rather than concealing their worthlessness beneath dialectal rags. The Niçards will hence forgive us a justified contempt for their über-illustrious Rancher.'

(4)   L'atencion pòrta mai que mai—e n'en siam aürós—sus lo periòdi contemporan, mau coneissut [...]. **Serà** qu'aicí la matéria es nòva e abondosa. (from 'Cronicas' by Michel Miniussi, in *Oc* 19)

'Most attention—we are happy to see—is given to the modern period, which is poorly known [...]. This is surely because material here is new and abundant.'

In contrast to the French data, however, the SC in Occitan is not systematically attested with all four of these values. The SC is typically used to express possibility (5) and attenuation (6).

(5)   Se ni Moïses, ni Josué, ni el, non tornavan dau grand sèrre, de qué **farián** ? (from *Ciutats dins l'Azur* by Jean-Frédéric Brun)

'If neither Moses, nor Joshua, nor himself, came back from the mountain, what would they do?'

(6)   Per començar, siás ma convidada. T'ai fach alestir quicòm de requist. **Deuriás** pausar lo grand cotèl aquí, **volriái** pas que te fagas mau. (from *Ciutats dins l'Azur* by Jean-Frédéric Brun)

'For a start, you're my guest. I've prepared something exquisite for you. You should put the big knife down there, I wouldn't like you to hurt yourself.'

Reliable examples of the SC expressing conjecture are, however, much harder to find than in French. One possible explanation is that of text type: in French, the conjectural SC is strongly correlated with journalism, a genre for which there is relatively limited production in Occitan, and in which much of the available material is produced by non-native speakers. As a result, it is difficult not only to find examples, but to establish whether these examples reflect genuine native speaker usage or the influence of L1 French. The normative grammar of Romieu and Bianchi (2005: 332) claims that the SC can be used with conjectural value in Gascon (7); however, in certain varieties of the Languedoc this usage does not exist (Xavier Bach, p.c.).

(7)   A çò qui pareish, que **seré** malaut.
      'It would appear he's sick.'

Finally, while in most varieties the SC is the exponent of future-in-the-past (8), in a number of Pyrenean varieties this value is associated instead with the conditional perfect (9), with an apparently back-shifted form of the periphrastic go-future (10), or with the form which I label 'COND2', the reflex of the Latin pluperfect indicative (11).

(8) Lo vilatge dins la matinada ja avançada èra tan pasible. Colors e bruches de fèsta, verai. Cledas de fèrre per clausir las carrièiras quand i **farián** córrer los buòus. (from *Ciutats dins l'Azur* by Jean-Frédéric Brun)
     'The village was so peaceful even at this late hour of the morning. Festival colours and sounds, though. Iron barriers to close the streets for when they would send the bulls running that way.'

(9) Que pensavi qu'**auré venut** la maison.
     'I thought he would sell the house.' (Field 2003)

(10) Que'm prometós qu'**anavas tornar**.
     'You promised me you would come back.' (Field 2003)

(11) Que'm prometós que **tornèras**.
     'You promised me you would come back.' (Field 2003)

The modern use of COND2 to express temporal posteriority is particularly striking, as in medieval times this form appears to have an almost exclusively modal value. In medieval Occitan, the function of FIP appears exclusively associated with the SC (12); it is far from certain that COND2 could express FIP at all. Quint's (1997) study gives no example of COND2 as FIP; Jensen (1994: 245) claims that COND2 may in very rare cases serve as FIP, but gives only a single, ambiguous example (13), in which *fera* might equally be interpreted as expressing possibility. I have not yet found any example in which COND2 solely and uncontroversially expresses FIP.

(12) mon frayre Paul, l'angel m'a dich / que vous **vendria** (from *Mystères provençaux du XVe siècle*, anonymous medieval text)
     'my brother Paul, the angel told me that he would come to you'

(13) et enquer se'n loingna ades, e **fera**, tro seaz feniz (from 'Amics Marchabruns' by Marcabru)
     'and it is still moving away, and would do so until your end'

In medieval Occitan, therefore, while COND2 shares the values of possibility and attenuation found for the SC, it expresses a greater degree of irrealis than the SC (Jensen 1994: 246) and most probably lacks the value of temporal posteriority. In modern Occitan, COND2 is absent from the majority of varieties, and appears to survive only in certain varieties of the Pyrenees and Piedmont; although Chabaneau (1876: 283–4) notes the presence of COND2 in a cluster of localities around Nontron in the Limousin, his account clearly indicates the progressive loss of this screeve.

For the majority of the Pyrenean area in which COND2 is present, Allières (1997: 20) claims that the principal function associated with COND2 is FIP. Although Allières's general description does not explicitly address the issue of whether the SC can be used as FIP over this area, the inference is that it cannot, a conjecture in agreement with Bouzet (1928: 69) and with Field's (2003) data for Bordères-sur-l'Echez. Allières (1997: 20) notes two varieties which differ from the basic pattern. In the variety of Ferrière-Arrens, both COND2 and SC may express possibility, but only COND2 may be used as FIP; while in the variety of Barèges (see also Massourre 2006), the SC is entirely absent, and COND2 is associated with both temporal and modal values. A further distribution is given for the variety of Campan by Field (2003), in which the SC has been restricted to modal usages, while the value of FIP is expressed either by COND2 or by a periphrasis of the form *anavi* 'I was going' + INF.

A schematic representation of the different distributions of form and function found in Pyrenean varieties, as compared to those found in French and many varieties of Occitan, is given in Table 6.12. While formal stem identity is maintained between the SF and SC, the two exponents of temporal posteriority, the SF (FUÈC stem) and COND2 (PYTA root) conspicuously do not share a stem. It may therefore be seen that the paradigmatic distribution of the FUÈC stem does not map directly on to the paradigmatic distribution of the semantic value 'futurity'.

TABLE 6.12 **Distribution of forms across functions**

	Temporal future	Modal future	FIP	Modal conditional
Barèges	SF	SF	COND2	COND2
Ferrière-Arrens	SF	SF	COND2	COND2/SC
General Cond2 area	SF	SF	COND2	SC
Bordères	SF	SF	COND2/*anavi*+INF	SC
Campan	SF	SF	SC+PST.PTCP/*anavi*+INF	SC
French	SF	SF	SC	SC

Although fewer data are available for the varieties of the Italian Alps, it is notable that here once again the semantic parallel is between SF and COND2, while the formal parallel is between SF and SC. In this area, COND2 has become specialized, not as a temporal marker, but as a marker of epistemic modality. Vignetta (cited in Sibille 1997: 16) considers it directly equivalent to the Italian future perfect—strongly associated with modal conjecture (Barceló 2004)—and glosses *mi aguéro* (have. COND2.1SG) as *io avrò avuto*; while dialect descriptions typically gloss COND2 as the equivalent of an imperfect indicative plus an adverb meaning 'perhaps' or 'probably' (14).

(14)   I **l'aougueiron** tro minjà
        'Ils avaient peut-être trop mangé' (Jayme 2003: 55)
        'They had maybe eaten too much.'

Descriptions of these varieties frequently analyse COND2 as among the exponents of a distinct mood labelled 'dubitative' or 'conjectural', which, like the indicative and subjunctive, occurs in four tense/aspect values: present, imperfect, perfect, and pluperfect. The exponents of these values are, respectively, the SF, COND2, the periphrasis SF + PST.PTCP, and the periphrasis COND2 + PST.PTCP, as shown in Table 6.13 with their original Italian glosses for the variety of Bardonecchia, where *forse* means 'perhaps'.

TABLE 6.13 'Dubitative' forms for *chantar* 'sing', Bardonecchia (Gleise-Bellet 2003: 42–4)

Present	*mi a ciantarèi*	'forse canto'
Imperfect	*mi a ciantéru*	'forse cantavo'
Perfect	*mi oréi ciantà*	'forse ho cantato'
Pluperfect	*mi ughéru ciantà*	'forse avevo cantato'

Analyses of this type consider that the principal function associated with the SF is now that of marking conjecture, while temporal posteriority is now expressed by periphrastic then-futures of the type *mi a chanto pòi*. Both possibility (15) and attenuation (16) are certainly associated with the SC:

(15)   S'ou l'aouguëssë loû mouion, ou l'**achtëri**
        'S'il avait les moyens, il l'achèterait.' (Jayme 2003: 53)
        'If he had the means to, he would buy it.'

(16)   Ä **vudríu** mek ëd pan e 'd ciocolà
        'Je voudrais seulement du pain et du chocolat.' (Gleise Bellet 2003: 8)
        'I would just like some bread and some chocolate.'

There is, regrettably, no explicit information on the function of FIP, though as this is not mentioned among the values of the 'dubitative' mood, one may assume that it is not associated with COND2. Although the value at stake is different—epistemic modality as opposed to temporal posteriority—the varieties of the Italian Alps, like those of the Pyrenees, present a strong semantic link between the SF and COND2, contrasting with the formal link which persists between the SF and SC.

Overall, there is undeniably some measure of functional commonality between the SF and SC. However, elements of the semantic values involved are on occasion common to other terms, such as COND2; the distribution of the FUÈC stem and that of these values are not coextensive. Although there is functional commonality, this is not sufficient to explain the distribution of the Fuèc stem. Interestingly, while the functional relationship between SF and SC is clearly different between a variety such as French, where the synthetic conditional still expresses temporal futurity (stronger functional commonality), and a variety such as Italian, where it no longer can (weaker functional commonality), this difference appears to have no bearing on the formal similarities of the synthetic future and conditional, since the identity of future and conditional stems in Italian is quite as strong and systematic as it is in French.

6.5 The relation between these functions

Aronoff (1994) describes how in the case of the English 'past' participle, a single morphological form is the exponent for two distinct and unrelated functions, past and passive. If either the SF or the SC were considered in isolation, one might envisage a similar approach, analysing, for example, the SC as a single screeve arbitrarily associated with the independent temporal and modal functions. However, the parallelism between the set of semantic values associated with the SF and that associated with the SC argues against such an analysis: if the set of values 'posteriority', 'possibility', 'attenuation', and 'non-assertion' were indeed arbitrary and coincidental, one would not expect to find this exact same set associated with more than one screeve. It accordingly seems more plausible to propose an analysis in which the temporal and modal values of the SF and SC are semantically related, either stemming from a common source, or deriving from each other; all the more so given the cross-linguistic tendency for 'future' forms to evolve from or into expressions of modality (Fleischman 1982: 23–4, Bybee and Pagliuca 1987).

6.5.1 *Temporality vs. modality as basic values*

In the literature specifically on French, it is most commonly assumed that the modal uses of the SF, and by implication those of the SC, are derived from their temporal meaning. A typical example is that of Vet and Kampers-Manhe (2001: 103), who assert that:

D'abord, il s'avère que le futur simple [SF] et le futur du passé [SC] connaissent les mêmes types d'emplois non temporels : l'emploi modal et l'emploi illocutionnaire. Ensuite il est plus facile de faire le lien entre leur emploi temporel et les emplois non temporels. Ainsi l'emploi modal du futur simple [. . .] s'explique-t-il par le fait qu'on situe l'évaluation de la valeur de vérité dans l'avenir [. . .] tandis que l'emploi illocutionnaire repose sur un déplacement, fictif bien sûr, de l'acte de langage dans l'avenir.[4]

---

[4] 'First, both the simple future and the future in the past present the same types of non-temporal uses: a modal use and an illocutionary use. The non-temporal uses may then be more easily linked to the temporal use. In this way, the modal use of the simple future [. . .] can be explained as situating in future time the moment at which truth value is determined [. . .] while the illocutionary use is based on a (fictitious) displacement of the speech act into future time.' (my translation)

Vet and Kampers-Manhe do not explicitly analyse the use of the SF to express possibility, but their analysis of the SC in this function suggests that it would be considered a subtype of posteriority, as the proposition in the apodosis may only occur after the fulfilment of the condition in the protasis. They are unusual in describing the attenuating future as illocutionary, but the underlying idea of the speaker metaphorically distancing himself from the proposition is a familiar one, as is the notion of ulterior verification commonly evoked to explain the epistemic use of the SF. What is most striking about all these analyses is that they present as axiomatic the assumption that the SF and SC have a basic value, and that that value is temporal rather than modal. The explanations given for the attenuating and epistemic futures are crucially reliant on this initial assumption: using the SF to indicate that the proposition will be verified at a later time, for example, is only possible if the SF intrinsically refers to later time, while using the SF to 'displace' the proposition into a time other than the moment of speaking is only an effective strategy if the SF intrinsically refers to non-present time.

The assumption that the temporal value of the SF is primary may be plausible in diachrony, assuming a meaning of temporal futurity which developed from a pragmatic inference of posteriority, and modal usages subsequently developing from the temporal uses.[5] However, applied to the synchronic system of modern French or Occitan, it might conceivably constitute a 'diachronic fallacy': there is as yet no conclusive evidence that temporal values of the SF are more basic than modal ones, or indeed vice versa, in the mind of the modern, linguistically naive, native speaker.

Barceló (2004) and Barceló and Bres (2006) argue for French that the epistemic uses are rarer, and lexically restricted to the items *être* and *avoir*; and certain of Loporcaro's (1999: 92) data for varieties of southern Italy likewise suggest that the epistemic future is in some sense marginal.[6] Loporcaro notes that the epistemic future paradigm in the variety of Agnone presents defectivity such that only the third-person forms remain, and proposes that this is because speakers are relatively unlikely to make epistemic conjectures about themselves or their hearers. In making this suggestion he follows Berretta (1994), whose corpus study on spoken Italian shows both that epistemic uses of the SF are rarer than temporal uses, and that these tokens are majoritarily third-person forms.

---

[5] Loporcaro (1999: 95) argues that modal values are primary, since in the diachronic development of future forms, temporal values develop from initial modal values (before modal values in turn emerge from those temporal values). However, the modal values involved are strikingly different: deontic modality gives rise to temporality, while epistemic modality appears to develop subsequently.

[6] Although there are clearly cross-linguistic differences: Barceló (2004) finds Italian admits a wider range of lexical items in epistemic SF contexts than French does, while Squartini (2010) describes the Italian epistemic SF as covering a wider range of semantic values than its French counterpart.

Taken together, these findings appear to indicate that it is indeed the temporal use of the SF which is basic. However, acquisition data for Italian discussed by Berretta (1994: 22) and Loporcaro (1999: 95) suggest a different view, since the epistemic use of the SF in Italian is acquired several months before the temporal use (in contrast to what one might expect given the respective frequency of the two uses in adult speech). One might also cite the cross-linguistic comparisons of Bybee and Pagliuca (1987), who find that temporal futurity is rarely the sole value associated with a given exponent, and that forms expressing this value typically also express one or more modal values.

Overall, in the absence of fuller empirical evidence, whether from typological, frequency, or acquisition studies, it is difficult to resolve the issue of which (if either) value of the SF/SC is primary. This point is well illustrated by the case of Vet and Kampers-Manhe (2001: 103): while the authors contend that an analysis treating the temporal value as primary 'présente un certain nombre d'avantages', and their analysis is certainly plausible and elegant, they provide no objective measure by which to judge how closely this analysis corresponds to the reality of the native speaker's grammar, and thus their approach can be neither confirmed nor falsified.

6.5.2 *Temporal futurity as an intrinsic component of possibility*

Iatridou's (2000) cross-linguistic study makes the particularly strong claim that the modal use of 'conditional' forms to express possibility—conditionals which she labels 'present counterfactual', exemplified by sentences such as 'If Fred was drunk, he would be louder' (Iatridou 2000: 244)—is a conversational implicature, and can be reduced to the addition of futurity and a value which she terms 'exclusion feature' (ExclF). Comparing examples of present counterfactual conditionals in English and Greek, Iatridou observes that they consistently appear to share certain morphological features: forms which have the appearance of future morphology and past morphology. She considers the future morphology here to bear real future meaning. However, the apparently past morphology is more problematic, especially given Iatridou's implicit assumption that there are real morphemes of the classical type which directly and consistently associate a form with a meaning. In the English example 'If Fred was drunk, he would be louder', although the verbs display morphology which is associated with past tense, the functional content 'past' is absent, since the speaker's belief is in fact that 'Fred isn't drunk now' and the utterance thus refers not to past time, but to a time which overlaps with the present. Iatridou's solution is to redefine the semantic content associated with the 'past' morpheme as the 'exclusion feature', formulated as 'whatever x is the topic of the utterance, this x is not the x of the speaker' or, more formally, as 'T(x) excludes C(x)'. ExclF may be applied to time—the topic time is not the utterance time—in which case Iatridou claims that it should be interpreted as temporal past, though her formulation seems rather to refer to non-presentness. Alternatively, it may be applied to possible worlds—the topic world is not the speaker's (i.e. the actual) world—giving the interpretation of counterfactuality. Iatridou's overall contention is then that counterfactuality is an implicature which arises from the combination of real future morphology and ExclF, that is to say that futurity is a necessary element of the counterfactual conditional.

In the light of this hypothesis, Iatridou proceeds to an analysis of the Romance conditional derived from the infinitive + HABERE construction, arguing that despite its usual name this screeve does not in fact constitute a separate mood, but is instead part of the indicative. Within her account counterfactuality arises from the combination of future and ExclF; in Greek, where the future is analytic, these features may each have a distinct exponent, but in a language such as French, which has a synthetic future, Iatridou expects that both future and ExclF should be marked on the same word-form. As the French conditional presents a stem resembling that found in the future, and desinences resembling those found in the imperfective past, she finds in the forms of the conditional 'excellent candidates for what a French verb would look like if, in the indicative, the future and past morphologies combined' (Iatridou 2000: 267). Given this observation and her findings for Greek and English, she assumes that a segmentation into future stem (with future meaning) and imperfective past desinences (with ExclF meaning) can indeed be effected, leading to the conclusion that there is no need to invoke a third mood to account for the synthetic conditional, which is merely another indicative form.

There are a number of problems attendant on Iatridou's account, chiefly arising from theoretical assumptions. For instance, Iatridou assumes that the stem of the SC is a future stem with future meaning. Yet the stem in question is not a distinctively 'future' stem, precisely because it is the stem both of the SF and of the SC. This is not merely a synchronic, but also a diachronic, fact, concerning all Romance languages with have-futures and have-conditionals: at no point in the history of these forms has there existed a distinctive 'future stem'.

The choice of treating the SF as primitive and the SC as derived appears to arise less from any empirical observation than from an a priori assumption. For French (and many varieties of Occitan), it might be argued that it is preferable to derive the SC from the SF on the grounds that the formal mechanism of the derivation is more elegant: the SC may be straightforwardly derived by combining the stem found in the SF with the desinences found in the imperfect, whereas arriving at the SF from the stem found in the SC and a set of desinences resembling the present indicative forms of *avoir* 'have' involves more complex rules. However, this line of argument is much less persuasive for Italian, where the desinences found in the SC, derived from the preterite of *avere* 'have', are similar but crucially not all identical to those found in the preterite. Most questionable of all is the theory-driven assumption that either one of these forms must be derived from the other; there is no a priori reason why this should be the case, nor any compelling argument in the raw data to suggest it. Instead, the assumption must be imposed by the choice of a given theoretical framework: working within a morpheme-based theory is likely to require such a derivation, which would not be necessary within a Word-and-Paradigm approach.

The theoretical problems with Iatridou's account render the evidence which she adduces in support of her claim unconvincing as far as Romance is concerned. The Occitan data discussed above raise further difficulties: in cases of asymmetry, the SC (although expressing possibility) does not share the stem of the SF, while in many Pyrenean varieties the SC cannot be used to express futurity, and in the varieties of the Italian Alps the SF itself no longer expresses the value which Iatridou considers primary. Even with respect to her French data, she does not address the non-temporal uses attested for the SF; attempting to resolve this problem by redefining the meaning of the 'future' stem to a more general value would create a serious difficulty for the main insight which her study claims.

6.5.3 *Projection*

Precisely such a redefinition is made for French by Touratier (1996) and Revaz (2009), who consider that the modal and temporal values of the SF and SC represent contextual instantiations of a more general underlying value 'projection'.

Like Iatridou, Touratier adopts a strictly morpheme-based and compositional approach,[7] in which each verb form is assumed to consist of a stem and affixes, each associated with a distinctive meaning: the SC, for example, is analysed as lexical stem + future marker + imperfect marker + PN marker, making it a 'futur imparfait' and thus to be assigned to the indicative, as are the SF and imperfect indicative (Touratier 1996: 38). However, his discussion of both SF and SC is located under the heading of 'morphèmes de mode'; his argument for unifying the two originates in the assumption that the modal usages of the SF should be treated not as incidental to, but on a par with its temporal usages.

For Touratier (1996: 176–7), the basic meaning associated with what he considers a future morpheme is that of 'projection', referring to an event which is envisaged; its observed modal or temporal values result from context and interpretation. Although he considers temporal uses of the SF the most natural and intuitive, he finds that modal uses cannot easily be reduced to a basic temporal value. Revaz (2009: 153–5), who further develops this analysis, characterizes the temporal instantiation of the feature 'projective' as projection into future time, and the modal

---

[7] Touratier (1996: 11) is clearly aware that form and function are neither identical nor indissociable, as he explicitly makes the point that the traditional names of grammatical categories, while suggesting a semantic value, refer instead to morphological form. Nevertheless, his analysis endeavours to assign a consistent meaning to each form.

instantiation as projection into a possible world. She points out that this approach offers the advantage of capturing the intuition that the temporal and modal values of the SF are semantically close, and in practice difficult to separate. Touratier's classification of these values overlaps to some extent with Dendale's (2001), including temporal posteriority, conjecture, and attenuation; his additional class (Touratier 1996: 181)[8] of possibility (17), however, refers not to SC constructions, but to objections envisaged at and referring to the present moment, and may plausibly be considered a subtype of conjecture:

(17)   C'était, **penserez**-vous peut-être, participer à l'erreur que je dénonçais au début (*Europe*)
       'You may think this meant falling into the error which I criticized at the outset.'

Interestingly, while Touratier and Revaz generally concur in their classification, they differ in their analysis of the 'gnomic' future expressing universal truths (e.g. *Qui vivra verra* 'Time will tell'). Touratier assigns this usage to the class of temporal futures (assuming that it expresses advice drawn from experience for use thereafter, and that the universal bearing of the statement arises not from the SF but from universal or generic constituents such as *ne … jamais* 'never'), while Revaz considers it essentially modal. The disparity in their analyses might be taken to suggest that the difference between 'temporal' and 'modal' values associated with the SF is entirely one of contextual instantiation, and that the 'gnomic' cases constitute a grey area for which the context is simply not sufficient; thus rather than two discrete classes of values, the uses of the SF constitute a continuum within a single value 'projective'.

Since the SC may serve as FIP, and since it formally resembles the stem found in the synthetic future and the desinences found in the imperfect indicative, Touratier (1996: 111–12) attributes to the SC the values 'projection' (synthetic future) and 'non actuel' (imperfect indicative; the description of 'non actuel' is remarkably close to that of Iatridou's Exclusion Feature). The modal and temporal uses of the SC are therefore assumed to be unified as they are for the SF (Touratier 1996: 182–3).

Touratier's analysis, like Iatridou's, springs from a morpheme-based framework which assumes a direct association of form and function, and thus distributions of form which reflect natural classes. The assumption that the SF and SC necessarily share functional content because they share formal content, or vice versa, is clearly problematic in the light of the Occitan data examined above, in which the distributions of formal and functional content are not always coextensive. However, Touratier's basic insight that temporal and modal uses may stem from a single underlying

---

[8] Touratier also describes a class of futures of protestation, but finds no attestations later than the seventeenth century.

value offers an elegant and intuitively appealing account of the values associated with the SF and SC in French, and the SF in Occitan. It seems plausible that the semantic content common to SF and SC is the value 'projection' rather than temporal futurity, although the lack of evidential and temporal instantiations for the SC in certain varieties of Occitan remains to be accounted for. The lack of these instantiations, and cases such as that of COND2 in the Pyrenees, where a value stemming from projection is associated with a form outside FUÈC, show that even when the semantic content associated with the SF and SC is more accurately described, the mapping between form and function remains arbitrary.

6.6 Conclusion

Recent work on other Romance languages, particularly French, has shown that the basic value associated with the SF and SC is not uncontroversially temporal futurity. The SF is used for values of temporal posteriority, but also of eventuality, epistemic modality, and attenuation; these may plausibly be regarded as context-sensitive temporal or modal interpretations of a more general value, such as 'projection'. In French, the SC shares these values; however, in Italian the SC has long been replaced as exponent of FIP by the periphrasis SC + PST.PTCP. In varieties of Occitan, the functional asymmetry is equally pronounced: in some varieties, as in Italian, the SC is no longer the exponent of FIP, while in others it is doubtful that the SC can have an evidential reading. Although it seems clear that there is semantic content common to both SF and SC, some elements of this content may be shared with other forms, such as COND2, and not all the semantic content of the SF is shared by the SC: a natural class defined by projection or by any of its constituent values does not correspond exactly to the distribution of the FUÈC stem. The distribution of the FUÈC stem cannot therefore be considered as exclusively determined by a semantic value; instead, the stem identity most commonly observed for FUÈC is at least partially formal and arbitrary.

The formal coherence of the distribution FUÈC is likewise a more complex affair in Occitan than has been observed for standard Romance varieties. In the majority of cases, the identity of stem between SF and SC resulting from regular historical change is preserved; where analogical change reshapes the FUÈC stem, it tends to affect the SF and SC equally, or even, more rarely, to reinforce the identity between them. However, there are also many attestations of asymmetry, constituting further evidence for the arbitrary nature of the formal identity between SF and SC stems: the fact that the identity can be broken suggests that coherence elsewhere is not solely due to extramorphological factors. Furthermore, even where asymmetry is due to regular phonological change, speakers do not invariably 'repair' the resulting difference of stem, to the extent that the new pattern becomes morphologized and spread by analogy to other lexemes, sometimes creating very stark disparities between the stem of the SF and that of the SC. Interestingly, the novel, asymmetrical distributions do not appear to align with distinctions of function: they are not significantly more common in the varieties in which the functional commonality of SF and SC is weakest, nor do they seem to involve formal splits between the individual semantic values of each screeve. The patterns produced are arbitrary, as is the mapping between distributions of forms and distributions of functions.

The data are thus highly problematic for morphemic analyses: not only does the relation between form and function not appear isomorphic, it is not even necessarily consistent, as the distribution of stems across paradigm cells can vary extensively between lexemes. Equally, although diachronically the distribution Fuèc does seem to have psychological reality to the speaker, Fuèc resists a canonical morphomic analysis: unlike canonical morphomes such as PYTA, Fuèc still presents some measure of functional commonality, while displaying lesser formal coherence than would be expected of a morpheme.

The difference between Fuèc and canonical morphomes should not, however, be taken as grounds for rejecting a morpheme analysis entirely, as the notion of autonomous morphology has significant explanatory value for handling the arbitrary mapping between SF/SC forms and their respective functions. Indeed, Aronoff's initial characterization of the morpheme predicts the existence of distributions partly resulting from autonomous morphology and partly determined by extramorphological criteria, while Maiden (2011c) identifies just such a case at the interface between phonology and morphology, leading one to expect the existence of weakly morphomic phenomena in which syntactic/semantic criteria interact with morphological motivation. It seems most reasonable to consider Fuèc as an example of precisely such a phenomenon, in which an essentially arbitrary stem distribution is partially underwritten by functional motivations. This new attestation of a weakly morphomic pattern, previously attributed solely to the functional motivations which partially determine it, suggests that there may be more extant cases of autonomously morphological distributions than previously thought—i.e. cases in which a distribution hitherto ascribed to purely extramorphological factors may be partially determined by purely morphological factors.

7

Compositionality and change in conditionals and counterfactuals in Romance*

NIGEL VINCENT

7.1 Introduction

In a seminal contribution to the theory of morphology, Mark Aronoff (1994: 25) argued that 'the mapping from morphosyntax to phonological realization is not direct but passes through an intermediate level' and he coined the term 'morphome' for the entities that populate this level. He went on to note that '[i]t is possible to have a singleton morphosyntactic set mapped onto a singleton morphomic set, which is itself mapped onto a singleton morphophonological set' concluding nonetheless that 'it is morphomes like F_{en} [= English perfect and passive participles] that truly earn their name'. Characteristic of such an element on Aronoff's analysis is that there is no shared content to the features [PERFECT] and [PASSIVE] which map onto the morphome. Similarly, the realizations of this morphome are phonetically various, including the suffixes -ed and -en, ablaut of the stem vowel, zero, and various other minor irregular patterns. Yet for every verb in the language the perfect and passive participles have the same form, however various the modes of constructing that form may be. Hence, the only unity is at the level of the morphology, which to that extent is, or can be, autonomous.

* This chapter was first presented at the 2nd Oxford Workshop on Romance Morphology, 8–10 October 2010. I am grateful to the organizers for inviting me to participate, to all those who offered comments and suggestions at the time, and to the editors for their comments on the written version. Thanks in particular to fellow enthusiasts for conditionals Jennie Parkinson and Louise Esher for supplying me with copies of their work and for the inspiration I have drawn from them. Needless to say, I am alone to blame for any errors or misinterpretations this chapter may contain. Unless otherwise indicated, all translations, both from primary and secondary sources, are my own.

Martin Maiden has developed this argument for autonomy in the diachronic domain in a number of important studies, adding force to Aronoff's original claims by showing how morphological formations which lack semantic, syntactic, or phonological motivation may nonetheless survive and prosper over time. Thus, for example, already in early French for a number of verbs the same irregular stem is found in the present subjunctive and the participle—e.g. *ayant* 'having' and *aie* 'have.sbjv' from the verb *avoir* 'to have' and *puissant* 'being able' and *puisse* 'be able. sbjv' from the verb *pouvoir* 'be able'—even though there is no set of morphosyntactic features the forms share and even though the presence of this stem in the participle is not justified etymologically in the way that it is for a pair like *sache* 'know.sbjv' and *sachant* 'knowing'. It seems, rather, as if the pair of forms 'present subjunctive and participle' have become linked in the morphology alone and that this pairing has spread to other verbs during the later history of the language (Maiden 1996a). Such diachronic evidence is important because the spread of the morphomically linked pair implies that it came to have psychological reality in the minds of successive generations of speakers despite the absence of syntactic or phonological motivation. Hence, we must be dealing with something more than a coincidence or a historical accident. The change has shape and direction of a kind that is only stable if we assume a model of grammar which recognizes Aronoff's morphomic level (Maiden 2005a).

In the course of developing this argument, however, Maiden and his co-workers have operated with a narrower definition of the morpheme, which now applies only to those instances that, in Aronoff's words, 'truly earn their name'. Thus, Maiden (2001b: 442) frames his discussion of the Spanish PYTA stem—another case where the unifying generalization holds only at the level of the morphology—around the definition of a morpheme as 'an autonomous distributional regularity of morphological paradigms which cannot be expressed either in terms of phonological structure or of meaning, yet which is nonetheless systematically predictable'. O'Neill (2011b: 70, and this volume) offers a similar definition, which he attributes to Aronoff, though, as we have seen, Aronoff himself is rather more nuanced. At first sight this may seem simply a definitional question, but wider issues come into play. Whereas Aronoff's account emphasizes the place of morphology within an overall model of natural language structure and function, Maiden's redefinition risks shifting the focus onto morphology alone, although, as he recognizes, there is always the need to examine the points at which morphological and other generalizations overlap (Maiden 2011c: 87). This is consistent with his general view that the morphomic level is potentially present even in cases which appear to be non-morphologically motivated (Maiden 2005a: 137–9). That said, the balance of the historical evidence appears to argue that motivation is the primary or default circumstance. While there may be cases such as the French subjunctive–participle pairing or the Spanish PYTA stem in which a morpheme in the narrow sense demonstrates its historical independence, there is a much larger body of cases—broadly those which fall under the heading 'grammaticalization'—in which semantic, phonetic, and morphological change appear to be inextricably linked. If we put aside such evidence, there is a danger that we will slip from arguing that morphology may at times display autonomous properties to treating morphology as an intrinsically autonomous domain. While the case for the former is entirely persuasive—not least because of the examples that Aronoff and Maiden have adduced—the latter seems to me untenable both methodologically and theoretically. Inflectional systems may display autonomous properties but they are not insulated from the remainder of the linguistic system, and indeed they are often, and maybe usually, motivated by the properties of other parts of that system.

What is required therefore is a dataset where we can study the interaction of these various mechanisms in an integrated way. The history of Romance conditional verb forms involves changes in all linguistic dimensions, syntactic and phonological as well as morphological, and thus suggests itself as a natural candidate for this kind of enquiry.[1] Moreover, the fact that this dataset is the product of changes between Latin and Romance makes it easier to set it against the larger picture of Romance inflectional morphology that Maiden and his colleagues have been studying (cf. the contributions to this volume and to Maiden *et al.* 2011). It is valuable too that the changes are well documented over a long historical span and across a wide range of different outcomes in the individual languages. In addition, we can benefit from the fact that the literature contains a number of explicit proposals for the syntax and semantics of these forms, something which is crucial if we are to be sure that semantic connections have been broken in particular instances.

The organization of the chapter is as follows. In Section 7.2, we review the structural space for changes within a model of grammar that recognizes three separate components or levels: syntax–semantics, morphology, phonology–phonetics, while Section 7.3 looks briefly at the issue of compositionality which underlies standard accounts of structure on the morphosyntactic level and the cross-linguistic semantic account of the conditional that has been proposed by Iatridou (2000) and

---

[1] There is one big downside to this choice, namely the vastness of the relevant literatures on the one hand on the history of the Romance patterns and on the other on the semantics and syntax of conditionals. It should be clear therefore that what is offered here is in no sense a fully referenced *historique du problème*, although I will try to cover the main avenues of recent research. For the older Romanist literature see Pountain (1983) and Harris (1986) among others; an excellent analysis and synthesis of more recent contributions is to be found in Parkinson (2009: chapter 2). The work of the leading theoretician of recent years on the semantics of conditionals is collected in Kratzer (2012). For reasons of space I will limit the focus here to conditional forms deriving from Latin infinitive + *habere*, and I will not address, or address only in passing, other conditional and counterfactual expressions deriving from the Latin pluperfect indicative—as exemplified in some southern Italian dialects (Rohlfs 1968: §603) and in the so-called second conditional of Occitan (Esher 2011)—or pluperfect subjunctive, as in Sicilian (Bentley 2000a, 2000b).

von Fintel and Iatridou (2008). We turn in Section 7.4 to the origin of the Romance verb forms, and consider the differences between the Italo-Romance forms that derive from the perfect of *habere* and those in Italy and elsewhere which involve the imperfect (Parkinson 2009), building particularly on the insights of Viara Bourova's work on later Latin texts. We also consider here the question of the syntactic representations to be assigned to these emergent forms (D'hulst 2004, Slobbe 2004). Section 7.5 is devoted to the issue of the range of different uses of the conditional forms in the modern languages and whether they can be subsumed under a single unified semantics (with appropriate interfaces to the pragmatics). In Section 7.6 we return to the issue of compositionality and the possibility, most clearly formulated by Dahl (1997), that forms may become internally non-compositional and yet continue to enter into compositional relations with other parts of the verbal system. In Section 7.7 we examine some particular issues that arise in the case of compound conditionals and in Section 7.8 we sum up and draw some overall theoretical conclusions.

7.2 The structural space for change

To appreciate the force and originality of Maiden's argument, it is instructive to see how it alters our understanding of the conceptual space within which language change operates. We may assume as a pre-theoretical given that languages consist of groupings of items which link form and meaning, signs in the Saussurean sense. We can assume too that while the sound–meaning relation for individual signs is arbitrary, complex signs will typically display a degree of motivation, to use once again de Saussure's term. These are the core conditions for any natural language and the norm against which to define divergences of various kinds.[2]

Such an ontology allows, of course, for classic Neo-grammarian sound change operating 'mit blinde Notwendigkeit', and leading to alternations such as Spanish *digo* 'I say' vs. *dice* 'he says' or Italian *muoio* 'I die' vs. *moriamo* 'we die'. In extreme cases, the effect of sound change may so obscure the connection between related forms as to create the potential for suppletion, as when the reduction of the initial consonant cluster in Latin *latum* 'carried' (< *tlatum) breaks the transparent link with *tuli* 'I have carried'. Operating in the other direction (Sturtevant's Paradox), analogy as traditionally understood and as recently revived, for example by Fischer

---

[2] I do not wish to prejudge here the issue of (im)perfectionism in natural languages (Maiden 2005*a*: 137–9). Whether or not one accepts Maiden's claim that there exists 'a seamless link between what seem to be erratically local morphomic phenomena and the fundamental and universal principles of iconicity', the fact remains that the natural semiotic condition for a language is constant associations of form and meaning and the combinations thereof (cf. our discussion of compositionality in §7.3 below)—given the goal of communication, things could hardly be otherwise.

(2007: §3.5), may lead to the (re-)establishment of motivation as in the Italian generalization of the first person singular present ending to the imperfect:

	old Italian	modern Italian
1st singular present	*canto*	*canto*
3rd singular present	*canta*	*canta*
1st singular imperfect	*cantava*	*cantavo*
3rd singular imperfect	*cantava*	*cantava*

In this context Maiden's contribution is to show how the morphomic layer can serve to shape and direct the course of sound changes, suppletions (whether phonetically or lexically derived), and analogies, thereby revealing itself to be an active force within the overall profile of change in linguistic form.

Just as phonetic change is driven by intrinsic tendencies linked to the nature of the human apparatus for the production and perception of sound, so on the content side of language there are developments due to natural semantic directions of travel, changes which can ultimately lead to new morphosyntactic material via the mechanism of grammaticalization, as when Latin *cantare habebat* 'he had to sing' becomes Spanish *cantaría* 'he would sing'. In such cases, a parallelism between form and meaning, a kind of iconicity, means that there may be linked patterns of semantic 'bleaching' (obligation > futurity) and phonetic reduction ([ha'beːbat] > ['ia]), though as we shall see these two developments do not necessarily operate in phase with each other. In such a situation the presence of a morphomic stratum could be revealed if a pattern of form persists even though the sustaining semantic links have disappeared. This possibility is envisaged in Esher (2012a) with respect to the development of the conditionals in some dialects of Occitan (see below for further discussion). In similar vein, once the semantic connections between the items that come together in the type of suppletion deriving from lexical merger rather than from phonetic opacity have been levelled out (cf. Börjars and Vincent, 2011, for the mechanisms at work here), there is room for the morphome to take over and shape future developments as argued in Maiden (2004a). Conversely, forms which have lost association with their earlier content may acquire a role in expressing new content via exaptation or refunctionalization (Lass 1990, Smith 2011a and this volume). This latter kind of development may be seen as anti-morphomic (again in the narrow sense of morphome) in that the purely formal structures do not survive as such but acquire instead new semantic supports.

In all the instances where a case for the morphome is argued it is then crucial to demonstrate lack of both semantic and phonetic motivation for the forms that are grouped together. For the most part we put the phonological dimension on one side in the present contribution and concentrate on the issue of semantic connectedness between the forms entering the claimed morphomic pattern and the core property of compositionality which underpins such connectedness.

7.3 Compositionality and the semantics of the conditional

Compositionality is a vast and complex issue, as the contributions to Werning *et al.* (2012) attest. Here we will have to make do with principle in its starkest form. The following classic formulation is from Szabó (2009: 1):

> The meaning of a complex expression is fully determined by its structure and the meanings of its constituents—once we fix what the parts mean and how they are put together we have no more leeway regarding the meaning of the whole. This is the principle of compositionality.

It is true that, as Higginbotham (2007: 426) observes, 'understood in this way, however, the compositionality thesis verges on the trivial. For, there being nothing else but the parts of a sentence or discourse, and the way they are combined [...] compositionality simply follows.' Both Szabó and Higginbotham go on to discuss some of the standard challenges to compositionality—context, opacity, and the like—that arise in the philosophical literature and render the issue less trivial. Our concern here, however, is with a different kind of non-triviality, namely the circumstance in which semantic compositionality can be shown to exist although this is not at first sight evident from the surface configuration of the morphosyntactic elements. A circumstance, in other words, in which the form–meaning iconicity alluded to above breaks down. A simple example is provided by von Fintel and Iatridou (2007), who demonstrate that the meaning components of an English sentence like *To get good cheese you only have to go to the store on the corner* require the word *only* to be interpreted as 'not (other) than', in short to have the same underlying semantic composition as appears transparently on the surface in the French expression *ne ... que*.

   Nearer to home for present purposes is another case study by the same scholars, in which they demonstrate a cross-linguistic tendency for what they call weak modality, the equivalent of English *ought*, to be expressed by a combination of strong modality (roughly English *must*) plus the appropriate morphosyntactic expression of counterfactuality in the language in question (von Fintel and Iatridou 2008). The Romance languages fall neatly under this typological umbrella. Counterfactuals are expressed by the conditional and the meaning 'ought' is indeed derived by taking the 'must' verb (*devoir, dovere, deber*, etc.) and putting it in the conditional: *devrait, dovrebbe, debería*, and so on, as exemplified in the pair of Italian sentences in (1):[3]

---

[3] Reasons of space do not permit detailed treatment here of necessity modals other than reflexes of *debere*, but it seems clear that von Fintel and Iatridou's generalization applies to these as well, both to items derived from different Latin sources such as Catalan *cal* 'must' vs. *caldria* 'ought' (< Lat. *calere* 'be warm') and to borrowings such as Romanian *trebuie* 'must' vs. *ar trebui* 'ought' (< OCSl *trěbovati* 'need, require'). My thanks to Max Wheeler, Anabella Niculescu, and Mary MacRobert for their advice on these items.

(1)   a. Giorgio deve   rispondere alla   lettera entro domani.
         George   must.PRS.3SG   reply.INF   to-the letter   by   tomorrow
         'George must reply to the letter by tomorrow.'
      b. Giorgio dovrebbe   rispondere alla   lettera entro domani.
         George   must.COND.3SG   reply.INF   to-the letter   by   tomorrow
         'George ought to reply to the letter by tomorrow.'

In turn, the counterfactual component of the meaning here can itself be further broken down, since it transpires that the expression of counterfactuality, as evidenced in a wide range of languages, is itself made up of two semantically more primitive terms: [PAST] plus [FUTURE] (Iatridou 2000).[4] Thus, consider the Italian example in (2), where the verb form *vincesse* in the protasis is in the past subjunctive:

(2)   Se vincesse   la   Juventus, i   tifosi   del   Milan
      if win.PST.SBJV.3SG the   Juventus   the supporters   of-the Milan
      sarebbero   molto   contenti.
      be.COND.3PL   very   happy
      'If Juventus won, the supporters of Milan would be very happy.'

In such a case it is natural to ask whether the hypothetical meaning derives from the past or the subjunctive property of the verb. Despite an intuitive sense that the subjunctive expresses unreality, Iatridou provides convincing evidence to support the view that it is the past value which is the constant companion of the counterfactual meaning cross-linguistically, and hence is the relevant property here. Indeed, staying within Romance, it suffices to translate (2) into French to see that the past value is indeed what counts:

(3)   Si la Juventus gagnait, les fans du Milan seraient très heureux.

The verb *gagnait* 'win.IMPF.IND' here is indicative but the hypothetical value remains. The reason is not hard to find and has often been observed before (see references in Iatridou 2000). The past in the antecedent of a CF expresses remoteness either in time or reality; it is this common semantic feature which accounts for the fact that pasts are used in the expression of conditionals and counterfactuals in so many languages. In the semantics that Iatridou proposes, this property is expressed through an exclusion feature, whereby if the topic time is excluded we get a past interpretation and if the topic world is excluded we get a counterfactual

---

[4] Here and in what follows we adopt the convention of using small capitals to indicate semantic components. It should be clear, although we will not go into details here, that these labels are themselves shorthand for a more precise analysis. In particular we will assume that tense features such as [PAST] and [FUTURE] can be cashed out in neo-Reichenbachian terms as reviewed and referenced in Vincent (2011) and developed in detail in Schaden (2007). On the larger issue of the semantic connectedness of time and modality, see Condoravdi (2002).

interpretation.[5] The future component is a subsidiary one which expresses the relation between the excluded time/world and the consequent action. It is worth noting, however, that this additional future component need not be overtly expressed. In many languages a counterfactual can be expressed by two past tenses or two pluperfects:

(4) a. Se Piero veniva   ieri,   vedeva   la   partita.
        if Piero come.IMPF.IND.3SG yesterday see.IMPF.IND.3SG the match
        'If Piero had come yesterday, he would have seen the match.'
     b. Hvis Peter købte   kage, lavede   Anne kaffe. [Danish]
        if   Peter buy.PST.3SG cake   make.PST.3SG Anne coffee
        'If Peter bought cake, Anne would make coffee.'
     c. Had he not resembled my father as he slept, I had done 't (*Macbeth* II, ii)

Adding the two parts of the story together, we can now derive the overall equivalence expressed in (5):

(5) OUGHT = MUST + PAST + FUTURE

Assuming von Fintel and Iatridou are right in their generalization about the link between the expression of strong and weak necessity, the important thing from our point of view is that it follows that this compositionality can continue to hold even when the separate identity of the individual morphosyntactic ingredients of the construction has long since been obscured. Thus, as Iatridou (2000: n. 42) observes, we would not wish to maintain that the synchronic conditional is derived from the infinitive, a conclusion already reached by Matthews (1982), nor on her account is it strictly necessary for the forms of the future and conditional to be connected. Such connections, when discernible, help to reinforce the argument but their absence is not a licence to ignore the semantic links between the forms and the compositional account by which they may be derived. We return to the question of what morphosyntactic structures should be postulated for this construction in Section 7.4.2.

7.4 The origin of the Romance conditionals

The etymology of the Romance conditionals is not contested: forms such as Spanish *cantaría*, French *chanterait*, Occitan *cantariá* '(s)he would sing' derive from Latin *cantare habebat*, that is to say the Latin infinitive plus the imperfect of the verb

---

[5] There is a traditional and rather sterile debate as to whether the conditional in Romance is to be considered a tense or a mood. It may appear at first sight that to follow Iatridou is to come down on the side of tense, but the semantics of exclusion she proposes operates at a level removed from the particularities of individual times and worlds. It therefore helpfully finds the common ground between temporal and modal properties rather than opting for one or the other.

habere 'have'. Although a form from the same source is attested in some Italian dialects and in early poetry, it seems in such cases to be a borrowing from Occitan and is mainly restricted to literary registers (Parkinson 2009). The autochthonous conditional in most northern and in central dialects, and hence the modern standard language, derives instead from the infinitive combined with the perfect of *habere*: thus *cantare habuit > canterebbe*. In southern dialects and in Sardinian, the periphrasis with *habere* appears not to have taken root and other strategies to express conditionality and counterfactuality prevail (cf. footnote 1 and references there).

7.4.1 *Semantics*

It will be clear that the etymology of both formations fits well into Iatridou's typological scheme discussed above, with compositionality being respected at the level of both form and content, a kind of iconicity. Nonetheless, there are three questions that need to be addressed. In the first place we may wonder what pressures led to the emergence of the periphrasis. The most persuasive answer, and one already suggested in Fleischman (1982), is the need to express embedded tense relationships occasioned by the rise of finite subordination patterns introduced by *quod* or *quia* which were replacing the Latin accusative and infinitive construction.[6] But why then, we may ask, was recourse to this formation necessary given that Latin had an existing periphrasis, namely the combination of the participle in -*urus* plus the past of *esse* 'be', a pattern moreover which equally respects the requirement for a combination of the ingredients [PAST] and [FUTURE] (Bourova 2008)? Consider the following (= Bourova's (25)):

(6) Moriturus   enim   erat,   nisi   fuisset   sanatus   a Christo
     die.FUT.PTCP in-fact be.IMPF if-not be.PLPF.SBJV cleanse.PST.PTCP by Christ
     'He would have died if he had not been cleansed by Christ'
                (Ambrosius Mediolanensis, *Expositio euangelii secundum Lucam*, 5)

Here the counterfactual meaning of the expression *moriturus erat* 'he would have died' is built out of a participle with a relative tense value of futurity and an auxiliary providing the deictic anchor of the absolute past tense (see Vincent, 2011: 426–9, for further discussion).

As Bourova shows, the overlap between this construction and the nascent Romance pattern is striking. She writes (2008: 278):

---

[6] Although we won't go into the matter in detail, it should be noted that if Fleischman's argument is correct, we have here a case of a grammaticalization pattern which originates in a subordinate context, contrary to the views of some theorists that grammaticalization always starts in main clauses and direct discourse situations (cf. most recently Detges, 2012).

[...] il est justifié de voir dans les constructions des participes futurs avec *esse* au passé une sorte de conditionnel. Il est d'ailleurs particulièrement frappant que ces exemples présentent les mêmes particularités que {Infinitif, *habere* au passé}, tant en ce qui concerne la gamme des significations couvertes qu'en ce qui concerne les marques lexicales qui les accompagnent et les contextes d'occurrence.[7]

We need not investigate here the reasons for the eventual loss of the *-urus* construction; see Vincent and Bentley (2001) for a suggestion and Bourova (2008: 279–80) for a counter-proposal.

Research based on the corpus of material collected by Bourova also sheds light on the question of the order of the elements in this periphrasis. Bourova and Tasmowski (2007) show that there is a clear correlation between the order 'infinitive + *habere*' and what they call alethic or epistemic modality, in which what is at stake is the source of our knowledge of how things are ('la modalité de l'ÊTRE'). In contrast, when what is at issue is deontic modality or how things can be made to be ('la modalité du FAIRE'), the more frequent order is for the auxiliary to precede the infinitive.

Finally, there is the question of what determines the choice between the items that in different ways realize Iatridou's [PAST] component of counterfactual meaning, the imperfect and the perfect of Latin *habere*, and which yield the difference between Italian as compared to Western Romance. In this connection, it should be noted that both perfective and imperfective forms of *habere* are consistent with Iatridou's typology. Since for her the key factor in counterfactuality is the exclusion feature associated with pastness, the aspectual properties of the verb are free to vary, in particular as between perfective and imperfective. It is significant therefore that the Romance developments show variation exactly where this claimed universal model admits it. And yet, as Bourova (2007) demonstrates, the variation in Romance is not free. There are noteworthy differences in the grammatical distribution of the *habui* and *habebam* types: the perfect auxiliary is more commonly attested in main clauses and with readings linked to the deictic coordinates of time and person while the imperfect occurs in subordinate constructions where relative time—the future with respect to the past—is at issue. In addition, '[...] il existe une connexion entre la forme à l'imparfait et une orientation prospective, la "prédestination", alors que ceci n'est pas le cas pour la construction avec le parfait qui, elle, s'associe à un sens déontique ou contrefactuel' (Bourova 2008: 272).[8] Given such a striking difference in

---

[7] '[...] it is justified to see in the constructions consisting of a future participle plus *esse* in the past a kind of conditional. It is moreover particularly striking that these examples present the same peculiarities as {Infinitive, *habere* in the past}, whether in relation to the meanings expressed, the lexical properties that accompany them or the contexts of occurrence.'

[8] 'There is a link between the form in the imperfect and a prospective orientation, "predestination", while this is not the case for the construction with the perfect, which is associated with a deontic or counterfactual sense.'

distribution it is surprising that the two patterns should with the passage of time have become synonymous.

There is no standard answer to the conundrum (see Parkinson, 2009: 10–12, for a clear assessment of the alternatives), but one possibility which has not to my knowledge so far been canvassed is that the changes are to be linked to the shifting balance between the perfect and the imperfect in Latin. The Latin perfect is in origin a simple past/aorist, while the imperfect develops from a periphrasis with a specifically progressive meaning.[9] However, a recent study by Haverling (2010) notes a number of examples in later Latin where the imperfect occurs in contexts where classically the perfect would have been expected. This phenomenon is found particularly in the translated Bible but also in later writers such as the fourth-century Ammianus Marcellinus. Thus:

(7)   a. et occultabat se mensibus quinque (Vulgate, Luke 1.24)
        'and she hid away for five months'
     b. Et pugnabatur [. . .] diebus aliquot (Amm 20.6.5)
        'the battle lasted for several days'

On the basis of evidence of this kind, Haverling concludes (2010: 20):

Ce changement dans la fonction du parfait porte à un nouveau chevauchement entre le parfait et l'imparfait dans la fonction d'indiquer un aperçu global d'une situation dans le passé et nous trouvons souvent l'imparfait là où le latin classique aurait préféré le parfait. Il y a donc un déplacement dans le rapport entre le parfait et l'imparfait, où l'imparfait semble conquérir un peu de territoire qui auparavant avait appartenu au parfait.[10]

In the context of such an erosion of the semantic barriers between the two parts of the paradigm, and in a construction where in the end the choice of aspect is less important than the temporal value, it is not implausible that different regions would come up with different solutions, and perhaps not surprising that Italy should opt for the more conservative, in a sense more classical, alternative while in the West it is the innovative construction which prevails.

7.4.2 *Syntax*

Like all periphrases, the construction with *habere* must at the outset have been an independent syntactic construction. And clearly in the end it has become integrated into the verbal paradigm. On the assumption, supported not least by the evidence for

---

[9] For a helpful summary of the pre-history of the Latin forms, see Haug (2008). I am grateful to the author for supplying me with a copy of his paper.

[10] 'This change in the function of the perfect leads a new overlap between the perfect and the imperfect when the function is to indicate a situation in the past viewed as a whole and we often find the imperfect in contexts where Classical Latin would have preferred the perfect. There is thus a shift in the relation between the perfect and the imperfect, with the imperfect appearing to have conquered some of the territory that had previously belonged to the perfect.'

morphomic (in the narrow sense) distribution, that paradigmatic patterning should be modelled in terms of a formal paradigm (Vincent, 2011, and references there) and not in terms of syntactic tree structure as in Distributed Morphology (DM), there must have been a transition from one sub-component of grammar to another. What then are the processes that led up to that?

In his Minimalist account, D'hulst (2004) argues that, since in the first stage of the development *habere* had independent lexical content as expressing possession or modality, the starting point must have been a biclausal construction with *habere* in the main clause and the infinitive in an embedded complement clause. Only once the future-in-the-past meaning has developed does *habere* come to occupy a functional projection within the same clause as the lexical infinitive leading to a monoclausal construction. Finally, infinitive and auxiliary fuse through the process of univerbation, though this shift in external form does not, within this theoretical framework, require any alternation in the overarching syntactic structure.

By contrast, Slobbe (2004), working within the same set of theoretical assumptions as D'hulst and drawing on the same corpus of material as Bourova, argues that the biclausal starting point is neither necessary nor helpful. She cites in her support an example such as (8), in which the Latin pluperfect *habueram* has the meaning future-in-the-past and yet on D'hulst's assumptions would have to be in a separate clause from the infinitival *peccare*.[11]

(8) Nisi   deus   admonuisset   me [...]
     if not   god.NOM.SG   warn.SBJV.PLPF.3SG   I.ACC
     habueram   peccare   in   te
     have.IND.PLPF.1SG sin.INF   against   you.ACC
     'If god had not warned me, I would have sinned against you'
                        (Arnobius Iunior, *Commentarii in Psalmos* 104,51, 5th cent CE)

Instead she argues that we should look at theoretical models which do not require the main verb and infinitive to be in separate clauses. She draws on the classification of infinitive constructions in Wurmbrand (2003) and concludes: '[...] it seems most likely that the Romance synthetic conditional verb forms have developed from the functional restructuring infinitive construction' (Slobbe 2004: 117). For our purposes, we do not need to go into the details of the different infinitival constructions, although it is worth noting that one consequence of Slobbe's analysis is to reduce the amount of hierarchical syntactic superstructure required to deal with this body of data. This is consistent with a view of syntax in which the key ingredients are the

---

[11] It is worth noting that this example goes against the tendency discussed above for alethic *habere* to follow the infinitive. Bourova and Tasmowski (2007: 34) suggest that the explanation is to be found in the fact that a pluperfect like *habueram* is too long to be placed in what is essentially a post-verbal clitic position.

features, that is to say the elements like [PAST], [PERFECT], [FUTURE] that we have been adopting here, and the feature structures that they generate. If the compositionality that is the key conclusion of this section can be stated simply in terms of features, there is much less disparity between syntax and morphology than might otherwise appear, and what difference there is can be stated at the level of surface realization. Once again therefore, and from a different perspective, we see that surface form and underlying content can evolve at different rates (Vincent and Börjars 2010: 288–90).

7.5 The semantic diversity of the conditional

Both Iatridou's semantics of conditionals and the diachrony of the Romance forma-tions converge on what are commonly taken to be their core uses in hypotheticals, counterfactuals, and reported speech, uses which Dendale (2001), in his valuable survey, groups together under the rubric 'conditionnel d'éventualité'. In the modern languages, however, the forms which derive through the grammaticalization of the infinitive + *habere* construction have a range of other functions. If these functions cannot be brought within the same semantic compass, it may legitimately be argued that the modern conditional has over time severed its links with its etymological sources and now requires to be analysed as an independent form within the modern verbal systems. This in turn would in principle facilitate formal divergence between the two patterns, and to the extent that such divergence is not attested, the links which are maintained would be solely at the level of the morphology and would thus be morphomic in the narrow sense identified in our introductory discussion. Three questions therefore need to be addressed: What are these other uses? Can they—and should they—be reconciled with Iatridou's account? What is the chronology of the emergence of such uses and are they associated with any breakdowns in the morpho-logical connections between conditionals and futures?

Remaining with Dendale's typology, in addition to the 'conditionnel d'éventua-lité', he distinguishes two further uses which he labels the 'conditionnel d'emprunt' and the 'conditionnel d'atténuation'. The former is that typical of journalistic registers in examples such as (9) to (12):

(9)   Est-il vrai que l'assassin habiterait toujours là.
      'Is it true that the murderer still lives there?'

(10) Il registro non sarebbe stato prelevato dalla polizia.
      'The logbook was allegedly not removed by the police.'

(11) El nombre de víctimes, segons les últimes informacions, s'elevaria a 67 morts.
      (Avui, 18.10.1997, p. 3)
      'The number of victims, according to the latest information, has risen to 67 dead.'[12]

---

[12] This example is cited in the chapter by Manuel Pérez Saldanya in J. Solà *et al.* (eds.), *Gramàtica del català contemporani*, vol 3, pp. 2644–5. My thanks to Max Wheeler for directing me to this source.

(12) Gregorius habría nacido en Glasgow. (J. Cortázar, Argentina)
      'Gregorius was apparently born in Glasgow.'[13]

Although such uses are considered unwelcome Gallicisms within the Spanish and Catalan prescriptive traditions (see for example Butt and Benjamin, 1994: §14.7.2), the fact that the patterns are constant across the whole family suggests that they are of a piece with other uses of the conditional to express supposition and inference:

(13) Tendría unos treinta años.
      'He must have been about thirty.'

(14) Serait-il au bureau?
      'Might/would he be at the office?'

Moreover it is not difficult to see how these uses can be grouped with hypotheticals, as a number of the contributors to Dendale and Tasmowski (2001) argue. Indeed, one of the names for it in the French grammatical tradition, the 'conditionnel de non prise en charge', makes clear that in using this form the speaker is constructing an alternative and hypothetical context to which he/she is not necessarily committed (Celle 2007).

Where the individual languages differ, however, is in the links between inferential uses in the conditional and future. Squartini (2004) shows in detail that a range of different patterns and distributions have developed over the centuries in different members of the family. He proposes to account for the differences by distinguishing two features [±PAST] and [±DUBITATIVE]. The conditionals cross-linguistically are all of course [+PAST] and the futures are [−PAST]; where the individual languages diverge is in the way the values for [DUBITATIVE] correlate with the futures and the conditionals. We will not go into the details of the intra-family variation here but in the context of the present chapter, two points are worth noting. First, the divergence between the languages seems to be relatively recent, that is to say post-medieval and probably post-Renaissance, although more work is needed to establish relative chronologies within the individual languages. Second, it is not generally the case that these semantic divergences are accompanied by a breaking of the formal links between future and conditional. The data adduced by Esher (2012a) are very much the exception from this point of view, and all the more valuable in consequence.

Dendale's third category of meaning associated with conditionals, which he calls 'attenuation' and which might also be called the conditional of politeness, is that found in French *je voudrais* 'I would like', *je dirais* 'I would say', or Italian *mi permetterei di dire* 'I would dare to say', and the like. Dendale (2001: 14) describes

---

[13] This example and its translation are from Butt and Benjamin (1994: §14.7.2).

this as the 'enfant terrible' of conditional uses, although an association of past verb forms with politeness or tentativeness is by no means uncommon across languages, and it is not difficult to see a link between the pragmatics of politeness and a wish to mitigate the immediate content of a remark or request by removing it to a hypothetical alternative world. What is clear is that this use does not have a natural companion in the future in the way that other uses of the conditional do.

From the morphomic perspective the issue then is whether all these different uses can be subsumed under a single overarching account or whether they are genuinely distinct meanings. If the latter was true, it could be argued that as the conditional develops these meanings it necessarily separates itself from the future, whose morphological formation it shares, thus leading to a potential morphome in the narrow sense.

7.6 Dahl's paradox

So far in this chapter we have emphasized two things: the importance of compositionality and its potential persistence even in the face of quite radical changes in the surface realization of the categories in question. Nonetheless, there can obviously come a point at which compositionality breaks down. At the same time, in such circumstances, the newly non-compositional item may legitimately enter compositionally into constructions with other items. We will call this phenomenon 'Dahl's paradox', in deference to the Swedish linguist who has formulated the issue most clearly. He writes:

What is not always appreciated is the extent to which grammaticalization processes may interfere with compositionality. Suppose [...] two elements, A and B, combine in a construction C, which [...] has a perfectly compositional semantics. C then acquires a new meaning, although A and B as used on their own preserve their old meaning. Then, C combines with D to form a new construction, whose interpretation is compositional in the sense that it can be derived from the meanings of C and D, but non-compositional in the sense that it is not derivable from the meanings of its ultimate constituents, A, B, and D together. (Dahl 1997: 103)

A case in point is the so-called *passé surcomposé* in French, as exemplified in (15) (cited from Apotheloz, 2010):

(15)   aussitôt que Monsieur l'a eu quitté [...] (Dumas *Les Trois mousquetaires*, 1844)
        'as soon as Monsieur had left him ...'

In a context such as this the *passé surcomposé* formation *a eu quitté* is an alternative to the pluperfect *avait quitté* and realizes the same feature cluster [PAST, PERFECT]. While the pluperfect does so in a straightforwardly compositional way—*avait* [PAST] plus *quitté* [PERFECT]—the *surcomposé* requires us to assign the feature [PAST] to the string *a eu*, even though formally *a* is the present tense of the verb *avoir*, and indeed in other contexts can express the value [PRESENT]. This double value of the string *a eu* as realizing either [PAST] or [PRESENT, PERFECT] is consistent with the more general development in modern French according to which the etymological present perfect construction *il a quitté* has taken on the additional value [PAST].

From a theoretical perspective, the type of situation that Dahl diagnoses allows two options. The first is to develop a tense ontology which will accommodate such formations, as in their different ways Paesani (2001) and Schaden (2007) each seek to do, thus eliminating the paradox and rendering the construction compositional at every stage. The alternative is to accept the opacity of the auxiliary + participle combination, treat it as non-compositional internally but allow it to combine externally with a second participle in a compositional fashion. This would yield a result which is, as it were, the opposite of the conclusion arrived at above for forms like *devrait* and *dovrebbe*. In those instances, accepting von Fintel and Iatridou's theory of the relation between strong and weak modality requires a compositional account of a morphologically synthetic formation; here instead we can envisage the possibility of a non-compositional account of an analytic form. In the next section we will see that such a move is indeed necessary when we come to analysing the past conditional *surcomposé*, further supporting our initial assumption that conclusions about compositionality of meaning are independent of conclusions about the corresponding linguistic form(s).

7.7 Compound forms of the conditional

In our discussion so far we have deliberately left out of account the compound conditional or what is sometimes called the conditional perfect, that is to say forms such as French *aurait mangé* 'would have eaten', Italian *sarebbe arrivato* 'would have arrived', Portuguese *teria cantado* 'would have sung', and the like. In many instances their uses will fall under one of the headings already reviewed but with an added dimension of pastness. And indeed in such uses the counterfactual in (16) and the indirect speech in (17) converge, both implying that Pierre was not able to come and thereby lending further support to a unified analysis of the two uses exactly as an account along the lines of Iatridou (2000) would predict.

(16)   Pierre disait qu'il serait venu au concert.
        'Pierre said that he would have come to the concert.'

(17)   Si Pierre n'avait pas perdu son billet, il serait venu au concert.
        'If Pierre had not lost his ticket, he would have come to the concert.'

Very much the same applies to inferential uses as in (18) and (19), in both of which the inference or the allegation is made with respect to a past rather than a present state of affairs:

(18)   Il terremoto non sarebbe stato un fatto naturale.
       'The earthquake was alleged not to be due to natural causes.'

(19)   Il ragazzo sarebbe stato svegliato dal suono del campanello di casa.
       'The boy is thought to have been woken by the sound of the doorbell.'

Compositionality seems therefore to be straightforwardly preserved and we will not consider such uses further. There are, however, two special circumstances involving compound conditionals which merit further discussion and which in different ways offer challenges to compositionality: the conditional *surcomposé*, which is attested in a number of Romance varieties, and the use of the compound conditional in reported speech in modern Italian.[14]

7.7.1 *The conditional surcomposé*

This construction, relatively little discussed in the literature, fits into the larger pattern of *surcomposé* constructions schematized by Ledgeway (2009: 596) as follows:

(20)   [finite auxiliary] + [participial auxiliary] + [participle of the lexical verb]

We have already seen examples of the best-studied member of this class, the *passé surcomposé*, in our discussion of Dahl's paradox above. Here now are some instances of the conditional member of the system:

(21)   J'aurais eu commis des crimes affreux que je n'aurais pas eu un sommeil plus bourrelé.
       'Even if I'd committed terrible crimes, my sleep wouldn't have been any more troubled.' (Eugène Sue; cited by Schaden, 2007: 46, following Imbs, 1960)[15]

(22)   Quand j'aurais eu appris la dactylo, j'aurais appris la steno.
       'Once I had learnt to type, I would have learned shorthand.'
                         (again cited by Schaden, 2007: 46, following Imbs, 1960)

(23)   si se havesse abstenuto dal vino [...] non siria stato morto.
       'if he had abstained from the wine, he would not have died'
                (Giovanni Brancati, 15th cent., cited by Ledgeway, 2009: 597)

There are a number of reasons to want to maintain a compositional account for these patterns. First, in those languages which have the *surcomposé* it is productive across the full paradigm of the verb, occurring not only in the perfect and as here in the conditional but also in the pluperfect (cf. the Sardinian example (24) below), the

---

[14] Something similar is found with the use of the so-called second conditional in reported speech in Pyrenean varieties of Occitan (Esher 2011, this volume).

[15] My thanks to J. C. Smith for the translation of this example.

subjunctive, and so on.[16] Second, the meaning of the relevant forms is what we would expect if we add a participle to an existing verb form. Third, the construction seems to have developed differently in different dialects, each with its own local constraints. Thus, within French it is standard to distinguish two subtypes, called by Schaden *antérieur* and *superparfait*, with different regional distributions. For old Neapolitan, Ledgeway notes that the construction is only found with unaccusative verbs, whereas in French and northern Italian dialects it is found with verbs of all lexical classes. Each subtype exhibits a mixture of local constraints beside overall combinability which would not be expected if the developments had led to arbitrary patterns or what might be called syntactic idioms.

Sardinian is particularly instructive in this connection and reinforces the case for a compositional approach. Jones (1993: 308) notes that both the following express the meaning 'If you had gone to Cagliari, you would have concluded the matter':

(24)   Si fis istáu andáu a Ccasteddu, kk'aías áppiu finíu sa cosa.

(25)   Si días ésser istáu andáu a Ccasteddu, kke días áer áppiu finíu sa cosa.

The difference is that in (24) we have an example of a double pluperfect *composé*— literally 'if you had been gone to Cagliari you had had finished the matter'— reminiscent of the Shakespearian example (4c) above, and one which reinforces Iatridou's claim that in such constructions it is more important cross-linguistically to express the [PAST] rather than the [FUTURE] meaning component. In (25), on the other hand, we find the reduced form *días* of the verb *dévere* used as a future/ conditional auxiliary (Jones 1993: 90–1), so the literal gloss is 'if you would have been gone to Cagliari, you would have had finished the matter'.

The temporal ontology proposed by Schaden (2007) in order to accommodate the *passé surcomposé* is already considerably richer than most neo-Reichenbachian systems, permitting as it does a theoretical maximum of forty-eight tenses (Schaden 2007: 44). Even so, the conditional *surcomposé* stretches it beyond its natural capacity. Schaden (2007: 194) writes that 'ce temps grammatical pose problème pour la raison suivante: s'il est purement temporel, on aura besoin de quatre relations temporelles pour en rendre compte, mais le système n'en fournit que trois'.[17] Space does not allow detailed discussion of his systems and the alternatives for coping with such tenses, but in any case for our purposes it suffices to show that there is a difficult trade-off between coverage of the data and richness of the analytical system deployed. However, following the logic of Dahl (1997), it is possible

---

[16] For details and full references on French, see Paesani (2001) and Schaden (2007). For old Neapolitan, Ledgeway (2009: 596) explicitly notes that these forms are found across 'the entire range of possible temporal and modal specifications including non-finite ones'.

[17] 'This grammatical tense poses a problem for the following reason: if it is purely temporal, we would need to have four tense relations to account for it, but the system only makes three available.'

to accept a degree of internal non-compositionality in a complex auxiliary form and still allow it to combine freely with a clause's lexical main verb. Either way we have a development that creates a potential for non-compositionality, but not one that, as far as I can see, opens the door to potential cases of new morphemes.

7.7.2 *Reported speech in Italian*

Another context in which compositionality appears to fail is reported speech in Italian. Compare the following French and Italian sentences, both of which mean 'Paul said that he would come later':

(26)   Paul a dit qu'il viendrait plus tard.

(27)   Paolo ha detto che sarebbe venuto più tardi.

Where French—as also Spanish, Catalan, and Portuguese—is like English in that a future statement 'I will come later' is reported by transposing the future of the direct speech into the conditional in reported speech, in Italian the required form is the compound conditional. Replacing the compound form *sarebbe venuto* in (27) with the simple conditional *verrebbe* would render the sentence ungrammatical, whereas exchanging the French simple form *viendrait* for the compound form *serait venu* yields a grammatical sentence but with a different meaning, the equivalent of English *he said he would have come (if he had been free)*. The Italian sentence is in fact ambiguous since it can also be used to convey the latter counterfactual meaning. The paradox that this pattern creates is that in some uses the compound conditional behaves in as compositional a way as its French and English counterparts. Thus, the difference between hypotheticals containing the simple form as in (28) and ones containing the compound form as in (29) is that the latter describe a situation that did not come about while the former merely imply that it is unlikely to come about:

(28)   a. S'il venait, il s'amuserait.
        b. Se venisse, si divertirebbe.
        c. If he came, he would enjoy himself.

(29)   a. S'il était venu, il se serait amusé.
        b. Se fosse venuto, si sarebbe divertito.
        c. If he had come, he would have enjoyed himself.

A semantics of the kind proposed by Iatridou accounts for the difference between (28a,c) and (29a,c) in French and English by assuming that in the (28) examples we have a past of unreality or an excluded world, whereas in (29) we are faced with an impossible circumstance since to the past of unreality is added a temporal past, that is to say an excluded time. There is no reason not to assume the same analysis of the relation in Italian between (28b) and (29b). And, as noted above, the three languages behave alike in that the reports of the sentences in (29) will all also contain the compound conditional. How then are we to explain the fact that this expected compositionality breaks down in Italian in the case of reports such as (27)?

It was not ever thus. In old Italian we find the same situation as in modern French or Spanish with simple backshift so that an utterance containing the future is reported with the conditional. Thus:

(30)   disse, dove ella a' suoi piaceri acconsentirsi volesse, la libererebbe.
        'he said that if she were willing to yield to his pleasure he would free her'
                            (Boccaccio *Decameron* 4.6, = example (30) in Squartini, 1999)

Maiden (1996*b*) identifies the point of transition to the use of the compound conditional in such contexts as occurring in the sixteenth century and links it to what amounts to a distinction in modality between complements of verbs of promising and the like in which there is a stronger commitment on the part of the speaker to the immediate fulfilment of the circumstance described. However, as Squartini (1999) observes, this cannot be the whole story since it relies on the contrast between a simple and a compound conditional in subordinate contexts, and it is precisely this possibility which is later lost. At the same time Squartini's own solution—that the simple conditional lost the possibility of past reference—is little more than a restatement of the change and does not account for the stability across languages and time of the patterns underlying the examples in (28) and (29). The pan-Romance picture painted in Squartini (2004) and discussed above in Section 7.5 does not fare much better when it comes to accommodating this shift in the history of Italian. Nor can we have recourse to a solution along the lines of Dahl (1997), as discussed in the previous section for the conditional *surcomposé*, since the forms of the verb are the same in both the compositional and the non-compositional contexts. There therefore appears to be no alternative but for the grammar of Italian to contain a statement overriding the expected rules for the combinatorial semantics of the conditional in indirect speech. What is of interest, however, in the context of the present chapter, is that the morphological links between future and conditional in Italian remain unsevered.

7.8 Conclusion

Inevitably, in order to draw the larger picture we have had in the foregoing to skate over many detailed and sophisticated analyses by the scholars whose work we cite. Nonetheless, certain general lessons can be drawn. In particular we have under-scored the importance of compositionality in natural languages as being what may be called the default condition or the null hypothesis. Arguments for the existence of morphemes, in the narrow sense defined in Section 7.1, must therefore show the failure of the expected compositionality in pairs such as future and conditional. To show such failure it will not suffice to adduce new meanings for items which had previously expressed this content, but it will also be necessary to show that the new meanings are not connectible to the old ones by deeper semantic principles. Moreover, in conducting such an argument it will not be possible to rely on the breakdown of formal links since we have seen in the case of conditionals, and in the special sub-case of modals of necessity, that formal coalescence is not necessarily accompanied by semantic dissociation. We have seen too that the case for compositionality in a given construction is very much dependent on the analytical primitives deployed, a point that had already emerged as one of the main conclusions of Vincent (2011). To that extent, such arguments cannot be conducted independently of the larger theoretical framework. Otherwise put, morphomes in the narrow sense must reconnect with the larger sense of the concept, already alluded to in Aronoff (1994), as the necessary interface between syntax and phonology, and need to be embedded in appropriate theories of those independently required domains of language.

8

Morphomes in Sardinian verb inflection*

MICHELE LOPORCARO

8.1 Introduction

In this chapter I intend to sift the evidence Sardinian provides for the effectiveness of morphomes (Aronoff 1994) in determining morphological change. In order to lay the ground for this discussion, I will first elaborate on the synchronic sketch of verb inflection provided in Loporcaro (2012) for one variety of Logudorese, the western Logudorese dialect of Bonorva.[1] After some preliminary information on Sardinian (and Bonorvese) verb inflection in general (§8.2), I shall move on to focus on (moderately)

* Thanks are due to many Bonorvese speakers, in particular Grazia, †Forica, and Antonello Porcu, Domenico Faedda, and Mariangela Serra, who shared their grammatical intuitions with me over the years. The same thanks are due to my Lurese friends, first and foremost Piero Depperu, as well as to the speakers of Cagliaritano M. Teresa Piga and Efisio Santus. I am also indebted to Ignazio Putzu for the data on Oristanese, as well as for joint fieldwork on that variety and on Cagliaritano, which is part of the project 'Repertorio plurilingue e variazione linguistica in uno spazio urbano mediterraneo: Cagliari' funded by Regione Sardegna. The following abbreviations are used throughout the chapter: S = stem, BS = basic stem, It. = Italian, Lat. = Latin, Log. = Logudorese, PL = plural, SG = singular. For verb tenses/moods, Leipzig-style glosses are only used when needed for clarification, and the following abbreviations are adopted: pres(ent), imp(er)f(ect), i(ndicative), imper(ative), s(ubjunctive), ger(und), p(a)st p(ar)t(iciple). As the focus of the chapter is not on the phonetics, in presenting Sardinian data current orthographic conventions are employed: z = [dːz] and tz = [tːs] (both long between vowels), s = both [s] and [z] (the latter intervocalically); palatal sounds are rendered with diacritic i, as in Italian. Contrary to common usage, though, k is employed for [k] and stress is systematically marked, with a grave accent on lower-mid vowels and an acute elsewhere. Whenever unreferenced, dialect data stem from my own field notes.
[1] Bonorvese, a heavily endangered language (like most of Sardinian), is spoken by a subset of the about 5,000 inhabitants of the town of Bonorva (in the province of Sassari). The sociolinguistic research of Rindler-Schjerve (1987), based on a quantitative study as well as on participant observation, reports on language shift among the younger generations of Bonorvese speakers in the early 1980s, when 2/3 of the people below the age of twenty spoke Sardinian with their parents. One generation later, Paulis (2010: 180) reports a figure of less than 2% for the entire island, based on the statistical figures published in Oppo (2007). This scenario concerns the whole of Sardinia, whereby urban varieties such as Cagliaritano and Oristanese, touched upon in §8.5.1 below, are more strongly endangered since cities are as expected at the vanguard of language shift (cf. Oppo 2007: 16).

irregular verbs, since it is in their paradigms that one finds the kind of stem allomorphy which morphomic partition classes in the Romance verb capitalize on (cf. Maiden, 2011*b*, for a recent overview). Section 8.3 will provide a synchronic sketch of the paradigmatic distribution of irregularity in this variety of Logudorese.[2] Section 8.4.1 then explores the consequences of the synchronic regularities described in Section 8.3 for the study of morphological change in the verb system, with special focus on the morphomic partition scheme Maiden (2003, 2005*a*, 2011*b*) dubbed the 'L-pattern'. In Section 8.5, finally, I shall turn to the N-pattern, taking into account selected comparative data from other varieties of Logudorese as well as from Campidanese Sardinian.

As will be shown, in-depth consideration of the L- and the N-patterns based on first-hand data holds some surprises in store. For the former, Maiden (2011*b*: 227, 235) quotes several examples from Sardinian illustrating both phonologically motivated root allomorphy and purely morphological innovations. The investigation to be presented here confirms that the L-pattern is observed in Logudorese Sardinian, but also shows that it has not quite the same status as in other Romance languages, since its integrity has been compromised by several converging changes. As for the N-pattern, on the other hand, this is claimed to be non-existent in Sardinian by Maiden (2003: 15, 2005*a*: 163–4, 2011*b*: 263), and its absence is traced back to the lack (in Logudorese, in particular) of stress-related vowel alternations. The present study will scrutinize putative instances of N-pattern distribution in some Sardinian dialects, trying to assess whether or not they can be interpreted as autonomously morphological. At least for some examples, the answer will be in the positive: crucially, none of those examples involves stress-related vowel alternations.

8.2 Verb inflection in Logudorese Sardinian

As shown in Table 8.1, Sardinian displays a less complex synthetic verb paradigm than other Romance languages, featuring only eight tenses/moods, as opposed to twelve in Italian or fourteen in Spanish. This is a product of diachronic development, since in Sardinian synthetic future and conditional did not arise (rather, those functions are expressed periphrastically, as in Romanian), whereas most varieties lost the preterite and many have also lost or are presently losing the imperfect subjunctive. The latter is displayed in Table 8.1 though, since it is still used by the most conservative Bonorvese speakers I have interviewed (born approximately before 1950).[3]

---

[2] The choice is arbitrary: in the absence of a well-established standardized variety of Sardinian, it is essential to analyse a coherent system at the level of detail required by current standards in morphological theory. This is precisely what is missing in research on Sardinian morphology, where most of the studies available either give an overview on whole dialect areas (Wagner 1938–1939, Blasco Ferrer 1984, 1986, Pisano 2004–2006), or, when focusing on specific dialects (e.g. Pittau 1972, on Nuorese, Piras 1994, on Sulcitano), do not provide enough detail for an investigation of the paradigmatic organization of morphological irregularity.

[3] Bonorvese is classified as northern Logudorese by Wagner (1941: 261f., 1950: 387f.), whereas for Spano (1840) it belongs to 'common Logudorese'. Note that several of the traits of verb inflection described for

TABLE 8.1 The overall distribution of basic stems in Logudorese

		1SG	2SG	3SG	1PL	2PL	3PL
Finite forms	Imperfect subjunctive						
	Present subjunctive			S3			
	Imperative				S3>S1		
	Present indicative	S2					
	Imperfect indicative			S1			
Non-finite forms	Gerund						
	Infinitive			S4			
	Past participle			S5			

The synopsis in Table 8.1, motivated in Loporcaro (2012), is built on the model of the Overall Distribution Scheme of stem allomorphy provided for Italian by Pirrelli and Battista (2000: 337, 359) (comparable representations of the verb paradigm are provided for Spanish by Boyé and Cabredo Hofherr 2006, for French by Bonami and Boyé 2003). It lists tenses/moods in an order such that different basic stems (henceforth BS)—i.e. stems that have to be stored in the lexical entry of an irregular verb—can be displayed orderly, and it neglects derived stems, built regularly on basic ones. Thus, for instance, just one BS occurs in the subjunctive mood, since the impf_s is always formed from the pres_s stem: compare e.g. *bènz-a* 'come.SBJV.PRS.1SG' and *benz-èr-a* 'come.SBJV.IMPF.1SG'.[4]

As is readily apparent, the list of BSs to be assumed for Logudorese is more restricted than in Italian, where eight BSs may be assumed (cf. Pirrelli and Battista 2000). The reader is referred to Loporcaro (2012) for a full discussion of regular verb inflection and of highly irregular verbs (the only ones to display form, rather than stem, suppletion in some cases). As for regular verbs, I shall assume, following Pirrelli's (2000) analysis of Italian, that their forms, exemplified in (1) for the present indicative of the three conjugations, are based on just the default stem S1:[5]

northern Logudorese by Wagner (1938–1939) are extraneous to Bonorvese which, for instance, forms the gerund on the default stem (e.g. *parínne* 'seeming', from *párrer*) as opposed to the northern dialects, which derive it from the 1SG pres_i or the subjunctive stem (cf. (35)–(36) and n. 27 below): e.g. *palzènde* 'seeming' in Luras, cf. 1SG pres_i *pálzo*, pres_s *pálze* (vs. S1 in e.g. the 2SG pres_i *páres*).

[4] In this respect, not all Sardinian and not even all Logudorese varieties coincide. In the dialects of Barbagia, where the Latin forms of impf_s were maintained (Wagner 1938–1939: 9), this tense shows the same stem as the infinitive: e.g. *pappáret* 'eat', *tèsseret* 'weave', *servíret* 'serve' (impf_s, 3SG). In Campidanese, on the other hand, the impf_s derives from the Latin pluperfect_s: thus, synchronically, it is usually built from S1 + *-éssi* (e.g. Cagliaritano *kreéssit* 'believed' 3SG < Lat. CRE(DI)DISSET, *podéssit* 'could' 3SG < Lat. POT(U)ISSET), though some remnants of forms sharing the same stem as the pres_s still occur: e.g. *protzéssit* alongside *proéssit* 'rain' 3SG, cf. the pres_s *pròtzat/pròat*, from *pròi* 'rain'.

[5] For the reader to be able to compute the phonetics of the Sardinian forms introduced here, some further information is needed. Sardinian regularly adds an epithetic vowel after (phonologically) consonant-ending word(-form)s: this is a copy of the preceding vowel, so that e.g. /ˈmɔris/, /ˈbɛnit/ in (2)–(3) are

(1)

1SG	2SG	3SG	1PL	2PL	3PL	pres_i (Log.)	
kánto	kántas	kántat	kantámos	kantádes	kántan	*kantáre*	'sing'
krèsko	krèskes	krèsket	kreskímos	kreskídes	krèsken	*krèsker*	'grow'
pálto	páltis	páltit	paltímos	paltídes	páltin	*paltíre*	'depart'

While highly irregular verbs such as *èsser* 'be' by definition escape the generalizations on the distribution of stem allomorphy mirrored in Table 8.1, we will now examine moderately irregular verbs to see that they display, as elsewhere in Romance, a systematic patterning of stem allomorphy.

8.3 The synchronic distribution of stem allomorphy

Compare the pres_i and the pres_s of the two (moderately) irregular verbs in (2)–(3):

(2)

1SG	2SG	3SG	1PL	2PL	3PL	*mòrrer*	'die'
mòlzo	móris	mórit	morímos	morídes	mórin	pres_i	
mòlza	mòlzas	mòlzat	molzémus	molzèdas	mòlzan	pres_s	

(3)

1SG	2SG	3SG	1PL	2PL	3PL	*bènner*	'come'
bènzo	bénis	bénit	benímos	benídes	bénin	pres_i	
bènza	bènzas	bènzat	benzémus	benzèdas	bènzan	pres_s	

The shape of the two partition classes determined by stem allomorphy corresponds to the L-pattern. This systematic allomorphy, found in several verbs of the 2nd class, justifies positing a second basic stem (S2), which is unpredictable from the default S1.[6] While in Italian the present indicative of irregular verbs may host up to four morphomic partition classes, as with the verbs *dolere* 'hurt' or *dovere* 'must', in Logudorese one finds maximally the bipartition seen in (2)–(3). Hence, given that the pres_s stem never displays allomorphy, the binary subdivision determined by the L-pattern would seem to be the maximal partition. However, the solidarity of the paradigm cells tied together in the L-pattern distribution (1SG pres_i + pres_s) is

pronounced ['moːrizi], ['beːniði]. These transcriptions (which imply the phonological analysis of stressed vowels maintained in Loporcaro 2003: 84) also show that the final consonant, having become intervocalic through epithesis, is lenited.

[6] Note that the 2nd class divides into two inflectional subclasses, as discussed in Loporcaro (2003: 96–107): thus, *krèsker* in (1) exemplifies subclass 2a (thematic vowel -*e*-), whereas the two verbs in (2)–(3) belong to subclass 2b (thematic vowel -*i*- in the pres_i).

not as tight in Logudorese as it is in, say, Spanish or Portuguese. On the one hand, there are cases in which allomorphy is not morphomic, but aligned with mood, the same way as e.g. in French verbs displaying a dedicated subjunctive stem (e.g. *que je fasse/veuille*, etc., with the stems /fas-/, /vœj-/ from *faire* 'do', *vouloir* 'want'):[7]

(4)

1SG	2SG	3SG	1PL	2PL	3PL	*krer*	'believe'
krèo	kres	kret	kreímos	kreídes	kren	pres_i	
krèa/	krèas/	krèat/	kreémus/	kreèdas/	krèan/	pres_s	
krètta	krèttas	krèttat	krettémus	krettèdas	krèttan		

(5)

1SG	2SG	3SG	1PL	2PL	3PL	*lassare*	'leave'
lásso	lássas	lássat	lassámos	lassádes	lássan	pres_i	
lásse/	lásses/	lásset/	lassémus/	lassèdas/	lássen/	pres_s	
lèsse	lèsses	lèsset	lessémus	lessèdas	lèssen		

(6)

1SG	2SG	3SG	1PL	2PL	3PL	*nárrer*	'say, tell'
náro	náras	nárat	narámos	narádes	náran	pres_i	
nèlze	nèlzes	nèlzet	nelzémus	nelzèdas	nèlzen	pres_s	

On the other hand, there is at least one case in which one finds three distinct stems here, as shown in (7):

(7)

1SG	2SG	3SG	1PL	2PL	3PL	*fágher*	'do'
fátto	fághes	fághet	faghímos	faghídes	fághen	pres_i	
fètta	fèttas	fèttat	fettémus	fettèdas	fèttan	pres_s	

In current studies on (Romance) verb inflection, the common analytical procedure has it that 'chaque paire d'indices de thème est motivée par au moins un contraste' (Bonami and Boyé 2003: 110). Therefore, contrary to Pirrelli and Battista's (2000) analysis of Italian, where one and the same stem index (S2) is assigned to the L-shaped collection of cells of Maiden's L-pattern, for Logudorese Sardinian, given the data in (7), one must assign different indexes to the stem occurring in the 1SG pres_i (S2), as opposed to the one occurring in the subjunctive (S3).

[7] As shown in (4)–(5), these verbs also display a regular subjunctive, based on S1: *krèa, lásse*, and, for some of my informants, also *náre* (not shown in (6)). Both the occurrence of a dedicated subjunctive stem for those verbs and the coexistence of regular subjunctive forms are encountered widely across Sardinian (cf. Pittau 1972: 113, Blasco Ferrer 1986: 136).

While *fágher* admittedly is the only Bonorvese verb displaying a categorical contrast between those three stems, upon closer consideration this turns out not to be an isolated irregularity in the system, as will be shown in Section 8.4.1. Note in particular that, unlike its Italian counterpart *fare* 'do' (cf. Pirrelli and Battista 2000: 338), *fágher* is not a highly irregular verb in this dialect: contrary to *èsser* 'be', *áer* 'have', or *dare* 'give' (cf. Loporcaro 2012: §3.2), *fágher* has no irregular endings anywhere in the paradigm.[8] This is shown in Tables 8.2 and 8.3 by comparing the paradigm of *fágher* with that of a regular 2nd class verb.[9]

TABLE 8.2 Inflectional paradigm of *bènner* 'sell' (2nd class regular verb)

		1SG	2SG	3SG	1PL	2PL	3PL
Finite	impf_s	bennère[a]	bennères	bennèret	bennerémus	bennerézis	bennèren
	pres_s	bènna[b]	bènnas	bènnat	bennèmus	bennèdas[c]	bènnan
	imper		bènne		bennímos	benníde	
	pres_i	bènno	bènnes	bènnet	bennímos	bennídes	bènnen
	impf_i	bennía/-o	bennías	benníat	bennímis	bennízis	bennían
Non- finite	ger				benvínne		
	infin				bènner		
	pst_pt				bénnidu		

[a] In the impf_s of all inflectional classes, the vowel in the final syllable in the SG and the 3PL persons may be either -e, as displayed in the table, or -a, in free variation.
[b] In the pres_s of -er and -íre verbs, the vowel in the final syllable in the 1–3SG and 3PL persons may be either -a or -e in free variation.
[c] In the 2PL pres_s, the endings -èdas/-èdes are interchangeable in all inflectional classes.

TABLE 8.3 Inflectional paradigm of *fágher* 'do' (2nd class moderately irregular verb)

		1SG	2SG	3SG	1PL	2PL	3PL
Finite	impf_s	fettère	fettères	fettèret	fetterémus	fetterézis	fettèren
	pres_s	fètta	fèttas	fèttat	fettémus	fettèdas	fèttan
	imper		fághe		faghímos	faghíde	
	pres_i	fátto	fághes	fághet	faghímos	faghídes	fághen
	impf_i	faghía/-o	faghías	faghíat	faghímis	faghízis	faghían
Non- finite	ger				faghínne		
	infin				fágher		
	pst_pt				fáttu		

[8] In other dialects, like Nuorese indeed, *fáker* is even used to exemplify the paradigm of regular 2nd conjugation, having a different stem only in the pst_pt *fattu* but S1 elsewhere, including the whole pres_i (*fako* 1SG, *fakes* 2SG, etc.) and the pres_s (*faka* 1SG etc.; cf. Pittau 1972: 109–10).
[9] Cf. Loporcaro (2012) for the details on regular inflections in the different inflectional classes of the verb in Logudorese.

Until now we have seen that (moderately) irregular verbs lead us to assume three distinct stems. If we now consider the infinitive, we see that a fourth basic stem must be assumed. As argued in Loporcaro (2012), to which the reader is referred for the details, inspection of the infinitive forms requires positing a fourth BS (S4), since a series of 2nd class verbs build their infinitive on a stem which is distinct from S1. This is illustrated in (8): (The thematic vowel, whose status is not discussed here, is given in brackets.)

(8)

	'come'	'hold/have'	'put'	'open'	'cover'	'want'
S1 (default)	bén(i)-	tèn(e)-	pòn(e-)	abbér(i)-	kobér(i)-	kèr(e)-
S2 (1SG pres_i)	bènz-	tènz-	pònz-	abbèlz-	kobèrr-	kèlz-
S3 (SBJV)	= S2	= S2	= S2	= S2	= S2	= S2/kèlf-
S4 (INF)	bènn(e)-	tènn(e)-	pònn(e)-	abbèrr(e)-	= S2	kèrr(e)-

The pst_pt too forces us to assume a separate BS (S5), as shown by the occurrence, in several 2nd class verbs, of the different kinds of irregular pst_pt, whose form is not predictable from other BSs:

(9)   Irregular pst_pt formation for *-er* verbs (S5):

    a. S5 (ending in *-(C)t-u*, *-(s)s-u*) weakly suppletive wrt S1

	tènner	'have/hold'	→ *téntu*
	konnòsker	'know'	→ *konnóttu*
	prènner	'tie'	→ *présu*
	fríer	'fry'	→ *fríssu*

    b. S3 + *id-u* → S5

	dòler	'hurt'	→ *dólfidu*
	báler	'be worth'	→ *bálfidu*
	kèrrer	'want'	→ *kélfidu*
	pòder	'be able to'	→ *póttidu*

    c. S4 + *id-u* → S5   *bènner*   'come'   → *bénnidu*

    d. S1 + *d-u* → S5   *bíer*   'see'   → *bídu*

    e. S5 + *id-u* → S5′   *sutzèder*   'happen'   → *sutzéssu* → *sutzéssidu*

(9a) shows the kind of irregular pst_pt common throughout Romance, where no regular ending is discernible synchronically, so that the stem is a cumulative exponent of lexical and TAM values: e.g. *traítt-u* 'betray.PST.PTCP.M.SG' (from *traígher* 'betray'). Note, however, that also (9b–e), although formed by means of the same ending occurring in 2nd class regular verbs (e.g. *nóghidu* from *nògher* 'harm', or *bénnidu* from *bènner* 'sell', cf. Table 8.3), require a stored S5, since the BS to which the ending *-idu* is affixed does not coincide with S1, and since for any specific verb lexeme in (9b–c), this choice of the stem is unpredictable.[10] Thus, in

---

[10]   A further argument (cf. Loporcaro 2012: 23) comes from word-formation, where S5 is needed as a base for several deverbal nouns (cf. the data in Pinto 2011: 81–2).

this specific dialect, one has the pst_pt *bénnidu*, rather than *béntu (with a suppletive S5 as in (9a)) or *bénzidu (as in (9b)), whereas such forms do occur in other Logudorese dialects such as those of Siniscola (*véntu*, Pisano 2004–2006: 224) and Orosei (*véttu*, Blasco Ferrer 1986: 214, n. 94), both preserving the original irregular Latin participial form *ventu(s)*.

This exhausts the list of the BSs that may be maximally stored in the lexical entry for a Logudorese verb, with the sole exception of 'be', the only verb lexeme to display more than five stems. No further complication is needed, in part because, as we have seen, the tense/mood system is poorer than those of, say, Italian or Spanish (synthetic future and conditional never arose, the preterite was lost), in part because all the remaining tense-stems can be derived regularly from one of those listed.

By way of intermediate summary, (10) reports some examples of moderately irregular verbs (all belonging to the 2nd class), listing their BSs:

(10) a. Two stems (S5 $\neq$ S1–S4)

infinitive	pres_i (2SG-)	1SG pres_i	1SG pres_s	pst_pt	gloss
attènner	*attènnes*	*attènno*	*attènna*	*attésu*	'treat kindly'
atzènner	*atzènnes*	*atzènno*	*atzènna*	*atzésu*	'light'
distrúer	*distrúes*	*distrúo*	*distrúa*	*distrúttu*	'destroy'
kògher	*kòghes*	*kògo*	*kòga*	*kóttu*	'cook'
kunfúnner	*kunfúnnes*	*kunfúnno*	*kunfúnna*	*kunfúsu*	'confuse'
iskúder	*iskúdis*	*iskúdo*	*iskúda*	*iskúttu*	'beat'
ispálgher	*ispálghes*	*ispálgo*	*ispálga*	*ispáltu*	'scatter'
istríngher	*istrínghes*	*istríngo*	*istrínga*	*istríntu*	'clasp'
língher	*línghes*	*língo*	*línga*	*líntu*	'lick'
prommítter	*prommíttis*	*prommítto*	*prommítta*	*prommíssu*	'promise'
suígher	*suíghes*	*suígo*	*suíga*	*suéttu*	'make bread'

b. Two stems (S1 $\neq$ S2–S5)

infinitive	pres_i (2SG-)	1SG pres_i	1SG pres_s	pst_pt	gloss
giúgher	*giúghes*	*giútto*	*giútta*	*giúttu*	'bring, carry'

c. Three stems (S1 $\neq$ S2 = S3 = S4 $\neq$ S5)

infinitive	pres_i (2SG-)	1SG pres_i	1SG pres_s	pst_pt	gloss
kobèrrer	*kobéris*	*kobèrro*	*kobèrra*	*kobéltu*	'cover'

d. Three stems (S1 = S4 ≠ S2 ≠ S5)

infinitive	pres_i (2SG-)	1SG pres_i	1SG pres_s	pst_pt	gloss
appòrrer	*appórris*	*appòlzo*	*appòlza*	*appóltu*	'hand over'
báler	*bális*	*bálzo*	*bálza*	*bálfidu*	'be worth'
dòler	*dòles*	*dòlzo*	*dòlza*	*dólfidu*	'hurt'
kúrrer	*kúrres*	*kúlzo*	*kúlza*	*kúltu*	'run'
pòder	*pòdes*	*pòtto*	*pòtta*	*póttidu*	'be able to'

e. Three stems (S1 = S2 = S4 ≠ S3 ≠ S5)

infinitive	pres_i (2SG-)	1SG pres_i	1SG pres_s	pst_pt	gloss
krè(e)r	*krès*	*krèo*	*krètta*	*kréttidu*	'believe'[11]

f. Three stems (S1 = S4 ≠ S2 = S5 ≠ S3)

infinitive	pres_i (2SG-)	1SG pres_i	1SG pres_s	pst_pt	gloss
fágher	*fághes*	*fátto*	*fètta*	*fáttu*	'do'

g. Four stems (S1 ≠ S2 = S3 ≠ S4 ≠ S5)

infinitive	pres_i (2SG-)	1SG pres_i	1SG pres_s	pst_pt	gloss
abbèrrer	*abbéris*	*abbèlzo*	*abbèlza*	*abbéltu*	'open'
bènner	*bénis*	*bènzo*	*bènza*	*bénnidu*	'come'
kèrrer	*kéres*	*kèlzo*	*kèlza*	*kélfidu*	'want'
kobèrrer	*kobéris*	*kobèlzo*	*kobèlza*	*kobéltu*	'cover'[12]
mòrrer	*móris*	*mòlzo*	*mòlza*	*mòltu*	'die'
muntènner	*muntènes*	*muntènzo*	*muntènza*	*muntésu*	'maintain'
párrer	*páris*	*pálzo*	*pálza*	*pálfidu*	'seem'
pònner	*pònes*	*pònzo*	*pònza*	*póstu*	'put'
preffèrrer	*prefféris*	*preffèlzo*	*preffèlza*	*prefferídu*	'prefer'[13]
tènner	*tènes*	*tènzo*	*tènza*	*téntu*	'hold, have'

---

[11] In the subjunctive, as shown in (4), S1 *krè-* may occur in free variation with the dedicated S3 form *krètt-*.

[12] For some speakers, the verb *kobèrrer* has the allomorphy indicated here whereas for other, more conservative, informants its paradigm only has three contrasting basic stems, as shown in (10c).

[13] This verb also inflects, in some forms, according to the 3rd class: cf. the alternative infinitive form *prefferíre* and the pst_pt in (10g).

Some of the verbs in (10) display variation of two stems in some parts of the paradigm: in those cases where this variation (and change) affects verbs of type (10g), a maximal partition ensues, with five distinct stems, as will be discussed in Section 8.4.1, when the diachronic development of such paradigms is considered.

8.4 The diachronic evolution of stem allomorphy

Having completed the review of stem allomorphy in Logudorese, as reflected in the distribution schema in Table 8.1, I now move on to explore the implications of this synchronic distribution for the diachronic evolution of Logudorese verb inflection.

One first observation is that stem allomorphy is mostly aligned with tenses/moods. While the default stem S1 is the only one that stretches over subsets of cells from different verb tenses, the occurrence of all remaining stems can be characterized in syntactic/semantic terms, which does not leave much room for an autonomously morphological (i.e. non-functionally motivated) distribution of distinct stems. The only potential source for non-alignment is the L-pattern, to which we shall return directly.

Before resuming the L-pattern issue, let me briefly comment on the imperative, in that this is the only other tense, in addition to the pres_i, which formerly hosted stem allomorphy. This was, however, smoothed away by change over the past century, as shown schematically by the notation S3 > S1 in the 1PL cell in Table 8.1. While 2SG/2PL imperative forms are invariably based on S1, the 1PL imperative used to be a suppletive form from the present subjunctive, as in Italian, Spanish, or Portuguese (cf. e.g. Swearingen 2011: 130). Although this suppletion, as in standard Italian, is also found in the 3SG/3PL, there is a synchronic difference in that only 1PL imperatives display imperative syntax, as shown by the enclitic position of pronominal clitics (see below, in (12)), the same way as in e.g. Italian *mangiàmolo* 'let's eat it', *cantiàmola* 'let's sing it[F]', etc. (cf. Graffi 1996: 135). Strictly speaking, it may thus be said that synchronically the imperative has a defective paradigm consisting of the 2SG, 1PL, and 2PL cells (therefore the remaining ones are greyed out in Table 8.1). Now, as I said, the 1PL for irregular verbs used to be formed on S3, and also the endings were those occurring in the pres_s, not only for irregular but for regular verbs too, as exemplified in (11) with data from the nineteenth-century verses of the Bonorvese poet Paulicu Mossa (1818–1892):[14]

(11) a. *andemus como* 'let's go now', *isolvemus sas velas pro torrare* 'let's deploy our sails in order to return' (Mossa 1982: 81)

   b. *ponzemus pe' in mare* 'let's put our foot to the sea' (Mossa 1982: 81), *ponzemus paghes* 'let's make peace' (Mossa 1982: 87)

---

[14] The corresponding pres_s forms are homophonous. Note, however, that the pres_s form in (11a) is *annémus* in present-day Bonorvese, due to *nd* > *nn* assimilation, which takes place here like in many other Sardinian dialects.

Present-day Bonorvese speakers, however, normally use for this cell of the imperative paradigm a form coinciding with the pres_i, not (any longer) with that of the pres_s:

(12)   a. *manigámonnolla/*[??]*manigémunnolla nóis, kústa pètta* 'let's eat this meat ourselves'; *kantámola/*[??]*kantémula nóis, kusta kantòne* 'let's sing it ourselves, this song'

   b. *ponímolu/*ponzémulu innòghe* 'let's put it here' (cf. pres_i *ponímos* vs. pres_s *ponzémus*); *muntenímola/*muntenzémula nois, kústa kadrèa* 'let's hold this chair ourselves'

With regular verbs (12a) the subjunctive form, which is only affixally distinct from its indicative counterpart, is judged by some informants as less strongly ungrammatical than with irregular verb lexemes (12b) which display stem allomorphy. However, I have never heard forms such as those in (12a) produced in spontaneous speech by my informants. This suggests that, probably in the early twentieth century, the allomorphy in the imperative was disposed of so that stem selection was realigned with mood in this verb tense too. In sum, the imperative nowadays displays only S1 throughout.

8.4.1 *Diachronic change and the L-pattern in Logudorese*

After what has been said in the preceding sections, it is clear that the L-pattern is the only exception to regular alignment of stem allomorphy with tense/mood in (this variety of) Logudorese. In order to discuss the peculiarity of this morphomic partition in Logudorese, with respect to the rest of Romance, let us recall the diachronic sources that ultimately gave rise to morphomic partition classes in the Romance verb according to Maiden (2003, 2005*a*: 146–58, 2011*b*: 223):

(13)   Diachronic sources of the L-/U-/N-patterns
   a. 'yod-effect': e.g. It. *faccio* ['fat:ʃo] 'do.PRS_I.1SG' < PRom ['fakjo] < Lat. FACIO ['fakio(:)] (likewise, Log. *fátto* < Lat. FACIO);
   b. palatalization/affrication of velar consonants: e.g. It. *fa*[tʃ]*eva* < Lat. FA-[k]IEBAT (but Log. *faghíat* < Lat. FACIEBAT, *rúghe* 'cross' < Lat. CRUCEM);
   c. differentiation in quality between stressed and unstressed vowels (> stress-related alternations): e.g. It. *vieni* vs. *venite* 'come.IMPER.2SG/PL' (but Log. *béni* vs. *beníde* < Lat. VENI vs. VENITE).

As Maiden observes, Sardinian underwent the changes recapitulated under the label 'yod-effect' (13a), which is where the L-pattern is rooted, whereas it did not undergo (13b–c), which explains the non-occurrence of the U- and N-patterns. When introducing the data on the L-pattern in Section 8.3, I have shown (cf. (7)) that the verb *fágher* has three BSs where the L-pattern usually provides for just two (S1 vs. S2, e.g.

in Pirrelli and Battista's (2000) analysis of Italian). Diachronically, S2 (in *fátto*) is the expected result of the 'yod-effect' (cf. (13a)), whereas S3 (*fètt-a* pres_s) results from analogical reshaping of the regular outcome of Lat. FACIAM (> *fátta*), which is still preserved in other Logudorese dialects such as that of Buddusò (*fátta/*fètta*, *fáttas/*fèttas* pres_s 1–2SG, with the same stem occurring in the pres_i 1SG *fátto*; cf. Molinu 1999: 135). Thus, Bonorvese must also once have had a 'regularly irregular' L-pattern here, before the subjunctive of *fágher* was reshaped on the model provided by *krètta* (cf. (4) and (10d) above), whose -*è*- is etymological (cf. Wagner 1938–1939: 155, 169).[15] Note that though this is not a general situation across Sardinian, co-occurrence of three stems in this area of the paradigm of *fágher* is not an isolated peculiarity of the Logudorese variety of Bonorva: for instance, the same is true of the dialect of Luras, where one finds *fátto* (S2), *fághes* (S1) pres_i 1–2SG vs. *fètte, fèttes* pres_s 1–2SG.

In what follows, I will first show that the L-pattern did act as a catalyst for morphological change in Logudorese, as elsewhere in Romance, but then that change also happens to have disrupted the L-pattern in other cases. The data in (14) illustrate the rise of stem allomorphy via regular sound change (the 'yod-effect'):[16]

(14)		1SG			3SG		
Lat. 2nd conj.	DOLEO	> Log.	*dòlzo*	vs. Lat.	DOLET	> Log.	*dòlet*
	PAREO	>	*pálzo*		PAR(E)T	>	*párit*
	VALEO	>	*bálzo*		VAL(E)T	>	*bálit*
3rd conj.	FACIO	>	*fátto*		FAC(I)T	>	*faghet*
	MORIO(R)	>	*mòlzo*		MORIT(UR)	>	*mórit*
4th conj.	APERIO	>	*abbèlzo*		APERIT	>	*abbérit*
	VENIO	>	*bènzo*		VENIT	>	*bénit*
	FERIO	>	*fèlzo*		FERIT	>	*férit*

Thus, the L-pattern in, say, *mòrrer* 'die' or *bènner* 'come' (cf. (2)–(3) above) is etymologically justified. In addition, stem allomorphy spread to several other 2nd conjugation verbs, where it was not etymologically motivated. As shown in (15), their 1SG pres_i forms (as well as the whole subjunctive) display a stem that would be expected, had yod been there etymologically:

---

[15] S3 *krètt-* of *krè(e)r* 'believe' has in turn made its way into the subjunctive, coming from the perfect (cf. (18) below): (late) Lat. *CREDUIT > OLog. *kréttit*, which does not seem to be attested (it is not reported in Meyer-Lübke 1902: 47–8, Wagner 1938–1939: 11–21, or Blasco Ferrer 2003: 213, 231) but must have existed alongside the pst_pt *kréttidu* (cf. e.g. *cretidu* in Blasco Ferrer 2003: 189, from the *Statuti di Castelgenovese* 190.5, about 1334–1336; or in Lupinu 2010: 116, *Carta de logu* 71.5, 13).

[16] Except for *fèlzo* 'injure, wound', glosses for the data in (14)–(15) have been provided in (10) above. In the Latin etyma, I include in brackets the theme vowels which do not appear in the Bonorvese outcome due to analogical change (cf. Loporcaro 2003: 92–107).

(15) Lat.   CURRO   > Log.   *kúlzo*   (as if from *currio*)

                       PONO   *pònzo*   (as if from *ponio*)

                       DUCO   *giútto*   (as if from *ducio* [x *iugum*])

                       PRAEFERO   *preffèlzo* (as if from *praeferio*)

                       QUAERO   *kèlzo*   (as if from *quaerio*)

        alongside   POTEO   *pòtto*[17]

This is a typical manifestation of the L-pattern effect, via analogical extension of allomorphy, or a case of 'irregularity as a determinant of morphological change' (Maiden 1992), as shown in (16):

(16) a.
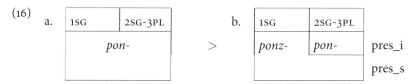

However, as seen in Section 8.3, (16b) is not the only possible distribution of stem allomorphy in the pres_i/s: this justifies the assumption of three distinct stem indexes $S_1 \neq S_2 \neq S_3$, which are needed since it is not the case that 1SG and subjunctive always share the same stem allomorph, unlike, say, in Italian.

One might expect this tripartition to have consequences for diachrony, which is indeed the case. Consider some of the irregular verbs listed above in (10d) and (10g) (*kèrrer*, *párrer*, *báler*, *dòler*), exemplified with *kèrrer* in (17):

(17)

	1SG	2SG-3PL
S_4 *kèrr(er)*	S_2 *kèlz-*	S_1 *kèr-*
'want'	($S_3 = S_2$)	

S_5 *kélfid-u*

As shown in (17), this verb has four distinct stems, with the familiar L-pattern distribution historically due to the yod-effect.[18]

Consider now the diachronic changes that involved what nowadays occurs as S_5 in the pst_pt (*kélfid-u*). Originally, the S_5 of those verbs was formed on the preterite stem (Wagner 1938–1939: 24, Pisano 2004–2006: 220) (cf. (18a–b)):

(18) a. Lat. *QUAERUI (replacing QUAESĪVI) > OLog. *kerui* (CSP 183) > *kerfi* > †

      b. pst_pt (S_5) formed on the preterite stem: *kérw-itu* > *kérfitu* > *kélfidu*

      c. SBJV (S_3) formed on the preterite stem: *kérw-at* > *kèrfat* > *kèlfat*

---

[17] Log. *pòtto* (< (late) Latin *poteo*) should be listed under (14), since it is an analogical form (on the model of regular *-ere* verbs) which ousted Classical Latin POSSUM not only in Sardinian (cf. central-southern Italian *pòttso, -u*, Rohlfs 1968: 283).

[18] The same goes for *párrer*, whereas *báler* and *dòler* had three inherited stems, before the change to be described directly.

As seen in (18c), this stem was also extended to the subjunctive, yielding kèlfat (Wagner 1938–1939: 15). After the preterite disappeared, the pst_pt stem S5 can be analysed synchronically as formed by applying the 2nd class participial ending -idu to the subjunctive stem S3, as shown above in (9b). Diachronically, though, the reverse was the case, as it is the subjunctive which is a later formation, based on the preterite stem that nowadays survives in the pst_pt after the demise of the preterite.

In some cases, the original preterite and subjunctive stems merged due to sound change. This is exemplified in (19) with pòder 'be able to', in whose paradigm the phonetic strings [tw] (occurring in the proto-Romance successor of Lat. POTUI > OLog. potti, cf. Wagner 1938–1939: 15) and [tj] (occurring in the proto-Romance successor of Lat. POTEAM > Log. potta), have merged into a geminate [tt]:

(19)	1SG	2SG-3PL		Lat. POTUI > OLog. potti
pòd(er) (S4 = S1)	S2 pòtt-o	S1 pòd-es		POTEAM	pòtta
'be able to'	pòtt-a, -as, -at … (S3 = S2)	S5 póttid-u	POTEO	pòtto

However, stems ending in a coronal sonorant like that of 'want' do preserve the distinction, so that one can still tell which stem allomorphs come from a w-preterite and which are original to the subjunctive. Given these circumstances, it is possible to observe that the spread of the preterite stem into subjunctive has disrupted the L-pattern:

(20) a. free variation S2 / S3   kèlz-at   /   kèlf-at   'want'
          in the pres_s: pálz-at   /   pálf-at   'seem'
                                   bálz-at   /   bálf-at   'be worth'
                                   dòlz-at   /   dòlf-at   'hurt'
      b. no free variation (only S2) kèlz-o   /   *kèlf-o   'want'
          in the pres_i: pálz-o   /   *pálf-o   'seem'
                                   bálz-o   /   *bálf-o   'be worth'
                                   mi dòlz-o /   %mi dòlf-o 'complain'

Free variation of the two stems has become established only in the subjunctive ((20a) shows the pres_s, and the same applies to the impf_s: e.g. kelz-èra-t/kelf-èra-t, etc.), because the stem originally associated with the preterite did not creep into the 1SG pres_i (20b).[19] Reciprocally, the originally subjunctive stem which had arisen via the yod-effect did not compete with the pst_pt stem S5:

---

[19] From Wagner (1938–1939: 154) it seems as though at least some Logudorese dialects restored the L-pattern here, in that bálfo and dòlfo are given as possible 1SG pres_i alternatives to inherited bálzo and dòlzo (not, however, *kèrfo, *pálfo). Indeed the L-pattern has resisted this analogical change in the northern Logudorese dialect of Buddusò, for which Molinu (1988–1989: 51, 169) reports free variation between the stem allomorphs of these verbs not only in the subjunctive but also in the 1SG pres-i (bálfo/bálzo, pálfo/pálzo, kèlfo/kèlzo). The same dialect, as noted earlier in this section, did not develop an S2 vs. S3 contrast in the verb fágher (Molinu 1988–1989: 151).

(21) no free variation in S5:   *kélfid-u / *kélzid-u*   'want'
                                 *pálfid-u / *pálzid-u*   'seem'
                                 *bálfid-u / *bálzid-u*   'be worth'
                                 *dólfid-u / *dólzid-u*   'hurt'

Note that in the case of *kèrrer* and *párrer*, listed in (10g) among the verbs displaying four distinct stems, this brings to a maximum exploitation of the stem contrasts provided for by the system, i.e. to five distinct stems:

(22) Five stems

infinitive	pres_i (2SG-)	1SG pres_i	1SG pres_s	pst_pt	gloss
kèrrer	*kéres*	*kèlzo*	*kèlza/kèlfa*	*kélfídu*	'want'
párrer	*páris*	*pálzo*	*pálza/pálfa*	*pálfídu*	'seem'

The asymmetry in (20a) vs. (20b)/(21) is not in line with the facts in (15)–(16), and attests to contradictory tendencies within the system. The same conflict is also observed in idiolectal variation, as shown in (23) with the example of the verb *kúrrer* 'run':

(23) a.

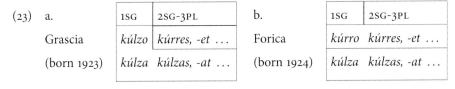

	1SG	2SG–3PL			1SG	2SG–3PL
Grascia	*kúlzo*	*kúrres, -et ...*	b. Forica		*kúrro*	*kúrres, -et ...*
(born 1923)	*kúlza*	*kúlzas, -at ...*	(born 1924)		*kúlza*	*kúlzas, -at ...*

The data in (23a–b) are representative of the linguistic competence of two sisters. Grascia has the L-pattern in the conjugation of this verb, which is no doubt the conservative option, being attested widely throughout Logudorese: cf. *kúlzo, kúrres* in the dialect of Bosa, *kúrzo, kúrres* in Macomer, etc. As shown in (15), this is one of the effects of the productivity of the L-pattern. Forica, on the other hand, displays morphosyntactic alignment of allomorphy, on the model provided by the verbs in (4)–(6): this is an innovation which, again, disrupts the L-pattern, in a way that is not documented in (the history of) other Romance languages such as Italian. Here, for instance, when the old Tuscan paradigm of *vedere* 'see' *veggio, vedi* 1–2SG pres_i, *veggia* 1SG pres_s was regularized, S1 (*ved-*) was extended uniformly to all cells previously hosting S2 (*vegg(i)-*).

To sum up, on the one hand we have evidence that the L-pattern has spread over time, in Logudorese just as in Spanish, Portuguese, Catalan, old French, and old Romanian (cf. Maiden 2011*b*: 225–38). This demonstrates that 'speakers make structural generalizations [...] over a disjunct set of morphosyntactic categories, in which first person singular present indicative, and present subjunctive [...] share a distinctive root' (Maiden 2011*b*: 241).

On the other hand, Bonorvese data such as those in (20b), (21), and (23b) also show that this 'disjunct set', in several instances, has been disjoined again. In the final analysis, it seems that Logudorese Sardinian did share from the outset this important organizing principle of the Romance verbal paradigm, but it also seems that its speakers had alternative models at their disposal: not only the alignment of allomorphy with mood, as in (4)–(6) and (23b), but also the three-way contrast S1 ≠ S2 ≠ S3 that we saw at work in (7) and (23) and which seems to be unique to Sardinian across Romance. These alternative arrangements were an option available to Logudorese speakers (contrary to, say, speakers of Italian or Spanish, where they are missing altogether) and apparently had the power of counterbalancing, to an extent, the impact of the L-pattern on the verb inflection system.

8.5 Incipient N-pattern in Sardinian?

In a section under the title 'Indo-European, Sardinian and the N-pattern', Maiden (2011*b*: 263) stresses that Logudorese Sardinian completely lacks this kind of morphomic class partition and argues that this can be explained through the fact that its phonological system did not undergo the vowel quality differentiation processes (such as diphthongization) that elsewhere provided the original phonologically motivated nucleus 'which attracted and channelled other kinds of allomorphy', giving rise to this morpheme elsewhere in Romance. From this, the prediction ensues that 'any Romance variety that had escaped stress-conditioned vowel differentiation should not show the N-pattern'.[20]

8.5.1 *The N-pattern in Campidanese*

The only case of N-pattern distribution considered by Maiden regards root suppletion in the conjugation of the verb 'go' in a Campidanese dialect, that of Villacidro (AIS pt. 973) (24a). With slightly different distributions, suppletion in the same verb is described for other Campidanese dialects as well, such as Sulcitano (Wagner 1938–1939: 166–7, Piras 1994: 276):

(24)

	1SG	2SG	3SG	1PL	2PL	3PL	*andái* 'go'
a.	bándu	bándas	bándada	andáus	andáis	bándanta	pres_i Villacidro
b.	bándu/báu	bázi	bári	andáus	andáis	bánti	pres_i Sulcis

---

[20] The same point had already been made by Maiden (2003: 15, 2005*a*: 163–4).

Occurrence of 'occasional examples of the N-pattern in the verb "go"' in Campidanese is explained by Maiden (2011*b*: 712–13, n. 70) by appealing to the circumstance
that Campidanese has departed from Logudorese in developing non-predictable
vowel alternations, due to the phonologization of the contrasts /e $\neq$ ɛ/, /o $\neq$ ɔ/
(Virdis 1988: 900). Indeed, Campidanese shows several more examples of N-pattern
distribution, independently from vowel alternations. Consider the following data
from Oristanese (I. Putzu, p.c.):

(25)

1SG	2SG	3SG	1PL	2PL	3PL	*krèi* 'believe'
krèu	krèisi	krèidi	kreéusu	kreéisi	krèinti	pres_i
krètta/ krètza	krèttas(ta)/ krètzasta	krèttada/ krètzada	krejáusu	krejáisi	krèttanta/ krètzanta	pres_s

(26)

1SG	2SG	3SG	1PL	2PL	3PL	*lassài* 'leave'
lássu	lássasa	lássada	lassáusu	lassáisi	lássanta	pres_i
lèssi	lèssis(ti)	lèssidi	lasséusu	lasséisi	lèssini	pres_s

These irregular verbs show regular inflections (1st class for *lassài*, 2nd class for *krèi*),
the irregularity being limited to stem allomorphy. This singles out the 1–2PL cells in
the pres_s, in a way that cannot be traced back to sound change. As for (26), the stem
lèss- arose through analogy on other subjunctive forms with etymological stressed
-*è*-, just like in Logudorese (cf. (5) above, and Wagner, 1938–1939: 170). Thus,
occurrence of the S1 *lass-* in the 1–2PL, where **lesséusu*, **lesséisi* are judged ungrammatical, has no phonological explanation and must be regarded as a bona fide
example of N-pattern distribution, since S1 occurs, by definition, not only in the
pres_i (as shown in (26)) but throughout the paradigm, a requirement emphasized
by Maiden (2003: 5).[21]

Compared with *lassái*, the case of *krèi* is slightly less telling, since the stem
allomorph occurring in the 1–2PL pres_s (*krej-*) is not exactly identical to S1 (*kre-*),
neither synchronically nor diachronically.[22] Yet the crucial fact is that the competing

---

[21] Note that while many of the instances of N-pattern discussed by Maiden involve the collection of
cells 'singular + 3PL' in the pres_i, examples of pres_s also feature in the database (cf. Maiden 2003: 9). In
this chapter, I adopt the broader definition (cf. e.g. Smith 2011*b*: 320: 'one stem is found in all three persons
singular and the third person plural of the present tense') rather than the more restrictive one, which also
is in circulation (e.g. Swearingen 2011: 119: 'a set of paradigmatic cells comprising the present indicative of
the 1SG, 2SG, 3SG, and 3PL in allomorphic contrast to the 1PL and 2PL').

[22] While *kre-* is a regular outcome of Lat. CRED- (e.g. *krèu* 'believe.PRES_I.1SG' < CREDO), *krej-* can be
traced back to an analogical subjunctive stem *CREDE(AM), with the regular change /dj/ > /j/ (Wagner
1941: 86, 143).

pres_s allomorphs *krètt-* and *krètz-* appear in the paradigm only in the N-pattern collection of cells, so that 1PL **krettéus/*kretzéus* and 2PL **krettéis/*kretzéis* are ungrammatical. None of those developments has any relationship with (phonologically motivated) vowel alternation.

In the dialect of Cagliari (Cagliaritano, Sardinian *Casteddaju*), the verb *krèi* 'believe' has stem allomorphy aligned with mood (27) rather than the N-pattern, like its Logudorese (4) and unlike its Oristanese (25) counterparts:[23]

(27)

1SG	2SG	3SG	1PL	2PL	3PL	*krèi* 'believe'
krèu	krèisi	krèiri	kreéusu	kreéisi	krèinti	pres_i
krèttara	krèttas	krèttara	krettáusu	krettáisi	krèttanta	pres_s

The N-pattern occurs again, on the other hand, in the Cagliaritano paradigm of *nái* 'say, tell':

(28)

1SG	2SG	3SG	1PL	2PL	3PL	*nái* 'say, tell'
náu	nárasa	nárara	naráusu	naráisi	ná(ra)nta	pres_i
néridi	nérisi	néridi	naréusu	naréisi	nérinti	pres_s

Here, two sources of allomorphy combine, none of which has a phonological cause: on the one hand, one observes alternation and/or variation of long (*nar-*) vs. short (*n-*) stems in the pres_i; on the other, the pres_s displays a stem allomorph with stressed *é*, rather than *-a-* occurring elsewhere throughout all tenses/moods. For this verb, too, occurrence of stressed *é* in the subjunctive is explained by Wagner (1938–1939: 169) as due to analogy. Now, the interesting fact for us is that the *nér-* stem is limited to the N-pattern cells. The analogical extension, in other words, did not make it into the 1–2PL cells which—given the N-pattern partition—show a solidarity with the rest of the paradigm, rather than with the singular and the 3PL cells in the same tense.

The collection of similar data for Campidanese could be expanded. But already the few examples discussed here show that the N-pattern seems to have acted as a moulding force in the verbal paradigm in this Romance variety too.

---

[23] There is variation in both stems and the form of some endings: my informant for *Casteddu* (Cagliari alta) preserves intervocalic *-d-* which turns to *-r-* in more popular pronunciation (reflected in (27)). As to stems, some speakers also have regular subjunctive forms built on S1 (*krèara* 1=3SG) or forms built on a distinct pres_s stem (*krètzara* 1=3SG). While this is not germane to our present concerns, note that the pres_s stem *krett-*, unlike in Oristanese, is not banned from the 1–2PL.

8.5.2 *N-pattern effects in Logudorese varieties?*

In this section, I will finally consider some possible candidates for an N-pattern distribution from Logudorese. The first case in point comes from the alternation of long vs. short stem forms in the verb 'say, tell' which, in some dialects of Logudorese, shows a solidarity of 1–2PL vs. the remaining cells of the pres_i that appears to be the mirror image of the Campidanese data in (28). In the dialect of the Planargia area, according to Wagner (1938–1939: 167), the short forms (*n*-) are in free variation with the long ones (*nar*-) only in the 1–2PL:

(29)

1SG	2SG	3SG	1PL	2PL	3PL	*nárrer* 'say, tell'
náro	náras	nárat	narámos/námos	narázis/nádes	nárana	pres_i

However, contrary to the Campidanese case in (28), there is no stem sharing between the 1–2PL pres_i and the rest of the paradigm.

Another case in point might be that of verbs like the following in Bonorvese:

(30)

1SG	2SG	3SG	1PL	2PL	3PL	*bíer* 'see'
bí-o	bí-es	bí-et	bid-ímos	bid-ídes	bí-en	pres_i
bí-a	bí-as	bí-at	bid-émus	bid-èdas	bí-an	pres_s

As in most of Logudorese (apart from the central-eastern dialect area centring on Nuoro; cf. Wagner 1941: 79), intervocalic voiced stops (plus -v-, which merged with -B- throughout Romance) were deleted via regular sound change (e.g. Log. *còa* < rustic Lat. CODAM). Among them, -D- was the most resistant, as it was irregularly preserved in some lexemes, including the verb *bí(d)er* 'see' < VIDERE, which has both variants across Logudorese (Wagner 1941: 80). Now, in Bonorvese, as seen in (30), the two variants were specialized for different paradigm cells, and the same -*d*-/-Ø-alternation was extended to verbs in which a labial or velar voiced obstruent had been deleted originally, such as *iskríer* 'write' < SCRIBERE or *fríer* < FRIGERE: (Variation, observed in some cells, will be addressed directly.)

(31)

1SG	2SG	3SG	1PL	2PL	3PL	*iskríer* 'write'
iskrí-o	iskrí-es	iskrí-et	iskrid-ímos	iskrid-ídes	iskrí-en	pres_i
iskrí-o	iskrí-es	iskrí-et	iskri(d)-émus	iskri(d)-èdas	iskrí-an	pres_s

(32)

1SG	2SG	3SG	1PL	2PL	3PL	*fríer* 'fry'
frí-o	frí-es	frí-et	frid-ímos	frid-ídes	frí-en	pres_i
frí-a	frí-as	frí-at	frid-émus	frid-èdas	frí-an	pres_s

At least as a first step, the ensuing *-d-/-Ø-* alternation is motivated phonologically, as seen in the verb *ríer* 'laugh' < RIDERE:

(33)

1SG	2SG	3SG	1PL	2PL	3PL	*ríer* 'laugh'
rí-o	rí-es	rí-et	rid-ímos	rid-ídes	rí-en	pres_i
rí-a	rí-as	rí-at	ri-émus	ri-èdas	rí-an	pres_s

d-insertion occurs, synchronically (and *-d-* < -D- was preserved, diachronically) where otherwise an *i+i* hiatus would have arisen. This generalization is largely borne out by inspection of the remaining forms of the paradigm:

(34)

	a. bí-er	b. rí-er	c. frí-er	d. iskí-er
Impf_i	bidía	ridía	fridía	iskridía
Impf_s	bidère	rière	frière	iskrière
Ger	bidínne	rinne	fridínne	iskrínne

Abstracting away from differences in the gerund, where selection of a shorter stem in *rínne*, *iskrínne* occurs unpredictably as an alternative hiatus-preventing strategy, *-d-* always occurs between stem-final *-i* and an initial *i-* of a following ending/stem formative.

Note, however, that this phonologically motivated distribution is preserved categorically only in *ríer* (cf. (33), (34b)), whereas *-d-* in *bíer* has been extended to all arrhizotonic forms of the subjunctive (cf. (30), (34a)), with *iskríer* and *fríer* lying in between.[24] A further question is whether pairs such as *ri(e)-/rid-* have to be listed as allomorphs, or can still be derived phonologically from one and the same underlying form: the latter position is endorsed in Loporcaro (2012: 27–8), whereas stem allomorphy, as argued there, would presumably follow under stem-maximizing assumptions such as Taylor's (2008). If one considers *bíer*, though, with extension of *bid-* to (subjunctive) forms not displaying the appropriate phonological context, it is clear that *-d-* insertion has become correlated with a certain subset of paradigmatic cells. While readers can compute by themselves whether or not this has to be considered—for the different verbs involved—as an instance of the N-pattern, it is clear that some arbitrary (hence purely morphological) collections of cells are at stake here.

---

[24] No doubt a systematic quantitative study over larger samples of Bonorvese speakers would reveal finer-grained variation within this area of paradigmatic instability. Yet, for the point to be made here, even these preliminary data, based on the competence of a dozen speakers from different generations, may be enough.

Finally, an even more compelling case for the occurrence of the N-pattern in Logudorese can be made based on data from the northern variety of Luras (in the province of Olbia-Tempio). Here, a group of 2nd class verbs whose stem ends in -*n(n)*- display a singleton/geminate alternation in the pres_i/imper along the following lines:[25]

(35)

1SG	2SG	3SG	1PL	2PL	3PL	*tènner* 'hold'[26]
tenío	tenías	teníat	teniámus	teniádes/-ázi(s)	tenían	impf_i
	tènne			teníde		imper
tènzo	tènnes	tènnet	tenímus	tenídes	tènnen	pres_i
tènze	tènzes	tènzet	tenzémus	tenzèdes	tènzen	pres_s
			tenzènde			gerund

(36)

1SG	2SG	3SG	1PL	2PL	3PL	*pònner* 'put'
ponío	ponías	poníat	poniámus	poniádes/-ázi(s)	ponían	impf_i
	pònne			poníde		imper
pònzo	pònnes	pònnet	ponímus	ponídes	pònnen	pres_i
pònze	pònzes	pònzet	ponzémus	ponzèdes	pònzen	pres_s
			ponzènde			gerund

Compare the (relevant part of) the paradigm of those two verbs in Bonorvese:

(37)

1SG	2SG	3SG	1PL	2PL	3PL	*tènner* 'hold'
	tène		tenímos	teníde		imper
tènzo	tènes	tènet	tenímos	tenídes	tènen	pres_i
tènza	tènzas	tènzat	tenzémus	tenzèdas	tènzan	pres_s

---

[25] In Lurese, the synthetic impf_s has been replaced by a compound tense, serving both imperfect and pluperfect functions: e.g. 1SG *essère téntu/ténnidu*. I have no data on 1PL imperative.

[26] The verb *manténner* 'hold, maintain' inflects the same way, apart from the pst_pt *mantésu*, as opposed to *téntu/ténnidu* 'held, kept'. Note in passing that the gerund shares the same stem (S3) as the 1SG pres_i and the subjunctive, in those cases where there is no S2 ≠ S3 distinction: when on the contrary there is a contrast, the gerund is based on S2 as seen in *fattènde* 'doing', with the same stem as the 1SG pres_i *fátto* (vs. *fètte, fèttes* pres_s 1-2SG). Thus, compared with Bonorvese (cf. Table 8.1 and §8.4), the alignment of stem allomorphy with mood is less pervasive in Lurese.

(38)

	1SG	2SG	3SG	1PL	2PL	3PL	*pònner* 'put'
		pòne		ponímos	poníde		imper
	pònzo	pònes	pònet	ponímos	poníde̞s	pònen	pres_i
	pònza	pònzas	pònzat	ponzémus	ponzèdas	pònzan	pres_s

Here, the L-pattern is observed, which in Lurese (cf. (35)–(36)) cumulates with a contrast between the pres_i singular (minus the 1SG, which shares the same stem with the pres_s, given the L-pattern) and 3PL, plus the 2SG imperative (all displaying *tènn-, mantènn-, pònn-*) vs. the 1–2PL of the pres_i, which share the default S1 *ten-, manten-, pon-*. The latter occurs in other tenses (the impf_i), thus satisfying the structural description of the N-pattern.[27] The issue is, at this point, whether this stem alternation can be explained away as purely phonological: if not, it will have to be recognized as a bona fide instance of N-pattern.

Note that a phonological reason would seem to be available at first glance, if one compares the phonetic realizations of the verb forms in (39a) with that of the other words in (39b):

(39) a. ['tɛnːɛzɛ] 'hold.pres_i.2SG', ['tɛnːɛðɛ] 'hold.pres_i.3SG', ['pɔnːɛzɛ] 'put.pres_i.2SG', ['pɔnːɛðɛ] 'put.pres_i.3SG', etc.

   b. *bénnaru* 'son-in-law' < GENERUM, *ténnaru* 'soft' < TENERUM 'soft' (cf. Depperu 2006: 88, 599)[28]

As illustrated in (39b), any -N- following the stressed vowel of a proparoxytonic word was regularly geminated, and as seen in (39a) the verb forms at issue are realized as proparoxytones prepausally. However, this is due to epithesis, a synchronic rule which applies across the board (cf. n. 5 above). Consequently, the verb forms in (39b) are underlyingly paroxytonic, and have always been such.[29] And no

---

[27] Inclusion of the gerund in the set of the N-pattern cells in (35)–(36) is reminiscent of the solidarity of the gerund with the U-pattern cells in old Tuscan which, just as in Lurese, could be either motivated etymologically (cf. (ia)) or due to analogical extension of the stem originally found in the U-pattern cells (cf. (ib)) (cf. Maiden 1996a: 176–7):

		gerund	1SG/3PL pres_i	pres_s	
(i)	a.	*vegnendo* < VENIENDO	*vegno* < VENIO	*vegna* < VENIAM	'come'
	b.	*veggendo* not a regular outcome of VIDENDO	*veggio* < VIDEO	*veggia* < VIDEAM	'see'

The two cases correspond respectively to Lurese (41) below vs. (35)–(36).

[28] The same phenomenon has already been attested in old Logudorese (cf. Meyer-Lübke 1902: 35, reporting the same two examples *ienneru* and *tenneru*).

[29] The corresponding infinitives, on the other hand, have become paroxytonic as their final -E was reanalysed as epithetic in old Sardinian (cf. Wagner 1938–1939: 138), so that the underlying representation of 2nd class infinitive ending is /-er/ (cf. Loporcaro 1988b: 359, 2012: 28, Molinu 1999: 132).

underlyingly paroxytonic word(-form) which becomes proparoxytonic at the surface owing to epithesis ever undergoes *n*-gemination, as shown in (40):

(40) [ˈmanɔzɔ]/*[ˈmanːɔzɔ] 'hands'   /ˈmanɔs/, [ˈkanɛzɛ]/*[ˈkanːɛzɛ] 'dogs'
      /ˈkanɛs/

This also applies to verb inflection, as shown by the paradigm of *bènner* 'come':

(41)

1SG	2SG	3SG	1PL	2PL	3PL	*bènner* 'come'[30]
benío	benías	beníat	beniámus	beniádes/-ázi(s)	benían	impf_i
	béni			beníde		imper
bènzo	bénis	bénit	benímus	benídes	bénin	pres_i
bènze	bènzas	bènzat	benzémus benzènde	benzèdes	bènzen	pres_s gerund

By the way, gemination in the infinitive of verbs with sonorant-ending stems is not due to the phonological process under discussion: indeed, several other verbs with stems ending in another sonorant, viz. /r/, share this property in Lurese and elsewhere in Sardinian (cf. Lurese *kèrrer* 'want', *mòrrer* 'die'). This change had already occurred by the old Sardinian stage, and is explained by Meyer-Lübke (1902: 42) as an analogical extension from the perfect stem (which may work for cases like Log. *tènner*, cf. OLog. *tenni* 'held', not for *kèrrer* 'want', given the OLog. preterite *kerfi*; Wagner 1938–1939: 15).

In sum, once it is ascertained that a phonological motivation for the occurrence of geminate -*nn*- in (a functionally arbitrary collection of cells within) the Lurese paradigms in (35)–(36) is to be excluded, this stands out as a case of N-pattern effect. Apparently, geminate -*n*-, first arising in the infinitive stem for whatever reason (perhaps due to analogy on the perfect), was generalized to the N-pattern cells, which then showed joint behaviour under morphological change, as expected if they constitute a morpheme.

8.6 Conclusion

The results of the present study can be summarized as follows. On the synchronic side, I have provided a description of the paradigmatic organization of irregularity in one variety of Logudorese, thus filling a gap in research in Sardinian morphology.

---

[30] In the pres_s, the -*e* endings original to the 1st class (e.g. *kánte*, -*es*, etc.) are categorically extended to 2nd and 3rd class verbs, though for some speakers the original -*a* endings are still (irregularly) preferred for some cells. (41) mirrors the competence of one such speaker.

Capitalizing on this, I described (in §8.4.1) the diachronic behaviour of the L-pattern in Logudorese, showing that it has some properties which seem to be unique among the Romance languages. Finally, in Section 8.5 I presented a larger-scale (if shallower) investigation into two varieties of Logudorese and two of Campidanese, in order to verify whether they display N-pattern effects. The answer, at least in some cases, is in the positive.

9

The roots of language*

MARK ARONOFF

9.1 Introduction

In this chapter, I will try to cast light from several angles on the term *root* as it is used in current morphological theory and on the various notions that the term embodies. I will contrast two very different broad types of morphological theories that traffic in roots, which I will term *root-based* and *lexeme-based* theories. In root-based theories, morphological structure is built up from meaningful simplex roots. In lexeme-based theories, the starting point of morphological structure is lexemes, which are meaningful but need not be simplex; in this type of theory, roots may be part of morphological structure, but they play a less central role and their relation to meaning is more complex.

From a very general point of view, the major difference between the two lies in aesthetics. Root-based theories value reduction and perfection highly, both as analytical strategies and as aesthetic desiderata. For these theories, it is highly desirable on aesthetics grounds that the basic lexical elements of language be simplex signs. Lexeme-based theories give both these considerations much less privileged places in both theory and practice, so that it does not much matter whether the ultimate units of language are simplex signs or not. The apparent fact that simplex signs do not occupy a place of honour is interesting, but not surprising.

As exemplars of the two types of treatments of roots, I have chosen to contrast Distributed Morphology, because it is the most widely discussed root-based theory, with my own work, especially as exemplified in Aronoff (1994). Distributed Morphology (DM) has been around for some twenty years in a variety of slightly

* This chapter originated with a presentation at a workshop on roots organized at the Institute for Advanced Study at Hebrew University, Jerusalem, in June 2011. I thank the organizers of that conference and the participants who provided feedback. Olivier Bonami provided very helpful comments on an earlier version. I owe a great debt to Bob Hoberman, who taught me what little I know about the Arabic grammatical tradition and about Arabic morphology in general.

different incarnations. I will try to confine myself to the version presented in Halle and Marantz (1993), the *locus classicus* of the theory, but much of what I have to say applies more broadly.

My prejudices are well known, so it should not be surprising that I come down on the side of lexeme-based theories. My goal, though, is not simply to excoriate root-based morphology, but to understand its motivation and sources. In the first part of this chapter, I will explore how roots have been treated in modern linguistics, from both perspectives (§9.3). In the second part, which is more substantive in many ways, I will take a longer perspective and look at the development of the treatment of roots in the grammatical traditions surrounding the two languages where roots have figured most prominently: Arabic and Hebrew (§9.4). I began researching this question under the assumption that the origins of the grammatical theory of roots lay in the Arabic tradition, but I have concluded that it is not obvious that the root as we understand it today was isolated as a distinct entity by the early Arabic grammarians. Instead, it is only in the tradition of Hebrew grammar (itself a somewhat late historical offshoot of Arabic grammar) that we can conclude unequivocally that the root assumed the theoretical role that most linguists have assigned to it. In the last part of the chapter (§9.5), I will look at the evidence for roots in modern-day Semitic languages from more empirically oriented approaches: neurolinguistics, experimental psycholinguistics, and first language acquisition. I will show that this evidence comes down on the side of lexeme-based theories of morphological roots.

Overall, my aim is to show that roots are real linguistic entities but that there is no point in assuming that all instances of a given root have the same meaning in any language, that roots are semantically invariant. Roots are part of the autonomous morphological system of a language and what is special about Arabic and Hebrew are the obligatory templates for verbs, not the roots. Overall, this conclusion should not be surprising.

The idea that roots are semantically invariant is old and grows out of a grammatical tradition whose object of study was, in the eyes of its practitioners, the sacred language of the first known divinely-inspired book, the Old Testament, and even more specifically the Pentateuch. It should not be surprising that students of such a language might want to treat it as a perfect system. This tradition persisted into the nineteenth century in such fanciful ideas as those of Fabre d'Olivet (1815–1816), who believed that not only Biblical Hebrew roots but the Hebrew letters themselves had invariant meanings, a view that greatly influenced Benjamin Lee Whorf's work on inner meaning. What should surprise us is the persistence of such beliefs when considering the languages of humans rather than God.

9.2 Controversies

The discussion of roots has generated as much heat as it has light over the last twenty years. But hot debate among grammarians is nothing new. William Chomsky, in his book on David Kimḥi's grammar of Hebrew, tells the following story about a pair of medieval grammarians:

The versatile and brilliant statesman, soldier, and poet, Samuel ha-Nagid (11th century) found time amidst his multifarious duties and occupations to engage in verbal clashes on grammatical issues with the profound grammarian Ibn Janah and to write, according to Ibn Ezra's testimony, twenty-two books of 'supreme quality' (v'eyn lm'alah mimenu) on Hebrew grammar [...] The grammatical controversy between Ibn Janah and Samuel ha-Nagid is recounted at some length in the writings of some of the medieval Hebrew grammarians. Samuel ha-Nagid apparently aroused by Ibn Janah's criticism of some of the views of his teacher, Yehudah Hayyuj, sent a messenger from Granada to Saragossa, the place of Ibn Janah's residence, charged with the task of challenging Ibn Janah to a verbal duel on certain grammatical issues and of exposing publicly the 'fallacy' of his theories. On his arrival in Saragossa, the messenger stayed at the home of a communal leader in that city, named Abu Soleiman ben Taraka, a friend of Ibn Janah. A public reception was arranged in honor of the visitor, to which Ibn Janah was invited. The latter, without suspecting the chief purpose of the gathering, accepted the invitation. During the reception, the visitor began to inveigle Ibn Janah gradually and subtly into a discussion. Some of the questions raised by him were readily disposed of and adequately answered by Ibn Janah. But others followed, and Ibn Janah, unprepared for this barrage of questions, was befuddled, and he promised to reply at some future time. He did so and sent his reply to the visitor. The latter, however, superciliously remarked that it would be wiser for Ibn Janah to withhold his reply until the Nagid's book was published, where he would find even more serious criticisms leveled against him. This Ibn Janah refused to do. He issued his reply in book form and called it *Kitab at-Taswiya*. After the publication of the Nagid's attack on him Ibn Janah retorted with a violent counter-attack in a book, which he called *Kitab al-Tashwir*. Ibn Janah was very proud of this book, and he frequently referred to it in glowing terms, but, unfortunately, only a fragment of it is now extant. (Chomsky 1952: xv–xvii).

Similar tales are told about the Arabic grammarians from a much earlier time. Kufa and Basra are two cities in Southern Iraq founded by early Muslims, acknowledged to have been the intellectual centres of early Islam. The city names came to represent two schools of Arabic grammar, with the Kufan school being in the minority. The two schools differed on, among other matters, whether the *maṣdar* verbal noun was the *ʔaṣl* (base) of the verb or vice versa. The battle raged for centuries, though the Basrans are generally acknowledged to have won in the end.

Plus ça change, plus c'est la même chose. The battle between DMers and their opponents has raged with equal ferocity over the last two decades. Here is a small sample of the invective in Marantz (1997: 202):

This paper brings the reader the following news: Lexicalism is dead, deceased, demised, no more, passed on [...] The underlying suspicion was wrong and the leading idea didn't work out. This failure is not generally known because no one listens to morphologists. Everyone who has worked on the issues of domains—what are the domains for 'lexical phonological rules', what are the domains of 'special meanings', what are the domains of apparently special structure/meaning correspondences—knows that these domains don't coincide in the 'word' and in fact don't correlate (exactly) with each other. But the people that work on word-sized domains are morphologists, and when morphologists talk, linguists nap.

Marantz's opponents are more polite, but no less damning. Here are a few samples from Williams (2007):

These awkwardnesses all stem from the idea that idiomatic meanings can all be fixed on the 'roots' that occur in the idiom, and not on the idiom itself; and that stems from the decision that the lexicon(s) in DM do not list any derived forms, and that in turn stems from the decision that morphemes are the sole units of insertion. (Williams 2007: 360)

As DM stands, all applications of the Pāṇinian principle which are not morpheme vs. morpheme contests must be recast as one or another kind of rule of special allomorphy, turning gold into clay. (Williams 2007: 364)

There is no reason to accept any part of Marantz's analysis of nominalization. (Williams 2007: 367).

9.3 Roots in modern morphological theory

9.3.1 *Roots and the intellectual sources of DM*

Meaningful roots are central to DM. Marantz (1997: 212–13) proclaims that 'Things with special meanings are roots'. The source of DM's insistence on the centrality of roots lies in the linguistic ideas of Roman Jakobson. Jakobson was a staunch reductionist who was strongly influenced by the successes of physics in the early twentieth century and believed that linguistics consisted mainly of removing the surface variance of languages to reveal the underlying invariance. Jakobson admired Baudouin de Courtenay and Kruszewski for their work on invariance, which he often argued to be the main source of modern synchronic linguistics.[1] Jakobson applied this aesthetic of invariance most fully and famously to his analysis of Russian nominal cases, in which the various meanings and uses of each case were reduced to a single abstract meaning (Jakobson 1971*a*).

Classic generative phonology was most centrally an attempt to apply a radical version of Jakobsonian invariance to sound systems. Its goal was to reduce the

---

[1] They coined the term *morpheme*, among many others, and were the first to use *phoneme* in something like its standard sense. Stankiewicz (1972) is an anthology of Baudouin de Courtenay's work, with some discussion of Kruszewski's influence on his teacher. Kruszewski's work is anthologized in English in Kruszewksi (1993). See Jakobson (1971*b*) for an assessment of the contributions of both.

linguistic signifiers of a language to an underlying level at which there was a one-to-one correspondence between the forms and meanings of simple signs. The DM notion of the root is a direct outgrowth of this Jakobsonian vision of languages: lexical items should be reduced to roots and each root should have a single form and a single meaning at some underlying level.

I have found no mention of roots in Chomsky and Halle's (1968) *The Sound Pattern of English* (SPE), the great masterwork of classic generative phonology; not surprising, since SPE makes no theoretical distinction between morphology (where roots reside) and syntax. The internal structure of a word like *theatr-ical-ity* is not provided by morphology but by syntax, in the form of a bracketed phrase structure tree to which the rules of phonology apply cyclically, with the cycles determined by the tree structure. There is implicit morphology distinct from syntax in SPE, though. The affixes in this same word *theatricality*, for example, are provided with internal morphological structure: *ic + al* and *i + ty*. In a footnote, the analysis of *i + ty* is said to be 'well motivated on morphological grounds' (Chomsky and Halle 1968: 33), based on the existence of the noun-forming affix *-ty* and such sets as *sanctity–sanctify–sanctitude* and *clarity–clarify*, although it is noted in the next footnote that this analysis of *ity* is not required by the phonology.

SPE makes use of the term and notion *stem*. For example, the *dox* of *orthodox* and the *graph* of *photograph* are labelled as stems and given their own (initial) cycle. Elsewhere, in particular in the analysis of Latinate verbs of the form 'prefix–stem' such as *permit*, *transfer*, and *compel*, the authors do not give the stem its own cycle, marking this particular construction by the famous '=' boundary (which is identified formally as neither a formative boundary nor a word boundary). In conclusion, nowhere that I can find does SPE use the term *root*; and though *stem* occurs in SPE it seems to be used by and large for bound stems, and apparently those without much semantic content.

The DM distinction between a list of roots and a list of words can be traced directly to Halle (1973). Halle uses the term *root* on the second page of this article, noting that 'the list [of morphemes] must include not only verbal, nominal, and adjectival roots but also affixes of various sorts' (Halle 1973: 4). One of the main points of this article is to provide an account for the fact that not all possible words actually occur, and those that do occur are often idiosyncratic in form or meaning. Halle encodes these idiosyncrasies by means of a dictionary that he characterizes as a filter:

I propose that idiosyncrasies of the type just illustrated be listed in a special filter through which the words have to pass after they have been generated by the word formation rules. The special information given in the filter under each entry is then added to the representation of the word. In the case of semantic idiosyncrasies such as those exemplified by the special meaning of nouns like *recital* and *transmittal* the filter would supply the appropriate indications about their semantics. In the case of phonological idiosyncrasies like those exhibited by nouns like *obesity*, the filter would supply the information that the noun in question is not subject to the Trisyllabic Shortening Rule, or, more formally, would supply the noun with the feature [–Trisyllabic Shortening Rule]. Finally, 'gaps' in the dictionary [...] would be accounted for by providing the 'missing' words with the rule feature [–Lexical Insertion]. In other words, the fact that English lacks the nouns *derival and *arrivation would be reflected in the grammar by marking these words, which would be generated by the word formation rules, as not being subject to lexical insertion and therefore incapable of appearing in any actual sentence of the language, in spite of the fact that they are neither semantically nor syntactically or phonologically anomalous. (Halle 1973: 5).

In other words, I am proposing that the list of morphemes together with the rules of word formation define the set of potential words of the language. It is the filter and the information that is contained therein which turn this larger set into the smaller subset of actual words. This set of actually occurring words will be called the dictionary of the language. (Halle 1973: 6).

Lexical insertion, within this framework, selects fully inflected words from this dictionary.[2] Researchers outside DM have not pursued the idea that the dictionary is a filter, because it is difficult to understand what Halle meant by the term *filter*. Are the dictionary entries the words that make it through the 'exception filter' or the ones that remain behind, those that are filtered out? The filter cannot be uniform in texture in any sense, as normal filters are, because it singles out the words that actually occur, which presumably comprise some sort of list. Furthermore, the filter provides some of these words, at least, with additional information that the rules of word formation do not provide. Overall, the relation among the dictionary, the filter, and the morphemes is not at all clear in this framework, which is admittedly not meant to be more than a prolegomenon.

DM makes use of another traditional term, *morpheme*, albeit in a very untraditional way. For DM, morphemes are not signs, sound/meaning pairs, but rather 'terminal elements of the trees [that] consist of complexes of grammatical features', which 'are supplied with phonological features only after Vocabulary insertion at M [orphological]S[tructure]' (Halle and Marantz 1993: 114). In other words, what they call morphemes are what most others call morphosyntactic features or properties or values, and what they call Vocabulary insertion (or 'the addition of phonological material' (p. 131)) is what others call morphological realization.[3] But Vocabulary insertion does more: 'In addition to phonological features, Vocabulary insertion supplies morphological features that signal idiosyncratic properties of specific Vocabulary items' (p. 136).

---

[2] Halle notes, incidentally, that 'certain words presuppose the existence of other words' (1973: 13), a harbinger of lexeme-based theories of morphology.

[3] It is not clear to me whether DM Vocabulary insertion differs at all from morphological realization rules or constraints. Both match phonological material with morphosyntactic information. DM allows for the morphology to manipulate the syntactic tree in various ways and even add structure before reaching Morphological Structure, but there is nothing to prevent other theories from doing the same if they like.

Nowhere do Halle and Marantz discuss the term *root* in their 1993 paper. As far as I can tell, roots are introduced into DM by Marantz (1997), who 'explodes the Lexicon and includes a number of distributed, non-computational lists as Lexicon-replacements' (p. 203). The first list of three, which he calls the 'narrow lexicon', 'contains the atomic roots of the language and the atomic bundles of grammatical features' (p. 203). The second list is the Vocabulary of Halle and Marantz, i.e. morphological realization or spell-out. The third list is Halle's dictionary redux under another name: 'Encyclopedia—the list of special meanings. The Encyclopedia lists the special meanings of particular roots, relative to the syntactic context of the roots, within local domains' (p. 204) and includes not only words but also all idiomatic expressions. In short, it is a Bloomfieldian lexicon of idiosyncratic complex items.

I won't speculate as to why DM plays so fast and loose with traditional terminology, here conflating *dictionary* and *encyclopaedia,* elsewhere *morpheme* and morphosyntactic feature value. The problem in this instance is that there is a well-established dichotomy in lexicology between the two terms at issue here, which is lost by calling one the other: a **dictionary** is a list of words: a dictionary definition contains only what is necessary to distinguish one word from another; while an **encyclopaedia** is about concepts and things: its entries contains all that there is to know about the entity named in each. Contrast the *Oxford English Dictionary* of 1928 with the *Encyclopaedia Britannica* of 1911. The first sought to include everything there was to know about the words of English. The other sought to include everything there was to know about everything besides the words of English. The DM Encyclopedia is not an encyclopaedia, but instead a dictionary, in fact a direct descendant of Halle's dictionary, a Bloomfield lexicon of 'idioms', irregular entities, including words and phrases. But within a theory that wishes to give words no special place, there can be no dictionary of words, and so the former dictionary is now called an encyclopaedia, even though it is not one, or at least this is the only explanation I can provide for the peculiar use of terminology here.

Which brings us back to roots. Roots in DM are mysterious objects. They have no phonological form, at least not at first, since they only receive form at the point of Vocabulary insertion and they are also subject to readjustment rules, but they do bear meaning: 'Things with special meanings are roots' (Marantz 1997: 212–13). As Williams (2007) notes, for DMers, it is not the case that what DM calls idioms have idiosyncratic meaning, but rather that the roots have idiosyncratic meanings in the context of individual expressions (idioms). DM roots are apparently not just abstract meaning-bearing elements, but rather the only true bearers of lexical meaning. In a way, they are like lexemes, except for being simplex (Aronoff 1994). And, as Williams argues, it is this claim about simplex roots bearing meaning that brings DM to grief.

But why make such a claim, especially when the existence of the 'Encyclopedia' makes the claim empirically empty, given that roots can have 'special contextual meanings' (Marantz 1997: 213)? The answer is that DM is a last-ditch attempt to preserve the vision of Jakobsonian invariance of elementary signs in the form of roots. From a signifier point of view, DM abandons this invariance to Vocabulary insertion, but it apparently cannot go so far as to abandon the signified side and so resorts to the artifice of supplying roots with abstract meanings that are then somehow moulded in context by means of the Encyclopedia. The upshot is that DM roots, in truth, have neither constant form nor constant meaning.

9.3.2 *Roots within lexeme-based morphology*

On 29 May 2011, Simon Winchester published a piece in *The New York Times* on the three 'most complex' verbs in the English language: *set*, *put*, and *run*. The last has now assumed top position as the verb in the *Oxford English Dictionary* (OED) with the most senses: 645 according to the official OED count. I will not attempt to prove that none of these 645 can be reduced to any other one, but consider just a few, listed in (1):

(1)   a. He ran the table
      b. The trains run between Jerusalem and Tel Aviv (ambiguous)
      c. Run a bath
      d. Run before the wind (of a sailboat)
      e. Overrun
      f. Run over
      g. Run a seam
      h. Run up a bill vs. run up a hill
      i. Run someone through with a sword

Within a lexeme-based theory, each of the however many distinct senses of *run* we finally decide there are is a separate lexeme with its own meaning, even though all are listed together in the dictionary. And here is where the concept of root becomes useful. All these distinct senses share the same three idiosyncratic forms: *run, ran, run* (the last two forming the past tense and past participle). Within a lexeme-based theory, we say that all three share a single abstract root $\sqrt{RUN}$. $\sqrt{RUN}$ does not have a constant sense, because it occurs in all these distinct lexemes; nor does it have a constant form. But all these lexemes share this single root, because they all vary in the same way under the same morphological conditions. Within lexeme-based theory, then, a root is a purely abstract morphological entity, a morphome. I suspect that the same is true in DM.

This analysis extends to all highly frequent irregular root/lexemes in all languages, which show the same consistent irregularity across multiple senses. In (2), I have provided a list of the most common English irregular verbs in rank frequency order:

(2)   BE, HAVE, DO, SAY, GET, MAKE, GO, KNOW, TAKE, SEE, COME,
      THINK, GIVE, FIND, TELL, FEEL, LEAVE

Just like √RUN, all of these verbs are highly polysemous and not one of them has a regularized analogue. We therefore say in a lexeme-based theory that each of these irregular verbs is a root that occurs in a large number of homophonous lexemes. We can also now understand how polysemy and homophony apply within such a theory: the roots are polysemous (inasmuch as they each occur in many lexemes), but the lexemes are homophonous (inasmuch as they share a single root).

Roots like English √RUN identify the paradigm of the lexemes that share this root. The root is not a semantic or phonological entity. Compare the homophonous English roots √RING₁ (with past tense form *rang* and participle form *rung*), √RING₂ (with past tense and participle form *ringed*), and √WRING (with both past tense and participle forms *wrung*). The root is purely morphological and similar to the *flexeme* of Fradin and Kerleroux (2003), Spencer's (2005) *lexemic index*, and Olivier Bonami's *Paradigm Identifier*, which he has discussed in various presentations. All specify the idiosyncratic information about the shape of an inflectional paradigm that may be shared among multiple lexemes. A root, in this sense, is not just a sound form but a set of forms.

I now turn to the notion of a root in Semitic morphology, specifically verbal morphology. I will first present, perhaps for the first time for an audience of non-Semitists, the history of the notion of the root in the Semitic grammatical tradition, with special attention to the (mistaken) idea that roots and morphological patterns have meaning. I will then discuss how verb roots (understood as purely morphological objects in the sense established here for English roots) interact with the binyan system of patterns in Semitic languages, drawing mostly on Israeli Hebrew. I close with evidence drawn from outside the narrow domain of pure linguistic analysis for the claim that Semitic roots are purely morphological entities.

9.4 The origins of roots in Semitic grammatical study

I will explore the historical origins of the idea of roots through a brief survey of the earliest works on Semitic morphology and of the received tradition that has persisted to this day in both the Arabic and Hebrew grammatical traditions. My goal is to understand what the traditional views of Semitic morphology were, how they have developed up to the current time, and to then use these views, in the final section of this chapter, as an aid to understanding what Semitic verb morphology is really like. The main conclusion of this section will be that Arabic grammar operated on roots but did not recognize them as a special category separate from other 'bases'. The isolation of the root as a distinct concept began in early Hebrew grammar shortly after the turn of the millennium and hundreds of years after the establishment of the Arabic tradition.

9.4.1 *Arabic dictionaries*

The first significant linguistic work on Arabic was a dictionary, *Kitāb al-ʕayn* 'the book of ʕayn', by al-Khalīl ibn ʔAhmad al Basrī (718–791 CE), who lived in the century following the founding of Islam. Al-Khalīl used an Indian-style order for the letters of the Arabic alphabet, starting at the letter representing the farthest point back in the vocal tract, which is pharyngeal ʕayn, and ending at the furthest point forward, which is aleph. Al-Khalīl aimed at a comprehensive Arabic lexicon, though he never got past the first letter, hence the title of the book. His method was to put into one entry all words with the same root. He then grouped together all occurring roots that are permutations of the same set of consonants. So, all k-t-b words are grouped together, but then this root is grouped with all occurring permutations of these three consonants. The fact that the dictionary was organized around roots, as were all subsequent dictionaries of Arabic and other Semitic languages, is a prima facie argument for the value of roots in describing Semitic languages. The fact that roots sharing the same consonants were grouped together, regardless of order, is an indication that al-Khalīl was concerned largely with form.

Homophonous roots were grouped together in one entry, as in the following partial entry for ʕ-sh-q from al-Azhari's (d. 981) *Tahdhīb*, a later lexicon in the same tradition:

Abūl-Abbās Aḥmad ibn Yaḥyā was asked whether love or passion is more praiseworthy. He said: 'love, because passion includes a degree of exaggeration'. Ibn-al 'Aʕrābī said 'ʕushuq are the men who trim the sets of sweet smelling plants; when said of a camel, ʕushuq means one that keeps to its mate and does not desire any other'. He said: 'ʕashaq is the lablab-tree; the singular is ʕashaqa'. He said: 'ʕashaq is also the arak-tree. An ʕashiq "lover" is called thus because he withers from the intensity of his passion in the same way as the ʕashaqa "lablab-tree" when it is cut.' (Tahdhīb I: 170, from Versteegh 1997: 30)

Dictionaries of Arabic ever since have been arranged by the forms of roots, not their meanings. All senses of a given root are listed together. The Wehr/Cowan Dictionary of Modern Written Arabic (cf. Cowan 1971) lists the numbered senses listed in (3), among others, under the verb entry *najada* for the root *njd* (where verb measures or patterns are in bold). Essentially synonymous definitions are separated by commas; semicolons separate the major senses. Nouns derived from the same root are listed in (4.)

(3)   I: to, help, aid, assist, support; to sweat, perspire;
       II: to furnish, upholster; to comb, card, tease (cotton);
       III: to travel in the highlands (of Arabia);
       X: to ask for help, seek aid; to take liberties, make bold

(4)   highland, upland, tableland, plateau; help, aid, succour; emergency, crisis, trouble, difficulty, distress, calamity; courage, bravery, intrepidity, undauntedness; sword belt; upholsterer; upholsterer's trade; upholstery work; upholstery

Cowell (2005: 36–8) remarks about Arabic dictionaries in general:

Words with the same root commonly have related meanings [...] There are countless exceptions however. In Arabic dictionaries, for instance, which are alphabetized by roots—not by bases as Western dictionaries are—'homonymous roots' are sometimes entered separately [...] This policy has never been consistently carried out, however; the more usual type of entry is the purely 'formal' roots, whose sub-entries may include words of various word-families, arranged without regard to meaning.

It is often difficult, if not impossible, to decide without arbitrariness whether two words with the same (formal) root have 'related meanings' or not. The use of etymology to resolve some of these difficulties only makes the concept of 'root' still more ambiguous.

9.4.2 *The influence of the Greek grammatical tradition on Arabic grammar*

Versteegh (1977) has demonstrated that the Greek grammatical tradition is a major source for Arabic grammar, to some extent indirectly through Syriac, the Aramaic language in which many of the writings of the early Church fathers were composed, at a time when early Christians and early Muslims lived side by side. Some of his strongest evidence comes from terminology, where we can sometimes see a direct chain from Greek through Syriac to Arabic and even further to Hebrew. The terms for verbs with two arguments, for example, are remarkably similar in meaning in all these traditions, as well as in Latin grammar. All are calques on the Greek word meaning 'going across', as shown in (5):

(5)   Greek   diabas   'going across'
       Latin   transitivus   'going across, passing over'
       Syriac   mʃannya:ni: 'moved away'
       Arabic   muta'addi   'crossing'
       Hebrew   yoceʔ   'going out'
       Hebrew   mitʕabber   'crossing over'

Versteegh provides more extensive evidence for the intellectual continuity among the Greek, Syriac, and Arabic grammatical traditions, which I cannot rehearse here. But his claim makes eminent sense, given other well-known continuities between the Greek and Islamic intellectual traditions.

9.4.3 *The Arabic morphological tradition*

Sībawayhi (Abū Bišr ʿAmr ibn ʿUṯmān ibn Qanbar Sībawayhi) is generally considered to be the author of the first book on Arabic grammar. He studied Arabic grammar in Basra, at about the time that al-Khalīl was writing his dictionary in the same city, and died about 796 CE, soon after al-Khalīl. He wrote one book, known as *Kitāb Sībawayhi*, often called simply the *Kitāb*, a grammar of Bedouin Arabic, which is generally regarded as the founding work of Classical Arabic grammar.[4] He often refers to al-Khalīl. All subsequent traditional grammars of Arabic fall within the template of the *Kitāb*.

The *Kitāb* and subsequent traditional Arabic grammars are divided into two parts. The first part is devoted to syntax: parts of speech (noun, verb, particle) and their distribution, and includes inflection. The second part is devoted to the forms of words: morphology and morphophonology. The coverage of morphology is exhaustive. According to Carter (2004: 100), within this tradition 'The word is formed from a combination of its root consonants (called *ʔaṣl*, lit. "trunk or base", hence "radical") and the pattern (*wazn*, lit. "measure" or *bināʔ*, lit. "structure, building"), in which those consonants are embedded'. Each *bināʔ* gets its name from the third person masculine past tense form of the verb in that *bināʔ*, using the root f-ʕ-l, e.g. faʕala.

In traditional Arabic morphology, however, derivation does not operate directly from the consonantal root, as it does in traditional Hebrew grammar, but *de mot à mot* 'from word to word' (Bohas 1984). This type of word-based derivation makes sense if we assume the influence of the Greek and Syriac grammatical traditions, which were strictly word-and-paradigm and admitted of no morphemes. Thus, one word form is said to be the *ʔaṣl* of another, as follows:[5]

The maṣdar is the initial form of the verb
The maṣdar is the *ʔaṣl* of the past form of the verb
The past form of the verb is the *ʔaṣl* of the present
The present form is the *ʔaṣl* of the imperative

In short, traditional Arabic morphology is not root-based in the modern sense. Each form in a derivation was regarded as the base (*ʔaṣl*) of the next and there was no distinct term for the consonantal root as opposed to other bases. Yes, dictionaries from the start were organized around consonantal roots, but homophonous roots with different senses were never systematically distinguished.

---

[4] Earlier grammarians whose work has been lost or was never written down may have influenced Sībawayhi.

[5] Here *ʔaṣl* might best be interpreted as 'base' or 'source'. Recall that the direction of derivations between the *maṣdar* and the verb was a major aspect of the war between the Basrans and the Kufans.

9.4.4 *The Hebrew morphological tradition*

The first grammarians of Hebrew lived in the Golden Age of Jewish culture in Arab Iberia, Al-Andalus, from about the tenth to the twelfth centuries, centred around Cordoba. The earliest Hebrew grammarians were clearly influenced greatly by the Arabic grammatical tradition. Hebrew grammar as we know it was later codified by the members of the Kimḥi family, who lived in Provence, much further north. The *Michlol* of David Kimḥi (1160–1235) (Chomsky 1952) is the best known of their works. Kimḥi also wrote a dictionary, called *Sefer Hashorashim* 'the book of roots'. Traditional Hebrew grammar after Kimḥi largely lost contact with Arabic grammar, due in part to the fall of Muslim Andalusia to the Christians in 1236. Later Hebrew grammarians consequently had little knowledge of Arabic or the Arabic grammatical tradition.

Traditional Hebrew morphology is resolutely root-based. The names of the radicals are identical to those used in Arabic grammar, the three letters p, ʕ, l from the verb 'do, work', demonstrating clearly the Arabic origins of the tradition. But a special term *ʃɔreʃ* 'root' is used in Hebrew grammar to mean **only** the consonantal root of a verb or noun, which may consist of two, three, or four radicals.[6] There is no equivalent term in Arabic grammar and no Hebrew term equivalent to the Arabic *ʔaṣl* 'base, source', which has a much wider use, as we saw in the last section.

It is likely that the Western grammatical term *root* is a calque of the Hebrew grammatical term. Of the four earliest citations of the English word *root* in this sense in OED, three refer to Hebrew. Furthermore, only Hebrew grammar, not Arabic grammar, had a distinct term that referred just to the root, and Western Christian grammarians had little or no contact with the Arabic tradition, although some did know Hebrew well because of the sacred nature of the Old Testament. The Old Testament books of the King James Bible, for example, were translated directly from the Hebrew original.

In traditional Hebrew grammar, words are not derived from one another in the Word-and-Paradigm manner used in Arabic grammar and its precursors. Instead, words are derived by putting a root into a *binyan* 'structure' for verbs and a *miʃkal* 'weight' for nouns.[7] Hebrew grammar traditionally recognizes seven verb *binyanim* in which roots can occur and a larger number of noun *miʃkalim*. Each *binyan* is said to have a meaning or syntactic function. The meanings of the *miʃkalim* are not given as large a role. The term used for binyan in traditional Western grammars of Hebrew

---

[6] The word *ʃɔreʃ* in the sense 'root of a plant' is attested in Deuteronomy, which was probably composed about the seventh century BCE, and the word has since been in continuous use in various related senses.

[7] This term is clearly related to the Arabic term *bināʔ* and the two concepts are very similar. Compare also Arabic *wazn* 'weight, measure', used interchangeably with *bināʔ*.

(e.g. Gesenius *et al.* 1910) is *conjugation*. One binyan is termed *qal* 'simple'. It is equivalent to the *binā? aṣliyya* 'root structure' of Arabic grammar and is similarly not named by its form. All others have names corresponding to the third person singular past tense, as in Arabic, called the *ground form* by Gesenius *et al.* (cf. German *Grundform*).

In traditional Hebrew grammar, a binyan is not a pattern or template, terms that have been used recently. The literal translation is 'structure' but *conjugation* is used in English, because binyanim are treated like conjugations in traditional Hebrew grammar, with full paradigms provided for each. For some binyanim it is possible to argue that there is one pattern/template or ground form or principal part. For other binyanim, most prominently *qal* and *niffal*, there are at least two principal parts in the paradigm. For *qal*, there are also subconjugations, mostly vowel-driven, similar in spirit to the subconjugations of the Latin third conjugation, with and without the theme vowel *i*.

9.4.5 *Form and meaning in Hebrew morphology*

In traditional Hebrew morphology, each root is said to have a constant meaning and each binyan is said to embody a constant syntactic type, defined largely in terms of argument structure. The meaning of an uninflected verb (lexeme) is composed of the meaning of its root and the syntactic type of its binyan. In fact, little of this is cashed out in practice. Consider first the binyan system. First, the syntactic types of only three of the seven binyanim are reliable. *Puʕal* and *hoffal* are more or less restricted to being passives of *piʕel* and *hifʕil* respectively, and have always been fairly marginal. Of the five major binyanim, *hitpaʕʕel* is the only truly reliable one, being almost always reflexive. Of the remaining four, *Hifʕil* is the most reliable, being usually causative, while *piʕʕel* is frequently 'intensive', not a structural type (though see the discussion of Doron below) and is also used with all quadriliteral verbs, regardless of meaning; a usage that is clearly driven by phonological factors. *Qal* embodies no syntactic type (it is basic). *Niffal* is usually intransitive but sometimes the passive of *qal*, which surprisingly has no regular passive, though it is the most common binyan. Overall, there are many verbs whose binyan must be listed lexically. For example, *hitpaʕʕel* verbs include *hitpallel* 'pray', *histakel* 'look', and *hiftameʃ* 'use'. Berman (1978: chapter 3) provides a summary of the nuances of the binyan system in Modern Israeli Hebrew. Her conclusion is that the traditional treatment is incompatible with the facts of Hebrew. Instead, 'each binyan can be said to have certain salient or "unmarked" properties' (p. 93), with many verb senses listed lexically.

Much less reliable are the roots. No root occurs in every binyan, let alone every nominal mishkal. And, as I have discussed at length elsewhere (Aronoff 2007), many roots have quite distinct senses when they occur in different binyanim. Overall,

Hebrew roots are very similar to English strong verb roots. None may be quite so polysemous as *run*, but what unites all the uses of a given root is its participation in the morphology of the language, not its semantics.

Hebrew (and all Semitic languages) has what are called weak roots, which are completely analogous to what are called strong verbs in Germanic. The terminology is confusing, but in the Semitic tradition the consonants in these roots were called weak because they are subject to loss or change in certain cells in the paradigm, while those of 'full' roots persist unchanged throughout. As I demonstrated at length in Aronoff (2007), these verb roots, like the Germanic strong verbs of English, can be placed into subclasses, according to their alternations. For example, there is a class of roots that we may call *missing n-initial*. The members of this class consist of a subset of the roots whose initial consonant is /n/, along with several roots whose initial consonant is /j/, and one with initial /l/. These form an inflectional class because they all lose their initial root consonant under certain circumstances, while regular roots with these same initial consonants do not. Semantics is irrelevant, just as it is with Germanic strong verbs in English.

All Semitic languages investigated to date, except to some extent Maltese (Hoberman and Aronoff 2003), exhibit almost exceptionless root-and-binyan verbal morphology, just as with any other system of verb conjugations (e.g. Latin). Roots and binyanim are morphological entities first and foremost. The difference in the obligatoriness of patterns between verbs and nouns may lie in the fact that verbs are inflected in all Semitic languages, while nouns are not always. Overall, though, neither the verb roots nor the binyanim have constant meaning in any Semitic language so far investigated, despite or perhaps because of the robustness of the inflectional patterns.

9.4.6 *A modern analysis: Doron on Israeli Hebrew binyanim*

Doron (2003) makes an excellent case for the semantic value of the 'derived' binyanim in Israeli Hebrew (those other than *qal*). But Doron admits that many individual verbs are idiosyncratic. Overall, her analysis supports a theory in which certain binyanim may be used productively as part of the derivational morphology of the language, while simultaneously serving as inflectional classes:

All the meaning contrasts discussed above are achieved by the pairing of equi-rooted verbs [two or more verbs with the same root]. On the other hand, when a single verb is derived from a root, i.e. when the verb is not paired with another equi-rooted verb, then the contribution of the template is more erratic. Even then, a lot of systematicity can be shown to exist if one also takes into account equi-rooted nouns and adjectives. But when no contrast whatsoever is expressed by the choice of morphology, then, as often as not, the template is arbitrary. For example, verbs such as *listen*, *climb*, or *urge* are not semantically causative, despite their derivation by the causative template; neither do *perfume*, *end*, or *disperse* necessarily denote actions, despite their derivation by the intensive template. (p. 23)

The semantics of the templates only reveals itself when the choice of template is paradigmatic rather than idiosyncratic. (pp. 24–5)

It is well known that derivational morphology allows a certain amount of deviation from compositional meaning [...] Many intensive verbs are associated with rich encyclopedic knowledge [...] Crucially, templates can be specified to have marked features in the environment of certain roots [...] Therefore, idiosyncratic verbs have listed templates. The templates of these verbs are completely uninformative—that is, the form/meaning correspondence is rendered as opaque as in the more familiar languages with poorer morphology. (p. 38)

Doron's account is very similar to that of Cowell (2005) for Syrian Arabic, where a change in binyan is treated as a form of derivational morphology or word formation: each derivational process has a syntactic and semantic effect that is expressed through a change in binyan, but the binyanim have no constant meaning outside their use in derivational morphology. This type of account fits easily into any framework that distinguishes degrees of productivity in derivational morphology, e.g. Aronoff (1976). The idea that assignment to conjugation class can be part of derivational morphology is discussed in detail in Aronoff (1994), for both Israeli Hebrew and other languages, especially Latin. For example, the Latin intensive verb is formed by taking the past participle stem of a verb, e.g. *canere-* 'sing', whose past participle stem is *cant-*, and using it to form a verb of the first (-a:) conjugation: *cantare*. The desiderative verb suffix *ur-*, by contrast, forms verbs of the fourth (-i:) conjugation (as in *e:suri:re*) from *e:dere* 'eat'. Just like Latin conjugations, Hebrew (and Arabic) binyanim have no predictable meaning except when used to form new words. This is what lies behind Doron's observation about verbs that are 'not paired with another equi-rooted verb' being idiosyncratic. Doron frames her account in terms of DM. But in fact, nothing in Doron's account particularly supports DM over other theories and there is much in it that quite directly supports the observation that binyanim are inflectional classes that have been co-opted for purposes of derivational morphology, which goes as far back as at least Kuryłowicz (1962).

9.5 Findings from outside pure linguistic analysis

In this section, I will review very briefly findings on Semitic roots from allied fields: child language acquisition, aphasiology, and experimental psycholinguistics. Despite claims to the contrary, the overwhelming weight of evidence favours the sort of position that I am advocating here: Semitic roots are primarily morphological in nature. Whether they have constant meaning or not is beside the point.

9.5.1 *Evidence from child language acquisition*

The leaders in the study of native acquisition of Hebrew and Arabic are Ruth Berman and Dorit Ravid. Berman and Ravid agree that 'Hebrew-speaking children can perform consonantal root extraction from as young as age three both in interpreting and producing novel verbs based on familiar nouns and adjectives' and that the novel verbs that they produce conform to the standard morphological patterns (Berman 2003: 274). Ravid (2003: 303) concludes: 'Developmental studies indicate that the basic ability to manipulate nonlinear structures emerges early on in Hebrew speakers.' By kindergarten, 'young Palestinian Arabic speakers were easily able to identify pairs of words related through the root, and also to provide another word from the same root' (pp. 306–7).

9.5.2 *Evidence from aphasia*

Prunet *et al.* (2000) present a case study of a French–Arabic bilingual aphasic who showed root-sensitive metathesis in Arabic but no similar behaviour for French. They conclude that 'Arabic roots can be accessed as independent morphological units' (p. 610). Prunet *et al.* suggest that this finding supports a 'morpheme-based theory that forms words by combining roots and templates' (p. 609). Goral (2001) surveys a number of case studies of aphasia in Hebrew speakers (including one covered by Prunet *et al.* 2000). She concludes that 'these two abstract morphemes [roots and patterns] have a psychological reality for Hebrew speakers' (2001: 309).

9.5.3 *Psycholinguistic evidence*

In the last twenty years, there have been many psycholinguistic studies on Hebrew root and pattern morphology, using a variety of experimental paradigms: Feldman *et al.* (1995), Frost *et al.* (1997), Deutsch *et al.* (2000), Goral and Obler (2003), Shimron (2003), Berent and Shimron (2003), Velan *et al.* (2005), Bick *et al.* (2010). Prunet (2006) presents a valuable overview of work on Semitic languages more broadly. The overall conclusion to all this work is best expressed in the words of Joseph Shimron: 'the sensitivity to the roots is not necessarily affected by their meanings. Rather, the root as a morpheme has an independent effect unconstrained by semantic mediation' (Shimron 2003: 20). This conclusion applies equally well to the findings from child language acquisition and aphasia: speakers of Semitic languages are very sensitive to roots, but there is no evidence that these roots have constant meaning, only that they play an important role in the morphology of these languages.

9.6 Conclusion

9.6.1 *Semitic roots*

Roots are real linguistic entities, but there is no value in assuming that all instances of a given root have the same meaning. Roots are instead most centrally part of the autonomous morphological system of a language and they play as robust a role in the morphology of a language like English or Latin as they do in Hebrew or Arabic.

What is special about Arabic and Hebrew is less the roots than the complex ways in which these roots interact with the obligatory syllabic templates that undergird the conjugation system of verbs. There is also the large role that the conjugations themselves play in derivation, apart from affixation. In most languages, conjugations are distinguished from one another by having different affix patterns. In Semitic languages, the inflectional affixes are identical across conjugations, which are distinguished largely by complex syllabic templates, reminiscent of the ablaut patterns of Germanic languages, but much stricter in form, as Kuryłowicz (1973: 43) notes: 'The Sem[itic] ablaut is an essential ingredient of the morphological structure of the verb.'

It is time now to close the circle. I started off by comparing the role of the root in two quite distinct types of theories, one in which roots have constant meanings, of which DM is the modern archetype, and one in which roots play a purely morphological role, need not have constant meanings, and often don't. I then searched for the historical origins of the theory in which roots are meaningful by definition. Although I had previously long believed that these origins lay in Arabic grammar, I have become convinced that the grammatical tradition in which roots first played the fundamental role that we find in modern theories was that of the medieval Hebrew grammarians.

Behind this search, though, lies a more fundamental issue. The idea that roots and other morphemes have constant meaning has been axiomatic in modern linguistics ever since the term *morpheme* was first coined by Baudouin de Courtenay (1895). Modern generative phonology, beginning with McCarthy (1981), adopted traditional Hebrew morphology almost wholesale. And though McCarthy's phonological analysis did not depend at all on Semitic roots having a constant meaning, that traditional notion has been imported into the theoretical literature along with the rest of the framework.

Meanwhile, though, another group of linguists began to work about a half century ago on descriptions of the morphology of Semitic languages unfettered by traditional notions, notably structuralists like Cowell (2005) working on Arabic dialects and the group of Israeli linguists who deliberately approached Modern Israeli Hebrew with an open mind rather than from the point of view of traditional Hebrew grammar, including Shlomo Ariel, Aaron Bar-Adon, Haim Blanc, Ruth Berman, Shmuel Bolozky, Uzi Ornan, and Ora Schwartzwald, to name only a few. What they and their successors discovered was that the root and binyan system of these languages was more honoured in the breach than in the observance, and that it constituted a system of partial regularities rather than the perfect universe that had been depicted in traditional grammar, what Berman (1978: 100) calls a 'compromise view [. . .]

most appropriate to the semi-productive nature of the *binyan* system in contemporary Hebrew'. Others, notably Waltke and O'Connor (1990), have extended similar observations to Biblical Hebrew, where the binyanim are more regular, but still not nearly as systematic as the received tradition would lead one to expect.

In other words, if one looks at Semitic root and binyan systems as they actually function within real languages, rather than through the lens of a tradition that dates back a millennium, they turn out to manifest the sort of partial and default regularities characteristic of complex morphological systems that have become familiar to morphologists over the last forty years, rather than the invariant system so dearly desired by theoreticians since Baudouin de Courtenay. But we should not despair, because in these forty years we have developed an arsenal of tools meant precisely to attack these partial regularities in very precise ways as a network of ordered defaults (Aronoff 1994, Brown and Hippisley 2011). Yes, Semitic morphology is unusual, but it is not outside the universe of morphological systems that have occupied morphologists' attention of late. Furthermore, although roots are central to Semitic morphology, the roots of Semitic are in many ways analogous to those of English or Latin, inasmuch as their most interesting properties are purely morphological and have nothing to do with meaning, except in so far as they are realized through a lexeme. They are not identical, but the ways in which Semitic roots, English roots, Latin and Romance roots differ from each other will provide grist for the mills of theoretical concepts like flexeme, lexemic index, and paradigm identifier that have been proposed over the last decade.

9.6.2 *Roots, morphemes, morphomes, and lexical categories*

The most remarkable property of roots in any language is their formal stalwartness in the face of semantic variation. As I noted above, English irregular verbs like *run* always have the same irregular forms, no matter how wide the variation in meaning across senses. The same is true of suppletive Latin roots like *fer* and the weak roots of Hebrew. Much less remarked but more remarkable is the fact that this formal unity in the face of semantic variation is not a special property of irregular roots or roots in general; it is the hallmark of morphological units of every kind, including those that show no variation in form at all. Consider English derivational suffixes, like *-er*, *-ic*, and *-y*. If we peruse a reverse alphabetical dictionary and consider the meanings of all words ending in any one of these suffixes, it quickly becomes apparent that there is tremendous variation in the set. But their form remains constant, so much so that this formal constancy is never noticed. English derivational suffixes differ greatly from one another in productivity, as derivational affixes do in any language, and these differences are correlated closely with what I have called elsewhere *semantic coherence* (Aronoff 1976), the extent to which the meaning of any given word containing a particular suffix is predictable (Baayen 1992, Plag 1999, Bauer 2001).

Where they do not differ is in what we might call *formal coherence*. Between the most productive affixes such as *-ness* and the least productive like *-th* there is no difference in formal coherence, despite the gulf in semantic coherence. The constant heart of linguistic morphology is the form of words and this extends to roots as it does to all morphological elements. Even Alec Marantz seems now to agree, at least if I interpret one of his recent statements correctly:

This view of the relation between roots and lexical categories is generally consistent with the insights of 'lexeme-based' morphological theories such as Aronoff's (2001) [sic]. The word root plays an important role in an Aronoff-style theory as well as the present one, capturing facts associated with families of words sharing the same root. However, the meaning contribution of a root is never independently realized within this version of Distributed Morphology, since the objects of interpretation are the phases, not the roots. A root with a category-determining head corresponds to the lexeme of Aronoff's system, and such a constituent can have a particular meaning, a variety of uses, and a history, as Aronoff makes clear. (Marantz, no date: 5–6)

10

Morphomic stems in the Northern Talyshi verb: diachrony and synchrony*

STEVEN KAYE

10.1 Introduction

The varieties collectively known as Talyshi, spoken in the southern Caucasus in an area bordering the Caspian Sea, belong to the north-western group of the Iranian language family: better-known members of this large group include Kurdish and Balochi. Talyshi itself represents a dialect continuum, but within it three well-differentiated dialect groups can be distinguished: the Northern Talyshi-speaking area straddles the border between Iran and the Republic of Azerbaijan, while the Central and Southern Talyshi dialects are found in Iran only. In this chapter I will examine the morphology of the verb in the Northern Talyshi (NT) of Azerbaijan (home to the large majority of NT speakers), and specifically the distribution of stem forms over the verb paradigm, which is striking both in general terms and within the context of the Iranian languages in particular.

For an introduction to the central issue addressed here, see Table 10.1, which illustrates the principal finite and non-finite forms of the verb *kārdé* 'do'.[1] Morphological segmentation has been provided only for person–number marking: with the exception of the imperative (2SG), all finite forms are represented by the 1SG.

* I am grateful to many people for their part in the genesis of this chapter, including Don Stilo, Gerardo De Caro, Agnes Korn, Johnny Cheung, and the editors of this volume. I would especially like to thank Gilles Authier, who introduced me to Northern Talyshi and made my fieldwork possible, and Məmməd Piriyev and Jeyhun Heydar, my main linguistic consultants for the work presented here. My field trips to Azerbaijan were supported by the Centre national de la recherche scientifique (UMR 7192).

[1] In my transcription of the Talyshi dialects the letters *a* and *ā* represent front and back open vowels respectively, while in data from other languages the macron signals a distinction in length rather than quality. The Northern Talyshi *i* is a mid-high central vowel. The other letters employed here have their usual values.

TABLE 10.1 The paradigm of NT *kārdé* 'do'

Infinitive	*kārdé*	Imperative	*bíka*
Present	*kārdéda=m*	Present subjunctive	*bíka-m*
Future	*bakārdé=m*	Present optative	*bíkao-m*
Preterite	*kárd[ïm]e*	Imperfect	*akáy-m*
Perfect	*kārdá[m]e*	Imperfect subjunctive	*bákay-m*
Past participle	*kārdá*	Future negative	*akáni-m*
Gerundive	*kārdanín*	Present participle	*áka*

A number of striking features emerge from this table which will be touched on again in the course of this study. One of these is the existence of a special future negative form, *akánim*. Negative forms have not, in general, been provided here, as their structure closely mirrors that of their positive counterparts; *akánim*, however, is listed in its own right because it does not correspond structurally to any existing positive form. The future form *bakārdém* given in the table has its own negative counterpart, *nibakārdém*, which is apparently synonymous with *akánim*.[2]

Another is the intricate system of person agreement marking found in NT, which is explored in detail by Stilo (2008a). Some TMA forms make use of personal desinences, which can never be separated from the body of the verb and are thus labelled as affixes in the table (e.g. *-m* in *bíka-m*). Others, marked here with the sign '=', distinguish person by means of clitic auxiliary forms identical with the copula, which may detach from the verb and float to its left in the clause—but this is only the case in two of the four zones of Azerbaijani NT, while in the remaining two these forms are in fact immobile and, as such, largely indistinguishable from the personal desinences. A third set of agreement markers are floating clitics in all NT dialect zones, and are not genuinely verbal elements but oblique pronominal forms, usually hosted by clausal constituents other than the verb and only appearing as part of the verb form itself (as mesoclitics) under special circumstances. They are therefore marked in brackets in the table. I return to some of these points in Section 10.3.

But the feature of this verb paradigm which primarily interests us here concerns the elements marked out in bold, namely **kārd** and **ka**. As is clear from the table, all finite and non-finite forms in the paradigm of *kārdé* are characterized by one of these two basic stems: neither of them is further reducible into more primitive morphological elements, and between them they divide the paradigm into two parts, as reflected in the representation given in Table 10.1. And yet their distribution

---

[2] Although these two negative forms are sometimes described as belonging to different regional dialects within NT (Pirejko 1966: 321), they may coexist happily within the idiolect of individual speakers. I have detected no difference in meaning between the two.

has no obvious synchronic rationale. The presence of one stem or the other does not appear to involve natural classes of cells within the paradigm, that is, to be consistently motivated by any single external factor, or combination of factors, at a level of generality above a simple list of the cells involved. If this is the case, the patterning of these two stems over the paradigm of *kārdé* is of no interest to, and has no effect on, any part of the grammar outside the morphological system. I claim that the distribution of these stems over the paradigm is indeed a purely morphological phenomenon, and that the stems themselves are comparable to such classically morphomic elements as the 'third stem' of Latin (Aronoff 1994: 35) or the 'PYTA root' of Spanish (Maiden 2001*b*).

The existence of a paradigm as apparently 'confused' as that seen in Table 10.1 inevitably raises the question of how things came to be this way diachronically. Accordingly, one of the goals of this chapter is to shed some light on the historical developments which have given rise to the stem distribution in the paradigm of *kārdé* in its modern form. But it also raises synchronic questions. Linguists are accustomed to seeing idiosyncratic behaviour in very common verbs such as *do*, which need not reflect important characteristics of the verb system as a whole; while such cases can be revealing in their own right, if they are truly isolated and unsystematic phenomena there may be little to say about them synchronically. It is also worth asking, then, how representative of the general NT verb system the stem distribution seen in *kārdé* actually is.

Interestingly, in previous descriptions of NT this stem distribution has been treated neither as regular nor as totally irregular. The verb *kārdé* belongs to a small class with nine members, all very frequently used verbs, which employ two weakly (or in one case strongly) suppletive stems according to the same distributional pattern as is exemplified here, which is thus systematic at least over this small part of the lexicon. These verbs will be listed in Section 10.4. However, all other verbs in the language are said to possess either a single stem throughout the paradigm (Pirejko (1991: 152) places 55% of all NT verbs in this category), or two regularly related stems, one of which is becoming obsolete while the other takes over the whole paradigm. That is, it is generally taken as increasingly abnormal for an NT verb to make use of two stems in its paradigm at all.

Nothing else in the inflectional behaviour of NT verbs is affected by the number of stems they possess, and it will be clear from the table that no inflectional distinction is marked solely by the choice of *ka* rather than *kārd*, or vice versa: the opposition is entirely non-functional. But the existence of two distinct stems in the verb paradigm, as seen here, is not in itself unusual in Iranian. The verb systems of most Iranian languages are articulated in terms of a fundamental opposition between so-called 'present' and 'past' stems, upon which further distinctions may be overlaid, and this is the conservative situation preserved by verbs such as *kārdé* and apparently being lost elsewhere. The question arises, then, whether NT has abandoned the inherited two-stem system to such an extent precisely because the distribution of those stems is too opaque for speakers to deal with.

The following three sections will each address a different aspect of the stem system under investigation here. In Section 10.2, on the basis of attestations from the Old and Middle Iranian periods, I briefly outline how the characteristic Iranian two-stem verb paradigm arose: this in itself will provide evidence to suggest that autonomously morphological behaviour is of great antiquity in the Iranian verb. In Section 10.3, focusing my attention on Northern Talyshi in particular, I look at each of the forms of *kārdé* given in the table above, with a view to determining its origins and where necessary giving further detail on its usage. On this basis I will add some weight to my claim above that the distribution of stems over the paradigm of *kārdé* is genuinely morphomic and cannot be motivated at some other linguistic level. Finally, and at greatest length, in Section 10.4 I turn to consider the current state of stem distribution patterns across the verb lexicon of NT. Here I will show that NT possesses a class of verbs as defined by stem behaviour which has not, to my knowledge, been identified before: this class finds parallels elsewhere within Talyshi and potentially further afield in Iranian. I will also cast doubt on the idea that the morphomic pattern visible in *kārdé* has been widely lost for reasons of inflectional 'simplicity'. In fact, it may have survived much more extensively than has previously been recognized.

10.2 The development of the two-stem system

As mentioned just above, the division of the verb paradigm into two formal zones, each making use of a different stem, is by no means specific to NT or the Talyshi group within the Iranian languages. On the contrary, the two-stem verb system is a highly distinctive feature of Iranian as a whole: Haig (2008: 9f.) calls it 'a remarkably stable characteristic, one of the deepest traces of genetic unity across the family', and what is unusual about NT is the extent to which it has been lost. Although the labels of 'present' and 'past' for these stems are clearly unsuitable in the NT case, in some Iranian languages the use of one stem or the other may be the only difference between present and past tense verb forms (e.g. Modern Persian *mikonam* 'I am doing' vs. *mikardam* 'I was doing').

But verbs in the earliest-attested Iranian languages do not yet operate according to this two-stem system. Like other ancient Indo-European varieties, proto-Iranian inherited a verb paradigm in which each lexeme possessed at least three aspectual stems, which could be further marked for tense and mood distinctions, along with isolated non-finite forms; this state of affairs, also seen in Vedic Sanskrit and Ancient Greek, survives fairly successfully into the most conservative Iranian language, Old Avestan. The shift from this complex organization of the paradigm to a fundamental opposition between just two stems was accompanied by further important changes in verb morphology and morphosyntax, all of which help to explain the synchronic behaviour of the verb in NT. In the western branch of the Iranian family, to which Talyshi belongs, these changes can be traced in the three languages substantially attested in the pre-Islamic period: Old Persian and its descendant Middle Persian (belonging to the south-western group of languages) and the closely related Parthian (north-western). Although these are not directly ancestral to the Talyshi group, the developments illustrated here must also have taken place in the unattested pre-cursors of Talyshi.

10.2.1 *Old Persian*

Old Persian, the language of the Achaemenid empire, is attested in inscriptions from the sixth to the fourth century BC: this places it, along with the Avestan varieties, in the Old Iranian period, and in fact the end of this period is conventionally marked by the downfall of the Achaemenids. Like Avestan, Old Persian does at least formally continue the three IE aspectual stems known as 'present' (durative), 'aorist' (punctual), and 'perfect' (stative), as shown in Table 10.2, which lists some of the forms taken by the verb *čartanaiy* 'do'.

But it is clear that the IE system itself is already moribund at best by the time of our very earliest attestations of Old Persian, as both the aorist and the perfect series are already close to disappearing. In fact, the form *čaxriyā* given in Table 10.2 is the only verb form in the whole Old Persian corpus which continues the IE perfect; meanwhile the aorist formation is represented by a mere handful of items, and seems to have no distinctive function of its own at this point. The only one of the IE aspectual stems which continues to flourish in Old Persian is the present stem: this is shared by the majority of finite forms, including the imperfect, the main narrative past tense of the language.

TABLE 10.2 **Some inflected forms of Old Persian *čartanaiy* 'do'**

IE aspectual stems:

Present stem *kunav-*	**kunau**-*tiy*	(3SG present active)
	kunav-*āhy*	(2SG subjunctive active)
	a-**kunav**-*am*	(1SG imperfect active)
Aorist stem *ku-*	*a*-**ku**-*mā*	(1PL aorist middle)
	ku-*šuva*	(2SG imperative middle)
Perfect stem *čaxr-* (< **ke-kr-*, *vel sim.*)	**čaxr**-*iyā*	(3SG optative active)

Other stems:

Infinitive stem *čar-* (< **ker-*, *vel sim.*)	**čar**-*tanaiy*	
Verbal adjective stem *kr̥-*	**kr̥**-*ta-*	

However, the Old Persian paradigm contains certain non-finite items, also given in Table 10.2, which have arisen without any connection to the aspectual stem system. The infinitive in -*tanaiy*, like most infinitives in IE languages, is an innovation postdating the breakup of proto-Indo-European.[3] The participial form in -*ta*-, on the other hand, reflects a verbal adjective which did exist in proto-Indo-European but lay only at the periphery of the verb system proper (Szemerényi 1996: 323). By the Old Persian stage, this -*ta*- form has been fully integrated into the verb paradigm as a perfect participle; but a mark of its origin outside the paradigm—besides the fact that it lacks the old perfect stem—is its aberrant behaviour in terms of voice, as it has passive value for transitive verbs but active value for intransitives (cf. *kr̥-ta*- 'done, i.e. having been done' and *mr̥-ta*- 'dead, i.e. having died'). In other words, it shows ergative–absolutive alignment in an otherwise nominative–accusative system.

In predicative position, with or without an overt copula, this participle forms an innovative periphrastic perfect construction, as in example (1) from an inscription on the tomb of Darius the Great (cited with alterations from Skjærvø 2009a: 144):

(1) dūraiy   r̥štiš   parā-gmatā
     far   spear.NOM(F)   forward-go.PTCP.NOM.F
     'the spear [of a Persian man] has gone forward far' (DNa 44–45)

When this periphrastic perfect is found with transitive verbs, the agent may be specified in the genitive–dative case. Pronominal agents can be expressed by both full (2) and clitic (3) genitive–dative forms:

(2) ima   taya   manā   kr̥tam   Pārs-aiy
     this   what(NEUT)   1SG.GEN   do.PTCP.NEUT   Persia-LOC
     'this is what I have done in Persia' (DB III 52–53)

(3) avaθā   =šām   hamaranam   kr̥tam
     thus   =3PL.GEN   battle(NEUT).NOM   do.PTCP.NEUT
     'thus they did battle' (DB III 18–19)

Note that, as in the last example, this perfect can be used as a narrative past tense to sum up a preceding sequence in the imperfect. The precise status of this construction with specified agent is still a matter of debate, as it lends itself to both possessive ('of me is a done X', cf. English 'I have done X') and passive ('by me is X done') interpretations. In pragmatic terms, the construction is certainly unlike a typical passive in that it favours highly animate, topical agents. However this may be, it is notable that all attested examples where the agentive argument is present involve the same verb *čartanaiy*, perhaps suggesting that this innovative perfect is at a fairly early stage in its incorporation into the language.

---

[3] This was originally a dative case form of an action noun in *-tan*- (Rastorgueva and Molčanova 1981a: 130).

10.2.2 *Middle West Iranian*

With the benefit of hindsight, we can see that in Old Persian the stage is already set for the rise of a new organizational principle in the verb paradigm, and when our documentation of Iranian resumes in the Middle West Iranian languages of Middle Persian and Parthian, around the beginning of the Common Era, some important developments already underway in Old Persian have taken full effect. The old aorist and perfect stems have been lost altogether; meanwhile, the periphrastic construction based on the participle in -*ta*- has broadened in use, having undergone a familiar shift from perfect to simple past meaning, and it has now replaced the imperfect as the basic narrative past tense for both transitive and intransitive verbs. The participial element has been reduced to an indeclinable form ending in a dental, as in examples (4) and (5) from Parthian and Middle Persian respectively. Both languages have further past perfective tense forms also using this element, which are not exemplified here; what is more, in both languages it serves as the basis for a recharacterized past participle in -*ag* found in various uses, and also showing ergative alignment (e.g. substantive *paywastag* 'something created'; adverbial *taxtag* 'having run'). Forms with past value sharing a dental stem reflecting the *ta*-participle—from now on called the past stem—thus came to make up a substantial part of the paradigm, while virtually all the remainder continued the IE present stem: it was in these circumstances that the characteristic Iranian two-stem paradigm took shape.

(4) man   dišt   apadan
     1SG.OBL   build.PST(3SG)   palace
     'I built a palace'

(M 5, 17–18; Rastorgueva and Molčanova 1981b: 223)

(5) ēg   =išān   Ērij   ōzad
     then   =3PL.OBL   Ē.   kill.PST(3SG)
     'then they killed Ērij'

(Bundahišn 33; Skjærvø 2009b: 270)

Examples (4) and (5) also illustrate an important morphosyntactic phenomenon entailed by the rise to prominence of the old periphrastic perfect. In Middle Iranian, the participial construction seen here cannot be taken as passive, possessive, or marginal to the system in any other way: it is simply the unmarked past tense form. But these examples demonstrate that its morphosyntactic behaviour has not fallen into line with that shown by all other Iranian verb forms up to this point. Case marking is severely weakened in the MIr. period to an opposition between direct and oblique at best; but wherever the distinction can be made, it is clear that this construction (along with others based on the *ta*-participle) requires direct marking on the intransitive subject and transitive object arguments, while the subject of transitive verbs appears in the oblique case, and potentially as a clitic—just as in the Old Persian periphrastic perfect. MIr. thus shows a split in its morphosyntactic alignment, which is ergative–absolutive only in clauses which use the new past tense constructions. For our purposes, this will be relevant to an understanding of person-marking behaviour in the past perfective tenses of NT.

While the morphosyntax of the participial construction has been retained into the MIr. period, significant change can often be seen in the verb form itself. In Old Iranian languages, the formal relationship between the inherited present stem and other parts of the verb was far from predictable synchronically, owing to the effects of differential sound change and the multitude of inherited IE formations available for every stem category. Often this unpredictability survives into MIr., giving synchronically irregular alternations such as (Middle Persian) past tense *bast* 'tied' vs. present stem *band-*, (Parthian) past tense *nimušt* 'cleaned' vs. present stem *nimarz-*. However, for many verbs the transition to MIr. has seen a process of regularization whereby the past stem is remodelled by the addition of a suffix (*-ād, -īd, -ist*) to the present stem, giving e.g. the innovative Middle Persian form *vizīd*, in place of inherited *vixt*, alongside present stem *viz-* 'choose'. There is no consensus on the origins of these suffixes, but they are an important feature of the MIr. verb system, also applied in the case of productive formations such as causatives and denominatives. The two Western languages attested in the MIr. period diverge noticeably in their choice of regular suffixes: in Parthian *-ād* is the most productive suffix by far, while Middle Persian prefers *-īd* and, to a lesser extent, *-ist*. As will be seen, the Talyshi group inherited stem pairings of both the regular and irregular types.

The final MIr. development to be mentioned here is fundamental to the makeup of the verb system, and particularly to the facts of stem distribution in NT. It concerns the formal relationship of the infinitive with the rest of the paradigm. As was illustrated above in Table 10.2, in Old Persian the infinitive in *-tanaiy* showed no inherent affinity with the participle in *-ta*: although they both bear suffixes beginning with a dental, the original independence of the two formations is obvious from the difference in their vocalism, which in *kṛta-/čartanaiy* has affected the initial consonant too. But by the MIr. stage we find that all such differences have been levelled out. The past tense and infinitive reliably pattern together, in this case giving *kerd/kerdan* in Middle Persian; moreover, this is not just a historical effect, but a synchronically active feature of the morphology, as the innovative regularization of one form is always accompanied by the regularization of the other, by means of the same suffix (e.g. Middle Persian *pursīd* 'asked' / *pursīdan* 'to ask', Parthian *pursād/pursādan*).

What this means is that rather than surviving as an isolated formation in a paradigm otherwise divided between the old present and new past stems, the infinitive has fallen in with the latter. Although the infinitive is not descended from the *ta*-participle or any offshoot of it, the form it takes is in no doubt once the past stem is known: it simply consists of this past stem + *-an*. This secures the strict division of the paradigm into two halves, with no anomalous forms remaining outside the new two-stem system.

All the phenomena surveyed here are reflected in the current NT verb paradigm, as will be seen in the following sections. From the point of view of autonomous morphology, however, the most interesting of them is this formal levelling of the infinitive with the past stem, because nothing in the behaviour of the infinitive seems to follow from its formal affiliations. It does not have a specifically past or perfective value, nor does it show the distinctive ergative alignment seen in the *ta*-participle and the new form in *-ag* derived from it. Like these forms, the infinitive is of course non-finite, but this feature is not specific to forms employing the past stem, as a number of participles based on the present stem are also found. The MIr. infinitive is thus a 'Priscianic' or 'parasitic' formation in the terms of Matthews (1972): although it is derived from the past stem in formal terms, it does not inherit any correspond-ing content. Already in MIr., then, the contexts in which the past stem is used cannot be said to form a natural class. This ancient feature will go a long way towards explaining the stem distribution found in present-day NT.

10.3 Verb forms in Northern Talyshi

The developments sketched out in the previous section underlie several important features of the NT verb system, but in particular the morphological opposition between present and past stems which forms the focus of this chapter. This inherited opposition is unambiguously preserved in the group of morphologically conservative verbs exemplified here by *kārdé*, as shown in Table 10.3 (which repeats Table 10.1

TABLE 10.3 The paradigm of NT *kārdé* 'do'. Intransitive preterite and perfect forms are represented by *mārdé* 'die'

	Past stem			Present stem
Infinitive	*kārdé*	Imperative		*bǐka*
Present	*kārdéda=m*	Subjunctive		*bǐka-m*
Future	*bakārdé=m*	Optative		*bǐkao-m*
Preterite (tr.)	*kǎrd[ǐm]e*	Imperfect		*akáy-m*
(intr.)	*mǎrd-im*	Imperfect subjunctive		*bákay-m*
Perfect (tr.)	*kārdá[m]e*	Future negative		*akáni-m*
(intr.)	*mārdá=m*	Present participle		*áka*
Past participle	*kārdá*			
Gerundive	*kārdanín*			

above, with additions mentioned below). In the current section I look at the way in which the distinction came to operate in NT, by laying out what is known about the origin and behaviour of the TMA forms continuing these two stems. For reasons of space, I cannot argue at any length in support of the diachronic claims made here, but I provide references to more detailed treatments of specific issues.

10.3.1 *Present-stem forms*

A distinctive characteristic of NT, and the Talyshi group as a whole, among the Iranian languages is the existence of an imperfect formed on the present stem. Represented here by *akáym*, this has two basic functions: it expresses the habitual/ iterative past ('I used to do') and appears in the apodosis of irrealis conditional constructions ('I would do, would have done'). This is not connected with the IE imperfect: instead it is generally taken to descend from an earlier optative in *ē* which is found in MIr. and can be traced back to IE.[4] In NT this *ē* is usually continued as a stressed *í* following the present stem, but this in turn diphthongizes with preceding vowels, as in *akáym* itself. The initial *a-*, however, must originate elsewhere. Miller identifies it with the OIr. past tense marker *a-* (< the IE 'augment' *e-*), but this element is already poorly attested in MIr., and there is no independent evidence for its survival anywhere in the Western branch of the family.[5] In fact the NT prefix is more likely to be connected with a network of innovative imperfectivity-marking affixes found widely across finite forms in West Iranian, and in particular those found in the Central Plateau Dialects (*a-*, *at-*, *ed-*, etc.), which Windfuhr (1987: 393, 1992: 249) tentatively traces back to OIr. *aiwada* 'at the same time, all the time'.[6]

The future negative *akánim* is similar to the imperfect in form, but, contra Schulze (2000: 48), there is no reason to see it as synchronically or diachronically based on the latter, which has a negative counterpart of its own (*nákaym*). In fact, the future negative is more plausibly linked with the agent noun / substantivized present participle (*áka*). I follow Miller's (1953: 157) identification of *akánim* as historically made up of *áka* plus the negative of the copula, with the meaning 'I am not one-who-does', giving rise to 'I will not do' in the process of grammaticalization; this development is paralleled in Sanskrit (Cardona 2003: 130f.).

The ultimate origins of *áka* itself are unclear. Windfuhr takes the initial *a-* to be identical to the element found in the imperfect; however, Iranian participles and

---

[4] E.g. Miller (1953: 154), followed by Schulze (2000: 48) and Windfuhr (1995). The semantic development required is plausible, especially as optative forms bearing habitual past meaning can be seen already in Old Iranian (Skjærvø 2009a: 137).

[5] In modern Iranian it is found otherwise only in the preterite of Yaghnobi, which belongs to the Eastern branch (Rastorgueva and Èdel'man 2000: 70).

[6] On the other hand, Don Stilo (p.c.) has suggested that the stressed *i* itself may descend from this imperfectivity marker, which may also appear as a suffix (Stilo 2008b: 106–8), via a stage *ay* seen in some Tati dialects; the NT form would thus contain the same etymological element twice in different guises, presumably via two separate areal developments.

agent nouns do not usually display the imperfectivity markers seen on finite verbs, and the element in question here appears even in Southern Talyshi, which uses no such prefix in the imperfect, suggesting that the two *a-* elements are etymologically distinct. Whatever its history, though, the *áka* form is marginal in present-day NT (at least as spoken in Azerbaijan),[7] unlike the future negative it has given rise to; its functions have largely been taken over by the form listed here as the 'past participle' (see below), and, to the extent that it survives, it is found as an agent noun.

The remaining present-stem forms show strong similarities in both form and function. The imperative, subjunctive, and optative have the range of modal values expected for such forms in IE languages, and in their positive forms all bear the stressed modal prefix *bï-* (also found in the imperfect subjunctive). In specifically modal use this prefix finds parallels across West Iranian (e.g. Zazaki *bi-*, Modern Persian *be-*),[8] but it seems to have begun life as an adverbial element with a meaning akin to 'once and for all', and is accordingly found elsewhere as a perfective marker (Rastorgueva and Èdel'man 2003: 40, Skjærvø 2009*b*: 240).

This element aside, though, the morphological structures involved in these parts of the paradigm are highly conservative. The imperative uses just the bare present stem with no further characterization—as it has done from the time of our earliest Iranian attestations. The optative descends from the ancient present subjunctive in *-ā-*, which regularly gives *o* in NT. This survival of the ancient subjunctive is unusual in Iranian, however: much more commonly it is ousted by the newer form also displayed by NT (and called 'subjunctive' here), which continues the general Iranian present indicative with the addition of the modal *bï-*. This original present indicative itself does not survive in NT, but in Southern Talyshi it is preserved alongside the new subjunctive, and the parallelism between the two parts of the paradigm is clear, e.g. ST (Māsulei) *kar-ïm* 'I do', *bï-kar-ïm* 'may I do' (cf. Lazard 1978: 263). The use of the present stem, and affixal personal desinences where applicable, in these three forms is therefore of great antiquity, and analogous verb forms can be found across Iranian.

10.3.2 *Past-stem forms*

For the purposes of this presentation, the past-stem forms can be divided into those which are etymologically based on the participial forms of MIr. and those which continue the infinitive, although synchronically no such distinction exists. Among the former is the preterite, here represented by *kărd[ïm]e*, which serves as the basic past tense in NT: this is the modern reflex of the innovative periphrastic perfect construction which we traced earlier from Old to Middle Iranian. Accordingly, in the case of transitive verbs such as *kārdé*, the morphological structure of the preterite

---

[7] It may be more successful in the NT of Iran: cf. Paul (2011: 147) on the dialect of 'Anbarān.

[8] Paul (1998*b*: 80), Mace (2003: 103f.)

differs from that of all the finite forms seen up to this point. As mentioned in Section 10.1, although it acts synchronically as an agreement marker, the *ïm* element which appears in this form is an oblique clitic pronoun, as could be used in the OIr. and MIr. versions of this construction.[9] Although usually not found on the verb form itself, which is otherwise invariable for person and number, it is given here in order to demonstrate the morphological composition of the preterite: the past stem *kārd-* (which bears the stress) is followed by a suffix *-e*, and the pronoun may be inserted as a mesoclitic between these two otherwise inseparable elements.

The past stem here clearly continues the verbal adjective in **-ta*, while the *-e* element is etymologically the 3SG present tense copula: the formal elements of the original periphrastic construction are thus still present in the modern form.[10] However, the final *-e* is not identified with the copula, and unlike the copula it may even appear as *-ï* or be omitted altogether (Stilo 2008a). The same goes for the intransitive version of the preterite formation, represented in Table 10.3 by *mārd-im* from *mārdé* 'die': this takes the full complement of personal desinences, but although these are descended from the copular element in the periphrastic perfect construction, forms such as *mārd-im* are now entirely synthetic. Likewise, the past stem (*kārd*, *mārd*), although it comes directly from the participial element of the OIr. periphrastic perfect construction, cannot be used as a participle in NT.

However, NT does possess a participle built on the past stem, which for the verb *kārdé* takes the form *kārdá*: this continues the verbal adjective in *-ag* seen in Section 10.2. Unlike its ancestor, though, the NT participle is also in widespread use as part of various TMA forms, which must have arisen in just the same way as the preterite and accordingly follow it in showing ergative alignment. The most important of these is the perfect indicative, represented by *kārdá[m]e* (intransitive *mārdá=m*) in the table. The perfect differs from the preterite, though, in that the copular element of the original periphrasis retains its own identity as a clitic auxiliary in the modern form: this auxiliary can itself appear in various moods and tenses, giving rise to forms such as the perfect subjunctive and pluperfect, which will not be discussed here.

This 'past participle' itself, however, does not retain the particular set of characteristics which originally led to the creation of all these ergatively aligned forms. In MIr., the form in *-ag* (like the *ta*-participle on which it was based) expressed a state resulting from a past event, and thus had passive meaning with transitive verbs and

---

[9] The distinction between the verbal endings and the clitic pronouns is clearer in some other person/number combinations, where the pronoun bears no resemblance to the verbal ending (e.g. 3PL desinence/copula *-(i)n*, clitic pronoun *=(i)šon*; cf. MPers. *=išān* in example (5) above). This clitic pronoun is still found in possessive and other oblique uses, e.g. *sārd=ïm=e* 'I am cold', lit. 'it is cold to me'.

[10] This is made obvious by the Central Talyshi equivalent of this form, where this final element agrees in number with the object (*=a/=in*): see Paul (2011: 137). It is remarkable that the 3SG form of the copula has left any traces in the modern-day construction, as it is so frequently absent in the MIr. attestations.

active meaning with intransitive verbs, meaning it could not take an object itself. This gave rise to the morphosyntactic peculiarities associated with the parts of the paradigm based on it. However, in its independent use as a participle, the modern NT -*a* form behaves very differently from its ancestor. As shown in example (6), it is free to relativize on the subject argument of transitive verbs, and it may refer to actions simultaneous with, rather than preceding, the event expressed by the main verb. As a result, the behaviour of all the analytic forms based on this participle cannot be predicted from the behaviour of the participle itself.

(6) boğšav-i   šišt-a   ağil   ki   =e ?
     plate-OBL   wash-PTCP   child who   =COP.3SG
     'Who is the child washing the plate?'

The infinitive in NT, as in other Talyshi varieties and widely across West Iranian, continues the parasitic formation consisting of the past stem + -*an*; a halfway stage in the NT development of final -*an* to -*e* can be seen in ST (Māsulei), which has -*e(n)* (Lazard 1978: 266). The infinitive is not differentiated for tense/aspect, and its uses are not surprising in the Indo-European context: as a verbal noun, it can behave as the complement of certain predicates (*I forced him to do X*) or as an action nominal retaining verbal argument structure (*to do X is difficult*). A notable instance of the latter function is seen in a construction with the meaning 'while V-ing', in which the infinitive is followed by the clitic postposition =*ada* (which raises the preceding vowel), giving *kārdí=ada* 'while doing'. In connection with the infinitive, the form *kārdanín* listed here as the 'gerundive' should also be noted: this is also called the future participle, and most commonly appears with the copula in a proximate or necessitative future construction *kārdanín=im* 'I am to go, I am about to go'. In diachronic terms it derives from the application of the adjectival ending -*in* to the infinitive in -*an*; synchronically this relationship is no longer recognizable.

One of the main features distinguishing NT from most other West Iranian languages, though, is its use of the past stem in the present and future tenses. In each case this seems to result from the grammaticalization of a construction involving the infinitive. The present tense form represented here by *kārdéda=m* is best explained as deriving diachronically from a syntagm meaning 'I am in doing', which makes use of a suffix -*da* related to =*ada* above and ultimately reflecting proto-Iranian **antar* 'in' (Windfuhr 1987: 393); the suffix is much less likely to be borrowed from Azerbaijani as is assumed by Schulze (2000: 47).[11] As mentioned in Section 10.1, person–number marking is borne by a clitic auxiliary identical with the

---

[11] An alternative proposal (Henning 1954: 175, followed by Paul 1998a: 172–4) instead connects the form with the old present participle in **-ant-*, but this provides no explanation for the most salient characteristic of this present tense form—its use of the past stem (cf. Stilo 2013).

copula; this auxiliary can also appear in the preterite, resulting in a past progressive *kārdéda=bim* 'I was doing'. This suggests that the progressive meaning is original to the present-tense form too; however, *kārdéda=m* is now used with general as well as progressive present value.

Synchronically there is less reason to see the form *kārdéda* as retaining any particular connection with the infinitive. In particular, regardless of its etymology, in present-day NT it does not consist of the infinitive with locative marking—this in fact gives converbal *kārdíada*, as seen above, while *kārdéda* does not exist as a non-finite element in its own right. Moreover, *kārdéda* exists alongside a reduced variant *kárda*, in which the vowel *é* is removed with simplification of the resulting consonant cluster, and the stress automatically moves to the preceding syllable. Whatever the reason for this phenomenon, it affects verbs in the present tense but never the infinitive itself.

In the future tense, here *bakārdé=m*, we see what looks like the result of the grammaticalization of an allative construction based on the infinitive: its prefix *ba-* can be identified with the existing preposition *ba* meaning 'to, at', while the following clitic is the present of the copula. A future tense with origins in such a construction would be far from unexpected. On the other hand, there is evidence to suggest that the original role of this form may not have been future but present. For example, Muslim Tat, an offshoot of Persian spoken alongside NT in Azerbaijan, shows a present tense form *bæ-gæštæn-üm* equivalent in structure to the NT future (Stilo 2011, citing Grjunberg 1963: 69), which suggests an areal development. Moreover, within NT itself one salient characteristic of the future tense is its common use in gnomic statements referring to timeless truths. While such statements are, by definition, not incompatible with the use of a future tense form, this does suggest that the future in fact continues what was once a more all-purpose present tense form which counted the expression of futurity among its uses, before its domain was restricted by the rise of the new present tense in -*da* (cf. the cases examined in Haspelmath 1998). In this case, the original construction which gave rise to this form could be taken as the equivalent of 'I am at doing X', involving the locative rather than the allative sense of *ba*.

However this may be, *bakārdé=m* is by now a fully grammaticalized form rather than a syntagm. The preposition *ba* cannot govern the infinitive in this way synchronically, and the copular element has little independence: it cannot be negated directly or appear in any other tense, and as was mentioned in Section 10.1, the originally independent clitic element in *bakārdé=m* (as in *kārdéda=m* and the intransitive perfect *mārdá=m*) now acts as an affix in two of the four NT dialect areas in Azerbaijan.

10.3.3 *The synchronic status of the past and present stems*

In this section I have surveyed the finite and non-finite forms of the verb in NT from a diachronic perspective, as well as giving some idea of the uses they are put to in the modern language. While in some cases a great deal remains to be understood, in others it is clear that little has changed since the MIr. period, and in general we are able to account historically for the appearance of the present or past stem in the forms of *kārdé* and other verbs which pattern with it.

We are also in a better position now to determine the synchronic status of this stem distribution—whether speakers can be viewed as selecting one stem or the other on the basis of an external motivation of some kind, or whether instead the fact that any given part of the paradigm requires a particular stem is simply a brute fact about the morphological system. I claim that the first of these possibilities cannot be sustained, as there is no functional or structural property which unites all the forms taking one stem in opposition to all the forms taking the other.

Thus neither stem is associated with a particular grammatical context, whether this is defined phonologically or morphologically. Both are found bearing lexical stress, and while all forms employing the present stem show prefixes, the same is also true of *bakārdém*, which is based on the past stem. Earlier, Table 10.1 appeared to show a striking correlation, relevant to finite forms at least, between affixal person marking and the use of the present stem; however, we have seen in this section that affixal marking is also found in the preterite of intransitive verbs (*mā́rd-im*). Ergative morphosyntactic alignment, and thus mesoclisis, is only found in connection with past-stem forms, but it does not extend to clauses involving the present or future tense.

Likewise, neither stem can be ascribed a particular value in morphosyntactic or semantic terms. A notable feature of Talyshi is the opposition between the imperfect, which bears the present stem, and the past perfective tenses, which bear the past stem, but this aspectual relationship between the stems is not consistent across the paradigm. Tellingly, the originally perfective 'past participle' *kārdá* has been able to take on the imperfective functions of *áka*, suggesting that speakers do not see the difference between the two stems as generally encoding an aspectual opposition. Distinctions in tense and mood are similarly ill served by the morphological distinction between present and past stem forms. Indeed, the existence of two future negative forms, one of which is based on each stem, is a clear indication that the stems bear no distinctive value of their own.

Given the way in which the opposition between the present and past stems first emerged, as seen in Section 10.2, the morphomic nature of these stems in NT is not surprising. The pattern of stem distribution over the NT paradigm is strikingly anti-functional, but it has come about largely on the basis of the purely formal connection between the infinitive and the past perfective tenses which arose in the MIr. period.

Moreover, although NT is distinctive for the extent to which it has built new forms on the basis of the infinitive, many other modern West Iranian languages have also inherited an infinitive built on the past stem, and therefore show similar morphomic behaviour. Thus the distribution of stems over the verb paradigm of Modern Persian is explicitly described as morphomic in Bonami and Samvelian (2009a: 27), while in earlier treatments the same thing has often been recognized implicitly by the use of purely formal labels, such as 'stem 1' and 'stem 2', to refer to the two halves of the paradigm. In fact, among those languages which inherited the infinitive formation seen here, it is unusual to find the two stems distributed on anything other than morphomic grounds. Semantic motivation is reported for Juhuri (Jewish Tat), where the past and present stems can now be synchronically associated with 'factual' and 'virtual' meaning respectively (Authier 2012: 168); but the rarity of such cases suggests that there is no general tendency for speakers to favour the alignment of form and function over purely morphological principles of stem distribution.

However, it remains to be seen to what extent this inherited morphomic distribution is relevant in present-day NT, where many verbs have abandoned the distinction between past and present stems altogether. This is the subject of the final section, which looks at stem behaviour in verbs outside the *kārdé* group.

10.4 Stem behaviour across the NT verb lexicon

Up to this point my discussion of NT verb morphology has focused on the small number of verbs whose formal behaviour can be exemplified by the paradigm of *kārdé*. As was touched on in Section 10.1, what distinguishes the nine basic verbs of this type from the rest of the NT verb lexicon is not the morphological structure of their TMA forms or the identity of the inflectional affixes they bear, which are common to all verbs in the language (barring a few isolated irregularities) according to their status as transitive or intransitive, but the fact that their paradigm makes use of two distinct stems which do not stand in a consistent formal relationship with each other and cannot be broken down into smaller morphological units. That is not to say that all nine verbs have distinct and unpredictable patterns of stem alternation. In fact, the verb *omé* 'come', with present stem *(v)o-*, is alone in having two stems which are entirely suppletive in synchronic and diachronic terms, while the others can be placed into groups according to the relationship between their present and past stems: *žan-/ža-* 'strike' patterns with *s(t)an-/s(t)a-* 'take'; *da-/do-* 'give' with *na-/no-* 'put'; and *ka-/kārd-* 'do' with *ha-/hārd-* 'eat', *ba-/bārd-* 'carry', and *va-/vārd-* 'bring'. But there is no room for further morphological analysis here, and it is only lexical knowledge that tells a speaker that *ža-* is a past stem while *da-* and *ba-* are present stems, and that their counterparts have nothing formally in common.

In fact, these nine verbs—along with the genuinely anomalous *še* 'go' and *be* 'be, become', which are not discussed in this chapter—are the only verbs in NT which retain the 'irregular' formal relationship of the past stem with the present which had already begun to lose ground, in favour of regularization by means of past stem suffixes (*-ād*, *-īd*, *-ist*), in the early MIr. period. But the stronger claim has also been made that these are the only verbs whose present and past stems are reliably distinguished at all in the present-day language: that is, that the morphomic distribution which I have been considering here is relevant only to these few conservative and frequently used items, while the rest retain just a single stem or are currently in the process of generalizing a single stem across the paradigm.[12] Thus Stilo (2008*a*: 372), referring to the NT of Azerbaijan, states simply that 'in all but about eight rather common verbs [...] the present and past stems have fallen together in Northern Talyshi', and he is followed in this by Paul (2011: 104), who makes a similar claim for the NT variety of Anbarān (Iran). Pirejko (1991) and Schulze (2000) give a slightly more complex description. Besides this hard core of very conservative verbs, they note the existence of a large group in which distinctive past stems in *-i* do exist, but are apparently being lost in favour of the corresponding present stem forms, a topic I return to below in Section 10.4.2.

Accordingly, Schulze (2000: 45) speaks of a long-term diachronic trend in NT away from the 'diptotic paradigm' and towards 'stem stabilization', whose effects can be seen both in earlier developments (given the large number of single-stem verbs already established in the language) and in the present day. For Schulze, then, the scope of morphomic stem distribution in NT has undergone severe restrictions, and rather than organizing the paradigm of all the verbs in the language, as it does elsewhere in Iranian, the two-stem system seems to apply only to the most frequent items, i.e. just where one would expect to find entrenched irregularities of little relevance to the morphological system as a whole.

Given the lack of any functional coherence among the parts of the paradigm which etymologically share one stem or the other, it may not come as a surprise if such a trend towards a single-stem paradigm does exist, whereby speakers are gradually doing away with a pervasive inflectional contrast which serves no purpose in morphosyntactic or any other extramorphological terms. Indeed, Schulze (2000) refers to this development as freeing the lexical component from inflectional 'burden'. On the other hand, a great deal of work on autonomous morphology, including some presented elsewhere in this volume, has shown that speakers readily preserve such non-functional distributions and may even extend their range of operation over the lexicon. In the NT case, then, are we really seeing the breakdown of a morphomic stem distribution which has simply become too much trouble to retain?

---

[12] Note that the index to Cheung (2007) lists only one stem for all verbs cited from NT, uniquely among modern West Iranian languages.

It is worth noting at this point that none of the treatments of NT mentioned above is focused specifically on the behaviour of verb stems across the paradigm or across the lexicon. Stilo (2008*a*), for example, is primarily concerned with person–number agreement marking, and his discussion of stem distribution is not intended to be exhaustive—this is made clear by the fact that he gives examples using verbs with a past stem in *i* (e.g. *davuni-* 'spend (time)', *gini-* 'fall'),[13] although he does not mention the existence of this group of verbs at any point. Similarly, the stem forms given by Paul (2011: 104) in a table illustrating the relative paucity of two-stem verbs in NT are sometimes contradicted by forms and glosses given elsewhere in the work. It is therefore worth taking a closer look at stem behaviour in NT to see to what extent the observations just cited can be upheld. My claim in this section is that the true synchronic and diachronic picture casts doubt on the idea of a single long-term trend towards the elimination of the two-stem system; and that, despite playing no functional role, the distribution identified for *kārdé* continues to be recognized by speakers as an important principle of paradigm structure for all verbs that retain a distinction between past and present stems, which are more numerous than has generally been realized.

10.4.1 *Single-stem verbs*

The central claim made in all descriptions of stem behaviour in NT—namely that many of its verbs have abandoned the formal distinction between present and past stems—is certainly true. Lazard (1978), in a description of the Southern Talyshi variety of Māsule, gives a list of around twenty-five different types of stem alternation (and does not claim to be comprehensive); for the most part these are not ST innovations, but inherited patterns which find close parallels in other modern Iranian languages and can often be identified in Parthian and Middle Persian as well. A comparison with NT, however, shows that the latter has lost practically all of these inherited alternation patterns by generalizing one of the stems across the paradigm. Thus ST *soin-/sot-* 'burn' corresponds to NT single-stem *sut-*, and *xïs-/xït-* 'lie down' corresponds to NT single-stem *hït-* 'sleep'. Table 10.4 gives more examples.

As illustrated by this table, the ST evidence shows that the Talyshi group inherited many different stem pairings of the kind labelled 'irregular' in our discussion of the MIr. period in Section 10.2.2, the large majority of which are simply not found in present-day NT. What also emerges from Table 10.4, and even more clearly from the full list it is based on, is that when any such irregular alternation has been eliminated in NT, the form that survives is always the past stem etymologically. In rare cases, folk poetry from the early twentieth century provides examples of old present stems

---

[13] This verb is usually found in the slightly different form *gini-*, which is how it appears below (§10.4.2).

TABLE 10.4 Comparison of ST (Māsulei) present and past stems with NT single stems

	ST present stem	ST past stem	NT single stem
say	*vā-*	*vāt-*	*vot-*
cook	*pe-*	*pat-*	*pāt-*
lie down / sleep	*xïs-*	*xït-*	*hït-*
stand up	*ez-*	*ešt-*	*ayšt-*
burn	*soin-*	*sot-*	*sut-*
die	*mer-*	*mard-*	*mārd-*
see	*ven-*	*venn-*	*vind-*
sing	*xon-*	*xann-*	*hānd-*
take	*ger-*	*get-*	*gat-*

which are no longer used, such as *mi-* 'die' and *vin-* 'see' (Miller 1953: 199, 201), showing that the process involved was still operative in the fairly recent past. Many more examples could be given of single-stem verbs which continue the inherited past stem in this way, and these include some of the most commonly used verbs in the language: they all bear the characteristic stem-final dental which reflects their previous function in the system as past stems in particular. Notably, no verbs are found in which the past stem has spread beyond its original boundaries without taking over the whole paradigm; if the inherited distribution is not retained intact, the result is always a single-stem verb.

Given that only one of the two inherited stems was to be retained in these verbs, the past stem would have been expected to win out over the present as it did, rather than vice versa. In terms of text frequency, those parts of the paradigm which etymologically require the past stem—including the infinitive, the main participial form, and all indicative tenses except the imperfect and one future negative formation—significantly outweigh the remainder, making the past stem of such verbs the more likely candidate for analogical spread over the paradigm when this took place.

But this reasoning after the fact, along with any attempt to explain the phenomenon of stem loss seen here as one aspect of a more general trend towards simplification of the paradigm, is faced with a severe challenge. As noted explicitly by Pirejko and Schulze, the nine verbs exemplified by *kārdé* in this chapter are not the only ones to retain a distinction between present and past stems in NT: the language still possesses many verbs whose inherited past stem is characterized by a final *i* absent in the present stem. However, these 'i-stem' verbs are reportedly in the process of generalizing the *present* stem over the paradigm—the reverse of the tendency seen in the verbs just discussed. Even more problematic is the existence of many verbs which seem to have generalized a single stem across the paradigm, and are accordingly grouped with *suté*, *hïté*, etc. in all descriptions of NT, but show

TABLE 10.5 The paradigm of NT *dïzdié* 'steal', showing conservative *i*-stem forms. Intransitive preterite and perfect forms are represented by *gïnié* 'fall'

	Past stem		Present stem
Infinitive	*dïzdié*	Imperative	*bídïzd*
Present	*dïzdiéda=m*	Present subjunctive	*bídïzd-ïm*
Future	*badïzdié=m*	Present optative	*bídïzdo-m*
Preterite (tr.)	*dïzdí[m]e*	Imperfect	*adïzdí-m*
(intr.)	*gïní-m*	Imperfect subjunctive	*bádïzdi-m*
Perfect (tr.)	*dïzdiá[m]e*	Future negative	*adízdïni-m*
(intr.)	*gïniá=m*	Present participle	*ádïzd*
Past participle	*dïzdiá*		
Gerundive	*dïzdianín*		

no sign of the dental, suggesting that here too it is the present stem that has won out. How can these observations be explained? I will take the two groups in turn.

10.4.2 *The i-stems*

While the origins of the stem alternations seen in verbs of the *kārdé* type (and lost in verbs of the single-stem *suté* type) go back to the so-called irregular stem alternations of MIr., the alternation shown by the *i*-stem verbs of NT is descended from a regular formation in which the past stem was remodelled as present stem + suffix *-īd*, as seen in Middle Persian.[14] The lack of a dental in the NT form of this suffix is the regular result of sound change: dentals in intervocalic position were lost at a certain stage in the development of Talyshi (cf. NT *moa* < proto-Iranian **mātar* 'mother').[15] The *i*-stem group is large: one reason for this is that it includes all verbs bearing the causative suffixes *-n-* and *-ovn-* (e.g. *hïtovn-/hïtovni-* 'put to bed', from *hïté* 'sleep'), which are numerous, though the synthetic causative is no longer a productive formation in NT. An analogous *i*-stem group is seen in ST, also associated with the causative suffix (Lazard 1978: 261).

The etymological distribution of the two stems over the paradigm is just like that of the two stems of *kārdé*, as illustrated in Table 10.5 for the verb *dïzdié* 'steal' (along with *gïnié* 'fall' for the intransitive preterite and perfect)—and in the modern language, all these etymologically expected forms may be found. But alongside

---

[14] Agnes Korn (p.c.) has pointed out to me that the long *ī* seen in this M Pers. suffix, which is required etymologically in order to give the vowel *i* in NT, may come as the result of a Persian-specific sound change, as argued in Korn (2009). If this is the case, the *i*-stem formation is not native to Talyshi but must have been introduced to the language at some stage as a result of Persian influence.

[15] The dental stops are preserved in *suté*, *hïté* because they were preceded by consonants at the time this sound change took place: cf. M Pers. *sôxt-*, *xuft-*. Note that the dental has been lost, as expected, in the irregular past stems *do-*, *ža-* (cf. M Pers. *dād-*, *jad-*), etc.

these, it is also easy to point to instances where the *i* element does not appear, although the past stem would be expected. Thus Pirejko (1991: 141f.) describes the verb 'collect' as having two parallel infinitive forms, one based on the past stem (*čini-é*) and the other innovating by using the present stem (*čin-é*). The transcribed narrative text provided by Schulze (*Palangi ahvolot* 'The leopard story') contains several examples of the same phenomenon, such as *bagïné* '(the bullet) will fall' rather than *bagïnié* (Schulze 2000: 76, line 64). Data from my own fieldwork likewise suggest that forms such as future *badïzdé* and present *dïzdéda* are far more commonly observed than their more conservative counterparts formed on the past stem. Meanwhile, a recent NT dictionary (Mamedov 2006) makes no particular claim about stem behaviour in this group of verbs, but both its headwords and its numerous example sentences provide further evidence for the existence for *i*-less inflected forms of this kind.

There is definitely something to be explained here, and one way to explain it would be to suggest that the morphomic distribution of stems over the paradigm has simply broken down, because its arbitrariness placed an intolerable burden on users of the language. That is, faced with the choice between two stem forms whose selection was not motivated by coherent sets of contexts and which never served to distinguish one inflectional form from another, speakers solved the problem by treating the two stems as interchangeable and abandoning the idea that they play distinct morphological roles at all.

But this cannot be the whole story, because the strict division between the two parts of the paradigm which applies historically to these verbs undeniably remains in evidence in their present-day behaviour. Forms containing the characteristic *i* can still be found in all parts of the paradigm for which the past stem is etymologically appropriate; on the other hand, it is never introduced into those parts of the paradigm which are historically based on the present stem. Thinkable forms such as an imperative **bídïzdi!* 'steal!', or a future negative **adïzdínim* 'I will not steal', are entirely absent. The morphomic distribution found in the *kārdé* group is thus still operative in the *i*-stems at least to this extent. As noted above, some scholars have explicitly taken this asymmetry as signalling the obsolescence of the past stem and the generalization of the present stem over the whole paradigm, in accordance with a long-term trend towards single-stem status for NT verbs.

But a closer look at the innovative behaviour of the *i*-stems casts doubt on the idea that a general long-term pressure towards stem stabilization is leading to the demise of the past stem in *i*. It has not been made clear in previous descriptions that in the large majority of cases where this *i* is absent from the surface form, the verb is in the infinitive, present (/past continuous), or future—all parts of the paradigm which employ a stressed *é* immediately following the stem. This is a well-established phenomenon, and instances can already be noted in Miller (1953), although he does not comment on them. Meanwhile, in the past participle and gerundive, and finite forms built on them—that is, wherever the stem is followed by *a*—the absence of *i* is attested, but more sporadic; the phenomenon is not found in Miller or, apparently, recognized in modern dictionaries, and I recorded it comparatively rarely in the course of my fieldwork. Speakers also appear much more hesitant in labelling such forms as 'correct', suggesting sociolinguistic distinctions between the loss of *i* in these two parts of the paradigm. Finally, in the preterite, where neither of these conditions applies and the stem itself bears the lexical stress in positive forms, the *i* is always found, with the result that the apparent spread of the present stem at issue here does not affect this part of the paradigm at all. Forms such as **gïn-im* and **dïzd[ïm]e*, for genuine *gïní-m* and *dïzdí[m]e*, are not attested.[16]

However we account for this behaviour, it emerges that the obsolescence of the past stem has been overstated. Even bearing in mind the dangers of talking about synchronic variation in such teleological terms, we have grounds to say at most that the past stem may be changing in its distribution—though, as I have pointed out, all the past stem forms given in Table 10.5 can still be found. Moreover, the encroachment of the present stem seems to have taken place in two separate stages, which correspond to the phonological context in which the stem is situated; this does not support the idea that general speaker confusion over the morphological role of the two stems is to blame, as there would be no reason for the effect to take hold in a ubiquitous form like the present indicative while remaining largely absent in a rare form like the gerundive.

Instead, given the pattern seen above, it makes more sense to look for a phonetic origin for the optional absence of *i*. In this connection it is notable that the language independently shows a surface tendency to reduce the sequence *ié* to *é*, as can be seen in verb forms where the *i* involved is not the past stem suffix but part of the lexical root, such as the verb *firsié/firsé* 'slip'.[17] This provides a plausible starting point from which to account for the innovative behaviour seen in the *i*-stem paradigm: doublets such as *badïzdiém* and *badïzdém* existed in any case, for reasons unconnected with any pressure towards simplification in the paradigm.

But the full range of variation now shown by *i*-stem forms cannot be treated simply as a surface phenomenon of this kind. The combination *ia* is commonplace both within morphemes and across morpheme boundaries, and there is no corresponding tendency to reduce it to *a* which would explain the potential for loss of *i* which can be seen in the past participle and gerundive; similarly, the existence of the present tense form *dïzdam* alongside *dïzdédam* shows that the latter can itself serve

---

[16] The combination -*ie* found at the end of forms such as (3SG) intransitive *gïníe*, (clitic-free) transitive *dïzdíe* may coalesce to give *í* or even *é* for some speakers; but in the latter case, the stress on this vowel still marks the fact that the past stem has been selected.

[17] Unfortunately it is hard to find examples from unrelated grammatical contexts: this sequence is not found within morphemes, while suffixes beginning with *é* are rare outside the verb. Verbs such as *firsié* belong to the *a*-stem class, which will be discussed below.

as an input for the idiosyncratic process which creates *kárdam* alongside *kārdédam*. This means that speakers have reanalysed the presence or absence of *i*, in parts of the paradigm which etymologically require the past stem, as an effect at some underlying level.

One obvious question to ask at this point is why this reanalysis took place. But another is what precisely it consisted of: what is the morphological structure of a form such as the past participle *dïzdá*, existing alongside *dïzdiá*? Although I have cast doubt on the idea that a general diachronic tendency is operating in favour of reducing the NT paradigm to a single stem, it is certainly possible that the loss of *i*, phonetically motivated to begin with, was reanalysed as a morphological phenomenon, namely the removal of the past stem marker. In that case, forms such as *dïzdá* really do contain the present stem, meaning that the morphomic distribution traced for *kārdé* has ceased to operate in the *i*-stem verbs.

There is an alternative analysis, however, which I pursue here. That is to claim that the morphomic boundary between the two halves of the paradigm has been preserved, and thus the past stem marker is always found underlyingly where it is expected; but that this marker may be realized either as *i* or as zero. In the present state of the language, the realization *i* is always possible, but the zero realization is made more or less likely by a complex set of morphological, phonological, and sociolinguistic factors.

This may seem, at the very least, an unduly complicated way of stating the facts. However, what is truly complicated remains the same on both accounts, which is to specify the conditions which license the choice of one form or the other. These have not been explored in any depth before, and on the basis of the evidence available to me I have only been able to point at some of the considerations involved.

On the other hand, the two treatments are not simply notational variants. What is novel in my preferred analysis is that it ascribes the alternation at issue here to the morphophonological level: it treats the past-stem marker *i* as a morphological element with its own distinctive set of phonological properties, which do not follow from those of the segment *i*. This is not as ad hoc as it may appear. I suggest that an analogous morphological element is required in any case to explain the behaviour of the final group of NT verbs, which I label the *a*-stems for reasons which will become clear.

10.4.3 *The a-stems*

If there are good reasons to doubt that a morphological process of stem stabilization is taking place in the *i*-stems in favour of a single, etymologically present stem, it becomes all the more surprising that NT seems to possess a large number of verbs in which this process has already taken place. These are reported to have just one stem across the paradigm, but one which continues the present stem, rather than the past as was the case for the single-stem verbs discussed above. Examples include *tošé* 'shear' and *rasé* 'arrive': corresponding to these infinitives we find the imperative forms *bǐ-toš* and *bǐ-ras*, apparently showing the collapse of the formal distinction between past and present stems. Verbs such as *firsié* above, in which the *i* is not a past-stem marker but remains throughout the paradigm (e.g. in imperative *bǐ-firsi*), belong here too.

In diachronic and comparative terms these verbs tend to be closely associated with the *i*-stems. Thus Miller (1953: 197) notes that many of the verbs in question here have Modern Persian cognates with infinitives in *-idæn*, i.e. continuing the regular past-stem suffix *-īd* which underlies the *i*-stem class in NT. Similarly, Pirejko and Schulze state that the paradigm of verbs such as *rasé* attained its current uniformity as a result of the same process of stem stabilization which they identify as affecting the *i*-stems, though they stop short of identifying these verbs as descending from the *i*-stems themselves. But all synchronic descriptions of NT known to me describe the behaviour of *tošé*, *rasé*, and the like as being identical to that of single-stem verbs such as *hïté*: that is, in the modern language they are placed in this single-stem class, which is treated as the default for NT verbs.

The unanimity of scholars on this point is odd, though, because these verbs do not in fact behave identically to those in the single-stem group: instead they make up a class of their own, which has apparently not been recognized before.[18] The distinction between the two types is reliably visible in the preterite. In the intransitive verbs seen so far, the preterite is composed of the past stem (or single stem as appropriate) followed by the unstressed personal endings *-im*, *-iš*, etc., which were originally forms of the present-tense copula, reflecting the periphrastic origins of the formation: *hïtim* 'I slept', *vítim* 'I ran'. The 1SG preterite of *rasé*, however, is not **rásim*, but *rasáym*. A monophthongized version of this form, *rasém*, is also widely attested; whichever is found, the same distinctive vocalism and stress pattern appear throughout the preterite. The existence of *rasém*, and the analogous *bāmém* 'I cried', is noted by Pirejko (1991: 150, 158). However, she treats this *em* and the *im* found elsewhere simply as variants of the same ending, and does not observe that they are stressed differently (stress marking is not given) and apply to disjoint sets of verbs.

On the basis of the intransitive formation alone, Pirejko could in principle be right to treat the distinctive behaviour of *rasáym* (*rasém*) as a feature of the ending, rather than of the stem—though this would be unexpected given the well-understood connection between the preterite person markers and the copula, and it would still represent a striking difference between the *rasé* and *hïté* types. However,

---

[18] Strangely, Miller notes the divergent behaviour of certain verbs (which are in fact the *a*-stem verbs discussed here) in the preface to his *Talyšskie teksty* (Miller 1930: xxvi), but he makes no mention of their existence in his later grammar of the language (Miller 1953), and the hint is not picked up in later descriptions of NT.

corresponding transitive forms make it clear that the stem in particular is involved here: they show a stem-final *a*, which can be recognized as such because it appears before the pronominal clitic markers when these are present, e.g. *tošá[m]e* 'I sheared', *romá[m]e* 'I drove'.[19] Such forms are entirely parallel in structure with the *i*-stem *dïzdí[m]e* 'I stole' seen above. These verbs can therefore be identified as *a*-stems: they have a distinctive past stem characterized by the addition of a regular suffix *a* to the present stem.

Although it has gone unnoticed, the existence of such a class is not unexpected in the Talyshi context: Lazard (1978: 261) lists a very similar formation for the ST of Māsule, which likewise patterns with the *i*-stem group in that variety.[20] It is tempting to connect these Talyshi *a*-stems with the regular past stem suffix *-ād* which emerged in parallel with *-īd* in Middle West Iranian, though a development of *ā* > Talyshi *a* is unexpected. What is certainly clear is that the past stem of these verbs has been remodelled at some stage on the basis of the present stem; the regular relationship between the two stems is what links this group with the *i*-stems and distinguishes them both from the true single-stem group.

While the preterite unambiguously shows the presence of this *a*, though, the infinitives *tošé*, *rasé*, etc. listed above (rather than **tošaé*, **rasaé*) demonstrate that it is not always visible where the past stem would be expected on etymological grounds. In fact, if the preterite is left aside, *a*-stem verbs usually do seem to behave identically to single-stem verbs, with present *rasédam/rásdam*, future *barasém*, participle *rasá*, gerundive *rasanín*, and so on.

Although it is reasonable to assume that these forms did once contain the past stem, as is the case for all other NT verbs, the diachronic developments which gave rise to the current situation are inaccessible to us. Synchronically, though, we find ourselves in the same situation as with the *i*-stems: the etymological distribution of stems over the paradigm seems to have been disturbed, but only to the extent that the past stem marker is apparently missing where it would be expected, whereas it never appears outside its original zone (giving forms such as an imperative **bïrasa* or imperfect **arasáym* for *bïras, arasím*). Meanwhile, the existence of reduced forms such as *rásdam* from *rasédam* shows that we cannot treat the absence of the past stem *a* simply as a surface phenomenon in the current state of the language. The question again arises, then, whether the past-stem marker should be thought of as surviving underlyingly in all the forms where it is expected, as I have suggested for the *i*-stems; or whether, as is generally assumed, from the synchronic perspective we

---

[19] This incidentally leaves the preterite of such verbs indistinguishable from the perfect in many cases; misidentification of these preterites as perfect forms may be one reason why the separate identity of this group of verbs has gone unrecognized.

[20] I thank Gerardo De Caro for drawing this to my attention.

can say that the present stem has been adopted in all parts of the paradigm—except for the preterite, where this claim must certainly be abandoned.

Evidence in favour of the first option comes from an unexpected quarter. The verb *omé* 'come' is one of the verbs of the *kārdé* type; unlike *kārdé*, though, its two stems are etymologically unrelated, the present stem *(v)o-* going back to **āHai-* and the past stem (generally listed as *om-*) continuing **āgmat-* (Cheung 2007: 156, 100). The morphomic distinction between the parts of the paradigm descended from these two different formations remains quite clear in the modern language. However, alongside the infinitive *omé*, present *omédam* (*ómdam*), and future *bomém*, this verb has the preterite form *omáym*. This means that we are faced with the same question here as in the case of the regular *a*-stem verbs—how to account for the distinction between the formation of the preterite, which bears an overt stem-final *a*, and that of other forms such as the reduced present *ómda*, which do not.

In this case, however, it is easy to see that the phenomenon cannot be explained diachronically, or treated synchronically, in terms of the spread of the present stem over the paradigm. Whatever account is given of the infinitive form *omé*, and even the reduced present form *ómda*, they evidently continue the past stem *oma-* rather than the present stem *(v)o-* diachronically, thus demonstrating what was assumed above, namely that *rasé* etc. can descend from forms based on the past stem without any disruption in morphological terms. Synchronically, too, they clearly cannot be described as containing the present stem *(v)o-*.

On the other hand, to claim that these forms are now taken by speakers as built on a stem *om-*, separate from the *oma-* visible in the preterite, would be inelegant. The problem is not primarily that this would entail a three-stem paradigm unique to the language (as the verb *omé* already shows certain irregularities in its behaviour), but that this approach would miss an important fact: this particular aspect of the behaviour of *omé* is not unique or irregular within NT but is replicated identically throughout a large class of regular verbs, the *a*-stems. What the paradigm of *omé* actually tells us, I propose, is that it is possible for one stem to be shared across all parts of the paradigm which are expected to pattern together, while bearing an underlying final vowel which does not always appear on the surface.

If this account is acceptable for *omé* and the regular *a*-stem verbs, its potential as a treatment of the variation currently found in the *i*-stems is clear. Moreover, if the current behaviour of the *i*-stems does result from the reanalysis of a phonetic effect as belonging to an underlying level, the prior existence of such a morphophonological phenomenon in the *a*-stems would help to explain why this reanalysis took place. The analogies between the two groups are certainly strong, and there is some evidence that the *a*-stem group still demonstrates a certain amount of synchronic variation itself: for example, Schulze (2000: 71) records a form *tilada bim* 'I was running', rather than *tiléda bim*, and Paul (2011: 139) gives an example with *barasa* 'he will arrive' rather than *barasé*, while verbs outside the *a*-stems never show such forms. The existence of overt *a*-stem forms of this kind, like that of the much more prevalent preterite forms showing *a* in the stem, has not been described before, and the possible dialectal, sociolinguistic, or other conditions on the appearance of *a* across the paradigm are simply unknown to me. However, this behaviour further underlines the parallelism between the *a*-stems and the *i*-stems in NT.

10.5 Conclusion

Whether or not the *i*-stem and *a*-stem verbs can be taken to retain the morphomic distinction found overtly in verbs such as *kārdé* depends to a large extent on whether we are willing to countenance the existence of an underlying past-stem marker in forms such as the infinitive *omé*, and by extension in forms such as *rasé* and *dïzdé* as well. I support this analysis as giving the most natural account of the parallels between *omé* and the *a*-stem class; it also explains the fact that past-stem vowels may be absent where they are expected, but never inserted where they are not. According to the alternative view, meanwhile, the morphomic opposition between the two stems has been weakened in these verbs, and may be leading eventually to the restriction of the original past stem to preterite forms only. Such behaviour would run counter to the notion of morphomic patterns as diachronically coherent entities, which stand or fall as single units and do not allow for intermediate positions. However, precisely this all-or-nothing conception is epitomized by the coherent spread of the past stem across the paradigm seen in Section 10.4.1 above, leading to the sharp distinction between single-stem and *kārdé*-type verbs. Though it may not be possible to prove, I hope to have shown that a serious case can be made for the reality of morphomic behaviour with the same origins in the NT *i*- and *a*-stems as well.

Whatever the value of this proposal, this study certainly reveals a more complex state of affairs than has been recognized in earlier treatments of the NT verb. The facts do not bear out the claim that the past stem is becoming obsolete in the *i*-stems, and the existence of the *a*-stem class has not previously been documented at all. Verbs in the *i*-stem class show a great deal of synchronic variation in some of their forms, and I have pointed to textual evidence that the same is true for the *a*-stems.

Furthermore, the contrast between the behaviour of these two verb classes and that of the single-stem verbs casts doubt on the idea that NT is displaying a long-term trend away from morphomic distribution and towards stem uniformity throughout the paradigm. The developments which have affected the *a*- and *i*-stem verbs do not result from speaker confusion over the correct distribution of morphomic stems, but from sound change, and they are leading to the apparent spread of the present stem into new parts of the paradigm. By contrast, it is the past stem that has been generalized in the single-stem verbs, where the distinction between the two stems has genuinely been lost, and comparative evidence from elsewhere in the Talyshi group demonstrates that all these verbs inherited irregular formal alternations between their two stems. In other words, what speakers have a problem with is not the existence of morphomic patterns over the paradigm, but the existence of unpredictable formal relationships between the stems instantiating those patterns.

11

Overabundance in diachrony: a case study*

CHIARA CAPPELLARO

11.1 Introduction

This brief study is concerned with an under-investigated dimension of paradigmatic irregularity, namely the phenomenon of overabundance (Thornton 2011, 2012*a*, 2012*b*), or the possibility of a paradigmatic cell being 'filled by two or more synonymous forms which realize the same set of morpho-syntactic properties' (Thornton 2011: 359). Overabundance is 'canonical' (in the sense of Corbett 2005) when 'two or more forms that realize the same cell (i.e. the same set of morpho-syntactic features) in a lexeme's paradigm [...] can be used interchangeably, with the choice of one or the other form subject to no condition' (Thornton 2011: 362). Examples of highly canonical overabundance are given in (1)–(5):

(1) English *leaped, leapt*
         jump.PST.PTCP   (Haber 1976)

(2) Latin a. *rexēre, rexĕrunt, rexērunt*
                rule.3PL.PRF.PRS.IND
            b. *domō, domuī*
                house.DAT.SG   (Carstairs 1987: 30)

* The support of the AHRC under grant 2006/122137 is gratefully acknowledged. Versions of this chapter were read at the 14th International Morphology Meeting, Budapest, 13–16 May 2010 and at OxMorph 2, 8–10 October 2010; I wish to thank members of each audience for useful discussion, and all the following for helpful comments or relevant references at different stages: Martin Maiden, Anna M. Thornton, Nigel Vincent, Sandra Paoli, Michele Loporcaro, John Charles Smith, Silvio Cruschina and Louise Esher.

(3)   Finnish   a. *perunien, perunoitten*
                   potato.GEN.PL
             b. *ympyrien, ympyröitten*
                   circle.GEN.PL   (Carstairs 1987: 30, Acquaviva 2008: 33)

(4)   German   *Wortes, Worts*
                   word.GEN.SG   (Fehringer 2004: 314)

(5)   Italian   a. *sepolto, seppellito*
                   bury.PST.PTCP
             b. *possieda, possegga*
                   possess.3SG.PRS.SBJV   (Thornton 2011: 363f.)

Overabundance goes against the expectation that each cell of inflectional paradigms will be filled with no more than one form, is thus against the notions of 'inflectional parsimony' (Carstairs 1987: 31) and 'uniqueness of realization' (Thornton 2011), and goes more generally against what Natural Morphology would predict.

The phenomenon had not received thorough attention until very recently—with few exceptions such as the pioneering work by Haber (1976), and the more recent diachronic study by Fehringer (2004, 2011). Previous works do acknowledge the existence of 'polymorphy' (Anttila 1977), 'alternative inflexions' (Carstairs 1987), and 'doublets' (Acquaviva 2008). But very often the issue is treated as 'unusual, in the sense that in most inflected languages most if not all inflected words have only one form for each morphosyntactic slot' (Carstairs 1987: 30). The phenomenon, however, is not simply an artefact of grammar books and dictionaries. It is rare but attested, both at the level of the speech community and at the level of individual speakers (see examples (7)–(8) in §11.2). Thornton's study, carried out within the canonical approach to inflection (Corbett 2005, 2007*a*, 2007*b*), is the first attempt to investigate it systematically and to recognize fully its gradient nature.

This chapter investigates overabundance in the system of Italian third-person subject pronouns from a diachronic perspective. In particular, by looking at the behaviour of cell-mates *egli/esso* (3.M.SG.SBJ.PRON) and *ella/essa* (3.F.SG.SBJ.PRON) in a corpus of texts dating from the sixteenth century to the twentieth century, it claims the following:

    (i)   The diachronic maintenance of competing (near)-synonymous forms *egli/esso* and *ella/essa* correlates with lower frequency and lower salience, and affects items that are not acquired as core grammar/lexicon in early acquisition.

   (ii)   Overabundance, like defectiveness, can be motivated by speakers' uncertainty (Albright 2003, 2008, 2010). Uncertainty is not produced by low frequency alone, that is, quantitative lack of exposure to linguistic data. But rather, and more crucially, uncertainty is produced by qualitative lack of exposure, namely lack of exposure in the early stages of acquisition.

(iii)   The Principle of Contrast (Clark 1987, 1993) or a similar cognitive principle whereby 'wherever there is a difference in *form* there is a difference in *meaning*' (Clark 1987: 1), must operate in the early stages of acquisition. The data suggest that synonymy in fact appears to be tolerated at later stages of acquisition and in L2 acquisition.

The structure of the chapter is the following: in Section 11.2, I briefly discuss the notions of overabundance and canonical inflection. In Section 11.3, I present and discuss pronominal overabundance in Italian focusing on the diachronic perspective. Before concluding in Section 11.5, I put forward some observations on the relationship existing between the phenomena of overabundance and defectiveness in Section 11.4.

11.2 Overabundance and the canonical approach

Thornton investigates overabundance within the canonical approach to inflectional morphology. In this framework, the properties that identify a canonical paradigm are well known (Table 11.1). For example, all cells are expected to display the same stem, but each cell should exhibit different inflection. Deviation from canonicity results in non-canonical phenomena such as syncretism and suppletion, as illustrated in Table 11.2.

Overabundance is another kind of deviation, not listed in Table 11.2 'because the existence of multiple forms that realize the same cell adds a further dimension to the matrix' (Thornton 2011: 360), that is, deviation from 'uniqueness of realization' or the property whereby for any given lexeme every cell of its paradigm will be filled in a unique way. The forms in an overabundant cell are labelled 'cell-mates' in Thornton's study, and the crucial criterion of canonicity for cell-mates is 'no condition > condition' (where > = 'more canonical than').[1] Purely canonical cell-mates will also occur with the same frequency (Thornton 2011: 362). As with other non-canonical phenomena (cf. Corbett 2007a: 9), it is expected that 'pure' instances of canonical overabundance will be very rare and even non-existent:

Two completely interchangeable forms of equal frequency, whose use is not subject to any (speaker-related) diaphasic, diastratic, diamesic, diatopic, or diachronic conditions, or to any phonological, morphological, syntactico-semantic, or pragmatic conditions, do not exist. But breaking up the criterion relating to conditions into these several facets allows us to establish canonicity clines, classifying specific sets of forms as more or less canonical according to a certain sub-criterion, and to observe what sorts of factors, if any, tend to influence the appearance of a specific form from a set of cell-mates. (Thornton 2011: 362)

---

[1] For a full description of sub-criteria and their gradience, see Thornton (2011).

TABLE 11.1 Canonical inflection (Thornton 2011: 358; from Corbett 2007*a*, 2007*b*)

	COMPARISON ACROSS *CELLS* OF A LEXEME	COMPARISON ACROSS *LEXEMES*
COMPOSITION/STRUCTURE (≈ means of exponence)	same	same
LEXICAL MATERIAL (≈ shape of stem)	same	different
INFLECTIONAL MATERIAL (≈ shape of inflection)	different	same
OUTCOME (≈ shape of inflected forms)	different	different

TABLE 11.2 Deviations from canonical behaviour in single lexemes (Thornton 2011: 359; from Corbett 2007*b*)

	Canonical behaviour	Deviant behaviour	Type of deviation
COMPOSITION/STRUCTURE (of the inflected *word*)	same	different	fused exponence periphrasis
LEXICAL MATERIAL (≈ shape of *stem*)	same	different	alternations suppletion
INFLECTIONAL MATERIAL (≈ shape of *affix*)	different	same	syncretism uninflectability

Among the highly canonical instances of overabundance, Thornton discusses the Italian cell-mates *sepolto, seppellito* (bury.PST.PTCP). She provides both quantitative and qualitative data from the *Repubblica* on-line corpus and claims that while *sepolto* is preferred as an adjective and *seppellito* as a verb form, both forms can be used in both capacities, as in the following example:

(6) a. l'avvocato Enzo Storoni [. . .] **sarà seppellito** oggi dopo funerali privati.
     'The lawyer Enzo Storoni will be buried today after a private funeral.'
   b. Chagall **sarà sepolto** lunedì, nel cimitero del paese.
     'Chagall will be buried on Monday in the village cemetery.'

While the data above show that both cell-mates can be used interchangeably in Italian at the level of the speech community, one might still suspect that they could not be used interchangeably by a single individual. Consider, however, the following example uttered by the television presenter Federica Sciarelli,[2] where the speaker uses both forms as if they were synonyms and totally interchangeable:

(7) Ottavia, dodici anni, scomparsa, mai più trovata; una lettera che dice che è stata violentata, uccisa e … **sepolta, seppellita**. Ebbene, di lei raccontavano […]

'Ottavia, twelve years old, gone missing, never found again; a letter saying that she was raped, killed, and … **buried**. Well, people said about her […]'

Other examples of cell-mates used interchangeably by the same speaker are discussed in Fehringer (2004: 314f.). They are given below in (8)–(9):

(8) a. Das Reduplikativ muss nicht einmal auf derselben Seite des **Wortes** stehen wie der reduplizierte Teil.
'The reduplicating element does not have to be on the same side of the word as the reduplicated one.'
  b. Wie Vennemann 1986a […] bürde ich die Beschreibung der (nicht-kompositionellen) Nebenakzente eines **Worts** der Satzphonologie auf.
'Like Vennemann 1986a […] I take the description of the (non-compositional) secondary stress of a word to be a matter of sentence phonology.'

(9) a. Die Position nach dem Verb hat in diesen Sätzen mehr Gewicht, indem die im Standarddeutschen übliche Endstellungdes finiten **Verbs** im Nebensatz aufgehoben ist.
'The position of the verb has more weight in these sentences, since the verb-final word order in subordinate clauses, which is usual in standard German, has been abandoned.'
  b. Weder die Endstellung des finiten **Verbes** im Nebensatz noch die Vollklammer wurden ins Jiddische übernommen.
'Neither the verb-final word order in subordinate clauses nor the full verbal bracket was taken into Yiddish.'

In these examples, the same speaker 'go[es] on to use both forms apparently indiscriminately' (Fehringer 2004: 314). There is no difference in register between (8a) and (8b): '*Wortes* and *Worts* "word" appear in a context where the register is identical (the text deals with theoretical linguistics; one sentence discusses reduplication and the other word-stress).' Moreover, as the author adds with reference to (9), there appears to be no conclusive correlation between prosody and choice of variant.

---

[2] The TV programme 'Chi l'ha visto?' was broadcast on 26 April 2010. The video clip is available at the following link: http://www.rai.tv/dl/RaiTV/programmi/media/ContentItem-36f1c04d-819b-4402-892b-a81e6bba7bcc.html

Let us now turn to Italian data on pronominal overabundance in the system of third-person subject forms in the standard language.

11.3 Italian third-person pronouns

Standard Italian shows multiple forms for the third-person subject pronoun, as illustrated in Table 11.3. This coexistence of pronominal forms has been the object of considerable interest for its significance for the history of the Italian language, in the so-called *questione della lingua* (cf. D'Achille 1990: 313f.). Prescriptive grammars (since Fortunio's (1516) *Regole grammaticali della volgar lingua*, and Bembo's (1525) *Prose della volgar lingua*) have strongly opposed the use of *lui, lei, loro* as subjects, but these are in fact the forms used in modern Italian in everyday conversation. They are both anaphoric and deictic and can be used in all syntactic functions, unlike *egli, ella, esso, essa, essi, esse*, which are stylistically marked [+formal], extremely infrequent, and syntactically constrained (cf. Cordin and Calabrese 1988: 535f.), and are not acquired at an early stage by native speakers of Italian as part of their basic vocabulary (cf. Renzi 2012: 27–30, 66, for a very recent appreciation of the question).

In this study I am concerned with the pronominal forms given in level II of Table 11.3, namely the cell-mates *egli/esso* and *ella/essa*. They do not contrast in style, but while the masculine forms *egli* and *esso* contrast in semantic reference, *esso* being specialized as [−human] and *egli* as [+human], *ella* and *essa* can both refer to humans. According to the fundamental criterion of canonicity proposed by Thornton (2011),[3] *ella* and *essa* are highly canonical cell-mates, contrary to their masculine counterparts.

The specialization of *esso* as [−human] and the consequent semantic asymmetry between *esso* and *essa* is relatively recent, as the data in Table 11.4 show. The data on the occurrences of the two forms and on the nature of their antecedents have been collected from a corpus of twenty-nine texts by Tuscan and non-Tuscan authors dating between 1525 and 1923 and included in the *LIZ* 4.0 (Stoppelli and Picchi 2001) (the full corpus details are provided in the Appendix). The date 1840 is singled out in Table 11.4 because it marks the publication of the second edition of *I promessi sposi*

TABLE 11.3 **Third-person subject pronouns in modern Standard Italian**

	M.SG	F.SG	M.PL	F.PL
I	egli esso lui	ella essa lei	essi loro	esse loro
II	egli esso	ella essa		

[3] The criterion of no conditions > conditions (> = 'more canonical than'); in this case, no semantic condition > semantic condition.

TABLE 11.4 Occurrences of *esso/essa* as subjects with human and non-human reference

	esso vs. *essa* [+human]	*esso* vs. *essa* [−human]
1525–1840	93 vs. 64	14 vs. 33
1840	0 vs. 42	8 vs. 14
1840–1923	15 vs. 45	96 vs. 133

by Alessandro Manzoni, a text that was intended by the author as a model for the standardization of the Italian language. As I have claimed elsewhere (Cappellaro 2010), contra Böstrom (1972), the specialization of *esso* is in fact one of the innovations promoted by Alessandro Manzoni.

For centuries, *egli/esso,* as well as *ella/essa,* have been highly canonical cell-mates. Qualitative evidence for the interchangeable use of *esso* and *egli* as [+human] before 1840 comes from the quotations in (10), where the two pronouns refer to the same human antecedent, and from the entries in the first dictionary of the Italian language, the *Vocabolario della Crusca* (1612) in (11) where *egli* and *esso* are described as synonyms.

(10)   a.   A capo di altro poco tempo seppe **egli** ch'era salita in pregio la fisica sperimentale, per cui si gridava da per tutto Roberto Boyle; la quale, quanto **egli** giudicava esser profittevole per la medicina e per la spagirica, tanto **esso** la volle da sé lontana, tra perché nulla conferiva alla filosofia dell'uomo e perché si doveva spiegare con maniere barbare, ed **egli** principalmente attendeva allo studio delle leggi romane.

'After some time he ('**egli**') heard that experimental physics had gained in prestige and everybody was talking about Robert Boyle; but as regards experimental physics, while he ('**egli**') thought it would benefit medicine and spagyria, he ('**esso**') also wanted to distance himself from it, on the one hand because it did not benefit human philosophy and on the other because it had to be explained in barbaric ways, and he ('**egli**') was mainly interested in the study of Roman law.' (Vico *Vita.* 19)

   b.   Perciò che [...] vedute alcune carte scritte di mano medesima del poeta, nelle quali erano alquante delle sue rime, che in que' fogli mostrava che **egli**, secondo che **esso** le veniva componendo [...]

'[...] having seen some handwritten rhymes by the poet's own hand, because in those papers he ('**egli**') showed that, as he ('**esso**') was composing them [...]' (Bembo *Prose della volgar lingua* Book 2.6)

c. [...] **egli** mi fa dir quello che già mai non s'è detto né scritto; e mentre noi diciamo, che se la cometa si movesse di moto retto, ci apparirebbe muoversi verso il vertice e zenit, **esso** vuole che noi abbiamo detto ch'ella, movendosi, dovesse arrivare al vertice e zenit.

'[...] he ('**egli**') makes me say things that have never been said nor written; and while we claim that if the comet were moving in a straight line, it would appear as if it was moving towards the summit and zenith, he ('**esso**') wants us to have claimed that the comet, by moving, should reach the summit and zenith.' (Galileo Galilei *Il Saggiatore* 28.4)

(11) a. *egli* [...] primo caso del pronome corrispondente al Lat. *Ille.* e vale quegli, colui, esso, e dicesi tanto nel singular quanto nel plurale, quantunque si dica anche nel plurale *eglino* [...]

'first case of the pronoun continuing Lat. ILLE and equivalent to *quegli, colui, esso;* used for both singular and plural; however, in the plural the form *eglino* can also be employed'

b. *esso* Lo stesso, che EGLI. Lat. *ipse, ille*: e nel femm. ESSA, lo stesso, che ELLA [...]

'The same as *egli,* from Lat. IPSE, ILLE: in the feminine *essa* is equivalent to *ella*'

Further data for the decades 1940s to 1990s from Leone (2003) (see Table 11.5) confirm that *ella* and *essa* remain highly canonical cell-mates until the 1960s and later, while *esso* and *egli* cease to be so.

To sum up, the following general observations can be put forward:

(i) For centuries *egli/esso* and *ella/essa* have been highly canonical cell-mates and have been maintained in the system.

(ii) Until very recently, Italian was not the native language of most (dialect-speaking) Italians. For the writers included in the corpus, literary Italian

TABLE 11.5 **Subject pronouns in Leone's (2003) corpus for the decades 1940s to 1990s**

	EGLI	ESSO	ELLA	ESSA	LUI	LEI
1940s	697	2	207	49	357	254
1950s	419	3	177	175	419	237
1960s	213	2	5	29	681	303
1970s	179	2	0	17	446	220
1980s	40	1	0	42	419	480
1990s	80	1	5	9	271	218

was (to different degrees) an L2 variety. Even today, the stylistically marked pronouns *egli, esso, ella, essa, essi, esse* are not acquired at an early stage by native speakers of Italian as part of their basic vocabulary.

I claim that the diachronic maintenance of cell-mates *egli/esso* and *ella/essa* in Standard Italian is favoured by the status of these forms as not having been acquired as core grammar/lexicon in early acquisition. And here lies a parallel with Fehringer's observations on German genitive singular forms in *-(e)s* (see examples in (8)–(9) in §11.2): 'Some spoken varieties of German do not use these genitive forms at all, and when they are used in speech they tend to signal a more formal register. [...] [Genitive forms] are learned by native speakers when they learn to write, which indicates that [...] [they] have been internalized late' (Fehringer 2004: 307).

(iii)   When highly canonical overabundance is reduced, reduction affects masculine but not feminine forms. Thus, in diachrony, morphological competition for reference to male subjects is less tolerated than that for reference to female subjects in Italian.

(iv)   Data show that masculine pronouns occur much more frequently than feminine pronouns. See, for example, the total number of occurrences of masculine vs. feminine subject pronouns for the decades 1940s to 1990s in Leone (2003) in Table 11.6. This quantitative piece of data seems to confirm the prominence and salience of males as subjects (and agents, since subjects are prototypically agents), which is, more generally, in line with cross-linguistic observations on the unmarked status of masculine members of a morphological opposition (Greenberg 1966*a*).

Basing myself on this first survey, I claim that this maintenance of highly canonical overabundance in the feminine singular slot correlates with lower

TABLE 11.6 Total occurrences of subject pronouns for the M.SG and F.SG

	Total M.SG	Total F.SG
1940s	1056	510
1950s	841	589
1960s	896	337
1970s	627	237
1980s	460	522
1990s	352	232

frequency[4] (dry numbers) and lower salience (we can hypothesize in fact that agentivity was a more male rather than female territory). Further quantitative data will be collected in future research to test this hypothesis against a larger corpus.

11.4 Cell population in numbers: overabundance and defectiveness

Defectiveness and overabundance are both complex phenomena which involve deviation from the one form–one meaning principle at the level of the individual cell.[5] Recent studies on defectiveness have showed that the phenomenon is not homogeneous (Boyé and Cabredo Hofherr 2010) and appears to be motivated by different factors such as: (i) form avoidance (speakers have a candidate form for the defective form but do not use it); and (ii) form indeterminacy (speakers do not have a plausible candidate for the defective form). Instances of defectiveness of the latter type share interesting properties with the instances of overabundance discussed here. Consider, for example, Albright's studies on defectiveness (2003, 2008, 2010) and the claims the author puts forward (Albright 2008: 2–14):

- 'Gaps arise when speakers have too few relevant data to extract a rule that can be applied with any confidence.'[6]
- 'In general, words with gaps have overall lowish frequency.'
- Low frequency alone evidently does not create uncertainty: 'Pathologically little data [can cause] uncertainty.'
- 'Gaps target specifically that part of the paradigm that displays alternations.'

I propose that assuming a common motivation for both of these non-canonical phenomena is a hypothesis worthy of serious investigation. Such motivation could be the uncertainty speakers have in either (a) generalizing morphological patterns, which can result in defective paradigms (cf. Albright 2008), or (b) knowing which one to discard among competing forms, which can result in overabundant paradigms. Crucially, pathological lack of data leading to uncertainty is likely to be qualitative as well as quantitative (frequency). By qualitative lack of data I mean

---

[4] With reference to Italian see also the conclusions in Thornton (2012b), where it is claimed that 'overabundance tends to be better preserved in low frequency items'.

[5] Deviation from the one meaning–one form principle has generally been investigated at the level of the inflectional paradigm rather than at the level of individual cells. For example, 'one-to-many' is more easily associated with suppletion than overabundance. Within the canonical approach, defectiveness is considered as deviation from completeness ('for any given lexeme, every cell of its paradigm will be filled by the inflectional system' (Corbett 2005: 33)). It is visualized as a gap in its paradigmatic and geometrical dimension, rather than being considered 'zero' (i.e. not one-to-one).

[6] But see Sims (2008) on the fact that defectiveness can persist independently of low speaker confidence. See also Maiden and O'Neill (2010: 106), who claim that there are cases where 'there is not, and never was, any possibility of "morphological competition" or "speaker uncertainty", with regard to alternation in the specific lexemes affected' (for example the verb *blandir* 'to brandish' in Spanish).

lack of exposure to specific lexical or grammatical word-forms in early acquisition when a cognitive principle such as the Principle of Contrast (Clark 1987, 1993) has been shown to be operating. This leads me to advance the hypothesis that the Principle of Contrast stops operating in later stages of acquisition, and in the acquisition of L2.

11.5 Conclusion

There is a strong correlation between overabundance (and more generally between deviation from the one form–one meaning principle at the level of the individual cell) and some aspects of language use and acquisition.

Basing myself on data from Italian third-person pronouns, I have shown that diachronic maintenance of competing synonymous forms (a) correlates with lower frequency and lower salience, and (b) affects items that are not acquired as core grammar/lexicon in early acquisition.

I have proposed that highly canonical overabundance, like defectiveness, can be motivated by speakers' uncertainty (Albright 2008). Uncertainty is not produced by low frequency alone (quantitative lack of exposure). Crucially, uncertainty is also produced by qualitative lack of exposure, namely lack of exposure in the early stages of acquisition. Finally, I have put forward the hypothesis that the cognitive Principle of Contrast (Clark 1987, 1993) operates in the early stages of acquisition, and that, as data suggest, synonymy is tolerated at later stages of acquisition and in L2 acquisition.

Appendix: corpus details

Author	Title	Year	Location
Bembo, Pietro	*Prose della volgar lingua*	1525	Veneto
Gelli, Giovan Battista	*I capricci del bottaio*	1546	Florence
Grazzini, A. Francesco	*Le cene*	c.1550	Florence
Doni, A. Francesco	*I marmi*	1555	Faenza
Cellini, Benvenuto	*Vita*	1558–1565	Florence
Marino, Giovan Battista	*Dicerie sacre*	1614	Campania
Galilei, Galileo	*Il saggiatore*	1621	Tuscany
Brignole Sale, A. Giulio	*Maria Maddalena peccatrice e convertita*	1636	Liguria
Pallavicino, Ferrante	*Il corriero svaligiato*	1641	Emilia
Gravina, Gian Vincenzo	*Della ragion poetica*	1708	Calabria
Vico, Giovan Battista	*Vita scritta da sé medesimo*	1725–1728	Campania
Crudeli, Tommaso	*Arte di piacere alle donne e alle amabili compagnie*	1730–1745	Tuscany

(*continued*)

Appendix: (Continued)

Giannone, Pietro	*Vita scritta da lui medesimo*	1736–1737	Puglia
Verri, Pietro	*Sull'indole del piacere e del dolore*	1763	Lombardy
Alfieri, Vittorio	*Vita scritta da esso*	1790–	Piedmont
Foscolo, Ugo	*Ultime lettere di Jacopo Ortis*	1817	Veneto
Manzoni, Alessandro	*Fermo e Lucia*	1821–1823	Lombardy
Manzoni, Alessandro	*I promessi sposi*	1827	Lombardy
Manzoni, Alessandro	*I promessi sposi*	1840	Lombardy
Leopardi, Giacomo	*Lettere*	1810–1837	Marche
Verga, Giovanni	*Storia di una capinera*	1869	Sicily
De Sanctis, Francesco	*Storia della letteratura italiana*	1870–1871	Campania
Serao, Matilde	*Il ventre di Napoli*	1884	Campania
Pratesi, Mario	*L'Eredità*	1885	Tuscany
Fogazzaro, Antonio	*Piccolo mondo moderno*	1901	Veneto
Pirandello, Luigi	*Il fu Mattia Pascal*	1904	Sicily
Slataper, Scipio	*Il mio Carso*	1912	Ven. Giulia
D'Annunzio, Gabriele	'Notturno'	1921	Marche
Tozzi, Federigo	*Gli egoisti*	1923	Tuscany

12

The morphome and morphosyntactic/semantic features

PAUL O'NEILL

12.1 Introduction

Although there is much variation in the use of the term 'morphome' and the adjective 'morphomic', O'Neill (2011a: 44) noted the following recurrent basic definitions of this term[1] and the uses of the adjective:

(a) meaningless stems which show identical patterns of allomorphy and which cannot be reduced to any coherent phonological semantic or syntactic generalization (Aronoff 1994: 57, Maiden 2001b: 446, Sadler and Spencer 2001: 72);

(b) a semantically and syntactically incoherent set of paradigmatic cells which display a particular type of allomorphy (Aronoff 1994: 24–5, Maiden 2001b: 442);

(c) a cover term for phenomena which could be considered 'purely morphological' in the sense that they are not derived by semantico-syntactic features: e.g. stem formation, stem-indexing, inflectional classes (Aronoff 1994, Stump 2001: 169, 2010).

The most widespread usage of the term and the original definition of Aronoff (1994) is that of the morphome as a function which is the union of points (a) and (b); that is, the regular distribution of identical form, usually an allomorphic root/stem, which does not correspond to any coherent generalization or function, phonological, semantic or syntactic.

---

[1] At times the stems themselves are not termed morphomes but rather referred to as *morphomic* stems; likewise the groups of cells which display a particular type of allomorphy are referred to as *morphomic*, and the distribution of the allomorphy is called a *morphomic* distribution.

In this chapter, following the convention in linguistics of understanding and modelling the complexity of natural languages by recourse to features (Kibort and Corbett 2010), I formalize the morpheme as a purely morphological feature and I analyse to what extent morphomic features are different from those interface features which are considered to be relevant not only to morphology but also to syntax or semantics. In the literature, such features have been termed morphosyntactic, morphosemantic, or even syntacticosemantic. For the sake of brevity and so as not to enter the discussion as to whether a feature is morphosemantic or morphosyntactic or both (see Corbett 2010, and Kibort 2010, for a detailed discussion) I will use the term *morphemic features* to refer to these interface features. In analysing the difference between morphomic and morphemic features I also examine whether morphomic and morphemic phenomena are qualitatively different or merely quantitatively different.

12.2 A canonical morphome

Canonical examples of morphomes, and those which feature most prominently in the literature, are the cases in which a particular allomorphic root/stem is shared by a number of semantically heterogeneous categories. The classical example of one such morphome is what Aronoff (1994) refers to as the Latin 'third stem'. In traditional grammars and dictionaries, Latin verbs are always presented in their *principal parts*, which (usually) number four and are the forms of the verb for the 1SG present indicative, 1SG perfect indicative, infinitive, and the supine. These forms represent the different stem allomorphs which the verb displays, as well as its conjugational class. Thus, the verb 'eat' is cited as EDŌ, EDERE, ĒDĪ, ĒSUM, and is thereby a third conjugation verb with three stem allomorphs ED-, ĒD-, and ĒS-. The last of these allomorphic variants, which Aronoff terms the 'third stem', formed the base of the past participle, the supine, and the future participle and was used derivationally to form desiderative verbs, iterative verbs, and nouns with the suffixes -OR-, -ŪR-, and -IŌ(N)-. This can be appreciated in Tables 12.1 and 12.2; in the first table the Latin verbs are presented in their principal parts, in the second table I give the word-forms which traditionally are considered to be built on the form of the past participle.

The suffixes to which the Latin third stem attaches are diverse not only phonologically but also semantically, in that they convey very different information, yet all these different inflectional and derivational forms share the same root allomorph. Aronoff identifies this third stem as a morpheme—to be understood as a morphologically abstract function relating to the distribution of a morphological entity.

With respect to this definition of the morpheme, Maiden (2005*a*) noted that such regular distribution of form could be merely accidental, since speakers could have memorized the identical allomorphs separately without ever making the deeper

TABLE 12.1 **Principal parts of three Latin verbs**

Verb	1SG present indicative	1SG perfect indicative	Past participle	Infinitive
write	SCRĪBŌ	SCRĪPSĪ	SCRĪPTUS	SCRĪBERE
shear	TONDEŌ	TOTONDĪ	TŌNSUS	TONDĒRE
buy	EMŌ	ĒMĪ	EMPTUS	EMERE

TABLE 12.2 **Latin word forms which are built on the third stem**

	to write	to shear	to buy
Past participle	SCRĪPTUS	TŌNSUS	EMPTUS
Supine	SCRĪPTUM	TŌNSUM	EMPTUM
Future participle	SCRĪPTŪRUS	TŌNSŪRUS	EMPTŪRUS
Desiderative	–	–	EMPTŪRIO
Iterative	SCRĪPTITŌ	TŌNSITŌ	–
-OR-	SCRĪPTOR	TŌNSOR	EMPTOR
-ŪR-	SCRĪPTŪRA	TŌNSŪRA	–
-IŌ(N)	SCRĪPTIŌ	TONSIŌ	EMPTIŌ

grammatical generalization which the morphome supposes: that there exists a function which is related to a number of semantically diverse tenses, and this grouping of tenses forms a grammatical unit for the language, on the basis of a common shared form. This is opposed to each individual tense mapping onto different functions which coincidently produced the same morphological form.

Much of Maiden's work (2001*a*, 2001*b*, 2004*b*, 2005*a*, 2009*a*, 2009*c*, 2011*a*) has been devoted to proving, with reference to the inflectional verbal paradigm of the Romance languages, that the cases of a regular distribution of identical form which does not correspond to any coherent semantic or syntactic function are psychologically real for speakers. That is, they are morphomes. The evidence which has been advanced in support of this argument has been of a diachronic nature, since there are a number of historical developments in the Romance languages which presuppose the existence of a grammatically real and abstract connection between both the allomorphy in the various cells of a morphome and the cells themselves. First, the different types of allomorphy which occupy the cells of a morphome (defined in this case as a collection of cells) display a tendency towards sideways analogy (the principle of convergence; Maiden 2005*a*: 143), whereby all allomorphs come to resemble each other formally. Second, the cells of the morphome, with respect to their particular allomorphy, 'show persistent resistance to any morphological change liable to disrupt their peculiar paradigmatic distribution. If an analogical change affects one 'cell' of the paradigm in which the relevant allomorph occurs, it affects all the others in the same way' (the principle of coherence, see Maiden 2005a: 143). Maiden maintains that such evidence suggests that morphomes are 'psychologically real' for speakers since they can channel and condition morphological change.

12.3 The morphome as a feature: the Latin third stem

Although no diachronic evidence of the type that Maiden has offered for the Romance languages has been provided for the Latin third stem, upon the assumption that these cells do constitute a morphome, then the implication is that speakers did not memorize each of the inflectional forms which share this same stem allomorph but that they were aware of the distributional regularity and this formed part of the grammar. If this distributional regularity is formalized in accordance with Aronoff's initial definition of the morphome as a function, then the morphome could be represented pictographically as in Figure 12.1, in which there are a number of different and unrelated semantic/syntactic features which map onto the same function which triggers a rule to produce the same morphological form: in the present case of Latin, the formation or selection of the third stem.

The Latin third stem morphome is here formalized as a function that exists between a root and a distribution. Given the tradition in formal linguistics of having recourse to features in order to formalize complex associations, the relationship between these two components could be expressed in terms of a feature specification whereby there exists a purely morphological feature, called 3RD-STEM, and a morphological rule of stem formation or, in the case of those verbs which display irregular allomorphy in the third stem, a set of stored root allomorphs which are specified for this feature. Considering only examples from within the verb

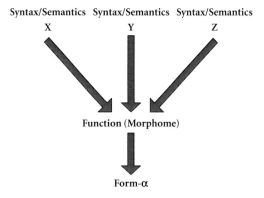

FIGURE 12.1 Pictographic representation of a morphome

morphology, the purpose of this feature is to act as a superordinate to the morpho-syntactic features of the past participle, the supine, and the future participle, and to stipulate the same allomorphic stem for these cells. In order for the appropriate allomorph to be selected or the stem created, however, it is necessary that the input to any word-formation rule contain the specifications of this feature. This feature, being purely morphological, would not be provided by the morphosyntax but rather by the morphology. Within a Word-and-Paradigm model which adheres to the Separation Hypothesis (e.g. Beard 1995) this is unproblematic, since form is not directly related to meaning. The formalization of this hypothesis by Stump (2001) is particularly illustrative and instructive for our present purposes.

Stump (2001) argues for the presence of two kinds of paradigm for inflection: the form paradigm and the content paradigm. The latter contains information which is relevant to morphosyntax whilst the former is relevant only to the inner workings of the morphology, usually information regarding inflectional class membership. In a revision of Paradigm Function Morphology, Ackerman and Stump (2004) develop the notion of Paradigm Linkage in order to explain a number of morphological phenomena, largely systematic whole-word syncretism or phenomena such as depo-nency, via different mechanisms whereby there is not a one-to-one matching between the content paradigm and the form paradigm. Such a distinction between content and form paradigms has been formalized in terms of features by Sadler and Spencer (2001). These latter authors distinguish between form features, which are internal to the morphological component, regulate the morphological form of words, and are termed *m-features*, and *s-features*, which are essentially syntactic and meaningful.

Following these theoretical assumptions, it could be hypothesized that all word-formation processes which make reference to the cells of the Latin third stem are assigned the purely morphological, or morphomic, 3RD-STEM feature by the form paradigm. In the case of regular verbs such a feature licenses a rule that concatenates -T to the end of the root or stem; for irregular verbs it selects the lexically stored allomorphs, which would have to be subcategorized for this feature.

In order to appreciate the exact workings of such features and how they are different from morphosyntactic/morphosemantic features, which I am calling mor-phemic features, it is illustrative to compare the process by which an allomorph is selected on the basis of both morphomic and morphemic criteria. Latin is a useful example in this respect since it marked aspectual differences on verbs morphologic-ally by a distinction between what were traditionally termed the *infectum* and *perfectum* stems, the former being realized in the imperfective forms of the verb and the latter in the perfective ones. For first, second, and fourth conjugation verbs, the most common way to form a *perfectum* stem was via the increment -v- [w] at the end of the root or stem. For third conjugation verbs and an array of verbs from other classes, this semantic distinction could also be marked by way of vowel

TABLE 12.3 A selection of perfective and imperfective forms of the regular Latin verb CANTĀRE 'sing'

	Imperfective		Perfective	
Present	CANTŌ	'I sing'	CANTĀVĪ	'I have sung'
Future	CANTĀBŌ	'I will sing'	CANTĀVERŌ	'I will have sung'
Infinitive	CANTĀRE	'to sing'	CANTĀVISSE	'to have sung'

TABLE 12.4 A selection of perfective and imperfective forms of the regular Latin verb SCRĪBERE 'write'

	Imperfective		Perfective	
Present	SCRĪBŌ	'I write'	SCRĪPSĪ	'I have written'
Future	SCRĪBAM	'I will write'	SCRĪPSERŌ	'I will have written'
Infinitive	SCRĪBERE	'to write'	SCRĪPSISSEM	'to have written'

lengthening, reduplication, and modifications of the final root consonant. This is shown in the examples in Tables 12.3 and 12.4 for the regular verb CANTĀRE 'sing' and the irregular third conjugation verb SCRĪBERE 'write'. For brevity and clarity I have only provided examples from the present, future, and infinitival forms. However, it is of crucial importance that the *perfectum* root occurred in all inflectional forms which expressed a completed action: the pluperfect indicative, perfect subjunctive, pluperfect subjunctive.

The *perfectum* stem of Latin verbs is traditionally represented as the second *principal part* via the form of the 1SG perfect indicative. For the verbs SCRĪBŌ 'I write', TONDEŌ 'I shear', and EMŌ 'I buy' in Table 12.1, the *perfectum* stems are SCRĪPS-, TOTOND-, ĒM-, respectively, and appear only in perfective forms of the verb, whilst the morphomic third stems for these verbs are SCRĪPT-, TŌNS-, EMPT-.

Thus for any lexeme, the production of any inflectional form which contained the semantic feature [+PERFECTIVE] would trigger the selection of the same stem. This process of stem selection or stem formation could be formalized in accordance with Aronoff's (1994: 68–9) notion of a realization pair,[2] which is the pairing of a

---

[2] The term 'realization rule' is a variation of the idea of Zwicky (1985) of a morphological realization, which Beard (1995) calls the 'morphological spelling component'. These are basically stipulations regarding how to create morphosyntactic word-forms. For example, the plural rule in Spanish of the type *casa* 'house', *casas* 'houses', *pato* 'duck', *patos* 'ducks' could be stated via the following morphological realization rule: X → Xs, where X is the default form of a noun. The other term, the 'morphosyntactic property array', is basically a list of features/categories. In the case of Spanish plural formation, the property array would consist of the feature 'plural' and the category 'noun' (N), and would be formalized in the following way: [PLURAL, NOUN].

morphosyntactic property array and realization rules. In Table 12.5, I have given the realization pair for perfective verbs in Latin. Note that I have slightly modified Aronoff's representation of a realization pair; I have omitted the word 'morphosyntactic' from the property array in order to be able to include semantic categories. Note, also, that the two different realization rules correspond to the formation of the perfective stem for regular verbs and the selection of an irregular stem allomorph for irregular verbs; the Pāṇini principle would apply to the application of these realization rules.

The realization pair for what could be considered a morphemic feature differs from that of the proposed morphomic feature in that there is no individual feature in the property array which is directly correlated with a realization rule. In the case of the Latin third stem, as illustrated in Table 12.6, three unrelated features all correspond to the same realization rules.

For the various perfective screeves of Latin, it is the common semantics of these forms that provides the feature of [+PERFECTIVE], which is directly correlated with the morphological realization rules on the right. In the case of the Latin third stem, there is no functional common denominator in the property array to ensure all

TABLE 12.5 **Realization pair for the Latin perfective tenses (a morphemic feature)**

Realization pair: X = default root/stem	
Property array [+ PERFECTIVE]	Realization rule (a) $(X \rightarrow Y)$ = select the stored allomorph which is subcategorized for [+ PERFECTIVE] (e.g. TOTOND-) (b) $(X \rightarrow XV\text{-})$ e.g. (e.g. CANTĀ > CANTĀV-)

TABLE 12.6 **Realization pair for the Latin third stem morphome (a morphomic feature)**

Realization pair: X = default root/stem	
Property array [+ PAST PARTICIPLE] [+ SUPINE] [+ FUTURE PARTICIPLE]	Realization rule (a) $(X \rightarrow Y)$ = select the stored allomorph which is subcategorized for [+ 3RD STEM] (e.g. TOTOND-) (b) $(X \rightarrow XT\text{-})$ e.g. (e.g. CANTĀ > CANTĀT-)

the features share the same realization rule. In Paradigm Function Morphology (Stump 2001), such morphomic phenomena, in which a special stem X is shared by a group of semantically and morphosyntactically unrelated features A B C, are formalized by each individual feature being indexed for the same stem form/same realization rule. However, such a formalization has been criticized (Blevins 2006: 554, Carstairs-McCarthy 2005: 267, O'Neill 2011*b*: 89–90), since it does not bestow any sense of unity upon the random group of paradigmatic cells. With such a formalization, the cells of a morphome are not linguistically marked as constituting a unit, and therefore no explanation can be given for the observable consistency of the distribution of allomorphy in diachrony and for how the cells of a morphome often act en bloc; that is, a change in the root in one cell often implies that change in all other cells (see Maiden 2005*a*: 143).

In order to capture this sense of grouping, it is hypothesized that there is an intermediate level in which the motley set of morphemic features of [PAST PARTICIPLE], [SUPINE], [FUTURE PARTICIPLE] are all assigned the purely morphological feature [$+3^{RD}$ STEM] at the level of what Stump (2001) defines as the form paradigm. This feature is then directly correlated with the realization rules for the selection/formation of the third stem. This expanded realization rule is represented in Table 12.7.

This intermediate level, which assigns to each one of the morphemic features in the property array the purely morphological feature of [$+3^{RD}$ STEM], ensures that the same stem is selected by all the cells in this morpheme and, more importantly, it captures the generalization that these cells act as a group and form a unit for the grammar.

In accordance with such a formalization, a preliminary hypothesis can be proposed as to the distinction between morphomic phenomena and morphemic phenomena. The former refer to recurrent phonological formatives, usually identical allomorphs of the root, which are not correlated with any homogeneous semantic or

---

TABLE 12.7 **Expanded realization pair for the Latin third stem**

Expanded realization pairs: X = default root/stem		
Property array	Form paradigm	Realization rule
[+ PAST PARTICIPLE]	[$+3^{RD}$ STEM]	(a)
[+ SUPINE]		(X → Y) = select the stored allomorph
[+ FUTURE PARTICIPLE]		which is subcategorized for [$+3^{RD}$ STEM]
		(e.g. TOTOND-)
		(b)
		(X → XT-) e.g. (e.g. CANTĀ- > CANTĀT-)

morphosyntactic property and which cannot be derived phonologically but whose distribution in the verb morphology is coherent and can be proved to be non-accidental. In terms of feature assignment, it is at the purely morphological level where these features are to be found and are assigned. The morphemic phenomena denote morphological formatives which correspond to morphosyntactic/morphose-mantic features and whose feature values are located at the interface between the morphology and the semantic/syntax. The realization rules for such phenomena display a single morphemic feature value in the property array.

In Figure 12.2 I present a schematic representation of the morphological compon-ent and how purely morphological features may be represented in this component. I have split the morphology into three levels: an interface level with the syntax and semantics, a level which is purely morphological and does not interact with any components external to the morphology, and a level which is morphophonological, in which reference is made to phonological material. The division of morphology into the first two different levels is analogous to Stump's distinction between the content and form paradigms.

In Figure 12.2, a number of different and unrelated semantic/syntactic features map on to different morphemic features at the level of the content paradigm which,

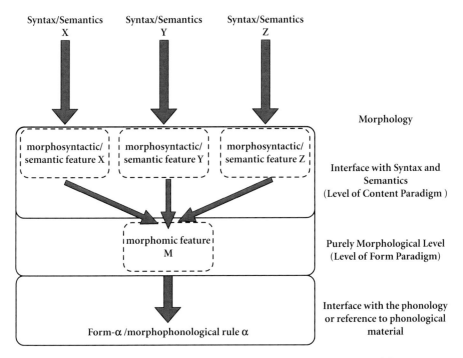

FIGURE 12.2 A schematic representation of the morphological component of the grammar, and morphomic features

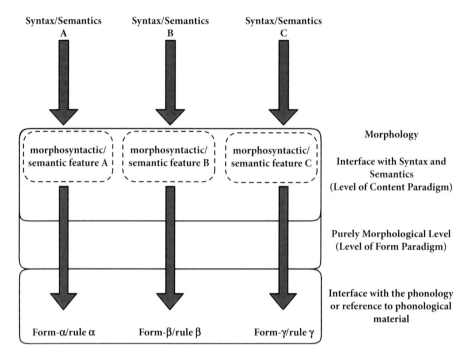

FIGURE 12.3 A schematic representation of morphemic features

in turn, all map on to the same morphomic feature, located at the level of the form paradigm. This morphomic feature produces the same morphological form or morphological realization rule for each of the different morphemic features. This diagrammatic representation of morphomic features contrasts with that in Figure 12.3 of morphemic features in which the different morphemic features do not map on to any morphomic feature at the purely morphological level but are correlated directly with a particular form or a morphophonological realization rule.

In what follows I assess the extent to which morphemic features can be considered to correspond to a homogeneous set of semantic/syntactic uses. The distribution of the *perfectum* stem in Latin was cited above as an example in which a paradigmatic distribution of form is determined by a coherent semantic usage: the *perfectum* stem is used in contexts and situation types which denote perfective aspect. This statement, however, is not entirely true, since Pinkster (1990: 229–42), in his study of Latin of the period 200 BCE–100 CE, notes that there are a number of uses of the *perfectum* forms which are employed in situations in which there is no perfective aspect. The most notable cases are the selection of Latin verbs, the famous examples being MEMINĪ 'I remember' and ODĪ 'I hate', which only possessed perfective forms of the verb and used these forms to refer to the present. However, Pinkster also notes a number of uses of the perfect subjunctive which do not correspond to non-anterior uses. In (1), I cite two of the examples from Pinkster (1990: 233), in which the verb forms in question, along with their translation in English, are in bold.

(1)   a.   cuius ego iudicium, pace tua **dixerim**, longe antepono tuo.
           'Whose judgement, if **I may say so** with your permission, I value more than yours' (Cicero, Seneca, 8)
     b.   ne vos quidem, iudices qui me absolvistis, mortem **temueritis**.
           'Not even you, judges, who have acquitted me, **should fear** death (Cicero, Tusculan Disputations, 1.98)

Likewise, Pinkster notes the use of the perfect infinitive in situations which normally require the present infinitive (1990: 236) and the use of the historic present in situations which would normally require explicit past tense perfective forms (pp. 239, 241).

Save these examples, all other uses of the *perfectum* stem in Latin, which constitute the great majority of uses, do correspond with some type of perfective aspect, and therefore it could still be maintained that the distribution of the *perfectum* stem corresponds to a more or less coherent semantics whilst that of the third stem does not. However, the introduction of such gradual or scalar terms which take into account frequency effects within the definition of phenomena being morphomic raises questions as to whether morphomic and morphemic phenomena are categorically different, as suggested by their formalization as features above, or whether the differences between the two phenomena are more gradual and scalar: a difference of degree and not of kind.

In the next section I analyse the different usages of the imperfect indicative in Spanish and demonstrate that the feature of imperfect indicative corresponds to a varied set of semantic usages which cannot be reduced to any useful and universal semantic generalization. I conclude that what are being termed here morphemic features often constitute a heterogeneous set of semantic and syntactic values and varied uses; their consistency and homogeneity in languages, I argue, derives from the common morphological forms or alternations which these screeves display and not some type of universal or common syntax or semantics formalized as a feature. I discuss the implications of these conclusions for the distinction between morphomic and morphemic features.

12.4 Questioning the functional coherence of morphemic features: the imperfect indicative in Spanish

Spanish verbs morphologically inflect for different combinations of tense, aspect, mood, person, and number; person and number are always realized cumulatively, as

TABLE 12.8 Paradigm of Spanish verb *cantar* 'sing'

	PRS IND	PRS SBJV	FUTURE	CONDITIONAL
1SG	canto	cante	cantaré	cantaría
2SG	cantas	cantes	cantarás	cantarías
3SG	canta	cante	cantará	cantaría
1PL	cantamos	cantemos	cantaremos	cantaríamos
2PL	cantáis	cantéis	cantaréis	cantaríais
3PL	cantan	canten	cantarán	cantarían
	IMPF SBJV (-RA)	IMPF SBJV (-SE)	PRETERITE	IMPF IND
1SG	cantara	cantase	canté	cantaba
2SG	cantaras	cantases	cantaste	cantabas
3SG	cantara	cantase	cantó	cantaba
1PL	cantáramos	cantásemos	cantamos	cantábamos
2PL	cantarais	cantaseis	cantasteis	cantabais
3PL	cantaran	cantasen	cantaron	cantaban
	IMPERATIVE	INFINITVE	GERUND	PARTICIPLE
2SG	canta	cantar	cantando	cantado
2PL	cantad			

are tense and aspect in the past; in non-past tenses, aspect is expressed via a periphrastic construction with the verb *haber* 'have', e.g. *habré cantado* 'I will have sung'. In Table 12.8 I give the paradigm of the regular first-conjugation verb *cantar* 'sing'.

Of importance to the present discussion is the imperfect indicative, which cumulatively expresses past tense and imperfective aspect. In regular -*ar* verbs the imperfect indicative is realized by way of the concatenation of the formative -*ba*- after the stem and before any markers for person and number. For -*er* and -*ir* verbs the formative is -*ía*; witness the forms of this tense for the verb *comer* 'eat': *comía, comías, comía, comíamos, comíais, comían.*

In Spanish a number of explanations have been offered for the difference between perfective and imperfective aspect including, but not restricted to, the following: viewing a situation as a unified whole as opposed to taking into account its internal structure (Comrie 1976); observing an action as finished as opposed to concentrating on its duration or progression (King and Suñer 2008); viewing the action as closed or bounded versus open or unbounded (González 1998, Montrul and Slabakova 2002). The present discussion does not enter into any arguments regarding the nature of aspect in Spanish but seeks to describe the different usages of the imperfect indicative and discuss the implications of its varied usages for the distinction between morphomic and morphemic features.

In modern Spanish the imperfect indicative has the following usages (in each example both the Spanish verb in question and its English translation are given in bold):

(a) Incomplete actions/states/processes in the past.
Al mediodía **llovía**. (Brucart 2003: 193)
'**It was raining** at midday.'

(b) Actions that coincide temporally with another action in a preterite context.
Los saludé cuando **se iban**. (Brucart 2003: 193)
'I said hello to them when **they were going**.'

(c) In sentences in which the focus is on the duration or progression of an event.
El capote amarillo del taxi que en aquel momento **doblaba** la esquina, la reconfortó. (Real Academia Española 2009: 1762)
'The yellow bonnet of the taxi which at that moment **was turning** the corner, comforted her.'

(d) Iterative or habitual actions.
Salía del trabajo a las seis. (Brucart 2003: 193)
'**I used to leave** work at six.'

(e) In expressions of an intention to realize an action which is conveyed immediately before the action is planned to be carried out.
Ya nos **íbamos**. (Brucart 2003: 194)
'**We were** just **going**.'

(f) In future expressions both to express intentions to realize an action which has been previously arranged but not carried out and to express events which are planned or scheduled but have not taken place yet.
Mañana **íbamos** al cine. (Brucart 2003: 194)
'Tomorrow **we are supposed to be going** to the cinema.'
En principio, mi avión **salía** mañana a las 23.50. (Real Academia Española 2009: 1751)
'In principle, my plane **will depart** tomorrow at 23.50.'

(g) Similar to the usage above but applied to past events/actions which were due to happen but did not. An adversative clause is necessary to disambiguate whether the predicate is to be interpreted in the future or the past.
Mi hermano **llegaba** ayer, pero algunos problemas de salud lo han obligado a posponer el viaje. (Real Academia Española 2009: 1752)
'My brother **was supposed to be getting here** yesterday, but health problems have forced him to postpone his journey.'

(h) In expressions in the present in which favours are asked or requests are made in a courteous way, and in which it is understood that the requests could be modified if the addressee is unable to carry them out.

Quería pedirte un favor. (Brucart 2003: 194)

'**I want** to ask you a favour.'

Yo **venía** a pedirle un favor. (Real Academia Española 2009: 1749)

'**I've come** to ask you a favour.'

(i) In situations to denote that the information that is being solicited has been relayed to the speaker by a third party.

¿Tú **jugabas** al fútbol, no es cierto? (Real Academia Española 2009: 1751)

'**You play** football, don't you?'

(j) Situations in which information which has already been provided is requested because it has been forgotten.

Perdón ¿Cómo **se llamaba** Ud.? (Brucart 2003: 195)

'Sorry, what **was** your name?'

(k) To express the difference between a dynamic and non-dynamic interpretation: actions vs. states.

El anuncio **decía**/*dijo que se había suspendido la función.

'The advert **said** (imperfect) / *said (preterite) that the function had been suspended.'

La radio **decía**/dijo que se había suspendido la función.

'The radio **said** (imperfect) / said (preterite) that the function had been suspended.'

El edificio **miraba**/*miró al oeste.

'The building **looked** (imperfect) / *looked (preterite) west.'

El policía **miraba**/miró al oeste.

'The policeman **looked** (imperfect) / looked (preterite) west.'

(l) To express surprise in the present when the speaker has just discovered an unknown situation.

Jolín, ¿pero, tú **trabajabas** aquí?

'God! **I didn't realize you worked** here.'

(m) In hypothetical imagined situations; often used in infant speech.

¡Vamos a jugar! Yo **era** la madre y te **cuidaba** y tú **eras** el bebé y tú **llorabas** mucho porque **tenías** hambre.

'Lets play! **I'm** the mum and **I look** after you and **you're** the baby and **you cry** lots because **you're** hungry.'

(n) As a substitute for the conditional (very common in spoken peninsular Spanish). See Vincent (this volume) for a semantic explanation as to how the imperfect comes to be used as a conditional.

Si me tocara la lotería, **me compraba** una casa en el campo.

'If I won the lottery **I would buy** myself a house in the country (straight away).'

Yo de ti no lo **hacía** eso.

'If I were you, **I wouldn't do** that.'

Aunque estuviera muriendo no le **pedía** ayuda.

'Even if I was dying **I wouldn't ask** him for help.'

Ahora me **tomaba** un café.

'**I'd have** a coffee right now.'

Me dijo que lo **hacía**.

'He told me **he'd do** it.'

(o) In narration with predicates which correspond to achievements even though they express punctual events. This usage, common to journalistic or literary texts, is akin to the historic present, which has the effect of making past punctual events more emphatic and the text more descriptive.

Dos aviones comerciales **se estrellaban** contra el World Trade Center, **estallaban** en una gran bola de fuego y las dos Torres Gemelas **se derrumbaban**.

'Two commercial planes **crashed** into the World Trade Center, **they burst** into a great ball of flames and the two Twin Towers **fell down**.'

Tras una lenta agonía, el 20 de Noviembre de 1975 **moría** Franco. (Taken from http://quedehistoria.blogspot.com/2010/05/el-testamento-de-franco.html)

'After a slow period in the throes of death, Franco **died** on 20 November 1975.'

Los corredores **cruzaban** la meta a las 12.34 tras una etapa agotadora.

'The runners **crossed** the finish line at 12.34, after an exhausting lap'.

From the above data it is clear that the imperfect indicative in Spanish has a number of different and varied uses. It can be used to refer to events/actions in the present (h, e, j, i, l), the past (a, b, c, d, g, k, o), and even in the future in which the action can be planned (f) or hypothetical (n). The different usages have varying frequencies, and, in general terms, it can be affirmed that the prototypical uses of the imperfect indicative in Spanish, and the ones which have attracted most academic attention, are those of (a)–(d) and (k), for which numerous scholars (Alarcos Llorach 1994, Bello 1847: §628–9, Brucart 2003, Gili Gaya 1943, Lenz 1920, Weinrich 1964, amongst others) have tried to come to a single overarching generalization, based usually on either temporal or aspectual criteria. My aim here is not to evaluate the suitability of such accounts but to note that they are not intended to capture all the uses of the imperfect. Certain uses have been discarded, by some authors, as marginal or metaphorical despite their frequency in the spoken language.

My contention is that what unites **all** the uses of the imperfect indicative in Spanish is not any type of coherent semantics but rather its dedicated morphological exponence. I am not espousing an extreme relativist view of the imperfect indicative in Spanish. That is, I do not claim that some of the most prototypical uses of the imperfect indicative in Spanish are not semantically related, nor that they are fundamentally different from the expression of imperfectivity in any other languages. The numerous studies on tense and aspect (Bybee *et al.* 1994, Croft 2003, Dahl 1985) militate against such a relativist view, as do similar and overlapping uses in other Romance languages. Indeed, from the examples above it is clear that certain uses of the imperfect indicative are semantically related: (a) to (b), (e) to (f) and (g), and these, in turn, to (l) and (m). In fact, it is often apparent that a particular usage X has evolved from a usage Y based on some type of common or overlapping conceptual semantics (see Vincent, this volume). However, my point is that once **all** the different usages are taken into account it is difficult if not impossible to come to some semantically valid and single generalization which captures **all** of them. Thus, whilst the semantic relation between usage (a) and (b) may be apparent, that between usage (a) and (f) is vague and that between (a) and (o) totally non-existent. The essence of what I am stating is not new, since it has long been recognized that semantic universal definitions of notions such as aspect and tense are infamously difficult to establish (see Binnick 1991, Sasse 1991, 2002), and single definitions suffer from being either too vague to be useful or too specific to capture cross-linguistic data and generalizations. Croft and Poole (2008: 1) note that 'a fundamental fact about grammatical structure is that it is highly variable both across languages and within languages'. They go on to observe that this variation 'is not sociolinguistic variation, but variation in the conventions of a language, that is, the conventional grammatical structures used by a community of speakers to describe a particular situation' (p. 1). These authors have highlighted that speakers can mark subtle and fine-grained linguistic differences between grammatical expressions which, from a universal perspective, or from the perspective of another language, could be considered as having the same feature value. That is, speakers can be sensitive to very specific criteria in order to mark the difference between the usage of one morphological form / grammatical construction and another. Such delimitations of different grammatical forms between semantically related situation types are essentially language-specific and can be arbitrary.

I must reiterate that my hypothesis is not intended as a challenge to the cross-linguistic generalizations with regard to tense and aspect. In fact, the conclusion of the aforementioned study by Croft and Pole (2008) is that the application of multidimensional scaling models on large and diverse datasets, involving the different uses of notions such as aspect and tense, does yield results in terms of the semantic clustering of functions which would suggest that language universals exist,

but 'they are not directly manifested as a set of universal linguistic structures. Instead, language universals are indirect. Language universals are constraints on grammatical variation, and grammatical variation is as necessary a part of language as the universals are' (pp. 47–8). With specific reference to the tense–aspect analyses of their cross-linguistic study of a large number of languages, the authors note that the results may not be indicative of universal grammatical categories but rather universal conceptual categories, and again they highlight the importance of individual grammatical variation and how their results 'argue[s] against both an extreme universalist and an extreme relativist theory of grammar'.

The relevance of these conclusions to my discussion of the imperfect indicative in Spanish and the difference between morphomic and morphemic features is that, although some of the uses of the imperfect indicative may be semantically related and there could even exist some type of semantic change connecting different uses (e.g. the use of the conditional; see Vincent, this volume), there is **no** semantic common denominator for **all** usages. In sum, the total set of usages for Spanish are particular to Spanish. My contention is **not** that the imperfect indicative in Spanish (or tense and aspect in general) corresponds to a set of meanings and situation types which are each individually unrelated and without parallels to uses in other languages. Rather, I make the point that once one analyses all the different situation types it becomes clear that there is no **one** conceptual or semantic feature which subsumes **all** usages. Such a situation is analogous to Wittgenstein's (1953) observation that common, unexceptional words such as *game* have few, if any, common properties which characterize all of their uses, although individual uses are generally semantically connected to other uses. This is the crux of my argument: that tenses, just like words, can function as forms which can map on to multiple semantic functions, and that even though there may be semantic relations between a number of functions, it is not necessary that this be the case for all functions.

The conclusion from the foregoing, therefore, is that morphemic features, such as the Spanish imperfect indicative, do not necessarily correspond to a consistent set of homogeneous semantic uses but can be correlated with a number of heterogeneous and even semantically unrelated uses. I maintain that the consistent element of the imperfect indicative lies not in its semantics but in its morphology; it possesses a dedicated morphological form in accordance with the conjugational class of the verb. Thus, in line with representing features as functions, and on the basis of the Spanish data, morphemic features can be represented as in Figure 12.4, in which a number of different semantic/syntactic uses all correspond to the same feature/function that displays the same morphological form, or triggers the same morphological realization rule. Note that this diagram for a morphosyntactic feature/function is identical to the diagram for the morphomic function in Figure 12.1.

Accordingly, the pictorial representation of a morphemic feature in Figure 12.3, in which the common morphological form / morphological rule was associated with a

homogeneous type of syntax/semantics, ought to be modified to allow for heterogeneous, and even overlapping, syntactic/semantic types and uses. Such a modified
diagram is given in Figure 12.5.

The startling similarities between the representations of morphemic and morphomic features/functions raise questions as to the importance of the formal

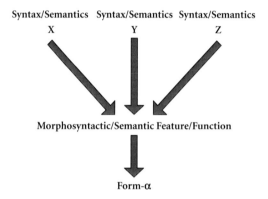

FIGURE 12.4   Basic representation of a morphemic feature

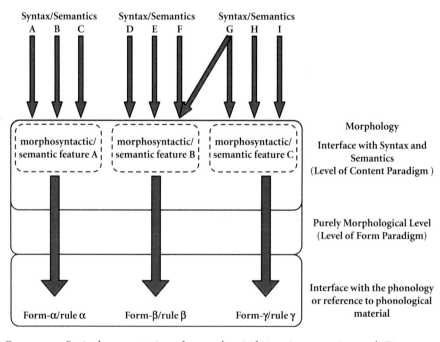

FIGURE 12.5 Revised representation of a morphemic feature in comparison with Figure 12.3

distinction between these features. Both features involve a common form / morpho-logical rule which is associated with a number of heterogeneous syntactic/semantic uses, and the relationship between the form and the syntax/semantics is mediated by the morphology. The question therefore is whether there are qualitative differences between the two types of features, and morphemic and morphomic phenomena themselves, which warrant a terminological distinction being made between them. In this respect, it is enlightening to analyse the English participle morpheme 'past' (or 'perfect') proposed by Aronoff.

12.5 The English PP morphome and morphomic features

The morphological forms referred to as the past participle are used both in perfective verb forms in periphrases with an auxiliary verb, and also in passives. Aronoff (1994: 25) notes that, synchronically, passives and analytic perfects cannot be said to share a constant significant functional property since they correspond to different syntactic and semantic values; however, they always share the same phonological form, as shown in the examples in Table 12.9.

On the basis of this systematic homophony, Aronoff (1994: 24–5) claims that there is a function linking verb stems to past participles which 'is neither morphosyntactic nor morphophonological but rather purely morphological—morphology by itself. Let us call the level of such purely morphological functions *morphomic* and the functions themselves *morphomes*.' This function is considered to occupy 'a cell in the morphological paradigm of English' (p. 25).

The interesting point here is that the morphological forms of the English past participle occupy only one cell in the paradigm. Thus, Aronoff has taken this single cell and has decomposed the different semantic and syntactic uses which map on to this cell and has identified two unrelated uses which, nevertheless, are always expressed by the same morphological form, albeit periphrastically with different auxiliary verbs. The same could be done for the imperfect indicative in Spanish, which occupies a single column in the paradigm of Spanish; the different semantic uses / situation types could be identified and these could be listed in different columns. Likewise, it could be claimed that there exists a morphomic function for

TABLE 12.9 The English PP-morphome

Present perfect	Passive
he has seen	it is seen
he has bitten	it is bitten
he has sought	it is sought

the imperfect indicative whereby the different semantic uses all map onto the same purely morphological function and are expressed by the same forms.

The reason why the morphology of the imperfect indicative is conventionally assumed to correspond to a common meaning, and why verbs are presented as having only one set of imperfective indicative forms, is the systematic formal syncretism over a plurality of meanings.[3] Morphologists traditionally assign formal identity to an assumed shared morphosyntactic feature. These features owe their existence to the common dedicated morphological form(s) and **not** any type of heterogeneous semantic uses or situation types. This point was made in classical grammars and was reiterated by Matthews (1991). In classical grammars, the parts of a word were divided in accordance with their *accidents*, their morphological for-matives. In many modern theories of morphology such *accidents* are formalized as features, but it is of crucial importance to remember that the feature exists because of the form; without a dedicated morphological form in a number of verbs there is no basis for proposing that a feature exists. Morphemic features are, therefore, depen-dent on the morphology and not vice versa.

Returning to the question of the difference between morphemic features and morphomic features, I think the answer lies in the extent of formal identity/consist-ency of an alternation over whole word forms. For morphemic features, total identity of form or consistency of an alternation is crucial (even though such an alternation may be subject to the conjugational class of a verb). Witness how the Spanish imperfect indicative forms for the regular first conjugation verb *cantar* 'sing' (*can-taba, cantabas, cantaba, cantábamos, cantabais, cantaban*) all share exactly the same stem[4] *cantaba-*, and the only difference between the forms are the person and number formatives (*-ø, -s, -ø, -mos, -is, -n*). Witness, too, how, although the future forms for the same verb (*cantaré, cantarás, cantará, cantaremos, cantaréis, can-tarán*) do not all contain the same dedicated stem, *cantará*, all verbs of this class share the same alternations whereby the final stem vowel of the 1SG and 1PL is /e/ and not /a/. Contrast this with the forms of Latin third stem which never appears solely followed by the exponents of person and number but always along with other formatives, those of the past participle, the supine, and future participle (-US, -UM, and –ŪRUS respectively) e.g. SCRĪPTUS, SCRĪPTUM, SCRĪPTURUS.

For morphosyntactic features, therefore, it seems unimportant whether they correspond to a set of varied syntactic/semantic uses but of significant importance that the phonological exponent of this feature does not co-occur in the same word

---

[3] In the case of the Spanish imperfect indicative the varied usages all display the same alternation of form in accordance with the conjugational class of the verb (concatenation of *-ba* or *-ía* to the root/stem).

[4] My definition of a stem does not correspond to the traditional definition of the root + thematic vowel but to Aronoff's (1994: 30) definition of a stem as 'the part of a complete word form that remains when an affix is removed'.

with any other exponents of other features, with the exception of the formatives for person and number.

In order to illustrate this point more clearly, it is instructive to present a hypothetical case: let us suppose that a language has two tenses (Tense A and Tense B), which are not semantically or syntactically related, and that the morphological structure of these two tenses is that in (2): (PN = person and number markers):

(2)   Tense A: ROOT + {f} + /pa/ + PN
       Tense B: ROOT + {f} + /re/ + PN

In such a hypothetical language, the formatives /pa/ and /re/ would be correlated with Tenses A and B respectively and be considered morphemic exponents of these features; the formative {f} in this language and its particular distribution could be considered morphomic (subject to diachronic confirmation), since it does not correspond to any coherent morphemic feature, but occurs after the root in two unrelated tenses and nowhere else in the paradigm.

However, if, due to historical phonological processes, the exponents /pa/ and /re/ were deleted, the result would be a syncretism between tenses A and B, as shown below in (3):

(3)   Tense A and Tense B: ROOT + {f} + PN

On account of the resulting syncretism between these tenses they could be classed as one tense, and {f} could be derived via a morphosyntactic/semantic feature; the distribution of {f} would no longer be morphomic but could be considered morphemic in that it corresponds to a morphemic feature. However, I stress once again that the consistency of this feature does not lie in its syntax or semantics but in its morphological form. The difference between the two diachronic stages lies not in the uses in which {f} appears, but that in the earlier diachronic stage, a subset of the uses of {f} also coincided with those of other morphological formatives on the word.

For the sake of clarity both diachronic stages as described in (2) and (3) are represented as Venn diagrams in Figures 12.6 and 12.7; the circles correspond to the common form and the letters within the circles to different semantic/syntactic usages.

There are two points to note regarding this hypothetical situation and the difference between morphemic and morphomic features:

(a) Morphosyntactic features may correspond to a varied set of heterogeneous uses.

(b) The morphomic phenomena which this chapter addresses and which have been formalized as features correspond to cases in which, like some morphemic features, there is a correspondence between a varied set of syntactic/semantic uses and a morphological form/alternation but a subset of these uses are also associated with another morphological form/alternation.

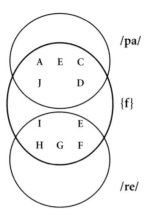

FIGURE 12.6 A Venn diagram illustrating the diachronic stages in (2) of a hypothetical language

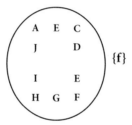

FIGURE 12.7 A Venn diagram illustrating the diachronic stages in (3) of a hypothetical language

With reference to the hypothetical data above, the formative {f} in Figure 12.7 is similar to /pa/ and /re/ in Figure 12.6, in that it corresponds to a number of different uses. More importantly, however, the formative {f} in Figure 12.7 is different from the formative {f} in Figure 12.6, not in respect of the different uses to which {f} corresponds, but rather in that, in Figure 12.6, a subset of the usages (A, E, C, J, D) are also associated with the formant /pa/. Due to this partial overlap the consistent distribution of {f} would be licensed by a morphomic feature since (i) a subset of its uses does not only trigger the formative {f} but also the formative /pa/, and (ii) there is no semantic connection between the uses.

This final point (ii), is of maximal importance, since if there did exist shared semantic traits between the uses, then it would be irrelevant whether a subset of these uses were correlated with another formative because there was a functional common denominator. Such is the case with the morphological forms of the Latin perfective tenses.

TABLE 12.10 Perfective forms of two Latin verbs

Verb form	CANTĀRE	SCRĪBERE
Future perfect indicative	CANTĀVERŌ	SCRĪPSERŌ
Pluperfect indicative	CANTĀVERAM	SCRĪPSERAM
Perfect subjunctive	CANTĀVERIM	SCRĪPSERIM
Pluperfect subjunctive	CANTĀVISSEM	SCRĪPSISSEM

As elaborated in Section 12.3, Latin expressed perfective and imperfective aspect morphologically by way of a special allomorphic stem which was either lexically stored or created by the concatenation of -V- [w] to the root/stem. Witness the following pairs of words: CANTŌ 'I sing', CANTĀVĪ 'I have sung'; SCRĪBAM 'I will write', SCRĪPSERŌ 'I will have written' (see Tables 12.3 and 12.4 for more examples). Of relevance to the present discussion is that the *perfectum* stem, corresponding largely to situations denoting perfective aspect, co-occurred with other morphological formatives besides those of person and number. A selection of verb forms are given in Table 12.10 for the regular verb CANTĀRE 'sing' and the irregular verb SCRĪBERE 'write'.

The Latin *perfectum* stem and the third stem are similar in that they both occur in a number of different paradigmatic cells and occur before other morphological formatives than those of person and number. The *perfectum* stem, *inter alia*, appears before the cumulative markers of the values listed in the first column of Table 12.10, the third stem before the markers of the past participle, future participle, and supine. However, the crucial difference is that there is some type of semantic common denominator in the case of the *perfectum* stem: all forms usually share perfective aspect.

Thus, the distinction between morphomic and morphemic features is not that the former necessarily correspond to a set of heterogeneous syntactic/semantic uses and the latter to a homogeneous set. Rather, as with the imperfect indicative in Spanish, morphosyntactic/semantic features can all potentially correspond to multiple uses for which there is no functional common denominator. Thus, a common meaning is not a prerequisite of a morphemic feature. Nor is a single dedicated morphological form a prerequisite, since morphemic features can have multiple exponents and these can even occur simultaneously in the same word-forms, e.g. the Latin perfective tenses. In these forms a subset of the uses correlated with one formative, e.g. the cumulative marker of pluperfect subjunctive -ISSE-, also includes all the uses correlated with another formative, e.g. the perfective aspect of the *perfectum* stem.

In sum, multiple and varied uses do not pose a problem if these are correlated with a consistent morphological form/alternation, likewise multiple and simultaneous exponences do not pose a problem as long as there is a common semantic link. The distinction therefore between morphomic and morphemic features seems to be that the former are cases in which there is both an set of unrelated uses and multiple and simultaneous exponence. Thus the distribution of the third stem of Latin is considered morphomic because a subset of the uses correlated with this stem also includes all the uses correlated with another formative, e.g. that of the supine. In such cases, the formative with the larger set of uses, the third stem, is morphomic, and that which has a smaller set of uses, the supine, is morphemic.

Again, I stress that the third stem is *not* to be considered morphomic exclusively on the basis of its varied uses, since if these were all expressed by the same morphological form, say that of the participle, the distribution would be morphemic and the varied semantics would be disambiguated by other elements within the sentence. Thus, let us imagine a hypothetical variety of Latin in which the three different functions expressed by the Classical Latin verb forms in (4) could be rendered by the same form of the verb, and therefore the speaker would have to rely not on the morphology of the verb but on pragmatic factors and other elements in the sentence in order to recover the different meanings. Thus, the meaning of the second sentence could be made clear by additional information such as the phrase 'but Brutus comes in and interrupts him':

(4)   a. Epistula scripta est.
         'The letter was/has been written.'
      b. Caesar epistulam scripturus est.
         'Caesar is about to write the letter.'
      c. Caesar it epistulam scriptum.
         'Caesar goes to write the letter.'

Such a reliance on other linguistic factors to establish the meaning of a morphological form is commonplace in languages, as is attested by the three Spanish phrases in (5), all of which use the same morphological form of the verb, the imperfect indicative. There are, however, important differences in meaning: in the first sentence the adversative clause indicates a past planned event which was not realized, whilst in the second sentence the planned event is interpreted to take place in the future; in the third sentence the event is not interpreted as being planned but having happened in the past and coinciding with another event. In the examples, the Spanish verb in question and the English translation are in bold.

(5)   a. Mi hermano **llegaba** ayer, pero algunos problemas de salud lo han obligado
         a posponer el viaje. (Real Academia Española 2009: 1752)
         'My brother **was supposed to get here** yesterday, but health problems have
         forced him to postpone his journey.'

> b. Mi hermano **llegaba** a las tres, creo, así que si quieres podemos ir juntos a la estación a recogerle.
> 'My brother **is getting here** at three, I think, so if you want we can go and pick him up from the station together.'
> c. Mi hermano **llegaba** a casa justo cuando yo salía de casa.
> 'My brother **was getting home** just as I was leaving home.'

Therefore morphomic and morphemic phenomena are not, I maintain, qualitatively different since both can represent the discontinuous relationship between form and meaning. Morphemic features can relate various meanings or situation types to one common form or set of morphological rules. Likewise, these features can also relate different forms/rules simultaneously to one common meaning. Morphomic features take this discontinuous relationship one step further, since the formatives which they predict are not only correlated with heterogeneous semantic uses but, more-over, a subset of these uses can be simultaneously associated with another morphological exponent in the same word.

Here, my claim is that morphomic phenomena such as the Latin third stem can, in fact, correspond to certain (non-homogeneous) semantic uses but that this relationship is rendered opaque by the other suffix in the word which is simultaneously related to a subset of these uses. Note that my claim is not that the suffix is meaningful but that it is correlated with the different uses and situation types. This claim is in direct contradiction with the assumption that morphomic formatives are only relevant to the particular workings of the morphology. In this respect, it is instructive to analyse the definition of a purely morphological feature by Kibort and Corbett (2010: 6).

These authors, with reference to the study by Corbett and Baerman (2006), define morphological features as irrelevant to both syntax and semantics and state that they are features 'whose values are inherent only, are not found on controllers of agreement, and additionally cannot be selected by the speaker based on the choice of meaning or function'. In what follows I assess the inability of morphomic features, as described in this chapter, to be chosen by the speaker based on choice of meaning or function.

It is clear that different morphological formatives can trigger differences in meaning. Compare the different semantic nuances between the forms of the imperfect indicative and preterite in the Spanish sentences below in (6):

(6)   a. De niño estudiaba mucho
        'As a child, I used to study a lot'
      b. De niño estudié mucho
        'As a child, I studied a lot'

It could be claimed that the speaker selects the feature which corresponds to the nuance they want to express and this feature then licenses the morphological form. This selection of such a morphemic feature can be contrasted with the selection of the morphomic feature for the Latin third stem. Observe the Latin sentences in (4) above. In each sentence there are different meanings associated with the verb 'write'. However, the same stem is used in all cases. Thus, it could be concluded that the difference in meaning comes from the selection of the additional suffixes (which are meaningful); the third stem is merely the common stem upon which a number of different tenses are built, and its selection is purely morphological (see Aronoff 1994: 44). Thus, the assumption is that the third stem is not correlated with the meanings of the word-forms in which it is used whilst the suffixes are. This distinction could be defined as the traditional morphomic vs. morphemic distinction.

However, what is the real evidence upon which this assumption is based? My argument is that the third stem is correlated with all the meanings/usages in (4) whilst the suffixes are only correlated with a subset. Note that the speaker can only recover the semantics of the word-form based on (a) the combination of the third stem *and* the suffix and (b) the situation type, or context, in which this morphological form occurs. Neither the third stem nor the suffixes ever appear in isolation; if either were not present the word would be ill-formed. The meaning is expressed by the whole word and not just one particular formative, and in this way the third stem is associated with and selected by a set of varied and unrelated functions. Thus, if the third stem is formalized as a feature, then I see no reason why this feature is not selected by the speaker based on choice of meaning or situation type.

I stress that such a conclusion does not imply that I consider the third stem to be meaningful, but merely that it is correlated with a large set of varied meanings and uses. I maintain that the relationship between form and meaning is discontinuous and that the reason the third stem poses problems for its classification as correlated with a set of varied meanings is merely because its uses are not exclusive to this third stem, but a subset of these uses are also correlated with other formatives which occur in the word together with the third stem. This fact does not, in itself, prove that the third stem is not associated with the different uses of the word-forms in which it occurs, but it does highlight how the construal of semantics is heavily determined by the morphological form.

In conclusion, I contend that the distinction between morphomic and morphemic phenomena is not one of kind but one of degree. This conclusion does not, in my opinion, render the notion of the morphome vacuous, but rather I would argue that it highlights the fact that the relationship between form and meaning is discontinuous. The examples of morphomes such as the third stem in Latin are canonical cases of this discontinuous relationship since two different forms (the third stem and the suffix) are correlated with the same semantic uses, but one of these forms (the third stem) is also correlated with other uses. Indeed, Aronoff states that all exponence is morphomic, whether the exponents have morphosyntatically coherent distributions or not, noting simply that the latter, canonical morphomes, are those which 'truly earn their name' (Aronoff 1994: 25)

13

The morphome as a gradient phenomenon: evidence from Romance*

JOHN CHARLES SMITH

13.1 Introduction

Aronoff (1994) famously proposed that morphology was not simply the intersection of syntax and phonology, but constituted an autonomous level of linguistic structure, a level he labelled the 'morphomic level'. The term 'morphome' then defines a mapping function (and more generally a structure or pattern) that exists at this level. Because the existence of such a level is crucially demonstrated by structures or patterns which do not correlate with syntax or phonology, the term 'morphome' has commonly been used to refer to a systematic distribution of morphological material within the paradigm which has no unique functional (or phonological) correlate. Aronoff's examples include the English 'past participle', which he claims combines the otherwise unrelated functions of active perfective participle (*They have seen the eclipse*) and passive participle (*The eclipse was seen by thousands*), and the 'third stem' of the Latin verb, which stands apart from the stems of the *infectum* and *perfectum*, and serves to form the past participle, the future participle, the supine, and a variety of derived nouns and verbs. However, it should be stressed that, despite this common usage, for Aronoff all morphology is morphomic. As he points out (Aronoff 1994: 25): 'It is possible to have a singleton morphosyntactic set mapped onto a singleton morphomic set, which itself is mapped onto a singleton morphophonological set.' For the sake of terminological clarity, I shall refer to the morphomes involved in this type of 'singleton' mapping as 'covert morphomes' and label

* Part of the research for this chapter was undertaken within the AHRC-funded project *Autonomous Morphology in Diachrony: comparative evidence from the Romance Languages*, in the Faculty of Linguistics, Philology, and Phonetics, University of Oxford. The support of the AHRC is gratefully acknowledged.

morphomes defined in the narrower sense above 'overt morphomes'.[1] For Aronoff (1994: 25) all morphological mappings involve morphomes, but it is the morphomes which I am terming 'overt' that 'truly earn their name'.

As already suggested, overt morphomes are significant because they demonstrate that regular patterns within paradigms may be undetermined by extramorphological factors, and therefore that morphology may sometimes constitute 'its own meaning'. Perhaps because of these important theoretical consequences, much research on autonomous morphology has proceeded as if the morphome were a relatively monolithic or undifferentiated concept, or, at the very least, as if there were a simple and clear-cut dichotomy between overt and covert morphomes (even though Aronoff, 1994: 25, suggests that there are 'cases intermediate in complexity' between the two)—a point also made by Vincent (this volume). In this chapter, I shall suggest instead that morphomehood is a gradient phenomenon, and that a given morphome may be situated on a cline of 'coherence', or 'motivation'. For instance, I shall distinguish between overt morphomes defined in terms of features which are internal to the grammatical category involved and those defined in terms of features which are external to this category. Thus, for instance, in the morphology of the verb, a morphome which can be defined simply in relation to tense and/or aspect and/or mood will (at least in a language in which these features are restricted to the verb) be more coherent than one which requires definition in terms of person and/or number, which are not purely (or even essentially) verbal features. Moreover, I shall suggest that collections of features may in themselves be more or less coherent. I shall show that a characterization of morphomes along these lines is not merely a descriptive device, but that it may have explanatory value, as well, in that a correlation arguably exists between this continuum and a scalar approach to morphological phenomena such as suppletion and defectiveness, with these phenomena being more likely to exhibit a morphomic distribution precisely when the morphome in question is more 'coherent' or 'motivated', in the terms defined above. In short, morphological autonomy is a matter of degree, and morphological processes appear to be sensitive to this fact. At the same time, I shall note that suppletion and defectiveness do not interact with the morphome cline in identical ways, and will examine possible reasons for this discrepancy.

13.2 Towards a typology of morphomes

13.2.1 *Class morphomes ('whole-paradigm' morphomes)*

I use the term 'class morphome' to define an overt morphome in which every cell of the paradigm of a particular subset of a lexical category behaves in the same way. In other words, these morphomes (traditionally referred to as 'conjugation classes' or 'conjugations' when verbs are involved, 'declension classes' or 'declensions' when

---

[1] I am grateful to Martin Maiden for helpful discussion of the appropriate terminology to use here.

nouns or adjectives are involved) involve a subset of the lexicon rather than a subset of the paradigm. In Romance, the most salient examples of class morphomes are conjugation classes. It is technically possible for noun or verb classes to have some semantic or other extramorphological homogeneity. For instance, Luís (2011) identifies a conjugation class in two Indian Portuguese creoles which contains exclusively loan verbs from substrate languages (Gujarati or Marathi). However, such precise correlation between a class morphome and some non-morphological feature seems to be rare. More often, correlations exist merely as informal and partial generalizations. For instance, in French, intransitive or transitive 'change-of-state' verbs derived from an adjective will tend to belong to the regular *-ir* class (what traditional French grammar calls the second conjugation, although diachronically it corresponds to the Latin fourth)—thus intransitive *grandir* 'become big, grow', transitive *agrandir* 'enlarge' (compare *grand* 'big'); intransitive *faiblir* 'weaken', transitive *affaiblir* 'weaken' (compare *faible* 'weak'); *vieillir* 'grow old, age' (compare *vieux, vieille* 'old'); *rougir* 'redden, blush' (compare *rouge* 'red'), etc. But this conjugation class is no longer productive (the last new forms are, famously, *alunir* 'land on the moon', first attested in 1921, and *amerrir* 'land in the sea', first attested in 1928, both by analogy with existing *atterrir* 'land'; the last 'change-of-state' verb derived from an adjective appears to have been *rosir* 'grow pink' (compare *rose* 'pink'), first attested in 1823 (all dates of first attestation from *TLF*)); even before it ceased to be productive, there were 'change-of-state' verbs derived from adjectives which belonged to other conjugations (such as *rapetisser* 'make small', more rarely 'grow small' (compare *petit* 'small') and *hausser* 'raise' (compare *haut* 'high')); and many verbs in the regular *-ir* class are not 'change-of-state' verbs or derived from an adjective (*applaudir* 'applaud'; *languir* 'languish', etc., including the relatively recent onomatopœic neologism *vrombir* 'buzz'). For some discussion, see Kobayashi (1988: 398–9) and Hewson (1997: 149). In other words, although correlations may exist between class morphomes and non-morphological features, they are the exception rather than the rule and rarely represent biunique entailments.

Class morphomes, then, present interesting properties. However, most overt morphomes are defined in terms of a subset of the paradigm.

13.2.2 *Paradigm-subset morphomes*

13.2.2.1 *Functionally coherent distribution of stems* Functionally coherent distributions of stems are clear cases of 'covert' morphomes, in the definition given above, precisely because they **do** have a unique extramorphological correlate. For instance, the imperfect indicative may have a unique stem, as in Spanish *ser*, 'be' (*era* 'I was', etc.). It is worth noting that distributions of this type may represent 'proto-overt morphomes': that is, one way for overt morphomes to arise is through functional divergence of a hitherto functionally or semantically homogeneous subset of the paradigm (compare the origins of the functionally heterogeneous PYTA morphome (Maiden 2001*b*; see below) from the functionally homogeneous Latin *perfectum*).

13.2.2.2 *TAM morphomes*   TAM morphomes, as the label implies, are defined in terms of tense and/or aspect and/or mood. (I am interested here, of course, in overt morphomes which are so defined; covert TAM morphomes have already been discussed in the previous section.) Although semantically and syntactically these categories may lie outside the VP or 'nuclear predication', and despite the existence in some languages of adjectives (see Kuno 1973), nouns (see Nordlinger and Sadler 2004), and complementizers (see Cottell 1995) which are marked for 'tense' (etc.), tense, aspect, and mood are the prototypical categories of verb morphology. They are in some sense 'grammatical categories of verbs' (Dahl and Velupillai 2005: 266). It follows that TAM morphomes can be seen as relatively coherent, in that they are verb morphomes defined in terms of prototypical categories of verb morphology.

Combinations of TAM features may be more or less coherent. In most Romance varieties, the future and conditional share a stem, which is sometimes not found elsewhere in the paradigm (compare French *aller* 'go', *je vais* 'I go'; *j'irai* 'I shall go', *j'irais* 'I would go'). For discussion of the morphomic status of these cells of the paradigm (and the use of the Occitan acronym FUÈC to refer to them), see Esher (2010, 2012*b*). It is not clear a priori what the functional or semantic link between future and conditional might be. One possible analysis would involve markedness (although we should be aware of the issues surrounding this notion—see Haspelmath 2006). For Greenberg (1966*b*: 87), the past is quasi-universally marked with respect to the present; it exhibits lower frequency and greater morphological complexity. By the same token, the future is more marked than either present or past. However, global analyses of this type are perhaps of limited value. If text-type is taken into account, nuances emerge—for instance, historical narrative may favour the past tense (although the 'historic present' can also be used in this context), whilst texts which are essentially predictive (from Nostradamus to tabloid horoscopes) may well use the future more frequently than other tenses. Likewise, Greenberg (1966*b*: 86) notes that 'the indicative may be considered the unmarked category as against the marked character of the one or more hypothetical modes'; but, once again, text-type may be relevant: prayers, imprecations, and directive texts are doubtless more likely to use non-indicative forms (subjunctives, optatives, hortatives, imperatives) than descriptive prose. So, whilst, globally speaking, the future is a highly marked tense (and the 'future in the past', inasmuch as it is a separate tense, is even more marked), and the conditional is amongst the most marked moods, this fact of itself does not make them a coherent set. It could also be argued, less rigidly, that the future and the conditional are less frequent and conceptually complex. Rather more convincing is Iatridou's claim (cf. Iatridou 2000) that there is some degree of semantic coherence to the future and the conditional, with the conditional continuing to be definable in terms of 'future' and 'past' (see the more detailed discussion of this issue by Vincent, this volume).

If this is the case, then the future and conditional taken together will not represent a completely arbitrary or 'incoherent' morphome.

The PYTA morpheme (see Maiden 2001*b*, 2011*a*, who derives the acronym from Spanish *perfecto y tiempos afines*), especially prevalent in Ibero-Romance, unites all the forms which have their origin in the Latin *perfectum*: thus, the preterite, the synthetic pluperfect, the past subjunctives, and the future subjunctive (or the subset of these forms which survives in a given variety). Compare Spanish *ser* 'be': preterite *fue*, past subjunctives *fuera/fuese*, future subjunctive (archaic) *fuere*; Portuguese *ser* 'be': preterite *foi*, synthetic pluperfect *fora*, past subjunctive *fosse*, future subjunctive *for* (for both languages, all forms other than the infinitive are given in the third person singular). Despite the common origin of their stem, these forms now exhibit highly diverse meanings as a result of semantic/pragmatic divergence, and it is difficult to see any unique semantic or functional feature which unites them. One could argue that all PYTA forms are marked (past tense and/or subjunctive mood; see above), but it is difficult to claim they are the most marked forms of the verb (they do not include the future indicative or the past imperfective indicative, for instance). PYTA is therefore arguably a less coherent morpheme than FUÈC.

13.2.2.3 *Person-related morphomes*

As the label implies, these morphomes require some definition in terms of person (and sometimes number), categories which are nominal (see especially Beard 1995: 135); in terms of verb morphology, these are agreement categories. It might be argued that this type of verb morpheme is less coherent than a TAM morpheme, because it is defined in terms of a category which is not intrinsically (or essentially) a category of the verb. Additionally, person-related morphomes (at least in Romance) are complex, in that all of them also appear to require some definition in terms of tense, mood, and/or aspect. This is another sense in which person-related morphomes are less coherent than those which are defined simply in terms of TAM.

Maiden (see especially Maiden 2011*b*) has identified three types of person-related morpheme in the paradigm of the Romance verb. In the N-pattern (cf. Maiden 2011*b*: 241–63), one stem is found in all the singular persons and the third person plural of the present, and a different stem elsewhere, as follows:

1 SINGULAR PRESENT INDICATIVE	1 SINGULAR PRESENT SUBJUNCTIVE	
2 SINGULAR PRESENT INDICATIVE	2 SINGULAR PRESENT SUBJUNCTIVE	
3 SINGULAR PRESENT INDICATIVE	3 SINGULAR PRESENT SUBJUNCTIVE	'ELSEWHERE'
1 PLURAL PRESENT INDICATIVE	1 PLURAL PRESENT SUBJUNCTIVE	
2 PLURAL PRESENT INDICATIVE	2 PLURAL PRESENT SUBJUNCTIVE	
3 PLURAL PRESENT INDICATIVE	3 PLURAL PRESENT SUBJUNCTIVE	

The N-pattern may be exemplified from Spanish *mostrar* 'show':

PRS.IND	PRS.SBJV	
muestro	*muestre*	IMPF *mostraba*
muestras	*muestres*	PRET *mostró*
muestra	*muestre*	FUT *mostrará*
mostramos	*mostremos*	COND *mostraría*
mostráis	*mostréis*	PST.PTCP *mostrado*
muestran	*muestren*	etc.

Note also that the N-pattern is the template for the distribution of the 'augment' (originally a marker of inchoativity) in many *-ire* verbs in Italian, such as *finire* 'finish':

PRS.IND	PRS.SBJV	
finisco	*finisca*	IMPF *finiva*
finisci	*finisca*	PRET *finì*
finisce	*finisca*	FUT *finirà*
finiamo	*finiamo*	COND *finirebbe*
finite	*finiate*	PST.PTCP *finito*
finiscono	*finiscano*	etc.

In Maiden's L-pattern (cf. Maiden 2011*b*: 223–41), the first person singular of the present indicative and the whole of the present subjunctive behave in the same way.

1 SINGULAR PRESENT INDICATIVE	1 SINGULAR PRESENT SUBJUNCTIVE
2 SINGULAR PRESENT INDICATIVE	2 SINGULAR PRESENT SUBJUNCTIVE
3 SINGULAR PRESENT INDICATIVE	3 SINGULAR PRESENT SUBJUNCTIVE
1 PLURAL PRESENT INDICATIVE	1 PLURAL PRESENT SUBJUNCTIVE
2 PLURAL PRESENT INDICATIVE	2 PLURAL PRESENT SUBJUNCTIVE
3 PLURAL PRESENT INDICATIVE	3 PLURAL PRESENT SUBJUNCTIVE

This pattern is found in many Spanish, Portuguese, and Italian verbs; it may be exemplified from Spanish *conocer* 'know, be acquainted with'.

PRS.IND	PRS.SBJV
conozco	*conozca*
conoces	*conozcas*
conoce	*conozca*
conocemos	*conozcamos*
conocéis	*conozcáis*
conocen	*conozcan*

Finally, in Maiden's U-pattern (cf. Maiden 2011*b*: 223–41), the third person plural of the present indicative is added to the L-pattern cells.

1 SINGULAR PRESENT INDICATIVE	1 SINGULAR PRESENT SUBJUNCTIVE
2 SINGULAR PRESENT INDICATIVE	2 SINGULAR PRESENT SUBJUNCTIVE
3 SINGULAR PRESENT INDICATIVE	3 SINGULAR PRESENT SUBJUNCTIVE
1 PLURAL PRESENT INDICATIVE	1 PLURAL PRESENT SUBJUNCTIVE
2 PLURAL PRESENT INDICATIVE	2 PLURAL PRESENT SUBJUNCTIVE
3 PLURAL PRESENT INDICATIVE	3 PLURAL PRESENT SUBJUNCTIVE

This pattern is somewhat rarer; as an example we may take *potere* 'be able' in old Tuscan:

PRS.IND	PRS.SBJV
posso	*possa*
puoi	*possi*
può	*possa*
potemo	*possiamo*
potete	*possiate*
possono	*possano*

Although sound change can be shown to have played a role in the emergence of some of these person-related morphemes, many verbs (such as, for example, old Tuscan *potere*) have been attracted into these patterns by subsequent quasi-analogical developments (compare the spread of the augment in the N-pattern), or as the result of suppletion or defectiveness (which we discuss below). The morphomes appear to be synchronically unmotivated. Is this in fact the case? Or do they have a more or less coherent identity which might be expressed in terms of frequency, markedness, or some similar notion? In the discussion of TAM morphemes above, I have already drawn attention to the view that present tense and indicative mood are unmarked. What of person and number? I deal with these issues in Smith (2011*a*: 290–5), and summarize the arguments below.

Considerable debate surrounds the notion of 'unmarked person'. After surveying data from a variety of languages, Greenberg (1966*b*: 84f.) is led, on the basis of frequency and morphological structure, 'to posit, tentatively at least, a hierarchy in which the third person [is] the least marked, and the second person the most marked, with the first person intermediate'. However, in an alternative, discourse-based, view, discourse participants would be less marked than non-participants, and the speaker, as the necessary participant in every utterance, would be less marked than the hearer, yielding a hierarchy 'first person > second person > third person'. Such a view underlies the work of Bühler (1934: 79–148) and Benveniste (1956), and is explicitly articulated by Dixon (1994: 84–90). Perhaps the most detailed exposition of this view is Silverstein's agentivity hierarchy (Silverstein 1976), in which first- and second-person forms lie above third-person forms; he further draws attention to the fact that some languages may invert the order of first and second persons in this hierarchy, apparently treating the second person as more animate or agentive than the first.

What does seem clear is that, just as what constitutes the unmarked tense or mood may be sensitive to text-type (see §13.2.2.2 above), so the unmarked person may vary from one text-type to another, and even, perhaps, from one society to another. In personal narratives, we expect to find a large proportion of first-person forms, given the central role of the narrator. Interpersonal texts, such as instruction manuals, pedagogical textbooks, or love poetry, will likewise be orientated towards the hearer/reader, and will in consequence contain large numbers of second-person forms. Finally, a descriptive text is likely to be written mainly in the third person. It is moreover probable that the social norms of particular societies will favour some types of discourse over others (compare some of the comments made by Manoliu 2011). In these circumstances, it is extremely difficult to make objectively verifiable (or falsifiable) statements about the unmarkedness of particular person-forms.

However, although there may be some uncertainty regarding the unmarked person in the singular, it is not unreasonable to claim that the third person is unmarked in the plural. Second- and third-person plurals correspond uncontroversially to the existence of more than one (potential) addressee or of more than one non-discourse-participant, respectively; but a plurality of first persons is a much less straightforward notion. So-called first-person plurals are rarely, if ever, literally that—they encode composite reference to the speaker and some other person or persons, including or excluding the addressee. An addressee might admittedly be confronted by a number of speakers using the same words simultaneously; but this is not the normal context in which first person plural forms are used. And for any individual speaker, a 'plurality of first persons' interpretation is impossible, except perhaps in highly metaphorical contexts or in science fiction. In this sense, then, the first person plural may be considered as an abnormal, or at least atypical, plural, and hence as marked. This view receives corroboration from frequency data. Greenberg's statistics on pronominal forms in the work of the second-century BC Latin playwright Terence (Greenberg 1966b: 78) give the following descending order of frequency in the singular (with the number of tokens in brackets): first person (1,786), third person (1,369), second person (1,267). However, in the plural, the order is: third person (197), first person (146), second person (98). Of course, these figures are small, and have no more than a heuristic value. But they are suggestive, nonetheless. In Smith (2011a: 291–3), I supplement them with data obtained from a search for present-tense forms on World Wide Web pages written in Italian, using the Google search engine, in February 2009. The results of this larger-scale survey show that, although the most frequent person in the singular may vary according to the verb, in the plural the most frequent form is the third person.

It is easier to make generalizations about number in this context. Greenberg (1966b: 75–80) discusses number in both nouns and verbs, concluding, on the basis of frequency and syncretization, that the singular is less marked than the plural (which is in turn less marked than other numbers, such as the dual and the trial).

Despite all the caveats, then, there is a strong case for regarding singular number, present tense, and indicative mood as the unmarked terms in contexts which are themselves unmarked.[2] Moreover, the third person seems to be the least marked person in the plural. The 'N–pattern', whereby one stem is shared by all the singular persons in the present and the third person plural in the present, with an 'elsewhere' stem in the remainder of the paradigm, might therefore be seen as a contrast between less marked forms (the unmarked number, and the unmarked person in the marked number, of the unmarked tense) and more marked forms. This interpretation is discussed—and dismissed—by Maiden (2011b: 258–9), who argues that, whilst it is 'initially seductive', '[t]he problem is that the appeal to "markedness" paints a deceptive veneer over the real arbitrariness of the phenonenon. [...] [T]hree parameters of markedness are involved, and nothing explains why they intersect in the way they do. [...] Above all, if the N-pattern diagrams some "natural", and presumably therefore universal, markedness relationship, how is it that this pattern seems not to recur repeatedly in other languages?'

---

[2] For further discussion of these issues, see Croft (2003) and Battistella (1990, 1996).

Maiden's point is well taken, and it indeed seems implausible to suggest that the N-pattern arose because it targeted what were in some sense the least marked cells of the paradigm. However, the proposal I am making is a slightly different one. My claim is not that the N-pattern morpheme originates as a result of (un)markedness or frequency, but that, once it has arisen, it can be rationalized in those terms, including by native speakers, regardless of its origins, in much the same way, perhaps, as the morphological structure of some words is rationalized after the event and in ignorance of historical developments by folk etymology. This fact gives the N-pattern a certain coherence.

The L-pattern, however, is considerably less coherent than the N-pattern. It is difficult to think of any meaningful link between the first person singular of the present indicative and the present subjunctive as a whole. If one were desperate, one might, given the modal (i.e. speaker-orientated) values of the subjunctive, argue that the forms were linked by the feature [+speaker] at some level of analysis, in the unmarked tense; but this is perhaps far-fetched. The U-pattern, in turn, is even less coherent than the L-pattern. The inclusion of the third person plural makes it impossible to discern any common feature linking the cells involved.

13.3 Suppletion and the morphome

In this section, I consider the interaction of suppletion with the typology of morphomes just outlined. In doing so, following earlier work (Smith 2011a), I shall treat suppletion as a special case of refunctionalization—the acquisition of a new function by a morphological opposition. I have suggested that, in refunctionalization, some vestige, however abstract, of the original functional or semantic opposition is carried over into the new one, and have claimed that the refunctionalization involves 'core-to-core' mapping, where the notion of 'core' value is associated with one or more of at least the following (in the spirit of Haspelmath, 2006): **qualitative unmarkedness; quantitative unmarkedness (higher frequency); default status.** (Often, these criteria will yield identical results; but not always.) I have illustrated this hypothesis with various case studies: the refunctionalization of the accusative and dative forms of the first and second person singular pronouns of Latin as conjunctive and disjunctive forms, respectively, in Spanish, Portuguese, and Picard (Smith 1999, 2006, 2011a); the refunctionalization of the first person plural inclusive and exclusive pronouns of proto-Austronesian as first person plural and first person paucal, respectively, in Tukang Besi and Lasalimu (Donohue and Smith 1998); and the refunctionalization of the first person plural inclusive and exclusive inflections of Tiwi (a non-Pama-Nyungan language of Northern Australia) as exponents of first person non-past and first person past, respectively (Smith 2008). In all of these refunctionalizations, quantitative and qualitative markedness appear to be maintained. Finally, the lexicalization of the nominative/oblique case opposition of Old Gallo-Romance gives rise in modern varieties to doublets, with a separate lexical item continuing each original case form (Smith 2005, 2011a); in each instance, it is the nominative, as the more agentive term of the original case opposition, which yields the lexical item with the more agentive meaning. Suppletion may be seen as the mirror image of this last process—rather than a morphological opposition becoming a lexical one, we have an opposition between two lexical items which becomes morphologized.

In Romance, suppletion is particularly associated with the verb (although see Maiden, 2012, for some examples of suppletion in the Megleno-Romanian adjective). I begin with class suppletion or whole-paradigm suppletion. Synchronically, this is a vacuous notion. We might tentatively suggest that examples of the replacement of entire verbal paradigms such as French *ardre* > *brûler* 'burn', *occire* > *tuer* 'kill', *ch(e)oir* > *tomber* > 'fall' are examples of **diachronic** class suppletion. However, a more accurate definition would see them as examples of **metachronic** class suppletion. The diachronic reality is that the suppletion takes place gradually and differentially, and forms of some of these verbs may still be found in elevated registers of the language, even though they have disappeared from everyday speech (compare the comments on *ardre* and *occire* below, §13.4).

Within the paradigm, we may find suppletion in a coherent subset of cells (a covert morphome, in the terminology I am adopting here). The existence of this type of suppletion is perhaps unsurprising. It occurs in, for instance, French, where the imperfect of *être* 'be' < ESSE(RE) is supplied by reflexes of the imperfect of STARE 'stand' (*il était* 'he was', etc.) (although the past participle is also affected, making the subset slightly less coherent). More relevant to our present argument is suppletion involving overt TAM morphomes. Suppletion occurs in the FUÈC cells of the paradigm—for instance, the use of the *ir-* stem in the future and conditional of French *aller* 'go'; thus present indicative *il va* 'he goes', present subjunctive *il aille* 'he go', imperfect *il allait* 'he went', preterite *il alla* 'he went'; but future *il ira* 'he will go' and conditional *il irait* 'he would go'. We also find suppletion in the PYTA cells of the paradigm (for instance, the use of the *fu-* stem 'be' in the PYTA of Spanish *ir* 'go'; thus, present indicative *va* 'he goes', present subjunctive *vaya* 'he go'; imperfect *iba* 'he went', future *irá* 'he will go', conditional *iría* 'he would go'; but preterite *fue* 'he went', past subjunctives *fuera/fuese*, future subjunctive (archaic) *fuere*).

Turning now to the person–number morphomes discussed above, we find that suppletion is possible in the N-pattern. I discuss this issue in detail in Smith (2011a), and will not repeat that material here, but merely illustrate the point with some relevant data. As examples of N-pattern suppletion, we may take Italian *andare* 'go', which patterns as follows (for further discussion, see Aski 1995):

	PRS.IND	PRS.SBJV	
1SG	*vado*	*vada*	IMPF *andava*
2SG	*vai*	*vada*	PRET *andò*
3SG	*va*	*vada*	FUT *andrà*
1PL	*andiamo*	*andiamo*	COND *andrebbe*
2PL	*andate*	*andiate*	PST.PTCP *andato*
3PL	*vanno*	*vadano*	etc.

or Italian *uscire* 'go out', which has the following paradigm:

	PRS.IND	PRS.SBJV	
1SG	*esco*	*esca*	IMPF *usciva*
2SG	*esci*	*esca*	PRET *uscì*
3SG	*esce*	*esca*	FUT *uscirà*
1PL	*usciamo*	*usciamo*	COND *uscirebbe*
2PL	*uscite*	*usciate*	PST.PTCP *uscito*
3PL	*escono*	*escano*	etc.

Significantly, we do not find (or do not find robust evidence) that the other person-related morphomic patterns proposed by Maiden (the 'L-pattern' and the 'U-pattern') serve as a template for suppletion. It is also the case that these patterns are less 'coherent', in terms of the cells they involve, than TAM morphemes and the N-pattern morphome. If suppletion, like other types of refunctionalization, involves a principle of 'core-to-core' mapping, then it may just be that the L- and U-patterns are simply too incoherent for any 'core' to be discerned, with the result that the process is blocked.

13.4 Defectiveness and the morphome

Having briefly discussed apparent correlations between suppletion and the morphomic patterns found in the Romance verb, I turn now to possible correlations between these same patterns and the morphological phenomenon of defectiveness, in which certain cells of the paradigm remain unfilled.

Class defectiveness or whole-paradigm defectiveness may seem as vacuous a concept synchronically as class suppletion. If all the cells of the paradigm are unfilled, then surely the verb simply isn't there? At a pinch, class defectiveness might be invoked to account for such phenomena as the 'covert verbs' which may realize 'little v' in Larson's VP-shell hypothesis (Larson 1988) and other proposals for 'silent verbs', from early Generative Semantics (see, for instance, Lakoff 1968) to, most recently, Kayne 2009—although such an analysis is by no means self-evident.

However, when discussing defectiveness in subsets of the paradigm, we are on much firmer ground. Defectiveness is found in coherent subsets of the paradigm (i.e. in some covert morphomes); compare French *ardre* 'burn', which has lost most of the full paradigm it had at earlier stages of the language, but survives in literary French solely in the imperfect *j'ardais*, etc. (Grevisse and Goosse 2011: §878). As far as overt TAM morphomes are concerned, examples of Fuèc-defectiveness are difficult to find, but a possible candidate for Fuèc-*complement* defectiveness (i.e. where the future and conditional are the only cells in the paradigm to be filled, rather than the only cells in the paradigm to be empty) involves French *occire* 'kill', which now exists only in the future and possibly the conditional (Grevisse and Goosse 2011: §878). PYTA-defectiveness is also found; compare French *traire* 'milk', *abstraire* 'abstract', *distraire* 'distract', *extraire* 'extract', *retraire* 'withdraw', 'milk again', *soustraire* 'subtract', etc.; *paître* 'graze' (Grevisse and Goosse 2011: §878). It should be stressed that these are cases of genuine defectiveness, and are not to be confused with the general disappearance of the PYTA forms of French (the preterite and the imperfect subjunctive) from the everyday spoken language (see, for instance, Foulet 1920, van Vliet 1983, Engel 1985).

Person-related morphomes may also serve as the locus of defectiveness. N-pattern defectiveness is found in Spanish and Portuguese (Maiden and O'Neill 2010, O'Neill 2011*a*), where it presupposes simultaneous L-pattern defectiveness. Thus, Spanish *abolir* 'abolish' has no present subjunctive and no singular persons or third person plural in the present indicative. An example of N-pattern-*complement* defectiveness (that is, where the singular persons and the third person plural of the present indicative are the only cells in the paradigm to be filled, rather than the only cells in the paradigm to be empty) involves French *clore* 'close' (Grevisse and Goosse 2011: §878). And, as just noted, L-pattern defectiveness is found in Spanish and Portuguese (Maiden and O'Neill 2010, O'Neill 2011*a*), sometimes, but not always, in conjunction with N-pattern defectiveness. However, U-pattern defectiveness appears not to exist (Martin Maiden, p.c.).

Finally, we can find defectiveness in several individually coherent subsets of the paradigm which, when taken together, do not have any coherent identity, yet which do not constitute a morphome (except by purely circular arguments of the type: 'This (single) instance of defectiveness affects this collection of cells; therefore this collection of cells constitutes a morphome'). Examples include French *frire* 'fry', which exists only in the singular persons of the present indicative and all persons of the future and conditional; and *gésir* 'lie', which exists in the present indicative and the imperfect indicative only (Grevisse and Goosse 2011: §878).

13.5 Some tentative conclusions

The foregoing constitutes more of a programme for future research than a basis for definite conclusions. However, certain threads emerge. I have distinguished between 'covert' and 'overt' morphomes, the former correlating with some extramorphological reality, the latter showing no such correlation. Within 'overt' morphomes, I have distinguished between class or whole-paradigm morphomes, which affect a subset of the lexicon, and paradigm-subset morphomes. These two categories of morphome are in a sense orthogonal to one another. Below, I present in tabular form the claims I have made in this chapter regarding paradigm-subset morphomes, whether covert or overt. The most coherent morphomes lie on the left, with coherence diminishing as one moves to the right. I am grateful to Grev Corbett (p.c.) for pointing out that a morphome which is 'canonical' (in the sense of Corbett 2007*a*) would lie on the extreme right of the table.

More coherent   Less coherent

covert   *overt*

Functionally coherent stems	TAM morphomes	Person-related morphomes		
		more coherent		less coherent
	Fuèc PYTA	N-pattern	L-pattern	U-pattern
suppletion				
defectiveness				

Defectiveness appears to operate in a less constrained set of environments than suppletion—it involves a greater range of non-class morphomes, and it may not be wholly vacuous to speak of synchronic class defectiveness. And, as we have seen, defectiveness can not only be clearly morphomic, it can also exist in patterns which are not otherwise morphomic (that is, patterns which could be defined as morphomic only on the basis of the defectiveness itself). In addition, some instances of morphomic defectiveness appear to involve complementarity, in that they affect either the set of cells which constitutes the morphome or its complement. Why should these differences between the two phenomena exist? I suggest that the answer may lie in the different motivation of defectiveness and suppletion. As noted by Baerman and Corbett (2010: 17): 'Any given instance of defectiveness likely involves multiple factors, whose individual contribution we are seldom in a position to sort out.' The implication is that there is seldom, if ever, a clear-cut opposition between 'core' and 'non-core' values in the distribution of defectiveness. Moreover, as one of the terms involved is 'zero', it is not really possible to see defectiveness as an example of refunctionalization, which requires an opposition between two full morphological entities. Suppletion, on the other hand, always represents a refunctionalization.[3] The notion of 'core' is therefore relevant—indeed, crucial—for suppletion, and if no 'core' can be discerned, then suppletion will arguably be blocked. In contrast, as just noted, defectiveness does not require a notion of 'core', even though it may be sensitive to the coherence of the cells involved, and is therefore found in a greater variety of contexts. For the moment, I advance this view as a tentative hypothesis— much more work is required on these issues.

[3] This statement holds diachronically. However, as Martin Maiden points out to me, there are rare instances of what appears to be suppletion synchronically (and hence presumably constitutes psychologically real suppletion for native speakers) which arise from phonological change. A case in point is the Romanian verb *a lua* 'take', in which regular sound change has yielded a present-tense paradigm which synchronically appears to exhibit N-pattern suppletion: *iau, iai, ia, luăm, luaţi, iau.*

14

Beyond the stem and inflectional morphology: an irregular pattern at the level of periphrasis

SILVIO CRUSCHINA

14.1 Introduction

Periphrases are traditionally understood as multiword constructions expressing a specific set of grammatical properties: in this respect, they clearly play the same role as inflection. However, when they are considered as a whole, periphrases typically straddle the border between two major linguistic components: morphology and syntax. Many scholars, especially in the Chomskyan tradition, have endorsed a reductionist approach that attempts to treat periphrasis as the product of ordinary syntax (cf. Belletti 1990, Cinque 1999, Giorgi and Pianesi 1997). Others have instead focused on the interaction between periphrastic constructions and morphology, and in particular on their integration within the inflectional paradigm (cf. Spencer 2001, Ackerman and Stump 2004). By adopting different perspectives, these approaches submit two divergent definitions of periphrasis. According to the reductionist approach, a periphrasis is really an instance of canonical syntax that includes one or more functional elements, and that expresses specific grammatical features. By contrast, in the inflectional integration approach a periphrasis is generally defined as a multiword combination that fills a cell in the inflectional paradigm of a lexeme (cf. Brown *et al.* 2012).

The reductionist approach has been criticized for leading to systematic overgeneralizations, and for failing to account for those periphrases whose meaning is characterized by combinatory opacity rather than being the predictable sum of the meanings of their parts. The definition formulated and adopted within the inflectional integration approach, on the other hand, rules out multiword constructions that are generally seen as periphrastic but that have no direct links to an inflectional paradigm. The idea of accounting for the relation between periphrastic and synthetic forms by extending the resources of morphology was first proposed by Börjars *et al.* (1997), and has been further elaborated in the framework of Paradigm Function Morphology by Sadler and Spencer (2001), Spencer (2001), and Ackerman and Stump (2004). More specifically, within this framework, scholars have concentrated on inflectional periphrases, namely, periphrastic constructions that are not the result of free syntactic combinations, but instead realize cells in the inflectional paradigms of lexemes. In order to qualify as an inflectional periphrasis, a syntactic construction must therefore express a grammatical property that is typically realized inflectionally, and must interact 'with inflectional morphology in such a way that it is best integrated in the inflectional paradigm' (Bonami and Samvelian 2009*b*: 1). Inflectional periphrases correspond to Haspelmath's (2000, 2002) *suppletive periphrases*, namely, gap-filling periphrases. If no synthetic form expressing the same grammatical categories exists in the language in which it occurs, the periphrasis in question will stand out as a *categorial periphrasis* (e.g. the French *aller*-future, and the Spanish *estar*-progressive, which are both entirely periphrastic).

While wholly syntactic accounts fail to capture the relation between the syntactic form of the periphrasis and its morphological function, the model of Paradigm Function Morphology runs into the opposite problem, in that the properties of a periphrasis that are not inflectional—at least not according to traditional grammars—and that are not directly related to its paradigmatic function are often disregarded. In the latter approach, syntax is overlooked and, in a sense, too unconstrained (cf. Bonami and Webelhuth 2011).

Their intermediate status between ordinary syntax and pure morphology has led to a special treatment for periphrases with reference to grammaticalization. If periphrases are seen as the result of a process of grammaticalization from lexical collocations towards new patterns of inflectional morphology, it must be acknowledged that they have a gradient nature, and the possibility of identifying intermediate states ranging from open syntactic combination to full morphologization must be accepted. In fact, different degrees, or types, of periphrasis have indeed been recognized. On the basis of the stage of grammaticalization and of the semantic transparency or opacity of the periphrasis, Vincent (2011: 424) distinguishes four logically possible and attested patterns:

  (i) purely syntactic constructions: e.g. *est amans* in early/Classical Latin;
  (ii) morphologically exploited but transparent periphrases: e.g. *amaturus est* in all attested stages and *est amans* in Biblical Latin;
  (iii) opaque periphrases: e.g. Lat. *amatus est,* and perhaps French *il a aimé* (in its preterite sense);
  (iv) morphologized periphrases: e.g. Italian *amerebbe* < Lat. *amare habuit.*

This approach has led grammaticalization theorists to observe that the distinction between periphrastic and non-periphrastic formations is not always clear-cut, as proved by the fact that a variety of intermediate combinatory stages are attested cross-linguistically (cf. e.g. Vincent 1987*b*, 2011, Hopper and Traugott 2003). Under this line of research, both paradigmatic (*suppletive*) and non-paradigmatic (*categorial*) periphrases are possible and may be connected with the morphological component of the grammar. The periphrastic expression may exist in order to fill a gap in the inflectional paradigm of a lexeme, but this function is by no means a prerequisite for a periphrasis to be treated as (partially or entirely) morphological. Other paradigm-independent factors should be analysed before determining whether a periphrasis is syntactic, morphological, or intermediate in nature, the prediction being that the more a periphrastic construction is grammaticalized, the more it can be claimed to have a morphological status.

This chapter examines the properties of a special periphrastic construction found in Sicilian and other southern Italian dialects. This construction does not meet the criteria proposed for the definition of inflectional periphrases within the framework of Paradigm Function Morphology; nevertheless, it displays properties typical of highly grammaticalized structures and shows features that are peculiar to the morphological domain. In particular, the irregular distribution of this construction in some dialects has been widely attested at the morphological levels of stem and inflection, and this is thus pertinent to the question of the boundary between phenomena that are purely morphological and those that are dependent on syntax. Our analysis will lead us to the conclusion that it is the degree of grammaticalization of a periphrasis, rather than its interaction and integration with a lexeme's inflectional paradigm, which is the deciding factor in determining whether the construction enters the morphological domain, and must therefore be treated morphologically.

14.2 The Sicilian doubly inflected construction (DIC)

The Sicilian doubly inflected construction (henceforth DIC) comprises, as the name suggests, two inflected verbs. The first must be a motion verb (i.e. *jiri* 'go', *viniri* 'come', *passari* 'come round (to someone's place)'), and must be followed by a second inflected verb. The two verbs are inflected for the same features and are connected by the preposition *a* 'to':

(1) Vaju   a mangiu.
     go.PRS.IND.1SG   to eat.PRS.IND.1SG
     'I am going to eat.'

(2) U   veni   a piglia   cu   a   machina.
     him.CL come.PRS.IND.3SG to collect.PRS.IND.3SG with the car
     'He is coming to pick him up by car.'

Periphrastic constructions involving a motion verb followed by another verb are very common in the Romance languages. However, the semantic evolution of this kind of periphrasis is varied: it has retained a movement meaning in Italian, has developed into a future tense in Spanish and in French, and has acquired a preterite function in Catalan (cf. e.g. Squartini 1998, Taylor 2011). Despite the specific semantic and functional properties of the periphrasis, in these languages the second verb is always an infinitive. By contrast, the peculiarity of Sicilian DIC lies precisely in the finite inflection of the main verb that follows the motion verb.[1] DIC is found in all Sicilian varieties, but with different paradigms in different parts of the island. In central and western Sicily, the construction is characterized by the defective paradigm shown in Table 14.1.[2]

No realizations correspond to the grey cells of Table 14.1. DIC is in fact used only in the present indicative, except for the first and second persons plural, and in the second person singular of the imperative. This distribution closely, and strikingly, resembles the irregular morphological patterns widely attested in Romance at the level of stem alternation and inflection (cf. Maiden 2004a, 2011a). This construction and its particular distribution raise a series of questions directly concerning the issue of the boundary between syntax and morphology: is DIC a canonical syntactic construction or is it instead a morphological periphrasis? Even if we assume that it qualifies as a periphrasis proper, in what sense would it be a morphological periphrastic construction?

The notion of inflectional paradigm does not prove very helpful in this respect. First of all, it is not immediately clear whether or not we are dealing with an

TABLE 14.1 **The defective paradigm of the Sicilian doubly inflected construction**

Mood	Indicative				Subjunctive	Imperative
Tense		Present	Imperfect	Preterite	Imperfect	
Sg	1	vaju a mangiu				
	2	va(i) a mangi				va (a) mangia
	3	va a mangia				
Pl	1					
	2					
	3	vannu a mangianu				

[1] The infinitival construction is also available in Sicilian, although it might be argued that its presence is due to an influence or a 'borrowing' from Italian. Some syntactic and semantic differences between DIC and the infinitival construction in Sicilian will be discussed below.

[2] The verb forms provided in Table 14.1 are from the variety spoken in Mussomeli, in the province of Caltanissetta. As stated previously, the distribution is the same in all dialects spoken in central and western Sicily, but the precise morphological endings may vary from dialect to dialect.

inflectional paradigm at all, in that the base element (i.e. the lexeme) of this supposed paradigm is by no means obvious, and no explanation for its defectiveness immediately presents itself. When compared to traditional inflectional paradigms, the paradigm of DIC can only with difficulty be integrated into the systematic arrangement of all the inflected forms of the main verb entering the construction. The inflectional integration approach relies on the assumption that a paradigmatic system must be either entirely synthetic, or partly synthetic and partly analytic (cf. the 'feature intersection' criterion in Ackerman and Stump 2004), but cannot be entirely analytic. An additional controversial issue is thus whether it is necessary to postulate an independent and autonomous paradigm at the level of the periphrasis.

Before addressing these questions, let us consider the syntactic properties of DIC that reflect its degree of grammaticalization. These properties will shed light on some of the questions above and will serve as a diagnostics for understanding the grammatical status of DIC and for identifying its proximity to morphologization.

14.2.1 *Syntactic properties and degree of grammaticalization*

In their analysis of DIC in Marsalese, the western Sicilian dialect spoken in Marsala, Cardinaletti and Giusti (2001, 2003) show that this analytic construction displays properties typical of monoclausal periphrastic structures whose first element (V1) is a functional verb or an auxiliary, and the second element (V2) is a lexical verb. These properties include obligatory clitic climbing, 'single event' interpretation, indivisibility, incompatibility with the arguments and the adjuncts typically associated with motion verbs, and phonologically reduced or invariant forms of V1.

Clitic pronouns that substitute for one or two arguments selected by the construction—by the second verb in fact, as will be shown below—can only be inserted to the left of V1, and are banned from any other position:

(3) U   veni   a   piglia   dopu.
     him.CL   come.PRS.IND.3SG   to   collect.PRS.IND.3SG   later
     'He is coming to pick him up later.'

(4) Ci   va   a   accatta   u   pani   tutti i   matini.
    there.CL   go.PRS.IND.3SG   to   buy.PRS.IND.3SG   the bread   all   the mornings
    'He buys the bread there every morning.'

(5) Ci-u   vaiu   a   dicu.
     to-him.CL-it.CL   go.PRS.IND.1SG   to   say.PRS.IND.1SG
     'I am going to tell it to him.'

This restriction clearly shows that, syntactically, DIC behaves as a single finite verbal constituent that requires the pronominal elements to appear in a proclitic position.[3] In this respect, DIC patterns with the other periphrastic structures found in the same language, such as the compound verb forms involving the auxiliary 'have' and the past participle of a lexical verb (e.g. the present perfect *aju mangiuatu* 'I have eaten').

From a semantic viewpoint, the motion verb does not contribute an independent event to the overall construction, which has thus a 'single event' interpretation. If we compare DIC with the infinitival construction, we observe that while with the latter the event expressed by the second verb can be negated or denied, the same is not possible with the inflected construction:[4]

(6) a. Vaju   a   accattari   a   cicoria   gnignornu,   ma   unn'
      go.1SG   to   buy.INF   the   chicory   every-day   but   not
      a   trovu   mai.
      it.CL   find.PRS.1SG   never

    b. *Vaju   a   accattu   a   cicoria   gnignornu,   ma
      go.1SG   to   buy.PRES.1SG   the   chicory   every-day   but
      unn'   a   trovu   mai.
      not   it.CL   find.PRS.1SG   never
      'I go to buy chicory every day, but never find it'.

The second sentence in (6a) negates the event denoted by the verb 'to buy', while the event expressed by the motion verb still holds. The speaker does not manage to buy the chicory, but still goes every day with the intention of doing so: only the buying-event is denied, not the going-event. In the corresponding DIC sentence, the motion verb and the main verb are interpreted as building a single event, so any attempt to deny part of it amounts to denying the event as a whole, creating a semantic contradiction, as in (6b).

---

[3] The infinitival construction also admits enclisis to the infinitive, regulated in accordance with the restructuring rule (cf. Rizzi 1982, Cinque 2006):

(i)   a.   U   veni   a   pigliari   dopu.
         him.CL   come.PRS.IND.3SG   to   collect.INF   later

     b.   ?Veni   a   pigliarlu   dopu.
         come.PRS.IND.3SG   to   collect.INF-him.CL   later
         'He is coming to pick him up later.'

In restructuring constructions, Sicilian generally exhibits a strong preference for proclisis, but the enclitic position of the pronominal form does not give rise to total ungrammaticality, as shown in example (ib).

[4] The examples in the rest of this section and the relevant discussion are from Cardinaletti and Giusti (2001). Also see Cardinaletti and Giusti (2001) for an interesting comparison between Sicilian DIC and similar constructions in English and in other Germanic languages.

V1 and V2 cannot be separated, except by the connecting preposition *a*,[5] and no intervening element can occur between the two verbs, be it a clitic pronoun (7) or an adverb (8):

(7) *Veni   a   u   piglia   dopu.
     come.PRS.IND.3SG to   him.CL collect.PRS.IND.3SG later
     'He is coming to pick him up later.'

(8) *Va   sempri a   accatta   u   pani.
     go.PRS.IND.3SG always to   buy.PRS.IND.3SG the   bread
     'He always goes to buy bread.'

The motion verb involved in DIC has lost its full lexical meaning of movement. The construction is therefore incompatible with the arguments (9b) or the adjuncts (10b) typically selected by this category of verbs, which are instead possible with their infinitival counterparts:

(9) a. Va   (agghiri   a   casa) a   mangiari (*agghiri a   casa).
         go.3SG towards   to   home   to   eat.INF   towards   to   home
     b. Va   (*agghiri a   casa) a   mangia   (*agghiri a   casa).
         go.3SG towards   to   home   to   eat.3SG   towards   to   home
         'He goes towards home to eat.'

(10) a. Peppe   va   a   mangiari   c'a   machina.
         Peppe   go.3SG to   eat.INF   with-the   car
     b. *Peppe va   a   mangia   c'a   machina.
         Peppe   go.3SG to   eat.3SG   with-the   car
         'Peppe goes to eat by car.'

A directional complement is acceptable in (9a) but not in (9b). Equally, a modifying adjunct can only appear in (10a), but not in (10b). The tests above show that DIC does not behave like a biclausal construction, and Cardinaletti and Giusti (2001) further argue that it should not be analysed as a structure involving coordination. Object extraction, which is generally barred from genuine coordination constructions, is in fact admitted with DIC:

(11) a. U$_i$ vajo   a   pigghio   t$_i$
         it.CL   go.1SG   to   fetch.1SG
         'I go and take it.'
     b. Cu   soccu$_i$ vai   a   aggiusti   a   machina   t$_i$?
         with what   go.2SG   to   fix.PRES.2SG   the car
         'What do you go and fix the car with?'

---

[5] I will return to the status of *a* in the next section.

Special features are also found at the morphological level. When inserted in DIC, the motion verb *jiri* 'to go' alternates, especially in fast speech, with an invariant reduced form, homophonous with the third person singular indicative, and with the second person singular imperative:

(12) 1SG *vaju*   a pigghiu   / *va* a pigghiu
      2SG *vai*   a pigghi   / *va* a pigghi
      3SG *va*   a pigghia   / *va* a pigghia
      3PL *vannu* a pigghianu / *va* a pigghianu

Despite the properties described so far, the periphrastic status of DIC is not uncontroversial. As mentioned previously, no corresponding synthetic forms of this construction exist in Sicilian. DIC is an inflectional or suppletive periphrasis because it does not fill a gap in the paradigm. In particular, Sicilian DIC does not conform to Ackerman and Stump's (2004) criteria for the definition of an inflectional periphrasis. These criteria are feature intersection, distributed exponence, and non-compositionality.

A periphrasis is said to be characterized by feature intersection when each of the property set denoted by the periphrasis is also expressed synthetically within the same language. The first problem with this criterion is the identification of the grammatical properties expressed by DIC. I will discuss the issue of the precise meaning of DIC in Section 14.5, but it is already clear from Table 14.1 that this construction is entirely analytic. Assessing the second criterion is also problematic. Distributed exponence refers to the situation in which the exponents of the features associated with the periphrasis are distributed over the elements of the construction. In regard to features such as person and number, Sicilian DIC in fact displays double morphological exponence, inasmuch as the morphological features conveyed by the inflection are repeated on both verbs. Compositionality obtains when the grammatical features of the construction as a whole are expressed by a combination of the features associated with its parts. Inflectional periphrases are non-compositional, in the sense that they do not build their meaning compositionally; rather, some features of the components often appear in contradiction with the overall features of the construction. In its most common use, the meaning of Sicilian DIC seems to be determined by the meaning of its constituents, but this is not always the case (see §14.5 below). On the basis of these observations, we can conclude that Sicilian DIC does not fall into the category of inflectional periphrases.

However, within the study of grammaticalization, several authors do not associate the term 'periphrasis' with inflectional paradigms (cf. Lehmann 1995: 29, Bybee *et al.* 1994: 133), and treat as a periphrasis any structure that expresses a grammatical meaning through a multiword construction. In this framework, the fundamental question shifts from the identification of defining criteria for periphrasis to the recognition of accepted defining criteria for a grammatical meaning, and hence for a grammaticalized structure. The question of what counts as a grammatical meaning is by no means trivial. In general, all and only the meanings that are clearly grammaticalized in a language with which linguists are very familiar (e.g. Latin or English) are considered as grammatical. Although there are evident problems with the defining criteria of a periphrasis from a grammaticalization point of view, many well-established and sound proposals can be found in the literature (cf. Heine 1993, Bertinetto 1990, Squartini 1998, Haspelmath 2000). If we take into account the well-studied mechanisms of grammaticalization, such as those discussed in Heine (1993) as basic parameters in the grammaticalization of auxiliaries, we realize that Sicilian DIC possesses all the hallmarks of a grammaticalized structure. The DIC motion verb shares all the essential elements of these parameters:

(a) desemanticization of the original lexical value;
(b) decategorialization, i.e. gradual loss of its morphosyntactic status as a full verb;
(c) cliticization, i.e. loss of autonomous word status;
(d) phonological erosion.

Although the motion verb does still contribute to the meaning of the construction as a whole, we have seen that it does not denote an independent event, nor does it preserve the thematic structure typical of the verbs of this class. The invariant form alternating with the fully inflected variants provides evidence for its decategorialization, as well as for phonological erosion and a tendency towards cliticization (cf. also §14.4). Under this view, Sicilian DIC would therefore count as a fully-fledged periphrasis.

14.2.2 *Sicilian DIC and serial verb constructions*

In this section I will explore the hypothesis that Sicilian DIC may be treated as a serial verb construction (SVC). Such an analysis would be able to capture both its morphosyntactic and its semantic properties. Cardinaletti and Giusti (2001) openly reject this possibility on the basis of the lack of object sharing and the presence of a connecting element. According to Baker (1989), and others after him, serial verbs must share the same object. This definition is rather strict, and would certainly exclude Sicilian DIC (cf. Manzini and Savoia 2005, I: 700).[6] A less rigid statement is provided by Aikhenvald (2006: 12): 'Prototypical serial verb constructions share at least one argument. Serial verb constructions with no shared arguments are comparatively rare, but not non-existent.' The two verbs in Sicilian DIC always, and necessarily, share the subject, as witnessed by the person and number agreement on

---

[6] Baker (1989) argues that serializing languages allow double-headed VPs. This property licenses a structure in which a V' contains both a V and a V' category. Since the two verbs are heads of the VP, they can both assign internal θ-roles to an NP within their shared maximal projection.

the ending of both verbs. The second issue that poses a problem for the classification of Sicilian DIC as an SVC is the presence of the connecting element *a*. Two hypotheses are found in the literature regarding the origins of *a*: (i) it comes from the Latin preposition AD; and (ii) it derives from the Latin coordinating conjunction AC used in spoken and late Latin (cf. Rohlfs 1969: §§710, 761). Indeed, in some cognate Calabrian dialects the connective element is the same as the coordinating conjunction *e* (cf. Rohlfs 1969: §759). However, the existence of an element connecting the two verbs is at odds with the classical definition of serial verb constructions. This emerges in Aikhenvald's outline of the main properties of a serial verb construction (SVC):

(13)   A serial verb construction is a sequence of verbs which act together as a single predicate, without any overt marker of coordination, subordination, or syntactic dependency of any other sort. Serial verb constructions describe what is conceptualized as a single event. They are monoclausal. [. . .] Each component of an SVC must be able to occur on its own

(Aikhenvald 2006: 1)

This definition strikingly includes all the other characteristics that we have observed for Sicilian DIC: it is monoclausal and expresses a single event. Moreover, its components can occur independently. The role of the element *a* within the construction is an interesting issue. Since it occurs in a monoclausal construction, this element clearly does not mark any sort of dependency between the two verbs, and its function is essentially equal to that of a desemanticized linker. As such, its presence does not impinge on the nature of DIC and on its possible identification as an SVC. This is acknowledged by Aikhenvald herself, who states that SVCs 'can, however, include a special marker which distinguishes an SVC from other types of constructions but does not mark any dependency relations between the components' (Aikhenvald 2006: 20).

In addition, the connecting element is absent in the imperative, and can be omitted in some Sicilian dialects such as Pantesco, spoken in the island of Pantelleria (cf. Tropea 1988):

(14)   a. vaju   vidu   b. vegnu   manciu
           go.1SG   see.1SG   come.1SG   eat.1SG

The variation observed with respect to the realization of this element could not be explained if a specific meaning or function was assigned to it. We can therefore conclude that the properties of DIC are best captured under the view that it constitutes an SVC, and more precisely an asymmetrical SVC. Aikhenvald (2006: 3, 22) distinguishes two types of SVC according to their composition: SYMMETRICAL serial verb constructions consisting of two or more verbs each belonging to a semantically and grammatically unrestricted class, and ASYMMETRICAL serial verb constructions, which involve one verb from a grammatically or semantically restricted class (e.g. motion or posture verbs) and one verb from an open class. The two verbs in the latter type of construction are sometimes known as the 'minor' verb and the 'major' verb, respectively. As is the case with the motion verb in DIC, the 'minor' verb of an asymmetrical SVC can still retain full lexical status in the language outside the construction in which it has been grammaticalized.

Despite its many advantages in accounting for the morphosyntactic and semantic properties of Sicilian DIC, the SVC analysis is not able to explain the peculiar defective distribution of this construction outlined in Table 14.1. In the next section, I will argue that the defective paradigm of DIC must be accounted for independently of its SVC features, and must be attributed to the application of a general morphological pattern found pervasively across Romance. The analysis of DIC as an SVC will again prove helpful in the discussion of the grammatical meaning of DIC (cf. §14.5).

14.3 Morphological properties and morphomic defectiveness

Cardinaletti and Giusti (2001, 2003) try to account for the morphological restrictions of Sicilian DIC in terms of allomorphy and markedness. They assume that the defective paradigm is an effect of the stem alternation of the two major motion verbs involved in the construction. Only the forms that are built on the allomorph *va-* for *iri* 'go' and *ve-* for *viniri* 'come' can combine with a second inflected verb. Interestingly, these forms are found in exactly the same cells of the paradigm as those that admit DIC. The paradigms of the present indicative and the imperative of these two verbs in Marsalese are given in Table 14.2 (from Cardinaletti and Giusti 2001: 381).

This inherited irregular distribution is explained by the two authors as a markedness phenomenon, in the sense that DIC is only possible with the less marked forms of the verbal paradigm, i.e. with specific persons of the present indicative and the imperative. The other tenses and moods are built on the other, allegedly more marked, allomorph. Present tense would thus be less marked than preterite,

TABLE 14.2 Paradigms of *iri* 'go' and *viniri* 'come' in Marsalese

Indicative	IRI	VINIRI	*Imperative*	IRI	VINIRI
1SG	vaju	vegnu			
2SG	vai	veni	2SG	va	veni
3SG	va	veni			
1PL	emu	vinemu			
2PL	iti	viniti	2PL	iti	viniti
3PL	vannu	vennu			

indicative less marked than subjunctive, singular less marked than plural, and, finally, third person less marked than first and second person.

It is undoubtedly true that the defective distribution of DIC parallels the stem allomorphy of the two motion verbs. However, the hypothesis that this distribution is simply 'inherited' historically or constrained by the inflectional paradigm of its components is not tenable. Other wholly regular motion verbs (i.e. *passari* 'come round') can be involved in the same inflected construction and retain the very same defective distribution.[7] Cardinaletti and Giusti (2003: 44) adopt a rather costly hypothesis to account for the fact that the other verb entering DIC does not display the same morphological stem alternation. They suppose that this verb also has two homophonous allophones in the lexicon, and that 'in Marsalese only the allomorphs which realize 1st, 2nd, 3rd singular, and 3rd plural are listed in the lexicon as functional verbs entering the inflected construction'.

I would like to propose an alternative explanation for the defective paradigm of DIC, which avoids the problems connected to the hypothesis of an inherited irregularity. As already mentioned (cf. §14.1), the paradigmatic distribution of DIC corresponds to a characteristic and recurrent pattern in verbal inflectional morphology in the Romance languages, including Sicilian, namely the N-pattern (Maiden 2004*a*, 2005*a*, 2011*a*), which is also present in defective paradigms (cf. Maiden and O'Neill 2010). The motivation for this distribution appears to be purely morphological in nature, i.e. the imposition and reproduction of a 'morphomic' subdivision of the cells of a paradigm (cf. Aronoff 1994), according to a pattern—the N-pattern— which is pervasively found in Romance and which does not align with any morphosyntactic meaning.

That no morphosyntactic restrictions or semantic principles can be considered responsible for the irregular distribution of DIC is further confirmed by both diachronic and synchronic data. Historically, more cells of the paradigm were filled with the expected forms, leading to the assumption that DIC had a more extended paradigm:[8]

(15) a. Ci   lu   **iju**   a   dissi   (Pitrè III, 229)
          to-him.CL   it.CL   go.PST.3SG   to   say.PST.3SG
          'I went to tell him.'

      b. **Iju**   a   vitti   lu   Cummentu   (Pitrè III, 232)
          go.PST.3SG   to   see.PST.3SG   the   convent
          'I went to see the Convent.'

---

[7] Cardinaletti and Giusti are aware of the weakness of this hypothesis, and openly state that 'allomorphy cannot be taken as the ultimate cause of the inflectional restrictions on the inflected construction' (Cardinaletti and Giusti 2001: 381).

[8] The following examples are cited in Wilson (1999) and are from the collection of Sicilian tales and short stories by Giuseppe Pitrè, published in 1875.

Table 14.3 DIC in the dialect of Modica

Present Indicative (V1 = 'go', V2 = 'eat')

'vaju a m'maɲʧu	1SG
'vai a m'maɲʧi	2SG
'va a m'maɲʧa	3SG
'jemu a mmaɲ'ʧamu	1PL
'iti a mmaɲ'ʧati	2PL
'vannu a m'maɲʧunu	3PL

Imperfect Indicative (it.CL + V1 = 'go', V2 = 'do')

u 'ia a ffa'ʃia	1SG
u 'jeutu a ffa'ʃieutu	2SG
u 'ia a ffa'ʃia	3SG
u 'jeumu a ffa'ʃieumu	1PL
u 'jeubbu a ffa'ʃieubbu	2PL
u 'jeunnu a ffa'ʃieunu	3PL

Preterite (it.CL + V1 = 'go', V2 = 'do')

u ji a f fiʃi	1SG
u 'jeru a f fiʃiru	3PL

Synchronically, moreover, some eastern Sicilian varieties display a full (or more complete) paradigm (cf. Sornicola 1976, Leone 1995, Manzini and Savoia 2005). Table 14.3 shows that in the dialect of Modica, DIC is also possible in the imperfect and in the preterite, with no person restrictions (cf. Manzini and Savoia 2005, I: 696).[9]

Under the N-pattern account, the distributional similarity between stem allomorphy (Table 14.2) and the defective paradigm of DIC (Table 14.1) is both less striking and less puzzling. Periphrases, at least grammaticalized periphrases, behave like other morphological formations, and are subject to the same distributional patterns of irregularity. We therefore expect to find at the level of periphrasis the same types of morphome and morphomic split as in inflectional morphology, an expectation supported by the evidence discussed in the next section.

14.4 Morphomic splits at the level of periphrasis

In the previous section, I put forward the hypothesis that the resource of irregular morphology should be extended to grammaticalized periphrases, which are therefore expected to display the same patterns of irregularity as stem and inflectional morphology. If we consider the N-pattern, there is evidence suggesting that this

---

[9] I report the partial paradigm here, as given in Manzini and Savoia (2005), of the forms with 'go' as V1, but the paradigm is actually complete in this Sicilian variety, as stated in the literature and as personally checked with native speakers.

morphomic irregular distribution is also found at the level of periphrasis, in the periphrastic equivalents of suppletion, allomorphy, and defectiveness.

We have already seen that the paradigm of DIC is characterized by a defective N-pattern distribution of the same type as found in fully synthetic paradigms (cf. Maiden and O'Neill 2010). The distribution of DIC is in fact internally motivated and does not find any external or semantic justification. This clearly contrasts with other periphrastic constructions in the same language with semantically motivated defectiveness, such as the progressive construction with *stari* 'stay' + gerund,[10] as well as with fully regular periphrastic constructions. An example of fully regular (and non-defective) categorial periphrasis is the deontic construction *aviri a* 'have to' + infinitive in Sicilian and other southern Italian dialects, which is used to express deontic modality (and sometimes future). In these varieties, deontic modality is expressed entirely and exclusively periphrastically, as no lexical verbs with a synthetic paradigm corresponding to 'must' exist in the language.

A possible case of periphrastic N-pattern suppletion is identified in Maiden (2004*a*: 240–2) for the verb 'to go' in the Romanian dialect of Fundătura. The verb *a merge* 'go' and the reflexive form of the verb *a duce* 'bring', namely *a se duce* 'take oneself, go' (where *se* is a reflexive pronoun, variable according to person and number), compete and alternate in different ways according to the dialect. A tendency towards an N-pattern distribution is visible in some dialects, including Fundătura, in which, as shown in Table 14.4, the forms of the verb *a merge* are replaced by the forms of *a se duce* in all the cells of the present tense except first and second plural.

A similar phenomenon of suppletion between a synthetic and a periphrastic paradigm has been observed for the verb *dvér* 'must' in Romagnolo, a dialect spoken in the Italian region of Emilia–Romagna. Pelliciardi (1977: 135) reports that the singular persons and the third person plural of the present indicative, and the persons of the present subjunctive and of the imperative are missing from the paradigm of this verb. They are replaced by the periphrastic locution 'have to' (e.g. *a j ò da* 'I have to', *t'è da* 'you have to', *l'à da* 'he has to'):

(16) tè   t'   è   da   stêr   zèt
      you   SCL   have.2SG   to   stay.INF   silent
      'You have to be quiet.'

It is clear from the description of the cells where the replacement occurs that this case of suppletion also leads to an N-pattern distribution.

Phenomena of N-pattern allomorphy are found in the paradigms of doubly inflected constructions similar to Sicilian DIC, and concern in particular the first

---

[10] The progressive construction is not possible in perfective tenses, but this is due to a semantic incompatibility and is therefore externally motivated (cf. Squartini 1998).

Table 14.4 The verb 'to go' in the Romanian dialect of Fundătura

PRESENT	SINGULAR	PLURAL
1	mə duk	'mɛrem
2	tʲe duc	'mɛrets
3	sə 'duce	sə duk

Table 14.5 The progressive construction in the dialect of Putignano

PRESENT INDICATIVE	V1 = 'stay'	V2 = 'do'	lexical STARE
u stok a ffattsə	1SG	1SG	'stokə
u ste f fafə	2SG	2SG	stiə
u ste f fafə	3SG	3SG	stiə
u sta ffa'ʃeimə	invariant	1PL	'stamə
u sta ffa'ʃeitə	invariant	2PL	'statə
u ston a ffaʃənə	3PL	3PL	'stɔnə
IMPERFECT INDICATIVE			
u sta ffa'ʃevə	invariant	1SG	'stavə
u sta ffa'ʃivə	invariant	2SG	'stivə
u sta ffa'ʃevə	invariant	3SG	'stavə
u sta ffa'ʃemmə	invariant	1PL	'stammə
u sta ffa'ʃivəvə	invariant	2PL	'stivəvə
u sta ffa'ʃivənə	invariant	3PL	'stavənə

verb of the construction. The doubly inflected progressive construction 'STARE ('stay') + inflected verb' in the southern Italian dialect of Putignano, in Puglia, displays an invariable form of V1 (i.e. *sta*) in all cells of the paradigm except the singular persons and the third person plural of the present indicative, where another inflected form is found (Manzini and Savoia 2005, I: 689). In Table 14.5, the invariant forms of functional STARE in the doubly inflected construction can be compared with the corresponding forms of the verb when it is used lexically.

A process of grammaticalization may be considered responsible for the phonological erosion observed. The grammaticalization of V1 in a doubly inflected construction is more evident in the dialect of Mesagne (Manzini and Savoia 2005, I: 691), in Puglia, both in the andative (cf. Table 14.6a) and in the progressive (cf. Table 14.6b) construction. In fact, in these cases it would be inaccurate to speak of doubly inflected constructions, as V1 has completely lost any trace of inflection. In the andative construction, however, two invariant forms alternate according to an

Table 14.6a The andative construction in the dialect of Mesagne

PRESENT INDICATIVE	V1 'go'	V2 'do'
lu va ffattsu	invariant 1	1SG
lu va ffatʃi	invariant 1	2SG
lu va ffatʃi	invariant 1	3SG
lu sa/ ʃa fa'tʃimu	invariant 2/ 3	1PL
lu sa/ ʃa fa'tʃiti	invariant 2/ 3	2PL
lu va ffannu	invariant 1	3PL
IMPERFECT INDICATIVE		
lu sa/ ʃa fa'tʃia	invariant 2/ 3	1SG
lu sa/ ʃa fa'tʃivi	invariant 2/ 3	2SG
lu sa/ ʃa fa'tʃia	invariant 2/ 3	3SG
lu sa/ ʃa fa'tʃiumu	invariant 2/ 3	1PL
lu sa/ ʃa fa'tʃiuvu	invariant 2/ 3	2PL
lu sa/ ʃa fa'ʃiunu	invariant 2/ 3	3PL

Table 14.6b The progressive construction in the dialect of Mesagne

PRESENT INDICATIVE	V1 'stay'	V2 'do'
lu sta ffattsu	invariant	1SG
lu sta ffatʃi	invariant	2SG
lu sta ffatʃi	invariant	3SG
lu sta ffa'tʃimu	invariant	1PL
lu sta ffa'tʃiti	invariant	2PL
lu sta ffannu	invariant	3PL
IMPERFECT INDICATIVE		
lu sta ffa'tʃia	invariant	1SG
lu sta ffa'tʃivi	invariant	2SG
lu sta ffa'tʃia	invariant	3SG
lu sta ffa'tʃiumu	invariant	1PL
lu sta ffa'tʃiuvu	invariant	2PL
lu sta ffa'ʃiunu	invariant	3PL

N-pattern distribution, with the second invariant form showing, in turn, a phonological variant.

In this dialect, V1 has evidently reached an advanced stage of grammaticalization, and can consequently be analysed as an invariable element, presumably a prefix, attached to the left of the main verb: it does not bear any inflection, and therefore does not carry any verbal information. Recall that a similarly invariable and impoverished form is possible with Sicilian DIC (cf. §14.2.1).

As far as inflection and the corresponding grammatical categories are concerned, different dialects display different variants of the periphrastic construction discussed in this chapter according to the state of grammaticalization of V1, which ranges from a fully inflected verb to an invariable and reduced preverbal element. It would be natural to wonder whether the dialectal variation observed could be significant in understanding the DIC paradigm change from full to defective. While a relationship between grammaticalization and the irregular distribution found in Sicilian and in other southern Italian dialects cannot be denied, it is far from clear how the process of grammaticalization could be seen as directly responsible for the patterns observed. It is more plausible to assume that during the process of change, the paradigm of the construction under consideration was 'attracted' to a recurrent pattern of irregularity, namely, the N-pattern.

14.5 The grammatical meaning of Sicilian DIC

Many authors, especially those working on grammaticalization (e.g. Bybee *et al.* 1994, Lehmann 1995, Hopper and Traugott 2003), do not presuppose any link between the use of the term 'periphrasis' and inflectional paradigms. According to these studies, a periphrasis is simply a multiword construction that expresses a grammatical meaning. We have so far discussed the syntactic and morphological status of the elements involved in DIC and in equivalent constructions in other southern Italian dialects, especially with respect to V1. It is now time to address the problem of the grammatical meaning associated with Sicilian DIC. Cardinaletti and Giusti (2001: 392) observe that in Sicilian DIC 'the motion verbs behave like lexical verbs in that they preserve their semantic content'. However, several scholars before them have pointed out cases in which the verb *jiri* 'go' in this construction has undergone desemanticization and has thus entirely lost its motion meaning (cf. Sornicola 1976, Leone 1973, 1978).

(17)	Vaiu	a	ssientu	ca	iddu	ci		fici	stu	tuortu
	go.1SG	to	hear.1SG	that	he	to-her.CL		made	this	wrong
	a	sso	mugghieri							
	to	his	wife							

'I heard that he did his wife such a wrong!'   (Sornicola 1976: 68)

Although it is generally true that it is difficult to find semantic differences between DIC and the corresponding construction with the infinitive, examples like (17) confirm that they are not always semantically identical. DIC cannot be replaced by the infinitival construction in this case:

(18) *Vaiu   a   ssentiri   ca   iddu   ci   fici   stu   tuortu
     go.1SG   to   hear.INF   that   he   to-her.CL   made   this   wrong

     a   sso   mugghieri
     to   his   wife

     'I heard that he did his wife such a wrong!'

I have collected further examples of DIC with a desemanticized V1 from the Sicilian dialect spoken in Mussomeli, in the province of Caltanissetta. The impossibility of an infinitival counterpart also holds for these examples:

(19) Cuannu   u   vitti   ca   sunava   nna   banna,
     when   him.CL   see.PST.1SG   that   play.IMPF.3SG   in-the   band

     vaju   a   pruvu   na   gioia!
     go.1SG   to   feel.1SG   a   joy

     'When I saw him play in the band, I felt such a joy!'

(20) Arrivammu   dda,   nn'u   ristoranti,   e   mi   vannu   a
     arrive.PST.1PL   there   in-the   restaurant   and   to-me.CL   go.3PL   to

     dunanu   na   pizza   accussì   ladia!
     give.3PL   a   pizza   so   ugly

     'We arrived there, at the restaurant, and they gave me such a bad pizza!'

(21) Ogellannu   va   a   capita   ca   ci   vinni
     last-year   go.3SG   to   happen.3SG   that   to-him.CL   come.PST.3SG

     a   frevi   tri   boti!
     the   fever   three   times

     'Last year it happened that he had a fever three times!'

It is important to note that in these examples DIC shows present tense inflection, but the reference time is actually past, as shown by the fact that the other verbs in the sentence are in the preterite. In addition, all these examples share a special emotional involvement of the speaker, which gives rise to an exclamative intonation. Let us first try to account for the instances in which DIC still preserves a motion meaning. I will then return to the cases of desemanticization in the past.

Once again, the parallelism with SVCs (serial verb constructions) is straightforward. SVCs with a motion meaning generally involve a so-called *andative* or *venitive* verb, that is, a deictic or directional verb (cf. e.g. Sebba 1987, Givón 1991, Aikhenvald 2006) that contributes a change of location and spatial deixis to the overall meaning denoted by the SVC. Andative verbs indicate movement away from the speaker or from the viewpoint location adopted by the speaker. Venitive verbs, instead, indicate movement towards the speaker or towards the viewpoint location adopted by the speaker. Cross-linguistically, venitive and andative verbs commonly derive from the verb 'to come' and 'to go', respectively, which appear to have undergone phono-logical reduction to auxiliary verbs or verbal affixes, and may ultimately be gram-maticalized to aspectual morphemes. We have already seen the variation concerning the different stages of grammaticalization and of phonological reduction in Sicilian and in other southern Italian dialects. Let us now consider the semantic contribution of the first verb according to the andative vs. venitive distinction:

(22)   a. Mangia!
          eat.IMP.2SG
          'Eat!'
       b. Va   mangia!
          go.IMP.2SG   eat.IMP.2SG
          '(Go to) eat!'
       c. Veni   mangia!
          come.IMP.2SG   eat.IMP.2SG
          '(Come to) eat!'

As expected, the main difference between DIC with an andative verb and DIC with a venitive verb is that the former expresses movement away from the speaker, while the latter indicates movement towards the speaker. This is clear in the imperative sentences in (22). When the main verb is used alone (22a), the imperative command or request does not imply a change of position or location. By contrast, in the two DIC sentences (22b, 22c) the first verb adds a motion requirement to the order or invitation conveyed by the second verb. The movement requisite entailed in DIC does not necessarily have to refer to the actual position of the speaker, but could simply follow the speaker's adopted viewpoint:

(23)   a. Maria u   va   a   pigglia   cu   a   machina.
          Maria him.CL   go.3SG   to   collect.3SG with   the   car
          'Maria is going to pick him up by car.'
       b. Maria u   veni   a   pigglia   cu   a   machina.
          Maria him.CL   come.3SG to   collect.3SG with   the   car
          'Maria is coming to pick him up by car.'

Sentence (23a) involves movement away from the speaker's viewpoint, while sen-tence (23b) indicates movement towards the speaker's adopted viewpoint.

Although the parallelism between the general meaning of DIC and the meaning of SVCs with andative and venitive verbs is direct and unequivocal, an explanation for the cases of desemanticization is still required. A further complication is the fact that desemanticized DIC typically refers to past time, whereas cross-linguistically, similar constructions tend to develop a future meaning when they are 'bleached' of their original movement meaning. The development of a future tense from a construction with the verb 'to go' constitutes a common path of grammaticalization (cf. Bybee *et al.* 1994) in Romance too (e.g. Spanish *va a cantar*, French *il va chanter* 'he will sing', 'he is going to sing'). When it retains its motion and deictic meaning, V1 in the Sicilian DIC may contribute an element of futurity or an inchoative aspect, but by no means does the construction encode a future tense. On the contrary, we have seen that when Sicilian *jiri* 'go' lacks any motion meaning, the construction refers to a past temporal frame. To account for this special use, I argue that V1 in the desemanticized DIC is an emphatic past marker employed in narrative contexts. Hence, even if morphologically present, V2 refers to an event in the past, and typically involves an emotional participation on the part of the speaker. This is thus a case in which DIC is related to temporal deixis, rather than to spatial deixis as in its canonical use.

The use of the verb 'to go' as a narrative past marker is not unprecedented. According to Pérez Saldanya and Hualde (2003), this is the function of Catalan *anar* 'go' in an intermediate stage along its grammaticalization path towards past marker or, more precisely, towards the periphrastic perfective past:[11]

(24)   verb of movement > <u>narrative past marker</u> > past marker

During this state, the *go*-construction is used as a narrative technique to foreground and emphasize punctual past events (cf. also Detges 2004):

(25)   Quant cels de la host ho viuren, meseren mans a cridar: –A armes, cavalers! Que·ls cavalers del castel se'n van! – E el rey, qui assò hac entès, *va prendre* ses armes, e muntà a caval e comensà a córrer aprés d'éls.
       'When those of the army saw it, they started to shout: To the arms, knights! The knights of the castle are running away! And the king, who heard it, *goes to take* (= goes to take and took) his weapons, and got on his horse and started to run after them.'
       (*Desclot, Crònica, vol. II, p.43*, in Pérez Saldanya and Hualde 2003: 54)

Pérez Saldanya and Hualde (2003: 48) point out that a narrative past value developed by constructions with the verb 'to go' has been documented in a number of languages, although often limited to specific styles and rhetorical effects, and that the periphrasis with 'to go' in narrative past contexts is also found in medieval French and medieval Occitan, and, to a lesser extent, in medieval Spanish. Emphasis, past narrative context, and reference to a punctual past event are indeed essential characteristics of the Sicilian desemanticized DIC.

14.6 Conclusions and final remarks

We have seen that recent studies have extended the paradigm model of inflectional morphology to periphrasis (Sadler and Spencer 2001, Spencer 2001, Ackerman and

[11] It must be noted, however, that the double inflection is a peculiarity of Sicilian alone, and that V2 in the other languages under discussion is always in the infinitive.

Stump 2004). The paradigm model has been applied not only to the synthetic forms of a lexeme, but also to analytic structures consisting of two or more elements—typically a functional and a lexical element—that may fill some of the cells of its paradigm. Entirely analytic paradigms have been disregarded within this approach, especially if they do not meet the criteria for the definition of inflectional periphrases. Sicilian DIC posits a series of problems when these criteria are considered. Feature intersection, non-compositionality, and distributed exponence are not obvious features of this construction, and a careful evaluation of these criteria is not possible without a full understanding of the grammatical features expressed by this periphrasis. The definition of its grammatical meaning must include two functions: a venitive or andative function, in its canonical use, and the function of an emphatic past marker, in narrative contexts. Only in the latter function can DIC be considered to be featurally intersective, in the sense that the properties PAST and EMPHASIS are not always expressed periphrastically rather than synthetically in Sicilian.[12] In its desemanticized function, DIC is evidently non-compositional. Even if we assume that the emphasis is contributed by the 'bleached' motion verb, the past meaning is conveyed by the construction as a whole, given that the individual verbs actually show present-tense morphology. As for distributed exponence, when V_1 is not phonologically reduced, both verbs morphologically realize person and number. As already observed, however, the past tense is not realized morphologically, at least not in a transparent and unequivocal manner.

By contrast, if we put aside the issue of the double inflection, and hence the distributed exponence criterion, it is clear that venitive and andative DIC is not featurally intersective and is fairly compositional, in the sense that the set of properties associated with the analytic formation is the composition of the property sets associated with its parts. From these observations it follows that only desemanticized DIC can be seen as an inflectional periphrasis or, in other terms, as a morphological periphrasis, while venitive and andative DIC cannot. However, this conclusion openly contrasts with the formal morphosyntactic characteristics discussed in Section 14.2, which I have described as direct reflexes of a process of grammaticalization, and which are not sensitive to the grammatical meaning distinction. Moreover, the paradigmatic defectiveness affects both functional types of DIC, and is also blind to the function served by the construction.

This contrast supports the claim that it is the degree of grammaticalization that must be considered as the main criterion for defining a morphological periphrasis, irrespective of whether synthesis competes with periphrasis as a mode of inflectional exponence. The more an analytic construction is grammaticalized, the more it

---

[12] I am aware that emphasis can hardly be considered a morphosyntactic feature or grammatical category. It is rather a narrative or pragmatic effect employed to focus on a particular aspect of the sentence.

becomes likely that it will be treated morphologically and will be subject to morphological rules and patterns of irregularity. Under this view, non-compositionality and distributed exponence simply reflect the grammaticalization status of the construction under consideration (cf. Vincent 2011). Morphology may influence periphrastic paradigms of any type, i.e. independently of whether the periphrasis is suppletive or not. As shown by the data discussed in this chapter, a periphrasis may be morphologically sensitive to the paradigms of its components, but may also give rise to its own independent paradigm.[13] In turn, this autonomous paradigm may be considered as part of the 'extended' paradigm of the lexeme, which must include not only the synthetic word-forms of the lexeme itself, but also its partially or entirely periphrastic paradigms according to their grammaticalization.

---

[13] The periphrastic constructions seen above could be analysed as cases of compound verbs (VV). Under such a view, a parallelism with compounding in the nominal domain could be envisaged. It has been shown that some nominal compounds are sensitive to the paradigms of their components, but may have their own independent (internally motivated) paradigm (Maiden 2010*b*). As for periphrases, therefore, certain aspects of Italian compound words are best understood if we accept that morphological word-forms sometimes play a role in grammar independent of the semantic and functional content of their parts.

References

Ackerman, Farrell and Stump, Gregory (2004). 'Paradigms and periphrastic expression: a study in realization-based lexicalism', in A. Spencer and L. Sadler (eds.), *Projecting Morphology*. Stanford, CA: CSLI, 111–57.

Acquaviva, Paolo (2008). *Lexical Plurals. A Morphosemantic Approach*. Oxford: Oxford University Press.

Adams, James N. (1991). 'Some neglected evidence for Latin *habeo* with infinitive: the order of the constituents', *Transactions of the Philological Society* 89: 131–96.

Aikhenvald, Alexandra Y. (2006). 'Serial Verb Constructions in Typological Perspective', in A. Y. Aikhenvald and R. M. W. Dixon (eds.), *Serial Verb Constructions: A Cross-Linguistic Typology*. Oxford: Oxford University Press, 1–68.

AIS: Jaberg, Karl and Jud, Jakob (1928–1940). *Sprach- und Sachatlas Italiens und der Südschweiz* (8 vols.). Zofingen: Ringier.

Alarcos Llorach, Emilio (1994). *Gramática de la lengua española*. Madrid: Espasa-Calpe.

Albright, Adam (2003). 'A quantitative study of Spanish paradigm gaps', in G. Garding and M. Tsujimura (eds.), WCCFL 22: Proceedings of the 22nd *West Coast Conference of Formal Linguistics*. Somerville: Cascadilla, 1–14.

Albright, Adam (2008). 'Cautious generalization on inflectional morphology, and its role in defectivity.' Paper presented at the *Defective Paradigms Workshop*, London, 10–11 April 2008.

Albright, Adam (2010). 'Lexical and morphological conditioning of paradigm gaps', in C. Rice and S. Blaho (eds.), *Modeling Ungrammaticality in Optimality Theory*. London: Equinox, 117–64.

Alibèrt, Loís (1976). *Gramatica occitana segon los parlars lengadocians*. Montpelhièr: CEO.

Alkire, Ti and Rosen, Carol (2010). *Romance Languages. A Historical Introduction*. Cambridge: Cambridge University Press.

Allen, Andrew (1995). 'Regrammaticalization and degrammaticalization of the inchoative suffix', in H. Andersen (ed.), *Historical Linguistics 1993*. Amsterdam & Philadelphia: John Benjamins, 1–7.

Allières, Jacques (1997). 'Note sur le "futur du passé" en gascon moderne', *Estudis Occitans* 21: 19–20.

ALLOc: *Atlas Linguistique du Languedoc Occidental*, unpublished *cahiers d'enquête*.

ALLOr: *Atlas Linguistique du Languedoc Oriental*, unpublished *cahiers d'enquête*.

ALMC: Norton, Pierre (1957–1963), *L'Atlas linguistique et ethnographique du Massif Central* (4 vols.). Paris: Editions du CNRS.

ALRII: Pătruţ, Ioan (ed.) (1972). *Atlasul lingvistic romîn: serie nouă. Vol. VII*. Bucharest: Editura Academiei române.

Anderson, Stephen R. (2006). 'Verb second, subject clitics, and impersonals in Surmiran (Rumantsch)', to appear in *Proceedings of the Annual Meeting of the Berkeley Linguistics Society* 32.

Anderson, Stephen R. (2008). 'Phonologically conditioned allomorphy in the morphology of Surmiran (Rumantsch)', *Word Structure* 1: 109–34.

Anderson, Stephen R. (2010). 'Failing one's obligations: defectiveness in Rumantsch reflexes of DEBERE', in M. Baerman, G. G. Corbett, and D. Brown (eds.), *Defective Paradigms: Missing Forms and What They Tell Us*. Oxford: Oxford University Press & British Academy, 19–36.

Anderson, Stephen R. (2011). 'Stress-conditioned allomorphy in Surmiran (Rumantsch)', in M. Maiden, J. C. Smith, M. Goldbach, and M.-O. Hinzelin (eds.), *Morphological Autonomy: Perspectives from Romance Inflectional Morphology*. Oxford: Oxford University Press, 13–35.

Anderson, Stephen R. and Lightfoot, David W. (2002). *The Language Organ: Linguistics as Cognitive Physiology*. Cambridge: Cambridge University Press.

Anttila, Raimo (1977). *Analogy*. The Hague: Mouton.

Apfelstedt, Friedrich (ed.) (1881). *Lothringischer Psalter*. Oxford: Henninger.

Apotheloz, Denis (2010). 'Le passé surcomposé et la valeur de parfait existentiel', *French Language Studies* 20: 105–26.

Aronoff, Mark (1976). *Word Formation in Generative Grammar*. Cambridge, MA: MIT Press.

Aronoff, Mark (1994). *Morphology by Itself: Stems and Inflectional Classes*. Cambridge, MA: MIT Press.

Aronoff, Mark (2007). 'In the beginning was the word', *Language* 83: 803–30.

Aronoff, Mark and Fudeman, Kirsten (2011). *What is Morphology?* Malden, MA: Wiley-Blackwell.

Aski, Janice M. (1995). 'Verbal suppletion: an analysis of Italian, French, and Spanish *to go*', *Linguistics* 33: 403–32.

Authier, Gilles (2012). *Grammaire juhuri ou 'judéo-tat', langue iranienne des Juifs du Caucase de l'est*. Wiesbaden: Reichert.

Baayen, Harald (1992). 'Quantitative aspects of morphological productivity', in G. Booij and J. van Marle (eds.), *Yearbook of Morphology 1991*. Dordrecht: Kluwer, 109–49.

Baerman, Matthew and Corbett, Greville (2010). 'Introduction: defectiveness—typology and diachrony', in M. Baerman, G. G. Corbett, and D. Brown (eds.), *Defective Paradigms: Missing Forms and What They Tell Us*. Oxford: Oxford University Press & British Academy, 1–18.

Baker, Mark (1989). 'Object sharing and projection in serial verb constructions', *Linguistic Inquiry* 20: 513–53.

Barceló, Gérard Joan (2004). 'Lo(s) futur(s) occitan(s) e la modalitat: elements d'estudi semantic comparatiu', *Lingüistica occitana* 2: 1–10.

Barceló, Gérard Joan and Bres, Jacques (2006). *Les Temps de l'indicatif en français*. Paris: Ophrys.

Bartoli, Matteo Giulio (1906). *Das Dalmatische*. Wien: Alfred Hölder.

Battistella, Edwin L. (1990). *Markedness: The Evaluative Superstructure of Language*. Albany, NY: State University of New York Press.

Battistella, Edwin L. (1996). *The Logic of Markedness*. Oxford & New York: Oxford University Press.

Baudouin de Courtenay, Jan (1895). *Versuch einer Theorie phonetischer Alternationen: Ein Kapitel aus der Psychophonetik*. Strasbourg: Trübner.

Bauer, Laurie (2001). *Morphological Productivity*. Cambridge: Cambridge University Press.

Beard, Robert (1995). *Lexeme-morpheme Base Morphology: A General Theory of Inflection and Word Formation*. Albany, NY: State University of New York Press.

Belletti, Adriana (1990). *Generalized Verb Movement*. Turin: Rosenberg & Sellier.

Bello, Andrés (1847). *Gramática de la lengua castellana destinada al uso de los americanos*. Madrid: Arcolibros.

Bentin, Shlomo and Feldman, Laurie B. (1990). 'The contribution of morphological and semantic relatedness to repetition priming at short and long lags: evidence from Hebrew', *Quarterly Journal of Experimental Psychology* 42A: 693–711.

Bentley, Delia (2000*a*). 'I costrutti condizionali in siciliano: un'analisi diacronica', *Revue Romane* 35: 3–20.

Bentley, Delia (2000*b*). 'Semantica e sintassi nello sviluppo dei costrutti condizionali: il caso del siciliano', *Revue romane* 35: 163–76.

Benveniste, Émile (1956). 'La nature des pronoms', in M. Halle, H. G. Lunt, H. McLean, and C. H. van Schooneveld (eds.), *For Roman Jakobson: Essays on the Occasion of His Sixtieth Birthday*. The Hague: Mouton, 34–37. Reprinted in Émile Benveniste (1966), *Problèmes de linguistique générale*. Paris: Gallimard, 251–57.

Berent, Iris and Shimron, Joseph (2003). 'What is a root? Evidence from the obligatory contour principle', in J. Shimron (ed.), *Language Processing and Acquisition in Languages of Semitic, Root-based, Morphology*. Amsterdam: John Benjamins, 201–22.

Berman, Ruth Aronson (1978). *Modern Hebrew Structures*. Tel Aviv: University Publishing Projects.

Berman, Ruth Aronson (2003). 'Children's lexical innovations: developmental perspectives on Hebrew verb structure', in J. Shimron (ed.), *Language Processing and Acquisition in Languages of Semitic, Root-based, Morphology*. Amsterdam: John Benjamins, 243–91.

Bermúdez-Otero, Ricardo (forthcoming). *Stratal Optimality Theory*. Oxford: Oxford University Press.

Bernardi, Ruth (2002). *Curs de gherdëina. Trëdesc lezions per mparé la rujeneda de Gherdëina*. San Martin de Tor: Istitut Ladin "Micurà de Rü".

Berretta, Monica (1994). 'Il futuro italiano nella varietà nativa colloquiale e nella varietà d'apprendimento', *Zeitschrift für romanische Philologie* 110: 1–36.

Bertinetto, Pier Marco (1986). *Tempo, aspetto e azione nel verbo italiano*. Florence: Accademia della Crusca.

Bertinetto, Pier Marco (1990). 'Perifrasi verbali italiane: criteri di identificazione e gerarchia di perifrasticità', in G. Bernini and A. Giacalone Ramat (eds.), *La temporalità nell'acquisizione di lingue seconde*. Milan: Angeli, 331–50.

Bianchi, Bianco (1888). *Il dialetto e la etnografia di Città di Castello*. Città di Castello: S. Lapi.

Bianconi, Sandro (1962). 'Ricerche sui dialetti di Orvieto e di Viterbo nel medioevo', *Studi di linguistica italiana* 3: 3–175.

Bick, Atira S., Frost, Ram, and Goelman, Gadi (2010). 'Imaging implicit morphological processing. Evidence from Hebrew', *Journal of Cognitive Neuroscience* 22: 1955–69.

Binnick, Robert I. (1991). *Time and the Verb*. Oxford: Oxford University Press.

Blasco Ferrer, Eduardo (1984). *Storia linguistica della Sardegna* [Beiheft 202, *ZRPh*]. Tübingen: Max Niemeyer.

Blasco Ferrer, Eduardo (1986). *La lingua sarda contemporanea. Grammatica del logudorese e del campidanese*. Cagliari: Della Torre.

Blasco Ferrer, Eduardo (2003). *Crestomazia sarda dei primi secoli*. Nuoro: Ilisso.

Blaylock, Curtis (1975). 'The Romance development of the Latin verbal augment -SK-', *Romance Philology* 28: 434–44.

Blevins, James (2006). 'Word-based morphology', *Journal of Linguistics* 42: 531–73.

Bohas, Georges (1984). *Études des théories des grammairiens arabes 1: morphologie et phonologie*. Damascus: Institut Français de Damas.

Bonami, Olivier and Boyé, Gilles (2003). 'Supplétion et classes flexionnelles dans la conjugaison du français', *Langages* 152: 102–26.

Bonami, Olivier and Samvelian, Pollet (2009a). 'Inflectional periphrasis in Persian', in S. Müller (ed.), *Proceedings of the 16th International Conference on Head-Driven Phrase Structure Grammar*. Stanford: CSLI, 26–46.

Bonami, Olivier and Samvelian, Pollet (2009b). 'The diversity of inflectional periphrasis in Persian.' Unpublished ms., Université Paris-Sorbonne.

Bonami, Olivier and Webelhuth, Gert (2011). 'Inflection as collocation.' Paper presented at the *8th Mediterranean Morphology Meeting*, 16 September 2011.

Bonet, Eulàlia, Lloret, Maria-Rosa, and Mascaró, Joan (2007). 'Allomorph selection and lexical preferences: two case studies', *Lingua* 117: 903–27.

Börjars, Kersti and Vincent, Nigel (2011). 'The pre-conditions for suppletion', in A. Galani, G. Hicks, and G. Tsoulas (eds.), *Morphology and its Interfaces*. Amsterdam: John Benjamins, 239–65.

Börjars, Kersti, Vincent, Nigel, and Chapman, Carol (1997). 'Paradigms, periphrases and pronominal inflection: a feature-based account', in G. Booij and J. van Marle (eds.), *Yearbook of Morphology 1996*. Dordrecht: Kluwer, 155–80.

Boström, Ingemar (1972). *La morfosintassi dei pronomi personali soggetti della terza persona in italiano e in fiorentino*. Stockholm: Almquist & Wiksell.

Boucherie, Anatole (1871). 'La vie de sainte Euphrosyne', *Revue des langues romanes* 2: 23–62, 109–17.

Bourciez, Édouard (1956). *Éléments de linguistique romane* (fourth edition). Paris: Klincksieck.

Bourova, Viara (2005). 'À la recherche du 'conditionnel latin': les constructions Infinitif + forme de *habere* examinées à partir d'un corpus electronique', in C. D. Pusch, J. Kabatek, and W. Raible (eds.), *Romanistische Korpuslinguistik II: Korpora und diachrone Sprachwissenschaft*. Tübingen: Narr, 303–16.

Bourova, Viara (2007). 'Les constructions latines Infinitif + *habebam* vs. Infinitif + *habui* et le développement du conditionnel roman', in D. Trotter (ed.), *Actes du XXIVe Congrès International de Linguistique et de Philologie Romanes (Aberystwyth, 2004)*. Tübingen: Niemeyer, 461–74.

Bourova, Viara (2008). 'Les participes futurs en -*urus* /-*ndus* combinés avec *esse* au passé en latin tardif. Un conditionnel non abouti?', in R. Wright (ed.), *Latin vulgaire—latin tardif VIII. Actes du VIIIe colloque international sur le latin vulgaire et tardif, Oxford, 6–9 septembre 2006*. Hildesheim, Zürich, & New York: Olms-Weidmann, 271–80.

Bourova, Viara and Tasmowski, Liliane (2007). 'La préhistoire des futurs romans—ordre des constituants et sémantique', *Cahiers Chronos* 19: 25–41.

Bouzet, Jean (1928). *Manuel de grammaire béarnaise*. Pau: Marrimpouey Jeune.

Boyé, Gilles and Cabredo Hofherr, Patricia (2006). 'The structure of allomorphy in Spanish verbal inflection', *Cuadernos de Lingüística del Instituto Universitario Ortega y Gasset* 13: 9–24.

Boyé, Gilles and Cabredo Hofherr, Patricia (2010). 'Defectiveness as stem suppletion in French and Spanish verbs', in M. Baerman, G. G. Corbett, and D. Brown (eds.), *Defective Paradigms: Missing Forms and What They Tell Us*. Oxford: Oxford University Press & British Academy, 35–52.

Brown, Dunstan and Hippisley, Andrew (2011). *Network Morphology: A Defaults-based Theory of Word Structure*. Cambridge: Cambridge University Press.

Brown, Dunstan, Chumakina, Marina, Corbett, Greville, Popova, Gergana, and Spencer, Andrew (2012). 'Defining "periphrasis": key notions', *Morphology* 22(2): 233–75.

Brucart, José, M. (2003). 'El valor del imperfecto de indicativo en español', *Estudios Hispánicos* 6: 193–233.

Brugmann, Karl (1887). *Grundriß der vergleichenden Grammatik der indogermanischen Sprachen. Vol. 1: Einleitung und Lautlehre*. Strassburg: Karl J. Trübner.

Bühler, Karl (1934). *Sprachtheorie: die Darstellungsfunktion der Sprache*. Jena: Fischer.

Burzio, Luigi (2004). 'Paradigmatic and syntagmatic relations in Italian verbal inflection', in J. Auger, J. Clancy Clements, and B. Vance (eds.), *Contemporary Approaches to Romance Linguistics*. Amsterdam: John Benjamins, 17–44.

Burzio, Luigi and Di Fabio, Elvira (1993). 'Accentual stability', in M. L. Mazzola (ed.), *Issues and Theory in Romance Linguistics*. Washington: Georgetown University Press, 19–34.

Butt, John and Benjamin, Carmen (1994). *A New Reference Grammar of Modern Spanish* (second edition). London: Edward Arnold.

Bybee, Joan L. and Pagliuca, William (1987). 'The evolution of future meaning', in A. Giacalone Ramat, O. Carruba, and G. Bernini (eds.), *Papers from the 7th International Conference on Historical Linguistics*. Amsterdam: John Benjamins, 109–22.

Bybee, Joan L., Perkins, Revere D., and Pagliuca, William (1994). *The Evolution of Grammar: Tense, Aspect and Modality in the Languages of the World*. Chicago: University of Chicago Press.

Camps, Christian (1985). *Atlas linguistique du Biterrois*. Toulouse: Institut d'Estudis Occitans.

Cappellaro, Chiara (2010). 'Un aspetto della morfologia storica dell'italiano. L'evoluzione del pronome personale *esso* rispetto al tratto [+ /−umano].' Paper presented at the *26é Congrés internacional de lingüística i filologia romàniques*, Valencia, 6–11 September 2010.

Cardinaletti, Anna and Giusti, Giuliana (2001). 'Semi-lexical. Motion verbs in Romance and Germanic', in N. Corver and H. van Riemsdijk (eds.), *Semi-lexical Categories. On the Function of Content Words and the Content of Function Words*. Berlin: Mouton de Gruyter, 371–414.

Cardinaletti, Anna and Giusti, Giuliana (2003). 'Motion verbs as functional heads', in C. Tortora (ed.), *The Syntax of Italian Dialects*. Oxford & New York: Oxford University Press, 31–49.

Cardona, George (2003). 'Sanskrit', in G. Cardona and D. Jain (eds.), *The Indo-Aryan Languages*. London: Routledge, 104–60.

Carstairs[-McCarthy], Andrew (1987). *Allomorphy in Inflexion*. London: Croom Helm.

Carstairs[-McCarthy], Andrew (1988). 'Some implications of phonologically conditioned suppletion', in G. Booij and J. van Marle (eds.), *Yearbook of Morphology 1988*. Dordrecht: Foris, 67–94.

Carstairs[-McCarthy], Andrew (1990). 'Phonologically conditioned suppletion', in W. U. Dressler, H. C. Luschützky, O. E. Pfeiffer, and J. R. Rennison (eds.), *Contemporary Morphology*. Berlin & New York: Mouton de Gruyter, 17–23.

Carstairs-McCarthy, Andrew (2005). 'Affixes, stems and allomorphic conditioning in paradigm function morphology', in G. Booij and J. van Marle (eds.), *Yearbook of Morphology 2004*. Dordrecht: Kluwer, 253–81.

Carter, Michael G. (2004). *Sībawayhi*. London: I. B. Tauris.

Celle, Agnès (2007). 'Analyse unifiée du conditionnel de non prise en charge en français et comparaison avec l'anglais', *Cahiers Chronos* 19: 43–61.

Chabaneau, Camille (1876). *Grammaire limousine*. Paris: Maisonneuve.

Chenal, Aimé (1986). *Le Franco-provençal valdôtain. Morphologie et syntaxe*. Aosta: Musumeci.

Cheung, Johnny (2007). *Etymological Dictionary of the Iranian Verb*. Leiden & Boston: Brill.

Chomsky, Noam and Halle, Morris (1968). *The Sound Pattern of English*. New York: Harper and Row.

Chomsky, William (1952). *David Kimḥi's Hebrew Grammar (Mikhlol)*. New York: Bloch.

Cinque, Guglielmo (1999). *Adverbs and Functional Heads*. Oxford & New York: Oxford University Press.

Cinque, Guglielmo (2006). *Restructuring and Functional Heads*. Oxford & New York: Oxford University Press.

Clark, Eve Vivienne (1987). 'The Principle of Contrast: A constraint on language acquisition', in B. MacWhinney (ed.), *Mechanisms of Language Acquisition*. Hillsdale, NJ: Erlbaum, 1–33.

Clark, Eve Vivienne (1993). *The Lexicon in Acquisition*. Cambridge: Cambridge University Press.

Colle, Liotta, Constantini, Angelo, Majoni, Ernesto *et al.* (1997). *Vocabolario ampezzano*. Cortina d'Ampezzo: Cassa Rurale ed Artigiana di Cortina d'Ampezzo.

Comrie, Bernard (1976). *Aspect: An Introduction to the Study of Verbal Aspect and Related Problems*. Cambridge: Cambridge University Press.

Condoravdi, Cleo (2002). 'Temporal interpretation of modals: modals for the present and for the past', in D. Beaver, S. Kaufmann, B. Clark, and L. Casillas (eds.), *The Construction of Meaning*. Stanford: CSLI, 59–88.

Corbett, Greville G. (2005). 'The canonical approach in typology', in Z. Frajzyngier, A. Hodges, and S. Rood (eds.), *Linguistic Diversity and Language Theories*. Amsterdam & Philadelphia: John Benjamins, 25–49.

Corbett, Greville G. (2007*a*). 'Canonical typology, suppletion and possible words', *Language* 83: 8–42.

Corbett, Greville G. (2007*b*). 'Deponency, syncretism, and what lies between', in M. Baerman, G. G. Corbett, D. Brown, and A. Hippisley (eds.), *Deponency and Morphological Mismatches*. Oxford: Oxford University Press & British Academy, 21–43.

Corbett, Greville G. (2010). 'Features: essential notions', in A. Kibort and G. Corbett (eds.), *Features: Perspectives on a Key Notion in Linguistics*. Oxford: Oxford University Press, 17–36.

Corbett, Greville G. and Baerman, Matthew (2006). 'Prolegomena to a typology of morphological features', *Morphology* 16: 231–46.

Corda, Francesco (1983). *Saggio di grammatica gallurese*. Cagliari: Edizioni 3T.

Cordin, Patrizia and Calabrese, Andrea (1988). 'I pronomi personali', in L. Renzi (ed.), *Grande grammatica italiana di consultazione. Vol. I, La frase. I sintagmi nominali e preposizionali*. Bologna: Il Mulino, 535–92.

Cortelazzo, Manlio and Zolli, Paolo (1979–1988). *Dizionario etimologico della lingua italiana (DELI)*. Bologna: Zanichelli.

Cottell, Siobhán (1995). 'The representation of tense in modern Irish', *Geneva Generative Papers* 3: 105–24.

Cowan, J. Milton (ed.) (1971). *The Hans Wehr Dictionary of Modern Standard Arabic*. Wiesbaden: Harrassowitz.

Cowell, Mark W. (2005). *A Reference Grammar of Syrian Arabic*. Washington, DC: Georgetown University Press.

Crocco-Galèas, Grazia (1998). *The Parameters of Natural Morphology*. Padua: Unipress.

Croft, William (2003). *Typology and Universals* (second edition). Cambridge: Cambridge University Press.

Croft, William and Poole, Keith T. (2008). 'Inferring universals from grammatical variation: multidimensional scaling for typological analysis', *Theoretical Linguistics* 34: 1–37.

D'Achille, Paolo (1990). *Sintassi del parlato e tradizione scritta della lingua italiana*. Rome: Bonacci.

D'hulst, Yves (2004). 'French and Italian conditionals: from etymology to representation', in J. Guéron and J. Lecarme (eds.), *The Syntax of Time*. Cambridge, MA: MIT Press, 181–201.

Dahl, Östen (1985). *Tense and Aspect Systems*. Oxford: Blackwell.

Dahl, Östen (1997). 'The relation between past time reference and counterfactuality: a new look', in A. Athanasiadou and R. Dirven (eds.), *On Conditionals Again*. Amsterdam: John Benjamins, 97–114.

Dahl, Östen and Velupillai, Viveka (2005). 'Tense and aspect', in M. Haspelmath, M. S. Dryer, D. Gil, and B. Comrie (eds.), *The World Atlas of Language Structures*. Oxford: Oxford University Press, 266–7.

Davis, Stuart and Napoli, Donna Jo (1994). *A Prosodic Template in Historical Change: the Passage of the Latin Second Conjugation into Romance*. Turin: Rosenberg & Sellier.

De Rossi, Hugo (1999). *Ladinisches Wörterbuch. Vocabolario ladino (brach)—tedesco*. Vigo di Fassa: Istitut Cultural Ladin "Majon di Fascegn".

Deledar, Jòrdi (2006). *Les Parlers couserannais*. Villeneuve-sur-Lot: Massourre.

Dell'Antonio, Giuseppe (1972). *Vocabolario ladino moenese—italiano*. Trento: Grop de Moena dell'Union di Ladins di Fassa e di Moena.

Dendale, Patrick (2001). 'Les problèmes linguistiques du conditionnel français', in P. Dendale and L. Tasmowski (eds.), *Le Conditionnel en français*. Metz: Université de Metz, 7–18.

Dendale, Patrick and Tasmowski, Liliane (eds.) (2001). *Le Conditionnel en français*. Metz: Université de Metz.

Depperu, Piero (2006). *Vocabolario lurisinco. Dizionario logudorese della parlata di Luras*. Sassari: Libreria Koinè.

Detges, Ulrich (2004). 'How cognitive is grammaticalization? The history of the Catalan *perfet perifràstic*', in O. Fischer, M. Norde, and H. Perridon (eds.), *Up and Down the Cline—The Nature of Grammaticalization*. Amsterdam: Benjamins, 211–27.

Detges, Ulrich (2012). 'Grammaticalization, pragmaticalization, subjectification: what a look at diachrony can tell us about synchrony (and vice versa).' Paper presented at the conference on *Refining Grammaticalization*, Free University of Berlin, 24–26 February 2012.

Deutsch, Avital, Frost, Ram, Pollatsek, Alexander, and Rayner, Keith (2000). 'Early morphological effects in word recognition in Hebrew: evidence from parafoveal preview benefit', *Language and Cognitive Processes* 15: 487–506.

Dixon, R. M. W. (1994). *Ergativity*. Cambridge: Cambridge University Press.

Donohue, Mark and Smith, John Charles (1998). 'What's happened to us? Some developments in the Malay pronoun system', *Oceanic Linguistics* 37: 65–84.

Doron, Edit (2003). 'Agency and voice: the semantics of the Semitic templates', *Natural Language Semantics* 11: 1–67.

Dressler, Wolfgang U. (2002). 'Latin inflection classes', in A. M. Bolkestein, C. Kroon, and H. Pinkster (eds.), *Theory and Description in Latin Linguistics*. Amsterdam: Gieben, 91–110.

Ebneter, Theodor (1981). *Vocabulari dil rumantsch da Vaz*. Tübingen: Max Niemeyer Verlag.

Ebneter, Theodor (1994). *Syntax des gesprochenen Rätoromanischen*. Tübingen: Max Niemeyer Verlag.

Elwert, Theodor (1943). *Die Mundart des Fassa-Tals*. Heidelberg: Winter.

Engel, Dulcie M. (1985). 'The survival of the French *passé simple*: a reply to van Vliet', *Word* 36: 77–81.

Esher, Louise (2010). 'Asimetrias sistematicas entre futur e condicional dins les parlars occitans.' Paper presented at the *26é Congrés internacional de lingüística i filologia romàniques*, Valencia, September 2010.

Esher, Louise (2011). 'The "second conditional" in Old and Modern Occitan.' Paper presented at the *44th Annual Meeting of the Societas Linguistica Europaea*, University of La Rioja, 8–11 September 2011.

Esher, Louise (2012a). 'The morphological evolution of infinitive, future and conditional forms in Occitan', in A. van Kemenade and N. de Haas (eds.), *Historical Linguistics 2009: Selected Papers from the 19th International Conference on Historical Linguistics*. Amsterdam: John Benjamins, 315–32.

Esher, Louise (2012b). *Future, Conditional, and Autonomous Morphology in Occitan*. Unpublished D.Phil. thesis, University of Oxford.

Fabre d'Olivet, Antoine (1815–1816). *La Langue hébraïque restituée, et le véritable sens des mots hébreux rétabli et prouvé par leur analyse radical* (2 vols.). Paris: The author, Barriot, and Eberhart.

Fabre d'Olivet, Antoine (1931). *La Langue hébraïque restituée*. Edition augmentée d'un complément inédit rédigé en 1823 sous le titre de Théodoxie universelle, examens de la cosmogonie contenue dans le premier livre du Sepher de Moïse, appelé Beraeshith et réproduit en fac-simile sur le manuscrit de l'auteur. Paris: Dorbon-aîné.

Fanciullo, Franco (1998). 'Per una interpretazione dei verbi italiani a "inserto" velare', *Archivio glottologico italiano* 83: 188–239.

Fehringer, Carol (2004). 'How stable are morphological doublets? A case study of /ə/ ∼ Ø variants in Dutch and German', *Journal of Germanic Linguistics* 16: 285–329.

Fehringer, Carol (2011). 'Allomorphy in the German genitive. A paradigmatic account', *Zeitschrift für Germanistiche Linguistik* 39: 90–112.

Feldman, Laurie B. and Bentin, Shlomo (1994). 'Morphological analysis of disrupted morphemes: evidence from Hebrew', *Quarterly Journal of Experimental Psychology* 47: 407–35.

Feldman, Laurie B., Frost, Ram, and Penini, Tamar (1995). 'Decomposing words into their constituent morphemes: evidence from English and Hebrew', *Journal of Experimental Psychology: Learning, Memory, and Cognition* 21: 947–60.

Field, Thomas (2003). 'Décalages entre forme et fonction dans la morphologie verbale gasconne', in R. Castano, S. Guida, and F. Latella (eds.), *Scène, evolution, sort de la langue et de la littérature d'oc: Actes du Septième Congrès de l'Association Internationale d'Études Occitanes, Vol. II*. Rome: Viella, 889–94.

von Fintel, Kai and Iatridou, Sabine (2007). 'Anatomy of a modal construction', *Linguistic Inquiry* 38: 445–83.

von Fintel, Kai and Iatridou, Sabine (2008). 'How to say *ought* in foreign: the composition of weak necessity modals', in J. Guéron and J. Lecarme (eds.), *Time and Modality*. Dordrecht: Springer, 115–41.

Fischer, Olga (2007). *Morphosyntactic Change. Functional and Formal Perspectives*. Oxford: Oxford University Press.

Fleischman, Suzanne (1982). *The Future in Thought and Language. Diachronic Evidence from Romance*. Cambridge: Cambridge University Press.

Forni, Marco (2003). *Vocabuler Tudësch—Ladin de Gherdëina*. San Martin de Tor: Istitut Ladin "Micurà de Rü".

Foulet, Lucien (1920). 'La disparition du prétérit', *Romania* 46: 271–313.

Fradin, Bernard and Kerleroux, Françoise (2003). 'Troubles with lexemes', in G. Booij, J. de Cesaris, S. Scalise, and A. Ralli (eds.), *Topics in Morphology. Selected Papers from the Third Mediterranean Morphology Meeting*. Barcelona: Institut Universitari de Lingüística Aplicada–Universitat Pompeu Fabra, 177–96.

Frost, Ram, Forster, Kenneth, and Deutsch, Avital (1997). What can we learn from the morphology of Hebrew? A masked-priming investigation of morphological representation', *Journal of Experimental Psychology: Learning, Memory, and Cognition* 23: 829–56.

Funck, Anton (1886). 'Die Verba auf *-issare* und *-izare*', *Archiv für lateinische Lexikographie und Grammatik* 3: 398–443.

Ganzoni, Gian Paul (1977). *Grammatica ladina: Grammatica sistematica dal rumantsch d'Engiadin'Ota per scolars e creschieus da lingua rumantscha e tudas-cha*. Samedan: Lia Rumantscha.

Ganzoni, Gian Paul (1983). *Grammatica ladina: Grammatica sistematica dal rumantsch d'Engiadina Bassa per scolars e creschüts da lingua rumantscha e francesa*. Samedan: Lia Rumantscha.

Gartner, Theodor (1883). *Raetoromanische Grammatik*. Heilbronn: Henninger.

Gesenius, Wilhelm, Kautzsch, Emil, and Cowley, Arthur E. (1910). *Gesenius' Hebrew Grammar: as edited and enlarged by the late E. Kautzsch*. Second English edition revised in accordance with the twenty-eighth German edition (1909) by Arthur E. Cowley. Oxford: Clarendon.

Giacalone Ramat, Anna (1998). 'Testing the boundaries of grammaticalization', in A. Giacalone Ramat and P. J. Hopper (eds.), *The Limits of Grammaticalization*. Amsterdam: John Benjamins, 107–27.

Giammarco, Ernesto (1979). *Abruzzo*. Pisa: Pacini.

Gili Gaya, Samuel (1943). *Curso superior de sintaxis española*. Barcelona: Bibliograf.

Gilliéron, Jules (1880). *Le Patois de la commune de Vionnaz (Bas-Valais)*. Paris: F. Vieweg.

Giorgi, Alessandra and Pianesi, Fabio (1997). *Tense and Aspect. From Semantics to Morphosyntax*. Oxford & New York: Oxford University Press.

Givón, Talmy (1991). 'Some substantive issues concerning verb serialization: grammatical and cognitive packaging', in C. Lefebvre (ed.), *Serial Verbs: Grammatical, Comparative and Cognitive Approaches*. Amsterdam: John Benjamins, 137–84.

Gleise Bellet, Augusta (2003). *Appunti morfologici della parlata occitano alpina di Bardonecchia*. Oulx: Comunità montana alta valle Susa.

Goebl, Hans, Böhmer, Helga, Dautermann, Irmgard, Bauer, Roland, and Haimerl, Edgar (eds.) (1998). *Atlant linguistich dl ladin dolomitich y di dialec vejins, 1ᵃ pert. Atlante linguistico del ladino dolomitico e dei dialetti limitrofi, 1ᵃ parte. Sprachatlas des Dolomitenladinischen und angrenzender Dialekte, 1. Teil* (7 vols.). Wiesbaden: L. Steiner.

González, Edelmiro (1998). 'Spanish aspect and the nature of linguistic time', *Hispania* 81: 155–65.

Goral, Mira (2001). 'Aphasia in Hebrew speakers', *Journal of Neurolinguistics* 14: 297–312.

Goral, Mira and Obler, Lorraine K. (2003). 'Root-morpheme processing during word recognition in Hebrew speakers across the adult life span', in J. Shimron (ed.), *Language Processing and Acquisition in Languages of Semitic, Root-based, Morphology*. Amsterdam: John Benjamins, 223–42.

Graffi, Giorgio (1996). 'Alcune riflessioni sugli imperativi italiani', in P. Benincà (ed.), *Italiano e dialetti nel tempo. Saggi di grammatica per Giulio C. Lepschy*. Rome: Bulzoni, 133–47.

Greenberg, Joseph H. (1966a). *Language Universals, with special reference to feature hierarchies*. The Hague: Mouton.

Greenberg, Joseph H. (1966b). 'Language universals', in T. A. Sebeok (ed.), *Current Trends in Linguistics: Vol. III, Theoretical Foundations*. The Hague & Paris: Mouton, 61–112.

Grevisse, Maurice and Goosse, André (1980). *Nouvelle grammaire du français*. Paris: Duculot.

Grevisse, Maurice and Goosse, André (2011). *Le Bon Usage: grammaire française* (fifteenth edition). Paris: Duculot; Bruxelles: De Boeck.

Grisch, Mena (1939). *Die Mundart von Surmeir*, Romanica Helvetica, vol. 12. Paris: Droz.

Grjunberg, A. L. (1963). *Jazyk severoazerbajdžanskix tatov*. Leningrad: Izd. Akademii Nauk.

Haber, Lyn (1976). 'Leaped and leapt: a theoretical account of linguistic variation', *Foundations of Language* 14: 211–38.

Haefelin, François (1879). *Les Patois romans du canton de Fribourg*. Leipzig: B. G. Teubner.

Haig, Geoffrey L. J. (2008). *Alignment Change in Iranian Languages: A Construction Grammar Approach*. Berlin & New York: Mouton de Gruyter.

Haiman, John and Benincà, Paola (1992). *The Rhaeto-Romance Languages*. London: Routledge.

Halle, Morris (1973). 'Prolegomena to a theory of word formation', *Linguistic Inquiry* 4: 3–16.

Halle, Morris and Marantz, Alec (1993). 'Distributed morphology and the pieces of inflection', in K. Hale and S. J. Keyser (eds.), *The View from Building 20*. Cambridge, MA: MIT Press, 111–76.

Harris, Martin (1986). 'The historical development of conditional sentences in Romance', *Romance Philology* 39: 405–36.

Haspelmath, Martin (1998). 'The semantic development of old presents: new futures and subjunctives without grammaticalization', *Diachronica* 15: 29–62.

Haspelmath, Martin (2000). 'Periphrasis', in G. Booij, C. Lehmann, and J. Mugdan (eds.), *Morphologie / Morphology. Ein internationales Handbuch zur Flexion und Wortbildung. An International Handbook on Inflection and Word-Formation*, Vol. 1. Berlin: Walter de Gruyter, 654–64.

Haspelmath, Martin (2002). *Understanding Morphology*. London: Hodder Arnold.

Haspelmath, Martin (2006). 'Against markedness (and what to replace it with)', *Journal of Linguistics* 42: 25–70.

Haug, Dag (2008). 'Aspectual oppositions from Proto-Indo-European to Latin', in F. Josephson and I. Söhrman (eds.), *Interdependence of Diachronic and Synchronic Analyses*. Amsterdam: John Benjamins, 61–72.

Haverling, Gerd (2000). *On sco-verbs, Prefixes and Semantic Functions*. Gothenburg: Acta Universitatis Gothoburgensis.

Haverling, Gerd (2010). 'Sur l'expression du temps et de l'aspect grammatical en latin tardif', *De Lingua Latina* 5: 1–23.

Heine, Bernd (1993). *Auxiliaries*. Oxford & New York: Oxford University Press.

Henning, W. B. (1954). 'The ancient language of Azerbaijan', *Transactions of the Philological Society* 53: 157–77.

Hewson, John (1997). *The Cognitive System of the French Verb* (Current Issues in Linguistic Theory 147). Amsterdam & Philadelphia: John Benjamins.

Higginbotham, James (2007). 'Remarks on compositionality', in G. Ramchand and C. Reiss (eds.), *The Oxford Handbook of Linguistic Interfaces*. Oxford: Oxford University Press, 425–45.

Hirsch, Leopold (1886). 'Laut- und Formenlehre des Dialekts von Siena, VIII. Verb', *Zeitschrift für romanische Philologie* 10: 411–46.

Hoberman, Robert D. and Aronoff, Mark (2003). 'The verbal morphology of Maltese', in J. Shimron (ed.), *Language Processing and Acquisition in Languages of Semitic, Root-based, Morphology*. Amsterdam: John Benjamins, 61–78.

Hopper, Paul J. and Traugott, Elizabeth Closs (2003). *Grammaticalization* (second edition). Cambridge: Cambridge University Press.

Iannace, Gaetano A. (1983). *Interferenza linguistica ai confini fra Stato e Regno. Il dialetto di San Leucio del Sannio*. Ravenna: Longo.

Iatridou, Sabine (2000). 'The grammatical ingredients of counterfactuality', *Linguistic Inquiry* 31: 231–70.

Imbs, Paul (1960). *L'Emploi des temps verbaux en français moderne. Essai de grammaire descriptive*. Paris: Klincksieck.

Jakobson, Roman (1971a). 'Beitrag zur allgemeinen Kasuslehre: Gesamtbedeutungen der Russischen Kasus', in *Selected Writings: Word and Language*, vol. 2. The Hague: Mouton, 32–71.

Jakobson, Roman (1971*b*). 'The Kazan school of Polish linguistics and its place in the international development of phonology', in *Selected Writings: Word and Language,* vol. 2. The Hague: Mouton, 394–428.

Jaquenod, Fernand (1931). *Essai sur le verbe dans le patois de Sottens.* Lausanne: Payot.

Jayme, Giovanna (2003). *Appunti morfologici della parlata occitano provenzale alpina di Oulx.* Oulx: Comunità montana alta valle Susa.

Jensen, Frede (1994). *Syntaxe de l'ancien occitan.* Tübingen: Niemeyer.

Job, Léon (1893). *Le Présent et ses dérivés dans la conjugaison latine d'après les données de la grammaire comparée des langues indo-européennes.* Paris: Bouillon.

Jones, Michael A. (1993). *Sardinian Syntax.* London: Routledge.

Kaisse, Ellen M. and Shaw, Patricia (1985). 'On the theory of lexical phonology', *Phonology* 2: 1–30.

Kamprath, Christine (1987). *Suprasegmental Structures in a Raeto-Romansh Dialect: A Case Study in Metrical and Lexical Phonology.* Unpublished Ph.D. dissertation, University of Texas at Austin.

Kayne, Richard S. (2009). 'A note on auxiliary alternations and silent causation', in L. Baronian and F. Martineau (eds.), *Le Français d'un continent à l'autre: mélanges offerts à Yves Charles Morin.* Québec: Les Presses de l'Université Laval, 211–35.

Kelly, Reine Cardaillac (1973). *A Descriptive Analysis of Gascon.* The Hague & Paris: Mouton.

Kibort, Anna (2010). 'Towards a typology of grammatical features', in A. Kibort and G. Corbett (eds.), *Features: Perspectives on a Key Notion in Linguistics.* Oxford: Oxford University Press, 64–106.

Kibort, Anna and Corbett, Greville (eds.) (2010). *Features: Perspectives on a Key Notion in Linguistics.* Oxford: Oxford University Press.

King, Larry D. and Suñer, Margarita (2008). *Gramática española: Análisis y práctica* (third edition). Boston: McGraw-Hill.

Kiparsky, Paul (1982). 'Lexical morphology and phonology', in I.-S. Yang (ed.), *Linguistics in the Morning Calm.* Seoul: Hanshin Publishing Company, 3–91.

Kiparsky, Paul (1985). 'Some consequences of lexical phonology', *Phonology* 2: 85–138.

Kiparsky, Paul (2000). 'Opacity and cyclicity', *Linguistic Review* 17: 351–67.

Kobayashi, Kazue (1988). 'On the formation of the Romance inchoative conjugation: a new theory', *Romance Philology* 41: 394–408.

Korn, Agnes (2009). 'Lengthening of *i* and *u* in Persian', in Wender Sundermann, Almut Hintze, and François de Blois (eds.), *Exegisti monumenta. Festschrift in honour of Nicholas Sims-Williams.* Wiesbaden: Harrassowitz, 197–213.

Kramer, Johannes (1976–1977). *Historische Grammatik des Dolomitenladinischen* (3 vols.). Würzburg: Wissenschaftlicher Verlag Lehmann.

Kramer, Johannes (1988–1993). *Etymologisches Wörterbuch des Dolomitenladinischen* (8 vols.). Hamburg: Helmut Buske.

Krämer, Martin (2009). *The Phonology of Italian.* Oxford: Oxford University Press.

Kratzer, Angelika (2012). *Modals and Conditionals.* Oxford: Oxford University Press.

Kruszewski, Mikołaj (1993). *Writings in General Linguistics: On Sound Alternation. An Outline of Linguistic Science.* Amsterdam: John Benjamins.

Kuno, Susumo (1973). *The Structure of the Japanese Language.* Cambridge, MA: MIT Press.

Kuryłowicz, Jerzy (1949). 'La nature des procès dits "analogiques" ', *Acta Linguistica Hafniensa* 5: 15–37.

Kuryłowicz, Jerzy (1962). *L'Apophonie en sémitique*. The Hague: Mouton.

Kuryłowicz, Jerzy (1973). *Studies in Semitic Grammar and Metrics*. London: Curzon Press.

Labov, William (2006 [1966]). *The Social Stratification of English in New York City*. Cambridge: Cambridge University Press.

Lakoff, Robin Tolmach (1968). *Abstract Syntax and Latin Complementation*. Cambridge, MA: MIT Press.

Lanly, André (1971). 'Sur des formes occitanes de conditionnel sans -r-', in I. Cluzel and F. Pirot (eds.), *Mélanges de philologie romane dédiés à la mémoire de Jean Boutière (1899–1967)*. Liège: Soledi, 795–800.

Larson, Richard (1988). 'On the double object construction', *Linguistic Inquiry* 19: 335–91.

Lass, Roger (1990). 'How to do things with junk: exaptation in language evolution', *Journal of Linguistics* 26: 79–102.

Laurent, Jean-Pierre (2001). *Le Dialecte de la vallée de Massat*. Montséron: J-P Laurent.

Laurent, Jean-Pierre (2002a). *Les Dialectes du Séronais, suivi de Le Séronais, histoire exemplaire d'un pays occitan*. Montséron: J-P Laurent.

Laurent, Jean-Pierre (2002b). *Le Dialecte gascon d'Aulus*. Montséron: J-P Laurent.

Laurent, Richard (1999). *Past Participles from Latin to Romance*. Berkeley: University of California Press.

Lausberg, Heinrich (1939). *Die Mundarten Südlukaniens*. Halle: Niemeyer.

Lausberg, Heinrich (1956–1962). *Romanische Sprachwissenschaft* (3 vols.). Berlin: De Gruyter.

Lausberg, Heinrich (1969). *Romanische Sprachwissenschaft, Vol. 1* (third edition). Berlin: De Gruyter.

Lazard, Gilbert (1978). 'Le dialecte tāleši de Māsule (Gilān)', *Studia Iranica* 7: 251–68.

Ledgeway, Adam (2009). *Grammatica diacronica del napoletano*. Tübingen: Niemeyer.

Lehmann, Christian (1995). *Thoughts on Grammaticalization*. Munich: LINCOM Europa.

Lempereur, Jules and Morayns, Jacques (1974). *Li Walon d'Lîdge. Tôme III: La Conjugaison*. Liège: Imprimerie Wagelmans.

Lenz, Rodolfo (1920). *La oración y sus partes*. Madrid: Centro de Estudios Hispánicos.

Leone, Alfonso (1973). 'Vattel'a pesca, vieni a piglialo', *Lingua Nostra* 34: 11–13.

Leone, Alfonso (1978). 'Sullo scadimento semantico di *andare*', *Lingua Nostra* 39: 50–4.

Leone, Alfonso (1995). *Profilo di Sintassi Siciliana*. Palermo: Centro di studi filologici e linguistici siciliani.

Leone, Fulvio (2003). *I pronomi personali di terza persona*. Rome: Carocci.

Lepschy, Anna Laura and Lepschy, Giulio (1981). *La lingua italiana: storia, varietà dell'uso, grammatica*. Milan: Bompiani.

Leumann, Manu (1948). 'Griechische Verba auf -ίζειν im Latein', in *Mélanges de philologie, de littérature et d'histoire anciennes offerts à J. Marouzeau par ses collègues et élèves étrangers*. Paris: Belles Lettres, 371–89.

Lombard, Alf (1954–1955). *Le Verbe roumain. Étude morphologique* (2 vols.). Lund: C. W. K. Gleerup.

Loporcaro, Michele (1988a). *Grammatica storica del dialetto di Altamura*. Pisa: Giardini.

Loporcaro, Michele (1988*b*). 'History and geography of *raddoppiamento fonosintattico*: remarks on the evolution of a phonological rule', in P. M. Bertinetto and M. Loporcaro (eds.), *Certamen phonologicum, Papers from the 1987 Cortona Phonology Meeting.* Turin: Rosenberg & Sellier, 341–87.

Loporcaro, Michele (1999). 'Il futuro CANTARE-HABEO nell'Italia meridionale', *Archivio Glottologico Italiano* 84: 67–114.

Loporcaro, Michele (2003). 'Dialettologia, linguistica storica e riflessione grammaticale nella romanistica del Duemila. Con esempi dal sardo', in F. Sánchez Miret (ed.), *Actas del XXIII CILFR, Vol. 1*, Salamanca, 24–30 September 2001. Tübingen: Niemeyer, 83–111.

Loporcaro, Michele (2011). 'Phonological processes', in M. Maiden, J. C. Smith, and A. Ledgeway (eds.), *The Cambridge History of the Romance Languages.* Cambridge: Cambridge University Press, 109–54.

Loporcaro, Michele (2012). 'Stems, endings and inflectional classes in Logudorese verb morphology', *Lingue e linguaggio* 11: 5–34.

Luís, Ana R. (2011). 'Morphomic structure and loan-verb integration: evidence from lusophone creoles', in M. Maiden, J. C. Smith, M. Goldbach, and M.-O. Hinzelin (eds.), *Morphological Autonomy: Perspectives from Romance Inflectional Morphology.* Oxford: Oxford University Press, 235–54.

Lupinu, Giovanni (ed.) (2010). *Carta de logu dell'Arborea. Nuova edizione critica secondo il manoscritto di Cagliari (BUC 211). Con traduzione italiana.* Oristano: S'Alvure.

Mace, John (2003). *Persian Grammar: for reference and revision.* London: Routledge.

Maiden, Martin (1992). 'Irregularity as a determinant of morphological change', *Journal of Linguistics* 28: 285–312.

Maiden, Martin (1995*a*). *A Linguistic History of Italian.* London & New York: Longman.

Maiden, Martin (1995*b*). 'A proposito dell'alternanza *esce, usciva* in italiano', *Lingua Nostra* 56: 37–41.

Maiden, Martin (1996*a*). 'The Romance gerund and "system-dependent naturalness" in morphology', *Transactions of the Philological Society* 94: 167–201.

Maiden, Martin (1996*b*). 'Ipotesi sulle origini del condizionale analitico come "futuro nel passato" in italiano', in P. Benincà, G. Cinque, T. De Mauro, and N. Vincent (eds.), *Italiano e dialetti nel tempo: Saggi di grammatica per Giulio Lepschy.* Rome: Bulzoni, 149–73.

Maiden, Martin (2000). 'Il sistema desinenziale del sostantivo nell'italo-romanzo preletterario. Ricostruzione parziale a partire dai dialetti moderni (il significato storico di plurali del tipo amici)', in J. Herman and A. Marinetti (eds.), *La preistoria dell'italiano.* Niemeyer: Tübingen, 167–79.

Maiden, Martin (2001*a*). 'Di nuovo sulle alternanze velari nel verbo italiano e spagnolo', *Cuadernos de filología italiana* 8: 39–61.

Maiden, Martin (2001*b*). 'A strange affinity: "perfecto y tiempos afines"', *Bulletin of Hispanic Studies* 78: 441–64.

Maiden, Martin (2003). 'Il verbo italoromanzo: verso una storia autenticamente morfologica', in M. Giacomo-Marcellesi and A. Rocchetti (eds.), *Il verbo italiano. Studi diacronici, sincronici, contrastivi, didattici.* Rome: Bulzoni, 3–21.

Maiden, Martin (2004*a*). 'When lexemes become allomorphs—on the genesis of suppletion', *Folia Linguistica* 38: 227–56.

Maiden, Martin (2004*b*). 'Verb augments and meaninglessness in Romance morphology', *Studi di grammatica italiana* 22: 1–61.

Maiden, Martin (2005*a*). 'Morphological autonomy and diachrony', in G. Booij and J. van Marle (eds.), *Yearbook of Morphology 2004*. Dordrecht: Springer, 137–75.

Maiden, Martin (2005*b*). 'La ridistribuzione paradigmatica degli "aumenti" verbali nelle lingue romanze', in S. Kiss, L. Mondin, and G. Salvi (eds.), *Latin et langues romanes. Études de linguistique offertes à József Herman à l'occasion de son 80ème anniversaire*. Tübingen: Niemeyer, 431–40.

Maiden, Martin (2008*a*). 'Lexical nonsense and morphological sense. On the real importance of "folk etymology" and related phenomena for historical linguists', in T. Eythórsson (ed.), *Grammatical Change and Linguistic Theory. The Rosendal Papers*. Amsterdam & Philadelphia: John Benjamins, 307–28.

Maiden, Martin (2008*b*). 'Haunting and exorcism: autonomous morphology and phonological conditioning in the Romance (and especially the Romansh) verb.' Paper presented at *The Fourth Oxford–Kobe Linguistics Seminar: History and Structure of the Romance Languages*, Kobe, Japan, April 2008.

Maiden, Martin (2009*a*). 'From pure phonology to pure morphology. The reshaping of the Romance verb', *Recherches linguistiques de Vincennes* 38: 45–82.

Maiden, Martin (2009*b*). 'On the morphologization of some phonetic processes in the Oltenian verb', in S. Reinheimer Rîpeanu (ed.), *Studia linguistica in honorem Mariae Manoliu*. Bucharest: Editura Universității din București, 175–85.

Maiden, Martin (2009*c*). 'Un capitolo di morfologia storica del romeno: preterito e tempi affini', *Zeitschrift für romanische Philologie* 125: 273–309.

Maiden, Martin (2010*a*). 'Riflessioni comparative e storiche sulla sorte del congiuntivo presente nelle varietà italoromanze', in G. Ruffino and M. D'Agostino (eds.), *Storia della lingua italiana e dialettologia*. Palermo: Centro di studi filologici e linguistici siciliani, 129–49.

Maiden, Martin (2010*b*). 'Italian compound nouns and the autonomy of morphology.' Paper presented at the conference *Italian Linguistics in the UK*, University of Reading, 11 June 2010.

Maiden, Martin (2011*a*). 'Morphological persistence', in M. Maiden, J. C. Smith, and A. Ledgeway (eds.), *The Cambridge History of the Romance Languages, Vol. 1*. Cambridge: Cambridge University Press, 155–215.

Maiden, Martin (2011*b*). 'Morphophonological innovation', in M. Maiden, J. C. Smith, and A. Ledgeway (eds.), *The Cambridge History of the Romance Languages, Vol. 1*. Cambridge: Cambridge University Press, 216–67.

Maiden, Martin (2011*c*). 'Allomorphy, autonomous morphology and phonological conditioning in the history of the Daco-Romance present and subjunctive', *Transactions of the Philological Society* 109: 59–91.

Maiden, Martin (2011*d*). 'Morphomes and "stress-conditioned allomorphy" in Romansh', in M. Maiden, J. C. Smith, M. Goldbach, and M.-O. Hinzelin (eds.), *Morphological Autonomy: Perspectives from Romance Inflectional Morphology*. Oxford: Oxford University Press, 36–50.

Maiden, Martin (2011*e*). 'Glimpsing the future. Some rare anomalies in the history of the Italo-Romance future and conditional stem, and what they suggest about paradigm structure.' Paper presented at *Italian Dialects in Diachrony*, Leiden, May 2011.

Maiden, Martin (2012). 'Clubbing together: on number suppletion in Megleno-Romanian (and mainland Scandinavian) adjectives.' Paper presented at the *Conference on The Morphological Expression of Number (OxMorph 3)*, Trinity College, Oxford, 29 May 2012.

Maiden, Martin (forthcoming). 'The Latin "third stem" and its Romance descendants', *Diachronica*.

Maiden, Martin and O'Neill, Paul (2010). 'On morphomic defectiveness: evidence from the Romance languages of the Iberian Peninsula', in M. Baerman, G. G. Corbett, and D. Brown (eds.), *Defective Paradigms: Missing Forms and What They Tell Us*. Oxford: Oxford University Press & British Academy, 103–24.

Maiden, Martin, Smith, John Charles, Goldbach, Maria, and Hinzelin, Marc-Olivier (eds.) (2011). *Morphological Autonomy: Perspectives from Romance Inflectional Morphology*. Oxford: Oxford University Press.

Mamedov, Novruzali (2006). *Talyšsko-russko-azerbajdžanskij slovar'*. Baku: Nurlan.

Manoliu, Maria (2011). 'Pragmatics and discourse changes', in M. Maiden, J. C. Smith, and A. Ledgeway (eds.), *The Cambridge History of the Romance Languages, Vol. I*. Cambridge: Cambridge University Press, 472–531.

Manzini, Maria Rita and Savoia, Leonardo (2005). *I dialetti italiani e romanci. Morfosintassi generativa*. Alessandria: Edizioni dell'Orso.

Marantz, Alec (1997). 'No escape from syntax: don't try morphological analysis in the privacy of your own lexicon', in A. Dimitriadis, L. Siegel, C. Surek-Clark, and A. Williams (eds.), *Proceedings of the 21st Annual Penn Linguistics Colloquium*, University of Pennsylvania Working Papers in Linguistics 4.2. Philadelphia: University of Pennsylvania, 201–25.

Marantz, Alec (no date). 'Phases and words'. Available at https://files.nyu.edu/ma988/public/marantz_publications.html. Published as Alec Marantz (2007). 'Phases and words', in S. H. Choe (ed.), *Phases in the Theory of Grammar*. Seoul: Dong In, 191–220.

Masarei, Sergio (2005). *Dizionar fodom—talián—todësch*. Colle Santa Lucia: Istitut Cultural Ladin "Cesa de Jan"—SPELL.

Massourre, Jean-Louis (2006). *Le Gascon haut-pyrénéen. Vallées de Luz, de Barèges et de Gavarnie*. Villeneuve-sur-Lot: Massourre.

Matthews, Peter H. (1972). *Inflectional Morphology. A Theoretical Study Based on Aspects of Latin Verb Conjugation*. Cambridge: Cambridge University Press.

Matthews, Peter H. (1982). 'Two problems in Italian and Spanish verbal inflection', in N. Vincent and M. Harris (eds.), *Studies in the Romance Verb*. London: Croom Helm, 1–18.

Matthews, Peter H. (1991). *Morphology*. Cambridge: Cambridge University Press.

Maurer, Theodoro E. (1951). 'The Romance conjugation in –ēscō, (-īscō) –īre. Its origin in Vulgar Latin', *Language* 27: 136–45.

Mazzel, Massimiliano (1995). *Dizionario ladino fassano (cazet)—italiano*. Vigo di Fassa: Istitut Cultural Ladin "Majon di Fascegn".

McCarthy, John J. (1981). 'A prosodic theory of nonconcatenative morphology', *Linguistic Inquiry* 12: 373–418.

Meinschaefer, Judith (2011). 'Accentual patterns in Romance verb forms', in M. Maiden, J. C. Smith, M. Goldbach, and M.-O. Hinzelin (eds.). *Morphological Autonomy. Perspectives from Romance Inflectional Morphology.* Oxford: Oxford University Press, 51–69.

Meul, Claire (2010). 'The intra-paradigmatic distribution of the infix *-i/esc-* from Latin to Romance: morphomic patterning and beyond', *Morphology* 20: 1–40.

Meul, Claire (2013). *The Romance Reflexes of the Latin Infixes -i/esc- and -idi̯-: Restructuring and Remodeling Processes.* Hamburg: Buske.

Meyer, Paul (1878). 'La légende de Girart de Roussillon', *Romania* 25: 161–235.

Meyer-Lübke, Wilhelm (1902). 'Zur Kenntniss des Altlogudoresischen', *Sitzungsberichte des kais. Akademie der Wissenschaften in Wien. Philosophisch-historische Classe* 145, V.

Meyer-Lübke, Wilhelm (1974). *Grammaire des langues romanes* [Reprint of the French translation (1890–1906) of the original German version (1890–1902)] (4 vols.). Genève: Slatkine Reprints; Marseille: Laffitte.

Micheels, Laurent (1865). *Grammaire élémentaire liégeoise (française-wallonne).* Liège: F. Renard.

Mignot, Xavier (1969). *Les Verbes dénominatifs latins.* Paris: Klincksieck.

Miller, Boris Vsevolodovič (1930). *Talyšskie teksty.* Moscow: Ranion.

Miller, Boris Vsevolodovič (1953). *Talyšskij jazyk.* Moscow: Izd. Akademii Nauk.

Mischì, Giovanni (2001). *Vocabolar Todësch—Ladin (Val Badia).* San Martin de Tor: Istitut Ladin "Micurà de Rü".

Molinu, Lucia (1988–1989). *Morfologia verbale del buddusoino (Varietà Logudorese di Buddusò).* Tesi di laurea, Università di Pisa.

Molinu, Lucia (1999). 'Morfologia logudorese', in R. Bolognesi and K. Helsloot (eds.), *La lingua sarda. Atti del II Convegno del Sardinian Language Group.* Cagliari: Condaghes, 127–36.

Montrul, Silvina and Slabakova, Roumyana (2002). 'The L2 acquisition of morphosyntactic and semantic properties of the aspectual tenses preterite and imperfect', in A. T. Pérez-Leroux and J. Muñoz Liceras (eds.), *The Acquisition of Spanish Morphosyntax: The L1/L2 connection.* Dordrecht: Kluwer Academic Publishers, 115–51.

Mossa, Paulicu (1982). *Tutte le poesie e altri scritti.* Cagliari: Edizioni della Torre.

Mourin, Louis (1980). 'L'infixe *-e-* des verbes de la 1ère conjugaison en ladin du Val Gardena', *Studii și cercetări lingvistice* 5: 585–89.

Mussafia, Adolf (1883). *Zur Präsensbildung im Romanischen.* Vienna: Kais. Akademie der Wissenschaften.

Neiescu, Petru, Rusu, Grigore, and Stan, Ionel (1969-). *Atlasul lingvistic pe regiuni. Maramureș. (Vol. IV).* Bucharest: Editura Academiei.

Nordlinger, Rachel and Sadler, Louisa (2004). 'Nominal tense in crosslinguistic perspective', *Language* 80: 776–806.

O'Neill, Paul (2011a). *The Ibero-Romance Verb: Allomorphy and the Notion of the Morphome.* Unpublished D.Phil. thesis, University of Oxford.

O'Neill, Paul (2011b). 'The notion of the morphome', in M. Maiden, J. C. Smith, M. Goldbach, and M.-O. Hinzelin (eds.), *Morphological Autonomy: Perspectives from Romance Inflectional Morphology.* Oxford: Oxford University Press, 70–94.

Oppo, Anna (ed.) (2007). *Le lingue dei sardi. Una ricerca sociolinguistica* [co-authored by G. Lupinu, A. Mongili, A. Oppo, R. Spiga, S. Perra, M. Valdes]. Cagliari-Sassari: Regione autonoma della Sardegna – Università di Cagliari – Università di Sassari.

OVI: Opera del vocabolario italiano (CNR, Florence). http://www.ovi.cnr.it/

Paesani, Katherine A. (2001). *The Syntax and Semantics of the Passé Surcomposé in Modern French.* Unpublished Ph.D. dissertation, Indiana University.

Pallabazzer, Vito (1989). *Lingua e cultura ladina. Lessico e onomastica di Laste, Rocca Pietore, Colle S. Lucia, Selva di Cadore, Alleghe.* Belluno: Istituto bellunese di ricerche sociali e culturali.

Parkinson, Jennie (2009). *A Diachronic Study into the Distributions of Two Italo-Romance Synthetic Conditional Forms.* Unpublished Ph.D. thesis, University of St. Andrews.

Parodi, Ernesto G. (1901). 'Il tipo italiano *aliare aleggia*', in *Miscellanea linguistica in onore di Graziadio Ascoli.* Turin: Loescher, 457–88.

Paul, Daniel (2011). *A Comparative Dialectal Description of Iranian Taleshi.* Unpublished Ph.D. thesis, University of Manchester.

Paul, Ludwig (1998*a*). 'The position of Zazaki among West Iranian languages', in N. Sims-Williams (ed.), *Proceedings of the 3rd European Conference on Iranian Studies (held in Cambridge, 11th to 15th September 1995). Part I, Old and Middle Iranian Studies.* Wiesbaden: Reichert, 163–77.

Paul, Ludwig (1998*b*). *Zazaki: Grammatik und Versuch einer Dialektologie.* Wiesbaden: Reichert.

Paulis, Giulio (2010). 'Varietà locali e standardizzazione nella dinamica dello sviluppo linguistico', in G. Corongiu and C. Romagnino (eds.), *Sa diversidade de sas limbas in Europa, Itàlia e Sardigna. Atos de sa conferèntzia regionale de sa limba sarda. Macumere, 28–30 santandria 2008.* Casteddu: Editzione de sa Regione, 179–84.

Pelliciardi, Fernando (1977). *Grammatica del dialetto romagnolo: la lèngva dla mi tëra.* Ravenna: Longo.

Pérez Saldanya, Manuel and Hualde, José Ignacio (2003). 'On the origin and evolution of the Catalan periphrastic preterite', in C. D. Pusch and A. Wesch (eds.), *Verbalperiphrasen in den (ibero-)romanischen Sprachen / Perífrasis verbals en les llengües (ibero-)romàniques / Perífrasis verbales en las lenguas (ibero-)románicas* [Beihefte zu Romanistik in Geschichte und Gegenwart 9]. Hamburg: Buske, 47–60.

Pfister, Max (ed.) (1979–). *Lessico etimologico italiano* (11 vols.). Wiesbaden: Reichert.

Pinkster, Harm (1990). *Latin Syntax and Semantics.* London: Routledge.

Pinto, Immacolata (2011). *La formazione delle parole in sardo.* Nuoro: Ilisso.

Piras, Marco (1994). *La varietà linguistica del Sulcis.* Cagliari: Edizioni della Torre.

Pirejko, Lija A. (1966). 'Talyšskij jazyk', in V. V. Vinogradov (ed.), *Jazyki narodov SSSR, tom I. Indoevropejskie jazyki.* Moscow: Nauka, 302–22.

Pirejko, Lija A. (1991). 'Talyšskij jazyk. Dialekty tati Irana', *Osnovy iranskogo jazykoznanija, tom V. Novoiranskie jazyki.* Moscow: Nauka, 91–175.

Pirrelli, Vito (2000). *Paradigmi in morfologia. Un approccio interdisciplinare alla flessione verbale dell'italiano.* Pisa-Rome: Istituti Editoriali e Poligrafici Internazionali.

Pirrelli, Vito and Battista, Marco (2000). 'The paradigmatic dimension of stem allomorphy in Italian verb inflection', *Rivista di Linguistica* 12: 307–80.

Pisano, Simone (2004–2006). 'Il sistema verbale del sardo moderno: tra conservazione e innovazione', *L'Italia dialettale* 65: 73–104; 66/67: 137–244.

Pittau, Massimo (1972). *Grammatica del sardo nuorese, il più conservativo dei parlari neolatini.* Bologna: Pàtron.

Plag, Ingo (1999). *Morphological Productivity*. Berlin: Mouton de Gruyter.

Pountain, Christopher (1983). *Structures and Transformations: The Romance Verb*. London: Croom Helm.

Prunet, Jean-François (2006). 'External evidence and the Semitic root', *Morphology* 16: 41–67.

Prunet, Jean-François, Béland, Renée, and Idrissi, Ali (2000). 'The mental representation of Semitic words', *Linguistic Inquiry* 31: 609–48.

Quint, Nicolas (1997). 'Etude de l'emploi du conditionnel deuxième forme dans la seconde partie de *la Canso de la crozada*', *Estudis occitans* 21: 2–12.

Ramat, Paolo (1992). 'Thoughts on degrammaticalization', *Linguistics* 30: 549–60.

Rastorgueva, Vera S. and Èdel'man, Džoj I. (2000). *Ètimologičeskij slovar' iranskix jazykov. Tom I*. Moscow: Vostočnaja literatura.

Rastorgueva, Vera S. and Èdel'man, Džoj I. (2003). *Ètimologičeskij slovar' iranskix jazykov. Tom II*. Moscow: Vostočnaja literatura.

Rastorgueva, Vera S. and Molčanova, Elena K. (1981*a*). 'Srednepersidskij jazyk', in V. S. Rastorgueva (ed.), *Osnovy iranskogo jazykoznanija, tom II. Sredneiranskie jazyki*. Moscow: Nauka, 6–146.

Rastorgueva, Vera S. and Molčanova, Elena K. (1981*b*). 'Parfjanskij jazyk', in V. S. Rastorgueva (ed.), *Osnovy iranskogo jazykoznanija, tom II. Sredneiranskie jazyki*. Moscow: Nauka, 147–232.

Ravid, Dorit (2003). 'A developmental perspective on root perception in Hebrew and Palestinian Arabic', in J. Shimron (ed.), *Language Processing and Acquisition in Languages of Semitic, Root-based, Morphology*. Amsterdam: John Benjamins, 293–319.

Real Academia Española (2009). *Nueva gramática de la lengua española, Vol. 1*. Madrid: Espasa.

Renzi, Lorenzo (2012). *Come cambia la lingua. L'italiano in movimento*. Bologna: Il Mulino.

Revaz, Françoise (2009). 'Valeurs et emplois du futur simple et du présent prospectif en français'. *Faits de langues* 33: 149–62.

Reymond, Jules and Bossard, Maurice (1982). *Le Patois vaudois. Grammaire et vocabulaire*. Lausanne: Payot.

Rindler-Schjerve, Rosita (1987). *Sprachkontakt auf Sardinien. Soziolinguistische Untersuchungen des Sprachenwechsels im ländlichen Bereich*. Tübingen: Narr.

Rizzi, Luigi (1982). *Issues in Italian Syntax*. Dordrecht: Foris.

Rohlfs, Gerhard (1968). *Grammatica storica della lingua italiana e dei suoi dialetti. Vol. II: Morfologia*. Turin: Einaudi.

Rohlfs, Gerhard (1969). *Grammatica storica della lingua italiana e dei suoi dialetti. Vol. III: Sintassi e formazione delle parole*. Turin: Einaudi.

Romieu, Maurice and Bianchi, André (2005). *Gramatica de l'occitan gascon contemporanèu*. Bordeaux: Presses Universitaires de Bordeaux.

Rudes, Blair (1980). 'The functional development of the verbal suffix $+ esc +$ in Romance', in J. Fisiak (ed.), *Historical Morphology*. The Hague: Mouton, 327–48.

Sadler, Louisa and Spencer, Andrew (2001). 'Syntax as an exponent of morphological features', in G. Booij and J. van Marle (eds.), *Yearbook of Morphology 2000*. Dordrecht: Kluwer, 71–96.

Sadler, Louise, Spencer, Andrew, and Zaretskaya, Marina (1996). 'A morphomic account of a syncretism in Russian deverbal nominalizations', in G. Booij and J. van Marle (eds.), *Yearbook of Morphology 1996*. Dordrecht: Kluwer, 181–216.

Sasse, Hans-Jürgen (1991). 'Aspect and Aktionsart: a reconciliation', in C. Vetters and W. Vandeweghe (eds.), *Perspectives on Aspect and Aktionsart (Belgian Journal of Linguistics 6)*. Bruxelles: Éditions de l'Université de Bruxelles, 31–45.

Sasse, Hans-Jürgen (2002). 'Recent activity in the theory of aspect: accomplishments, achievements, or just non-progressive state?', *Linguistic Typology* 6: 199–271.

Scalise, Sergio (1994). *Morfologia*. Bologna: Il Mulino.

Schaden, Gerhard (2007). *La Sémantique du parfait. Étude des 'temps composés' dans un choix de langues germaniques et romanes*. Unpublished Ph.D. dissertation, Université Paris 8.

Scheitlin, Walter (1962). *Il pled Puter*. Samedan: Uniun dals Grischs.

Schorta, Andrea (1938). *Lautlehre der Mundart von Mustair*, Romanica Helvetica, vol. 7. Paris & Zürich-Leipzig: Droz & Niehans.

Schulze, Wolfgang (2000). *Northern Talysh*. München: LINCOM Europa.

Sebba, Mark (1987). *The Syntax of Serial Verbs*. Amsterdam: John Benjamins.

Shimron, Joseph (2003). 'Semitic languages: are they really root-based?, in J. Shimron (ed.) *Language Processing and Acquisition in Languages of Semitic, Root-based, Morphology*. Amsterdam: John Benjamins, 1–28.

Sibille, Joan (1997). 'Nòta sus la subrevivéncia de la segonda forma de condicional de l'occitan vièlh dins l'Auta Val Doira e la Val Cluson (Itàlia)', *Estudis Occitans* 21: 13–18.

Signorell, Faust, Wuethrich-Grisch, Mena, and Simeon, Gion Pol (1987). *Normas surmiranas*. Chur: Tgesa editoura cantunala per stampats e meds d'instrucziun.

Silverstein, Michael (1976). 'Hierarchy of features and ergativity', in R. M. W. Dixon (ed.), *Grammatical Categories in Australian Languages*. Canberra: Australian Institute of Aboriginal Studies, 112–71.

Sims, Andrea (2008). 'Why defective paradigms are, and aren't, the result of competing morphological patterns', *Proceedings from the Annual Meeting of the Chicago Linguistic Society* 43(2): 267–81.

Skjærvø, Prods Oktor (2009a). 'Old Iranian', in G. Windfuhr (ed.), *The Iranian Languages*. London: Routledge, 43–195.

Skjærvø, Prods Oktor (2009b). 'Middle West Iranian', in G. Windfuhr (ed.), *The Iranian Languages*. London: Routledge, 196–278.

Skousen, Royal (1975). *Substantive Evidence in Phonology. The Evidence from French and Finnish*. The Hague: Mouton.

Slobbe, Biance (2004). 'Restructuring and the development of the Romance conditional verb forms', in S. Blaho, L. Vicente, and M. de Vos (eds.), *Proceedings of ConSOLE XII*, University of Patras, 107–123.

Smith, John Charles (1999). 'The refunctionalization of a pronominal subsystem between Latin and Romance', *Oxford University Working Papers in Linguistics, Philology & Phonetics* 4: 141–56.

Smith, John Charles (2005). 'Some refunctionalizations of the nominative–accusative opposition between Latin and Gallo-Romance', in B. Smelik, R. Hofman, C. Hamans, and D. Cram (eds.), *A Companion in Linguistics: A Festschrift for Anders Ahlqvist on the Occasion of his Sixtieth Birthday*. Nijmegen: De Keltische Draak, 269–85.

Smith, John Charles (2006). 'How to do things without junk: the refunctionalization of a pronominal subsystem between Latin and Romance', in J.-P. Y. Montreuil (ed.), *New Perspectives on Romance Linguistics: Selected Papers from the 35th Linguistic Symposium on Romance Languages (LSRL), Austin, Texas, February 2005. Vol. II: Phonetics, Phonology and Dialectology*. Amsterdam & Philadelphia: John Benjamins, 183–205.

Smith, John Charles (2008). 'The refunctionalisation of first-person plural inflection in Tiwi', in C. Bowern, B. Evans, and L. Miceli (eds.), *Morphology and Language History: In Honour of Harold Koch*. Amsterdam & Philadelphia: John Benjamins, 341–48.

Smith, John Charles (2011a). 'Change and continuity in form–function relations', in M. Maiden, J. C. Smith, and A. Ledgeway (eds.), *The Cambridge History of the Romance Languages*. Cambridge: Cambridge University Press, 268–317.

Smith, John Charles (2011b). 'Variable analyses of a verbal inflection in (mainly) Canadian French', in M. Maiden, J. C. Smith, M. Goldbach, and M.-O. Hinzelin (eds.), *Morphological Autonomy: Perspectives from Romance Inflectional Morphology*. Oxford: Oxford University Press, 311–26.

Sonder, Ambros and Grisch, Mena (1970). *Vocabulari da Surmeir*. Chur: Leia Rumantscha.

Sornicola, Rosanna (1976). '*Vado a dire, vaiu a ddicu*: problema sintattico o problema semantico?', *Lingua Nostra* 37: 65–74.

Spano, Giovanni (1840). *Ortografia sarda nazionale ossia grammatica della lingua logudorese paragonata all'italiana dal sacerd. professore Giovanni Spano*. Cagliari: Reale Stamperia [Reprinted, Cagliari: GIA 1995].

Spencer, Andrew (2001). 'The paradigm-based model of morphosyntax', *Transactions of the Philological Society* 99(2): 279–313.

Spencer, Andrew (2005). 'Inflecting clitics in generalized paradigm function morphology', *Lingue e Linguaggio* 4: 179–94.

Spescha, Arnold (1989). *Grammatica sursilvana*. Chur: Casa editura per mieds d'instrucziun.

Squartini, Mario (1998). *Verbal Periphrases in Romance: Aspect, Actionality, and Grammaticalization*. Berlin: Mouton de Gruyter.

Squartini, Mario (1999). 'Riferimento temporale, aspetto e modalità nella diacronia del condizionale italiano', *Vox Romanica* 58: 57–82.

Squartini, Mario (2004). 'La relazione semantica tra Futuro e Condizionale nelle lingue romanze', *Revue romane* 39: 68–96.

Squartini, Mario (2010). 'Where mood, modality and illocution meet: the morphosyntax of Romance conjectures', in M. G. Becker and E.-M. Remberger (eds.), *Modality and Mood in Romance: Modal Interpretation, Mood Selection, and Mood Alternation*. Berlin: Mouton de Gruyter, 109–31.

Stankiewicz, Edward (ed.) (1972). *A Baudouin de Courtenay Anthology*. Bloomington: Indiana University Press.

Stilo, Donald L. (2008a). 'Two sets of mobile verbal person agreement markers in the Northern Talyshi language', in S. Karimi, D. Stilo, and V. Samiian (eds.), *Aspects of Iranian Linguistics*. Newcastle: Cambridge Scholars, 363–90.

Stilo, Donald L. (2008b). 'Isfahan, xxi. Provincial Dialects', in E. Yarshater (ed.), *Encyclopaedia Iranica, Vol. XIV*. New York: Encyclopaedia Iranica Foundation, 93–112.

Stilo, Donald L. (2011). 'The diachrony of the present, subjunctive and future formations and their derivatives in the Araxes-Iran linguistic area.' Talk given at ICIL4: Fourth International Conference on Iranian Linguistics, Uppsala University, Sweden.

Stilo, Donald L. (2013). 'The polygenetic origins of the Northern Talyshi language'. Unpublished ms., Max Planck Institute for Evolutionary Anthropology, Leipzig.

Stoppelli, Pasquale and Picchi, Eugenio (2001). *LIZ 4.0—Letteratura Italiana Zanichelli*. Bologna: Zanichelli.

Stotz, Peter (1996). *Handbuch zur Lateinischen Sprache des Mittelalters. Dritter Band: Lautlehre*. München: C. H. Beck.

Stump, Gregory (1993). 'Rules of referral', *Language* 69: 449–79.

Stump, Gregory (2001). *Inflectional Morphology: A Theory of Paradigm Structure*. Cambridge: Cambridge University Press.

Stump, Gregory (2002). 'Morphological and syntactic paradigms: arguments for a theory of paradigm linkage', in G. Booij and J. van Marle (eds.), *Yearbook of Morphology 2001*. Dordrecht: Kluwer, 147–80.

Stump, Gregory (2006). 'Heteroclisis and paradigm linkage', *Language* 82: 279–322.

Stump, Gregory (2010). 'Associations between morphomic categories and morphosyntactic properties.' Paper presented at the workshop *Perspectives on the Morphome*, University of Coimbra, 29–30 October 2010.

Sturtevant, Edgar H. (1940). *The Pronunciation of Greek and Latin*. Philadelphia: Linguistic Society of America.

Swearingen, Andrew (2011). 'The Romance imperative, irregular morphology, syncretism, and the morphome', in M. Maiden, J. C. Smith, M. Goldbach, and M.-O. Hinzelin (eds.), *Morphological Autonomy: Perspectives from Romance Inflectional Morphology*. Oxford: Oxford University Press, 119–34.

Szabó, Zoltan (2009). 'Compositionality', in *Stanford Encyclopedia of Philosophy*. Accessible at http://plato.stanford.edu/entries/compositionality

Szemerényi, Oswald J. L. (1996). *Introduction to Indo-European Linguistics*. Oxford: Clarendon Press.

Taylor, Catherine (2008). 'Maximising stems', in M. Kokkonidis (ed.), online *Proceedings of LingO 2007*: 228–35.

Taylor, Catherine (2011). 'Periphrasis in Romance', in M. Maiden, J. C. Smith, M. Goldbach, and M.-O. Hinzelin (eds.), *Morphological Autonomy: Perspectives from Romance Inflectional Morphology*. Oxford: Oxford University Press, 401–16.

Teaha, Teofil, Ionică, Ion, and Rusu, Valeriu (1984). *Noul atlas lingvistic român pe regiuni. Oltenia*. Bucharest: Editura Academiei Republicii Socialiste România.

Tekavčić, Pavao (1972). *Grammatica storica dell'italiano* (3 vols.). Bologna: Il Mulino.

Thérond, Gustave (2002). *Éléments de grammaire languedocienne (1900): dialecte languedocien cettois*. Puylaurens: Institut d'études occitanes.

Thöni, Gion Peder (1969). *Rumantsch Surmeir: Grammatica per igl idioma surmiran*. Chur: Ligia Romontscha.

Thornton, Anna Maria (2011). 'Overabundance (multiple forms realizing the same cell): a non-canonical phenomenon in Italian verb morphology', in M. Maiden, J. C. Smith, M. Goldbach, and M.-O. Hinzelin (eds.), *Morphological Autonomy: Perspectives from Romance Inflectional Morphology*. Oxford: Oxford University Press, 358–81.

Thornton, Anna Maria (2012*a*). 'Overabundance in Italian verb morphology and its interactions with other non-canonical phenomena', in T. Stolz, H. Otsuka, A. Urdze, and J. van der Auwera (eds.), *Irregularity in Morphology (and beyond)*. Berlin: Akademie Verlag, 251–69.

Thornton, Anna Maria (2012*b*). 'Reduction and maintenance of overabundance. A case study on Italian verb paradigms', *Word Structure* 5: 183–207.

TLF = *Trésor de la langue française: dictionnaire de la langue du XIXe et du XXe siècle, 1789–1960*, edited by Paul Imbs (1971–1994). Paris: CNRS.

Touratier, Christian (1996). *Le Système verbal français*. Paris: Masson and Armand Colin.

Tropea, Giovanni (1988). *Lessico del dialetto di Pantelleria*. Palermo: Centro di Studi Filologici e Linguistici Siciliani.

Tscharner, Gion (2003). *Verbs valladers*. Chur: Chasa editura per mezs d'instucziun dal chantun Grischun.

Urech-Clavuot, Chatrina (2009). *Verbs puters*. Samedan: Gammeter Druck.

Väänänen, Veikko (1982). *Introduzione al latino volgare*. Bologna: Pàtron.

Vanelli, Laura (2010*a*). 'Congiuntivo presente,' in G. Salvi and L. Renzi (eds.), *Grammatica dell'italiano antico*. Bologna: Il Mulino, 1446–9.

Vanelli, Laura (2010*b*). 'Verbi con allomorfia e allotropia tematica nel tema di presente', in G. Salvi and L. Renzi (eds.), *Grammatica dell'italiano antico*. Bologna: Il Mulino, 1463–8.

Velan, Hadas, Frost, Ram, Deutsch, Avital, and Plaut, David (2005). 'The processing of root morphemes in Hebrew: contrasting localist and distributed accounts', *Language and Cognitive Processes* 20: 169–206.

Vendler, Zeno (1967). *Linguistics in Philosophy*. Ithaca: Cornell University Press.

Versteegh, C. H. M. (1977). *Greek Elements in Arabic Linguistic Thinking*. Leiden: E. J. Brill.

Vet, Co and Kampers-Manhe, Brigitte (2001). 'Futur simple et futur du passé: leurs emplois temporels et modaux', in P. Dendale and L. Tasmowski (eds.), *Le Conditionnel en français*. Metz: Université de Metz, 89–104.

Videsott, Paul and Plangg, Guntram (1998). *Ennebergisches Wörterbuch—Vocabolar Mareo*. Innsbruck: Wagner.

Vincent, Nigel (1987*a*). 'Italian', in B. Comrie (ed.), *The World's Major Languages*. London: Croom Helm, 279–302.

Vincent, Nigel (1987*b*). 'The interaction of periphrasis and inflection: some Romance examples', in M. Harris and P. Ramat (eds.), *Historical Development of Auxiliaries*. Berlin: Mouton de Gruyter, 237–56.

Vincent, Nigel (1995). 'Exaptation and grammaticalization', in H. Andersen (ed.), *Historical Linguistics 1993*. Amsterdam: John Benjamins, 433–45.

Vincent, Nigel (2011). 'Non-finite forms, periphrases, and autonomous morphology in Latin and Romance', in M. Maiden, J. C. Smith, M. Goldbach, and M.-O. Hinzelin (eds.), *Morphological Autonomy: Perspectives from Romance Inflectional Morphology*. Oxford: Oxford University Press, 417–35.

Vincent, Nigel and Bentley, Delia (2001). 'The demise of the Latin future periphrasis in -urus + esse', in C. Moussy (ed.), *De Lingua Latina Novae Quaestiones*. Louvain-Paris: Peeters, 143–55.

Vincent, Nigel and Börjars, Kersti (2010). 'Grammaticalization and models of language', in E. Traugott and G. Trousdale (eds.), *Gradience, Gradualness and Grammaticalization*. Amsterdam: John Benjamins, 279–99.

Virdis, Maurizio (1988), 'Sardo. Aree linguistiche', in G. Holtus, M. Metzeltin, and C. Schmitt (eds.), *Lexikon der Romanistischen Linguistik, Vol. 4: Italienisch, Korsisch, Sardisch*. Tübingen: Max Niemeyer, 897–913.

Vliet, E. R. van (1983). 'The disappearance of the French *passé simple*: a morphological and sociolinguistic study', *Word* 34: 85–115.

Vogel, Irene (1994). 'Verbs in Italian morphology', in G. Booij and J. van Marle (eds.), *Yearbook of Morphology 1993*. Dordrecht: Kluwer, 219–54.

Wagner, Max Leopold (1938–1939). 'Flessione nominale e verbale del sardo antico e moderno', *L'Italia dialettale* 14: 93–170; 15: 1–29.

Wagner, Max Leopold (1941). *Historische Lautlehre des Sardischen* [Beiheft 93 ZRPh]. Halle (Saale): Niemeyer.

Wagner, Max Leopold (1950). *La lingua sarda. Storia, spirito e forma*. Bern: Francke.

Waltke, Bruce and O'Connor, Michael (1990). *Biblical Hebrew Grammar*. Winona Lake: Eisenbrauns.

Weinrich, Harald (1964). *Estructura y función de los tiempos en el lenguaje*. Madrid: Gredos.

Werning, Markus, Hinzen, Wolfram, and Machery, Edouard (eds.) (2012). *The Oxford Handbook of Compositionality*. Oxford: Oxford University Press.

Wilkinson, Hugh E. (2000). 'Proto-Romance verb formation by suffixation', *Aoyama Journal of Business* 35: 157–74.

Willenberg, Gotthold (1878). *Historische Untersuchung über den Conjunctiv Praesentis der ersten schwachen Conjugation im Französischen*. Strasbourg: K. J. Trübner.

Williams, Edwin (2007). 'Dumping lexicalism', in G. Ramchand and C. Reiss (eds.), *The Oxford Handbook of Linguistic Interfaces*. Oxford: Oxford University Press, 353–81.

Wilson, Imogen (1999). 'Paratactic complementation in Sicilian.' Unpublished M.Phil. thesis, University of Cambridge.

Windfuhr, Gernot (1987). 'Convergence. Iranian Talishi and Turkic Azari', in E. Bashir, M. M. Deshpande, and P. E. Hook (eds.), *Selected Papers from SALA-7, South Asian Roundtable Conference*. Bloomington, Indiana: Indiana University Linguistics Club, 385–405.

Windfuhr, Gernot (1992). 'Central dialects', in E. Yarshater (ed.), *Encyclopaedia Iranica, Vol. V*. Costa Mesa, California: Mazda, 242–52.

Windfuhr, Gernot (1995). 'Dialectology', in E. Yarshater (ed.), *Encyclopaedia Iranica, Vol. VII*. Costa Mesa, California: Mazda, 362–70.

Wittgenstein, Ludwig (1953). *Philosophical Investigations*. Malden: Blackwell.

Wurmbrand, Susanne (2003). *Infinitives. Restructuring and the Clause*. Berlin: Mouton de Gruyter.

Wurzel, Wolfgang U. (1989). *Inflectional Morphology and Naturalness*. Dordrecht: Kluwer.

Yvia-Croce, Hyacinthe (1979). *Grammaire corse*. Ajaccio: Editions Cyrnos et Méditerranée.

Zamboni, Alberto (1980–1981). 'Un problema di morfologia romanza: l'ampliamento verbale in -idio, -izo', *Quaderni patavini di linguistica* 2: 171–87.

Zwicky, Arnold (1985). 'How to describe inflection', *Proceedings of the Annual Meeting of the Berkeley Linguistic Society* 11: 372–86.

Index

OXFORD STUDIES IN DIACHRONIC AND HISTORICAL LINGUISTICS

General editors
Adam Ledgeway and Ian Roberts, University of Cambridge

Advisory editors
Cynthia Allen, *Australian National University*; Ricardo Bermúdez-Otero,
University of Manchester; Theresa Biberauer, *University of Cambridge*; Charlotte
Galves, *University of Campinas*; Geoff Horrocks, *University of Cambridge*; Paul
Kiparsky, *Stanford University*; Anthony Kroch, *University of Pennsylvania*;
David Lightfoot, *Georgetown University*; Giuseppe Longobardi, *University of
York*; David Willis, *University of Cambridge*

IN PREPARATION

Diachrony and Dialects
Grammatical Change in the Dialects of Italy
Edited by Paola Benincà, Adam Ledgeway, and Nigel Vincent

Syntax over Time
Lexical, Morphological, and Information-Structural Interactions
Edited by Theresa Biberauer and George Walkden

The History of Negation in Low German
Anne Breitbarth

Pragmatic Markers from Latin to the Romance Languages
Edited by Chiara Ghezzi and Piera Molinelli

Nominal Expressions and Language Change
From Early Latin to Modern Romance
Giuliana Giusti

The Historical Dialectology of Arabic: Linguistic and Sociolinguistic Approaches
Edited by Clive Holes

A Study in Grammatical Change
The Modern Greek Weak Subject Pronoun τος *and*
its Implications for Language Change and Structure
Brian D. Joseph

Gender from Latin to Romance
Michele Loporcaro

Vowel Quantity from Latin to Romance
Michele Loporcaro

The Syntax and Semantics of Vedic Particles
John J. Lowe

Syntactic Change and Stability
Joel Wallenberg

The History of Negation in the Languages of Europe and the Mediterranean
Volume II: *Patterns and Processes*
Edited by David Willis, Christopher Lucas, and Anne Breitbarth